The Technology Factor
in International Trade

UNIVERSITIES—NATIONAL BUREAU
CONFERENCE SERIES

The Technology Factor in

International Trade

*A Conference of the
Universities – National Bureau Committee
for Economic Research*

EDITED BY
RAYMOND VERNON
Harvard University

1970

NATIONAL BUREAU OF ECONOMIC RESEARCH
NEW YORK

DISTRIBUTED BY
COLUMBIA UNIVERSITY PRESS
NEW YORK AND LONDON

77008

RELATION OF NATIONAL BUREAU DIRECTORS
TO PUBLICATIONS REPORTING CONFERENCE PROCEEDINGS

Since the present volume is a record of conference proceedings, it has been exempted from the rules governing submission of manuscripts to, and critical review by, the Board of Directors of the National Bureau.

(Resolution adopted July 6, 1948, as revised
November 21, 1949, and April 20, 1968)

This conference was financed by a grant from the Ford Foundation. General funds for the Economic Research Conference Program are supplied by the National Science Foundation.

CONTENTS

Hypotheses and the Tests of Trade Patterns

Case Studies

Introduction

RAYMOND VERNON

HARVARD UNIVERSITY

In the last decade or two, economic theory has struggled to understand and define the technology factor as an element in growth and change. A discipline that for so long had found it sufficient to think in terms of a taxonomy of factors consisting of land, labor, and capital has begun to see some utility in treating technology as a factor deserving separate analysis. This conference can be thought of as a step in that process— as a conscious effort to adapt and, if need be, to modify the received body of international trade theory to the existence of the technological variable.

The existence of a well-developed body of mutually consistent paradigms, it has often been noted, is both the prime strength of the discipline to which they relate and the prime weakness of that discipline. The strengths of a well-articulated taxonomy and an explicit set of models are obvious enough. They offer a structure by which new data may be observed and may be related to an existing body of observations. Lacking these tools, the observer would have to create some criteria for scanning the new data and for relating them to past experience. So trade theorists, scanning international trade out of a background to which Ricardo, Marshall, Heckscher-Ohlin, Samuelson, and others have contributed, tend to classify what they see in terms of capital-intensive, labor-intensive, or resource-intensive products, and tend to observe those flows in terms of their consistency or inconsistency with a set of theoretical expectations.

But there are also dangers in a set of well-developed models. Researchers have an extraordinary capacity to screen out the evidence that does not sit well with their preconceptions; to relegate uncomfortable observations to the dustbins of the subconscious; or, better still, to reshape the observations so that they may be perceived in a way that eliminates the discomfiture. "What a man sees," says Thomas S. Kuhn, "depends both upon what he looks at and also upon what his previous visual-conceptual experience has taught him to see."

Politicians, businessmen, journalists, and historians, possessing as a rule neither the strengths nor the vulnerabilities that go with an understanding of international trade theory, have been "seeing" the technological variable in international trade for a very long time. Economists, on the other hand, have been slow to incorporate that variable explicitly in the main body of trade theory. To assume that economists were not aware of the importance of that variable, however, would be a gross error. All one could say is that economists had great difficulty in finding a compatible and efficient way in which to handle the technological factor. As long as that was the case, there was a tendency to observe international trade and to analyze its causes in ways that did not require the specific manipulation of a technology variable.

International trade theory has been especially vulnerable to the risks of screening away inconsistent evidence, a vulnerability stemming from two factors. One is the great strength of the ruling models of trade theory. The doctrine of comparative advantage and the theory of the international equilibrating process have a simplicity, a strength, and a clarity that are not matched by many branches of economic theory. The second source of vulnerability has been the sheer physical difficulty, until quite recently, of testing trade theory hypotheses in any rigorous way. Rigorous tests of comparative advantage concepts generally require the handling of vast masses of data, on a scale that has only become feasible with modern data-handling devices. Accordingly, until a few decades ago, scholars were usually reduced to armchair speculation about the consistency between trade theory and trade patterns, selecting the illustrations that supported their preconceptions or provoked their doubts.

One might perhaps make out a case that the field of international trade theory has tended toward a certain complacency and sluggishness in development, turning inward to refinements on Marshall rather than outward to the developments suggested by other branches of theory and by changes in the conditions of world trade itself. It is true, for instance, that the main body of international trade theory was not greatly disturbed in the 1930's either by the impact of Keynes or by the development of the various theories of imperfect competition.

On the other hand, even at that early date, economists were not wholly unaware of the limitations of trade theory. By 1929, Williams was expressing his misgivings over the efficiency and adequacy of trade theory as a vehicle for explaining the observed patterns of international trade and was suggesting that different national propensities for innovation might have something to do with the creation of trade disequilibria. Ohlin, with his characteristic subtlety, recognized the potential importance to trade theory of differences in the quality of existing factors. A revisionist gleam, kept alive through the depression era of the 1930's, was strengthened after World War II by policy-oriented economists concerned with the problems of economic development, of regional trading blocs, and of the dollar shortage. Leontief's well-known paradox added to the mounting sense of inadequacy. His "solution," being couched in terms that superficially appeared loyal to the ruling paradigm, made revisionism respectable. The floodgates having been pried open, a torrent of speculation and empirical testing followed.

As the evidence developed, there were occasional efforts at synthesis. One of these efforts, for which M. V. Posner was responsible in 1961, proved especially rich in insights. By 1966, however, new materials were piling up at such a rate that the time seemed ripe for some more extensive efforts to relate theory and evidence. The initiative of the Universities-National Bureau Committee for Economic Research in proposing a Conference on Technology and the Theory of International Trade was eagerly seized as an appropriate opportunity. Harry G. Johnson, H. B. Lary, Edwin Mansfield, and Jacob Schmookler joined me in planning the Conference; and after Jacob Schmookler's untimely death, Alfred H. Conrad took a laboring oar in the enterprise.

Now that the Conference has made its modest contribution to the academic understanding of technology in international trade, it is clearer than ever how much still remains to be explored before that understanding is secured. Many of the unsolved problems that loom over this facet of trade theory are those that are endemic to economic theory in general. But some apply with very special force to the area of inquiry that is the subject of this conference volume.

The profession is still in its infancy, for instance, in its capability for the efficient theoretical handling of risk and uncertainty. Some exciting starts have been made, but there is still a considerable distance to go. Progress in this field is especially critical for the subject of this volume because, both empirically and intuitively, there are strong grounds for assuming that risk and uncertainty affect the trade in new products more than in old, and that these factors shape the behavior of exporters and importers more strongly than the behavior of traders within a single national market.

Related to questions of risk and uncertainty are questions of optimal investment in the acquisition of knowledge. The money-cost and time-cost of acquiring information affect all economic decisions in some degree. But there are grounds for supposing that they affect international trade, especially trade at the technological forefront, with special force.

On similar lines, the assumption of horizontal or rising cost curves proves an especially confining one for the international trade theorist concerned with the marketing of new products. It is one of the more firmly documented facts of international trade that such trade tends to be conducted by the larger firms in any industry; and it is fairly evident that scale economies play a role in that phenomenon. To make matters even more difficult, there are repeated hints in the empirical data that some of the scale economies that affect the international trade capabilities of national firms may be based in good measure on factors of agglomeration external to the firm. There are few concepts in economic theory more ill-defined and more resistant to precise formulation.

Finally, there is the difficult issue in international trade theory of defining the economic actor whose activities are to be explained and described. Few branches of economic theory can wholly disregard the fact that modern industrial processes usually involve a drawn out sequence of commodity transformations, rather than a single act of transformation. Sometimes these sequences—including the conversion of raw materials into intermediate products and components followed by incorporation in some final product—are undertaken from beginning to end within a single firm. The economics of these intrafirm transfers may be important, but they can often be disregarded by the theorist when the transfer occurs inside a single national market. Where international trade is concerned, however, intrafirm transfers become disconcertingly prominent. About one-quarter of U.S. exports of manufactured goods, for instance, has consisted of transfers of goods between affiliates; and the proportion has been especially high in technically advanced products. At that level, the implicit assumption that international trade is the product of the arms' length behavior of independent buyers and sellers begins to have its obvious limitations as a basis for relevant and efficient theory. The economic theorist may then be confronted with the question whether he will eventually be obliged to master and assimilate a theory of the organizational behavior of the firm with the main body of trade theory in order to generate a credible model of international trade.

Sufficient unto the day, however, are the theories thereof. Increased understanding in a field as complex as trade theory is bound to be a slow and costly process. One can only hope that the contributions in this volume represent a modest step forward.

Technology and the

Theory of International Trade

The State of Theory

in Relation to the

Empirical Analysis

HARRY G. JOHNSON

LONDON SCHOOL OF ECONOMICS
AND UNIVERSITY OF CHICAGO

The decision to hold the Universities-National Bureau Conference on Technology and Competition in International Trade was largely motivated by the beliefs that empirical research on patterns of international trade had revealed and confirmed important technological influences which were not recognized in the established theory of comparative cost, and that in the interests of scientific progress it would be highly desirable to confront empiricists and theoreticians with a stock-taking of the current treatment of the technology factor in international economics. The purpose of this paper is to discuss, in the light both of the literature prior to the Conference and the papers prepared specifically for the Conference, how far and in what respects there may be said to be a conflict between the empirical findings and the theoretical models, and to suggest ways in which any such conflict may be reconciled in establishing new foundations for future scientific advance.

To begin with, it is, I think, important and necessary to recognize a crucial difference between the role of theory in the context of empirical

NOTE: This is a revised and extended version of the paper actually presented at the Conference. This paper and the first version draw heavily on ideas developed in two earlier attempts of mine to come to grips with the problem of the technology factor in trade, my Wicksell Lectures of March 1968 [5] and my International Economic Association World Congress paper of September 1968 [6]. In discussing the state of theory in relation to the technology factor, however, I have regarded these efforts as not belonging to the literature relevant to the Conference.

research, and its role in economics generally.[1] In the context of economics as an empirical science, the function of theory is to cast up empirically testable and refutable explanatory hypotheses, and the value of a theory is to be judged by its explanatory power in comparison with its rivals. In the broader context of economics as a systematic approach to the understanding of economic phenomena and as the organization of disciplined thinking about these phenomena and about policies relating to them, however, the purpose of theory is to abstract from the complexity of the real world a simplified model of the key relationships between dependent and independent variables, and to explore the positive and normative implications of changes in the "givens" of this hypothetical system. For this purpose, the validity of the empirical foundations of a theory is, obviously within limits, not of such crucial importance, in the sense that the principles of interrelatedness, of systematic response to change, and of optimization remain valid in the face of wide variations in assumed economic structure.

The theory of international trade has always been primarily theory in the second sense. Specifically, it has not been much concerned with the empirical problems of predicting or prescribing which goods will or should be traded by particular countries, or of specifying the characteristics of such goods. Instead, it has tended to draw on prevailing models of the domestic economy, and particularly of the domestic production system, as the bases for analysis of the positive and normative aspects of trade between national economies with differing production opportunities. In this connection, the central contribution to both positive and normative economics of the theory of international trade has been the principle of comparative cost—a principle which is not dependent on any particular assumptions about the nature of production.

Although this way of constructing a theory is legitimate enough—again within limits—for the purposes at hand, it does court the definite risk of freezing into the theoretical apparatus a model of the production process which is gradually being revealed by further research conducted by specialists on domestic economics as inadequate, and consequently of appearing increasingly irrelevant, if not downright in error, as a guide to understanding, interpreting, and operating in the real world of experience. As is well-known, the theory of international trade

[1] The argument of this and the next two paragraphs was inspired by some comments by R. E. Caves on my World Congress paper.

retained the labor theory of value as an explanation of domestic production equilibrium long after that theory had been superseded by the marginalist revolution in the theory of domestic value. Moreover, the efforts of certain neoclassical trade theorists to "patch up" the labor theory of value with elements of marginalism and Marshallian partial equilibrium analysis resulted in an increasingly cumbersome theoretical structure, which was eventually discarded in favor of the Heckscher-Ohlin-Samuelson model of general equilibrium.

The Heckscher-Ohlin-Samuelson model—which, it should be noted, is in its contemporary form largely the work of Samuelson and disregards some of the more penetrating insights of the other two economists credited with its authorship—builds on the formalization of production theory in the mathematical concept of the production function. That concept, in its simplest textbook form of a constant returns-to-scale relation between output of product and inputs of the two homogeneous factors capital and labor, constitutes an extremely powerful but an equally extreme and restrictive simplification of production economics. Assuming perfect competition, international indentity of production functions and factors, nonreversibility of factor intensities, and international similarity of preferences, the constant returns-to-scale application to international trade theory leads to the dual key theorems—the differential factor-endowment explanation of trade theorem and the factor price equalization theorem. These are undoubtedly elegant theorems. But they are essentially mathematical theorems whose relevance and interest depend not only on the assumptions listed but more fundamentally on the relevance and usefulness of the production function concept itself.

The fundamental question, which has been raised in general by a large body of recent empirical and theoretical work on the economics of domestic industrial production and competition and on the role of technological change in economic growth, and which has been raised in particular by the recent empirical work on the technology factor in international trade, is whether orthodox international trade theory has once again reached a position of commitment to an antiquated and misleading model of the production process, which has to be rejected to further the progress of economic science.

This is a question which needs to be approached with considerable care, since there are natural pressures on everyone to arrive at an answer that justifies and if possible exalts his own choice of research activity, and it is only too easy to define the problem so as to arrive at a preconceived answer. For purposes of attack, orthodox theory can be identified with a specific textbook model designed to illustrate general principles but required by the critic to provide a detailed guide to empirical research and economic policy-making; for purposes of defense, orthodoxy can be endowed with a flexibility capable of absorbing any reasonable concept, or defined so broadly and vaguely as to be potentially consistent with all observed phenomena. These contrasting temptations can be illustrated by reference to certain papers prepared for this Conference.

Bruno, for example, identifies orthodoxy with the static analysis of the two-country model, assuming identical given production functions and no capital flows, and sets up in its place a dynamic linear programming optimization model for a single economy with foreign aid receipts as the key variable. This model, although ingenious in some respects and presumably useful to the Israeli planning authorities, not only involves the purely arbitrary constraints necessary to make a linear programming problem both interesting and computable, but so far as I can see contains nothing logically inconsistent with the application of orthodox theory to the same problem and also nothing that adds to our understanding of comparative advantage or the role of technology in determining and changing trade patterns.

On the other hand, Hall and Johnson assert, as if it proved something, that their paper illustrates that "international flows of technology can be studied profitably by means of conventional market-force analysis." In fact, however, all they show—though in admirably careful detail— is that technological transfers can be subjected to cost-benefit analysis. Their case, moreover, is a politically motivated, not market-directed, transfer; and their most striking finding is that, *contrary to prevailing opinion in the industry itself,* the transfer reduced the aircraft's cost of production. Apparently expert opinion in the industry overestimated the importance of engineering efficiency and underestimated the potential cost-saving from substituting cheaper Japanese for more expensive American labor. If such miscalculations of potential comparative cost are commonplace in industrial management circles, serious questions arise about (1) the amenability of technological transplantation to treatment as a rational economic process, and (2) the welfare implications of relying on the process of competition among large industrial firms to diffuse technical progress through the world economy.

Again on the side of orthodoxy, Ronald Jones' elegant paper demonstrates a point known to international trade theorists for over a decade,[2] that the Heckscher-Ohlin-Samuelson model can be readily adapted to place the emphasis of the analysis on technological differences, and goes on to discuss in a perceptive way how the approaches of recent research on the product cycle and the technology factor can be incorporated in formal theory. His analysis, however, markedly fails to capture the dynamic orientation of that research, but it does underline the key problem of making the connection between them the development of a satisfactory inducement mechanism for innovation. Moreover, the extension of the model in the ways he discusses reduces it perilously close to eclectic taxonomy.

The purely theoretical paper by Chipman goes beyond Jones' paper in applying recent developments in the theory of induced innovations in growth models of international trade. In so doing Chipman confirms the flexibility of theory and its power to absorb and apply ideas drawn from empirical work; but the paper's results are equally remote from the real stuff of the world of observation.

The fundamental problem, the conflict between the empirical findings and the theoretical models, can be seen in part as a continuation in the international trade field of the debate begun in the 1930's over the issue of monopolistic, as contrasted with perfect, competition— with the important difference that monopolistic competition is now viewed as a rational corollary of the evolution of technology in a free enterprise system rather than as a manifestation of consumer irrationality. The new empirical research stresses the influence on international trade patterns of factors determining monopolistically competitive ability—technological leadership, economies of scale, and product variation (nonstandardization). The orthodox theoretical tradition stresses differences in the classical determinants of wealth—specifically, capital per head— on the assumption of a broadly competitive international economy.

---

[2] For an early extension of the model to the case of technical changes, see my [3].

It may be observed parenthetically that the consternation caused to traditional theorists by the publication of the Leontief paradox can in the light of hindsight be attributed in large part to a misspecification, based on the identification in the English classical and neoclassical tradition of "capital" with capital equipment, and "labor" with human bodies regardless of skill, of the empirical counterparts of the arguments on the production function. The publication of the paradox led immediately, as Hufbauer rather scornfully points out, to tortuous efforts to rescue the factor proportions theorem by appeals to differences in demand conditions, or to the possibility of factor-intensity reversals. However, in the longer run, and partly in response to the development and application elsewhere in theory and empirical research of the concept of human capital, the outcome has been the recognition of human skills as an important constituent of capital together with material equipment and structures. This recognition goes a considerable way towards resolving the Leontief paradox; and, as I have suggested elsewhere (5), the paradox could probably be fully dispelled—at least formally—by extending the concept of capital to include the capitalized value of productive knowledge created by research and development (R&D) expenditure.

It must be admitted, however, that no one has yet performed the required calculations; and also that, as both the Hufbauer paper and the Gruber and Vernon paper have carefully confirmed, the Leontief paradox in its original form still stands. An explanation of it has been provided by proponents of the R&D explanation of U.S. comparative advantage in the form of an inverse correlation between material capital intensity and R&D effort in the United States (see [1] and [7]). Such a correlation is not necessarily a law of nature: Hirsch's paper finds a direct correlation in the case of Israeli industry.

Returning to the general framework of the debate in terms of classical comparative cost theory versus monopolistic competition theory, the difficulty and unsatisfactoriness of that debate in its late-1930's form arose from the fact that monopolistic competition theory is partial equilibrium theory—and therefore permits the insertion of a great deal of empirical detail—whereas comparative cost theory is general equilibrium theory—and therefore is useful and manageable only when it can be kept reasonably simple. The rock on which attempts to apply monopolistic competition theory to international trade theory—initially a hopeful enterprise—foundered, was the inability of theorists to translate monopolistic competition concepts into forms relevant for general equilibrium analysis.[3]

A parallel problem has emerged in the contemporary confrontation between empirical research emphasizing various aspects of the technology factor and its dynamic manifestations in international competition, and the grand simplicity of the neoclassical general equilibrium model of comparative advantage. Most of the empirical studies have been concerned with particular industries or the trade of the United States—by no means a typical country. And this has left to individual judgment the question of whether the empirical findings are to be considered as frontal contradictions of prevailing theory, or as curious or exceptional cases that are not inconsistent with the central theoretical propositions but require merely a more sophisticated interpretation and extension of them.

Hufbauer in his excellent paper emphasizes the dangers of testing hypotheses against a limited range of commodities or countries and the necessity of comprehensive testing of hypotheses against one another on a common (and extensive) set of data. The Gruber and Vernon study, though not explicitly devoted to testing rival hypotheses against one another, uses a comparable methodological approach. Hufbauer's study finds that the crude factor proportions theory performs surprisingly well according to the tests he runs. But so, embarrassingly, does every other theory proposed by a competent observing economist. The theories that cannot be confirmed empirically, to generalize beyond Hufbauer's study, are those proposed either in support of anti-orthodox policy prescriptions, or in more or less direct contradiction to comparative advantage theory in the broad sense—theories not really motivated by the spirit of scientific research and progress in understanding. The same eclectic conclusion emerges from the study by Gruber and Vernon: R&D expenditure as a surrogate for the technology factor is demonstrably significant as a determinant of international trade patterns, but it is not a powerful enough influence to supersede more conventional explanations of these patterns.

These results should be encouraging to all honest men—"little truths

[3] On this point, see my [4].

in every nook" is an undramatic but satisfyingly scholarly interim position to have arrived at, and one that opens up rather than closes off new avenues of theoretical and empirical research. It is, however, somewhat discouraging for those whose preference is for simple theories and for decisive testing of rival hypotheses against one another—especially if such testing can shatter orthodoxy in favor of heterodoxy or confirm the superiority of empirical-inductive over abstract-deductive approaches to international economic research.[4]

In the summary of his paper Hufbauer expresses something of this discouragement by posing again what I have described as the central issue of the Conference, in terms of the alternative "neofactor proportions" and "neotechnology" accounts of the determination of trade patterns, and suggests hopefully that if returns to scale, product age, and product differentiation could be combined into a single characteristic "that characteristic might prove as powerful as Lary's single measure (value added per man) of human and physical capital in explaining trade flows."[5] However, he adds rather wistfully, "the neotechnology approach is not geared to answering the traditional questions of economic inquiry. It can as yet offer little to compare with Samuelson's splendid factor price equalization theorem."

These remarks of Hufbauer's reveal a certain schizophrenia involving belief in the methodology of empirical testing to rival hypotheses (tempered naturally enough by concern for the chances of victory for one's favorite candidate) on the one hand, and admiration for the formal elegance of traditional theory on the other. In my judgment, they both sell the neotechnology approach short and obnubilate the theoretical and empirical issues. I conclude with three extended comments on these remarks.

First, it seems to me, as a rank amateur in empirical research in this field, that part of the power of Lary's statistic is that it picks up not only the neofactor proportion elements of material and human capital, but also to some extent the neotechnology elements of scale economies, and

---

[4] Actually, the difference is a matter of degree rather than of kind, for even the most abstract theory starts from some postulates about the nature of reality derived, however remotely, from observation, while even the most inductive approach requires some sort of theory specifying relevant facts.

[5] Editor's Note: See also the note by Lary in this volume for tests applying the value added variable to Hufbauer's trade data.

of product age and differentiation insofar as these are reflected in selling prices. Thus a composite neotechnology index, if one could be constructed, would be entered in a biased test against the Lary statistic, if the latter were identified uniquely with the neofactor proportions account of the courses of trade. If hypotheses are to be tested against each other on the basis of single indexes, the indexes must represent the hypotheses clearly. I would further suggest that something more might be learned about the neotechnology account from closer study of international differences in the Lary index, though I have not thought of a detailed research procedure that might be applied.

Second, the "adversary procedure" of testing one hypothesis against another is a useful scientific procedure up to a point; but, when both hypotheses perform well and seem to be fairly evenly matched, it is not necessarily the best scientific procedure to send the challenger back to training camp with good advice on how to prepare for the next month. In the realm of ideas, a conflict of equally well (or equally imperfectly) supported hypotheses may be more fruitfully resolved by merger into a composite hypothesis.

Specifically, as I have suggested above and elsewhere [5], the impression of strong conflict between the neofactor proportions and neotechnology accounts of international trade may reflect merely the domination of trade theory by the narrow concept of capital as material equipment, inherited from the English classical, neoclassical, and now neo-Keynesian economists. The concept of capital considered relevant has now been extended to include human capital—an extension which the neotechnology proponents in their roles as adversaries of the factor proportions theory may have accepted too easily for their own good— and could easily be extended further to include intellectual capital in the form of productive knowledge. Such an extension would be fully consistent with Irving Fisher's approach to the relation between capital and income. In that context, the neotechnology school can be interpreted as insisting on the importance of productive knowledge as a form of capital that is to be included in the theory of production, rather than as advancing a theory of international trade patterns to rival the factor proportions theory. Further, the neotechnology school can be viewed as emphasizing the process of obsolescence as well as the international mobility of capital in the form of productive knowledge, an aspect of capital which has generally been ignored in the neofactor proportions models.

More generally, a synthesis of the presumed rival hypotheses could be sought conceptually through revisions of the basic concept of the production function employed in standard trade theory. The standard concept implies capital equipment used by homogeneous labor to produce a given product according to a given technology. A more relevant concept would envisage capital embodied in various forms—natural resources, equipment and structures, human skills, and the productive knowledge used to combine them—cooperating to produce bundles of want-satisfying characteristics embodied in products whose nature changes as knowledge accumulates and demand changes. In this framework, the theory of comparative advantage would remain neoclassical in outline, resting on international differences in capital in the extended sense per unit of population, but would have to concern itself also with the influences governing the allocation of capital among the different forms in which it may be embodied, in countries of different economic sizes and with different institutions for the education of people and the support of knowledge production.

This observation brings me to my third comment. The appeal of the neotechnology account is not primarily that it is capable of explaining international trade patterns to a statistically satisfactory degree or better than an extended version of the factor proportions model, but that it accords more satisfactorily with prevailing ideas about, and observations of, the facts of competition in and between modern industrial states. Conversely, the dissatisfaction of empirical workers and policy advisers with the traditional factor proportions model is not so much that it does not explain trade flows to a satisfactory approximation as that its static and essentially mathematical formulation—and especially the production concept—is difficult to square with the apparent facts of competition in a dynamically evolving economy. What practical men—empirical workers and policymakers alike—see when they look at international competition is not national differences in factor endowments but corporations competing monopolistically either on the bases of superior technology, labor skill, managerial and selling techniques or on the more conventional bases of cheap labor and cheap capital.

This view is not, of course, sufficient to establish the neotechnology and dismiss the neofactor proportions theory; on the contrary, particularly in the field of international economic policy, preoccupation with the manifestations of neotechnology factors is likely to obscure understanding and facilitate erroneous conclusions. But it does suggest the need for a more sophisticated formulation of the Heckscher-Ohlin-Samuelson theory, and particularly for a more careful identification of the empirical correlates of its theoretical constructs, most notably with respect to "factors of production" and "products." More bridges need to be built between the abstract, theoretical model of trade, and the concrete phenomena that concern the practical man. I have suggested above how this problem might be approached.

Further, I would suggest that the neotechnology hypotheses embody both empirical and theoretical insights and point to both new problems and new formulations of old problems that ought to be pursued in their own right, unconstrained by the ambition to arrive at results as elegant as those of the Heckscher-Ohlin-Samuelson model. The Samuelson factor price equalization theorem is indeed a splendid proposition; but its chief practical relevance is to direct attention—by the indirect process of theoretical abstraction—to the many reasons why factor prices, and more still, incomes per head, are unlikely to be equalized in the real world as we know it. I believe that the neotechnological account offers a more direct and positive approach to this conclusion and also a more sophisticated and genuinely dynamic approach to the understanding of the persistence of inequalities of levels of development and of economic welfare in a developing world economy.

I would also suggest that the phenomena of modern international industrial competition, and the policy problems to which they give rise—especially those concerning policy toward science and policy toward foreign corporations—raise theoretical issues of far greater complexity than can be dealt with by the existing theories of tariffs. We are, as Ohlin emphasized in his paper for the Montreal World Congress [8], moving into a world of freer trade but much more direct governmental intervention in industry. Much of that intervention is directed at mastering the technology factor as a means of improving the comparative advantage and competitive power of the national economy, or of its nationally owned corporations. Traditional theory offers useful approaches to the analysis of some of these problems or apparent problems: conventional market analysis suffices to dispose of much popular nonsense. But as Posner [9] and Hufbauer himself [2] have pointed out (though in neither case with enough specificity to clarify the nature of the problem) there is a need for more fundamental analysis of the welfare effects of technological leadership and their diffusion, and correspondingly of the economics of government intervention in these matters. So long as one does not question the existing system of property rights in knowledge and in its productive application for profit, it is easy enough to elaborate on the traditional case for freedom of trade and freedom of factor movements and against government interference. But the essential problem is that reliance on the market principle of rewarding investment in the discovery of knowledge, which has the nature of a public good, by granting a temporary monopoly of the use of the knowledge, which makes the application of it suboptimal, is inherently inefficient. It is the recognition of questions of this kind and ultimately their solution, rather than the provision of new solutions to the traditional problems of "income distribution, migration, saving, and investment," that I would expect and hope to emerge from the challenge to traditional theory posed by the neotechnology approach.

REFERENCES

1. Gruber, W., Mehta, D., and Vernon, R., "The R&D Factor in International Trade and International Investment of U.S. Industries," *Journal of Political Economy,* February 1967, pp. 20–37.

2. Hufbauer, G. C., *Synthetic Materials and the Theory of International Trade,* London, 1965.

3. Johnson, Harry G., "Economic Expansion and International Trade," *The Manchester School of Economic and Social Studies,* May 1955, pp. 95–112.

4. Johnson, Harry G., "International Trade Theory and Monopolistic Competition Theory," in R. E. Kuenne (ed.), *Monopolistic Theory: Studies in Import,* New York, 1967, pp. 203–218.

5. Johnson, Harry G., "Comparative Cost and Commercial Policy Theory for a Developing World Economy," Wicksell Lectures of 1968, mimeographed.

6. Johnson, Harry G., "The Theory of International Trade," forthcoming in the Proceedings of the Third World Congress of the International Economics Association, or *The Future of International Economic Relations,* held in Montreal, Canada, September 2–7, 1968.

7. Keesing, D. B., "The Impact of Research and Development on United States Trade," *Journal of Political Economy,* February 1967, pp. 38–48.

8. Ohlin, G., "Trade in a Non-Laissez-Faire World," forthcoming in the Proceedings of the Third World Congress of the International Economics Association, or *The Future of International Economic Relations,* held in Montreal, Canada, September 2–7, 1968.

9. Posner, M. V., "International Trade and Technical Change," *Oxford Economic Papers,* October 1961, pp. 323–341.

10. Vernon, R., "International Investment and International Trade in the Product Cycle," *Quarterly Journal of Economics,* May 1966, pp. 190–207.

COMMENT

JAGDISH N. BHAGWATI
Massachusetts Institute of Technology

The papers of Harry Johnson and Ronald Jones [1] concur in the theme that trade theory has been somewhat left behind by the real world, especially in relation to the phenomenon of technological progress. While Jones essentially tries to develop the traditional Heckscher-Ohlin-Samuelson model of trade theory (which is basically a simplified general equilibrium model of the Hicksian variety) in directions implied by the consideration of technical change, the Johnson paper attempts to develop themes which are on a more "imaginative" scale but which seem to have no theoretical foundations as of the present moment.

Looking through the Johnson paper, one gets the strong impression of reading John Williams (a reference which, I assume, Harry Johnson would regard as complimentary): imaginative, insightful, stimulating, and pregnant with theoretical implications without actually offering a new theoretical framework for analysis. But one also gets an occasional impression of reading someone like Thomas Balogh (a reference which Harry Johnson would probably not approve of): imaginative and insightful but basically opposed to theoretical modes of reasoning, as when towards the end of his paper Johnson would gladly sacrifice such theories as those which yield powerful conclusions with respect to distributive shares in order to make his description of the real world move closer to observation.

I shall be returning to this question later, but let me say briefly at this stage that the real problem with Johnson's interesting paper is that the

[1] For comment on Jones see page 93 below.

"realistic" phenomena which he is dealing with, such as the development of new technologies in consumption and production, involve essentially phenomena of imperfect competition for which, despite Chamberlin and Joan Robinson, we still do not have today any serious theories of general equilibrium. Therefore, although we can certainly indulge in *partial* analyses of imperfectly competitive phenomena, we cannot yet replace the traditional value-theoretic models of general equilibrium on which even our welfare analyses are based. Unless therefore we have a new, powerful, theoretic system (built admittedly on many of the interesting insights about modern, affluent economies which Johnson offers us in his paper), we cannot really hope to make a dent in the traditional theoretical frames of analysis.

Having said this, however, let me offer some general remarks about the important point made by Johnson about the tendency of trade theory to get stuck with analytical models and questions that nontrade theorists have discarded in favor of more useful constructs. I *do* think that there are several problems for which the traditional Heckscher-Ohlin-Samuelson model has become obsolete: for example, those dealing with questions such as process, value-added or "effective" tariffs, as distinct from nominal tariffs, which require operating with a model involving traded factors of production or inputs rather than with the traditional model involving primary, nontraded factors producing traded consumer goods. But then, as we know, trade theory has indeed been adapting itself by using more variegated models, better suited to such problems. As for the kinds of questions asked, the recent introduction of dynamic analyses represents an important extension of traditional comparative-static treatments. For example, Michael Bruno's paper at this Conference represents an attempt at building a computational, planning model which takes into account the fact that comparative advantage shifts over time. The very fact that, if you had nonshiftable capital in a world where over time the foreign rate of transformation faced by a country could change, introduces the possibility that *someone* would have to "look ahead": the traditional, static models of gains-from-trade do not yield such insights, and recent interest in "structural" models has begun to penetrate through to trade-theoretic analyses as well to Jones.

But I do remain a pessimist at being able to handle the kinds of broader issues, such as imperfect competition, that Harry Johnson's stimulating paper raises. It would be valuable to hear from him what *precisely* is the manner in which he thinks we can begin to reconstruct our theories so as to bring them closer to his view of the role of technology in international trade in a developing world.

Models Incorporating

the Technology Factor

Development Policy

and Dynamic

Comparative Advantage

MICHAEL BRUNO

HEBREW UNIVERSITY

I. INTRODUCTION

It is now generally recognized that foreign exchange and international trade considerations should form key elements in the rational planning of development in most economies. However, it is also commonly believed that there is relatively little in the traditional theory of international trade that seems immediately applicable to development planning. We are often told, on the basis of theory or fact, that the received comparative cost doctrine, for example, has little to offer in this context because its assumptions and frame of reference are for various reasons irrelevant. This claim is not without foundation. Most formal theory is confined to two-country, static systems in which commodities, factor endowments, and (uniform) production functions are specified for both trading partners and the static optimal trade pattern is analyzed under the assumption of a trade balance. Only lip service is paid to the fact that any one country has numerous trading partners, that trade is in the present context hardly ever balanced, and that foreign aid and foreign investment is the rule rather than the exception. Last, but not least, trade like growth

NOTE: I wish to acknowledge the support of the National Bureau of Economic Research, New York, and the Bank of Israel, Jerusalem. Likewise I am indebted to Mordecai Fraenkel of the Bank of Israel for numerous very helpful discussions about some of the questions analyzed here. This paper is closely related to and was much inspired by a study that he, Christopher Dougherty, a student at Harvard, and I have recently conducted [6].

is a process that takes place over time, and dynamic considerations must play a central role in a theory of comparative advantage.

Between orthodox adherence to existing theories and summary dismissal of them, there should be some useful, intermediate standpoint. What seems most important as a first step is to set up systematic general equilibrium frameworks in which dynamic considerations of both development and trade could be dealt with simultaneously. Otherwise, there is no way of formulating empirically workable alternative hypotheses, and arguments of a rather imprecise kind can just flourish.[1]

Rather than grafting growth aspects to a two- (or multi-) country trade model, we shall look at trade from the point of view of the individual optimizing economy. In this situation foreign exchange is just another, albeit rather special, factor of production—largely complementary but partly substitutable—which possesses a given endowment (foreign aid), and certain intertemporal borrowing is allowed. Foreign exchange can be earned or saved by producing "trade" goods (exports or import substitutes). The economy produces other "final" goods (consumption, investment) and also directly and indirectly uses "primary" inputs (labor, capital of one or more kinds). The technology is assumed to be a discrete activity-analysis type technology. This is both flexible enough to allow for the introduction of some important nonlinearities and externalities and at the same time is of the kind that lends itself best to empirical implementation and verification.[2] Optimization takes the form of the maximization of some welfare function subject to the production, foreign exchange, and trade (and possibly institutional) constraints.

An important difference between the single country optimization approach and that of the usual two-country analyses of international

---

[1] The clearest and one of the earliest discussions of the dichotomy between the existing trade and development theory approaches is Chenery's [7]. Bhagwati in his excellent survey [3] also stresses the need for a more systematic analysis of the bordering fields. There certainly is more empirical work available now than there was four or seven years ago. Still one feels that a lot remains to be done, especially on improving the analytical tools to handle empirical situations falling outside existing theory. The rapid progress of the more systematic formal growth (as distinct from "development") theory in its preoccupation with closed economies only testifies to the same lacuna.

[2] In this connection one should mention the tools used in the analysis of the Leontief [10] paradox, and also the development planning literature of the linear-programming type.

trade is in the way comparative advantage ordering is established. A change in the availability of foreign exchange in relation to the endowment of other factors will call forth a change in the optimal bundle of foreign trade activities. The theory of comparative advantage in our analysis, whether in a static or dynamic context, consists of spelling out the resulting order of choice of these optimal bundles. In a static two-factor (plus foreign exchange) world, the result is something less simple but probably more generally applicable than Heckscher-Ohlin. However, an unambiguous ordering of activities can be established.

Section II of this paper briefly discusses a number of alternative static, single-period-optimization formulations of the problem. This is used in order to set the stage for the subsequent more realistic dynamic models and also helps to relate the development planning approach to the more common trade theory formulation. This is followed by a short digression (Section III) from the main theme—a discussion of the empirical possibility of interpreting the fixed coefficients approximation of a static model on the basis of *marginal,* rather than average, coefficients. This may have markedly different implications for the price structure and the pattern of comparative advantage and is probably worth exploring further in empirical work.

Section IV, entitled "An Intertemporal Analysis of Trade and Growth," forms the center of our study. In this section we also concentrate on the implications for comparative advantage of a number of important dynamic factors. Apart from the usual capital investment relations, these implications are the possibility of interperiod borrowing and lending of foreign exchange and the existence of externalities in the export process itself. Productivity changes and growth factors come in and trade goods can no longer be ordered independently of time. Nevertheless, under a fairly general set of assumptions a dynamic analogue of comparative advantage ordering can be established, involving both activities and the optimal time of their expansion. We also briefly discuss the possibility of incorporating labor training effects in the linear model.

In the subsequent and final section, (V), there are some empirical illustrations of the workings of the dynamic model based on Israeli data. This is not meant as a test of hypotheses but rather to show that such policy formulation can be given empirical content.

II. A STATIC PROLOGUE

This section deals with an optimization version of a number of alternative static production and trade models. These are related to the kinds of production frameworks also used in the trade theory literature. We start with a relatively straightforward Ricardian model.

A. A simple Ricardian system

Consider an open economy producing a composite consumption good (C) and choosing from among m foreign trade activities T_i ($i = 1, 2, \ldots , m$). These can be either exports or import substitutes and their net marginal foreign exchange revenue per unit is fixed ($= v_i$).[3] The economy is assumed to be small enough to take its import prices as given. At the same time this formulation allows for monopolistic export markets.

Apart from foreign exchange of which an equivalent of m_0 per incremental unit is used in producing the consumption good, suppose the economy uses a primary factor (labor) whose input coefficients in the various activities will be denoted by l_i ($i = 0, 1, \ldots , m$; the subscript 0 refers to the consumption good) and all refer to some given (future) planning period. We shall presently extend the technology to include capital goods, but for the moment we are sticking to the one-factor Ricardian case.

Let us now assume that our economy maximizes the single period consumption level C, subject to two net supply [4] constraints: a constraint on foreign exchange transfers (denoted by F); and a constraint on the primary input (L). To make for a more realistic choice of foreign trade activities, we also assume that the range of operation of each activity is bound by exogenously fixed minimum (T_i) and maximum ($\bar{T}_i$) levels (see constraint (1)). ("Trade activity" as used here is the production and sales of goods for export or for the substitution of imports, by specified industries.)

Our problem can now be expressed in the following form:

---

[3] This is "net" in the sense that we subtract from gross revenue all direct and indirect import requirements. In the case of an import substitute, v_i is net foreign exchange *saved* by one unit of the activity in question. (See also [5]—here we depart in a number of ways from the notation used in that paper.)

[4] "Net" here means that we subtract from the gross supply whatever fixed exogenous demand of the factor that is required (see [5]).

Maximize C subject to:

(1) $\quad\quad\quad \underline{T}_i \le T_i \le \overline{T}_i \quad\quad$ (trade activity constraints:

$$i = 1, 2, \ldots, m)$$

(2) $\quad\quad m_0 C - \sum_{i=1}^{m} v_i T_i \le F \quad\quad$ (foreign exchange constraint)

(3) $\quad\quad\quad l_0 C + \sum_{i=1}^{m} l_i T_i \le L \quad\quad$ (labor constraint)

No profound analysis is needed to see the nature of the solution in this case. The trade activities can be unambiguously ordered by their (Ricardian) comparative advantage ratios—v_i/l_i i.e., net foreign exchange revenue per unit of labor input. With a given supply of F and L the economy will produce its consumption level optimally if it follows the v_i/l_i scale for expansion of the trade activities, up to the point at which all labor is exhausted. Put in more formal terms, if we denote the shadow price of foreign exchange (in terms of consumption units) by q and that of labor (the real wage) by w, there will always be one trade activity (suppose it is the jth activity) that is just profitable at that price pair, so that we get:

(4) $\quad\quad\quad l_j w - v_j q = 0 \quad\quad$ (domestic costs in the jth

trade activity = its net

marginal revenue)

(5) $\quad\quad\quad l_0 w + m_0 q = 1 \quad\quad$ (total costs in consumption =

the price of consumption = 1)

from which we obtain:

$$w = \frac{v_j}{l_j m_0 + l_0 v_j}, \quad q = \frac{l_j}{l_j m_0 + l_0 v_j} \quad^5$$

[5] The full formal solution would be obtained by looking at the dual linear-programming formulation. Let us denote the shadow prices attached to the maximum and minimum constraint in (1) by $\overline{p}$ and $\underline{p}$ respectively. We then have:

$$Minimize \ wL + qF + \sum_{i=1}^{M} (\overline{p}_i \overline{T}_i - \underline{p}_i \underline{T}_i)$$

subject to

(7) $\quad\quad\quad\quad\quad\quad wl_0 + qm_0 \ge 1$

(8) $\quad\quad\quad wl_i - qv_i + \overline{p}_i - \underline{p}_i \ge 0 \quad (i = 1, 2, \ldots, m)$

Obviously for each good we will always have either $\overline{p}_1$ or $\underline{p}_i$ equal to zero with one case ($i = j$, say) at most in which both are zero and the good is just profitable. It is also the case that both (7) and (8) will always be satisfied with equality.

If we define the (static) *exchange cost* of an activity to be its real domestic costs of production per unit of foreign exchange earned (or saved) when it is just profitable (denoted by R_i), we obtain

$$(6) \qquad R_i = \frac{l_i w(i)}{v_i} = \frac{l_i}{l_i m_0 + l_0 v_i} = \frac{l}{m_0 + l_0(v_i/l_i)} \qquad {}^6$$

With the given F and L supplies, all trade activities i for which $R_i < R_j = q$ will be produced to the maximum ($T_i = \bar{T}_i$), i.e., they will be intramarginal, and all those for which $R_i > R_j = q$ will remain at their minimum values ($T_i = \underline{T}_i$).

The easiest way to describe the order and process of choice in such a model is to keep the supply of labor (L) fixed and change the relative scarcity of foreign exchange by varying F and watching the sequence of optimal "bases" in the linear programming solution. Clearly the order of expansion (or contraction) of the trade activities will be the order of R_i as measured by (6) above. Comparative advantage has an unambiguous meaning here and depends on a single technical coefficient, just as we would expect.

Before introducing more factors of production, let us make a few additional remarks on other aspects of the system represented by (1) to (3):

(i) As is explained elsewhere, our formulation of trade activities is quite general. They may represent physically different commodities or they may also represent stepwise linear portions of upward-rising supply curves or downward-sloping demand curves of a single export commodity. In the case of import substitutes the minimum bound formulation in (1) may allow for negative import substitution, and in the case of exports for the introduction of institutional limitations (e.g., vested

---

[6] A slightly different way in which we could define the "exchange cost" (also the form more likely to be used in cost benefit calculations) is to compare costs in terms of the *same* shadow prices (here w)—those which happen to hold at the point of comparison. For our present purpose, however, it is more meaningful to evaluate R_i in terms of the prices that will hold when *it* will be just profitable (here denoted by $w(i)$). In this way we can, whenever possible, try to obtain a complete measure of comparative advantage ranking that is independent of factor prices. The alternative procedure of using $l_i w/v_i$ (rather than $l_i w(i)/v_i$) to compare with q is consistent with the use of the simplex criterion to decide whether a given activity is or is not pofitable. It does not, in a more general model, necessarily help to establish ranking independently of prices.

interests forcing a minimum positive level of exports of certain unprofitable goods).

(ii) The primary input coefficients (here and in all the subsequent more general formulations) should be understood in the Leontief sense of *total* (direct and indirect) input coefficients, i.e., there are underlying intermediate inputs in our economy and their impact is embodied in our calculations of the total primary input coefficients. Ever since the Leontief paradox discussion this has become common practice. One might only note that the primary input coefficients for any future planning period should incorporate any known (or best practice) technological change, here assumed to be exogenously given.

(iii) Our economy is assumed to receive some amount of foreign exchange (F) from abroad at no direct cost. Borrowing costs could be incorporated without difficulty but this would distract our attention from the main issues (we shall return to a more satisfactory, dynamic view of foreign borrowing in Section IV). The explicit role of F here is to represent a policy variable whose change we use as a means of characterizing patterns of comparative advantage.

(iv) The aggregation of C in this framework can be justified empirically on the basis of linear approximations of Engel curves for the components of the consumption bundle. Moreover, the model could be generalized to allow for different ways of supplying aggregate utility, but this would not affect the main trade features with which we are concerned here.

B. *Incorporating capital in a Ricardian approach*

Let us now introduce capital goods and investment into the system in a specific form which will preserve the system's Ricardian nature. Suppose we have an underlying capital output matrix in the original interindustry system and suppose also that in maximizing total consumption we do so subject to a priori specified *rates* of growth of the various capital goods. As is shown in my previous study made in 1967 [5], the reduced form of our system will retain the same structural form given by constraints (1) to (3), providing we now give a new interpretation to our coefficients v_i, m_0, and l_i ($i = 0, 1, \ldots, m$). They will now incorporate not only the indirect effects of ordinary intermediate goods but also the direct and indirect allowance for the future steady growth of capital stocks.[7] These specified rates of growth can of course be adjusted by successive approximation so as to conform to an internally consistent development "program." We could thus retain the simple Ricardian nature of our system, even though we have introduced capital goods, providing we do so in a somewhat special form which will leave only one truly primary input in the system.

Even though this "Ricardian" way of looking at capital is more useful than might seem at first sight, our preliminary discussion would not be complete without discussing the alternative, more common, Heckscher-Ohlin way of introducing capital into our system. Moreover, we shall also make use of the Heckscher-Ohlin formulation in the subsequent dynamic analysis.

C. The static two-factor system

Let us now explicitly add one capital good to our system of which a fixed endowment K is available for use during the planning period. The economy also produces the investment good (I) (for use in later planning periods) with total input coefficients m_k, l_k, k_k. Capital per unit k_0 is used in consumption goods and k_i $(i = 1, 2, \ldots, m)$ in trade goods.[8]

Suppose that the economy now maximizes GNP $(= C + p_k I$, where p_k is given) subject to the extended set of constraints. So we have:

Maximize $C + p_k I$ subject to:

(1) $$\underline{T}_i \leq T_i \leq \overline{T}_i$$

(2c)* $$m_0 C + m_k I - \sum_{i=1}^{m} v_i T_i \leq F$$

(3c) $$l_0 C + l_k I + \sum_{i=1}^{m} l_i T_i \leq L$$

(9)† $$k_0 C + k_k I + \sum_{i=1}^{m} k_i T_i \leq K$$

---

* The numbers (2c), (3c), etc., refer to the new version of the original equations which are appropriate to the model contained in this section.

† Equations (7) and (8) are found in footnote 5.

[7] In this case one obtains a modified Leontief inverse matrix of the productive system $(I - A - HK)^{-1}$ where A is the ordinary input-output matrix, K is the capital stock-output matrix, and H is a diagonal matrix having the exogenously fixed rates of growth of the capital goods in the respective boxes.

[8] Again the understanding is that the k-coefficients are total (direct and indirect) in the Leontief sense and that K is "net" supply of capital.

To see the pattern of choice in this case we must again look at the price structure of our system. Let us denote the shadow price corresponding to (9), i.e., capital rentals, by s. Leaving out the less interesting corner solutions we shall assume that both consumption and investment goods are produced and that both labor and capital are fully utilized.[9] In that case there will again be *one* trade good that is just profitable, say the jth. Let us denote the shadow rate of exchange relevant for that case by $q = R_j$. We now have three equations to determine three prices $q \; (= R_j)$, w, s:

(4c) $$l_j w + k_j s - v_j q = 0$$

(5c) $$l_0 w + k_0 s + m_0 q = 1$$

(10) $$l_k w + k_k s + m_k q = p_k$$

and we obtain:

(6c) $$R_j = q = \frac{l_j w + k_j s}{v_j} = \frac{w + s x_j}{y_j} =$$

$$= \frac{(k_0 p_k - k_k) + (l_k - l_0 p_k) x_j}{(k_0 m_k - k_k m_0) + (l_k m_0 - l_0 m_k) x_j + (l_k k_0 - l_0 k_k) y_j}$$

where $$x_j = \frac{k_j}{l_j}, \; y_j = \frac{v_j}{l_j}$$

We note the following: If we keep the supply of capital (K) and labor (L) fixed and vary the amount of foreign exchange transfers (F) we go through a process of changing the relative scarcity of foreign exchange. As F changes monotonically the economy will choose its trade activities by order of comparative advantage which will be the order of

---

[9] The conditions for the latter to hold can be spelled out explicitly by looking at the solution of (4c), (5c) and (10). If the basic determinant (written out in full in the denominator, last expression of (6c)) is positive, the condition for w, s, and q, respectively, to be positive with the jth activity in the base, requires:

$$(k_j/v_j)(m_0 p_k - m_k) > (k_k - p_k k_0) \quad \text{(for } w > 0)$$

$$y_j(l_k - l_0) > (m_0 m_k) \quad \text{(for } s > 0)$$

$$x_j(l_k - l_0 p_k) > (k_k - k_0 p_k) \quad \text{(for } q > 0)$$

If the above determinant is negative, the signs must be reversed. If one of the conditions does not hold then the activity in question can be profitable only when we are back to a two-dimensional world. We ignore this possibility here since it does not add anything to what we already know.

the R_j's $(j = 1, 2, \ldots m)$ as given by the last expression of (6c). This order will depend on two intensive magnitudes, x_j $(= k_j/l_j)$ and y_j $(= v_j/l_j)$.[10]

As in the previous model (A) the economy will fully operate all T_i for which R_i is less than the exchange rate (q) corresponding to the given F and partially operate that T_j for which R_j just equals q.

Consider a set of activities which produce the same amount of foreign exchange per unit of labor (i.e., they have the same y). For this set the capital:labor ratio x can provide the sole measure of internal ranking.[11] This is reminiscent of Heckscher-Ohlin. But the important thing is to note that in general both x and y may vary as between different activities and the ranking will depend on *both* parameters,[12] and not on capital intensity alone.

Although our technology for the one economy is the same as in the Heckscher-Ohlin framework, the whole frame of reference is different. We don't have a simple two-country system but could have as many trading partners as we like; we don't make any assumptions about the production functions of the trading partners or about competition and the whole notion of capital or labor being relatively abundant is of little meaning here because, strictly speaking, we have a third factor (foreign exchange), a change whose quantity may alter the relative price of labor and capital in a nonmonotonic fashion. It seems to us that the present way of looking at the optimal trade pattern is empirically more relevant from the point of view of a single country.

There is, however, one important general conclusion that still remains correct here, and this is that in a static model trade activities can be ranked unambiguously and depending only on technology.

[10] As a check one can see that when $k_0 = k = 0$, we are back to (6) in terms of (v_j/l_j) only.

[11] This follows from the monotonicity with respect to x of the function $R = (ax + b)/(cx + d)$ where a, b, c, d are regarded as constants. (Proof: $dR/dx = (ad - be)/(cx + d)^2$, which is either positive or negative or zero throughout.)

[12] Leaving out cases of complete dominance in production, we can assume that across activities $dy/dk > 0$. It is easy to see, however, this is not enough to make for monotonicity of R with respect to x. More restrictive assumptions on the shape of the economy's technology would be required, and there is no reason to suggest that these conditions should hold in practice. (Examples of situations where such ranking becomes possible are: the case of a linear relationship between x and y, or if $l_k/k_k = l_0/k_0$ and in similar special cases).

D. *Adding more factors*

Nothing in principle will change if instead of one capital good we were to add more capital goods to the system, providing we assume that these are producible capital goods and for each K_s, say, we also add a final good, I_s, with price p_s. The dimensions of the problem will increase but from counting goods and constraints we can see that the nature of the solution will remain similar, except that now R_j will involve not only one capital intensity but capital intensity factors equal to the number of different capital goods in the system.

Things become much messier when we assume that there is more than one nonreproducible primary factor in the system. For example, consider adding another primary factor or domestic resource to our previous Ricardian system. We must now add a constraint, say,

$$(11) \qquad\qquad g_0 C + \sum_{i=1}^{m} g_i T_i \leq G$$

Let the relevant shadow price be donated by z. Domestic (combined) *resource* costs will now be $l_i w + g_i z$, and the exchange cost ratio R_i will now become

$$(6d) \qquad\qquad R_i = \frac{l_i w + g_i z}{v_i}$$

If both primary inputs are fully utilized we can no longer rank goods unambiguously. The ranking will not be independent of relative factor prices, or quantities. A related complication now will be the fact that we need a *pair* of trade goods to be just profitable at any optimal solution.[13] In theory we could now rank all possible *pairs* on the basis of their coefficients, but this will no longer be the simple notion of identifying comparative advantage by looking at single activities.

Much of my analysis in [5] consisted of the ranking of trade goods under two extreme Ricardian situations [14] in which only one of two primary input constraints is effective. This served to illustrate how the

[13] This follows from the *LP* property that in the optimal solution there will usually be as many activities as there are constraints in the system.

[14] The treatment of capital in that model was like the one indicated in Section IIB.

introduction of labor skills may change the optimal composition of foreign trade.

Finally it should be pointed out that comparative advantage might be affected by the existence of other institutional or political constraints in the system, as, for example, a constraint on the domestic savings ratio. When such constraints are introduced, comparative advantage will also involve each activity's differential claim on the additional institutional constraint. This is almost self-evident but may nonetheless be of practical importance in a policy context.

Before we move on to consider a fully intertemporal model, in which the above results have to be modified, we ought to discuss briefly a possible "dynamic" interpretation of the technical coefficients, still within a "static" framework.

III. DIGRESSION: MARGINAL LABOR COEFFICIENTS

So far we have said very little about the way in which the input coefficients l_i and k_i are estimated in practice. What is usually done in input-output analysis, and taken over in development planning, is to adopt a simple time-trend to represent technological improvement. Average labor and capital coefficients, both the original sectoral direct coefficients as well as the derived *total* (direct and indirect) coefficients in each final demand activity, are fixed at each point in time, independently of the scale of operation. This also is the view taken implicitly or explicitly in the computations performed in connection with the Leontief paradox.

There is a serious problem here which often tends to be overlooked: An assumption that may look rather harmless for purposes of prediction of approximate input levels of any one sector would produce wrong results for the *price* structure of a system and, for that reason, for the analysis of comparative advantage. Consider the following simple example:

For most industries in a growing economy a reasonably good approximation for predictions of capital and labor requirements of an industry would be to assume that the capital-output ratio remains constant and that the labor-output ratio falls at a constant rate over time. In other words, the following production function is assumed:

(12)
$$X = \text{Min}\left(\frac{K}{k}, \frac{L}{l_0} e^{\lambda t}\right)$$

where X = output level, K and L are the capital and labor inputs respectively, k and l_0 are fixed coefficients and λ is a fixed exponential time-trend. Suppose we use time series covering past years to estimate these coefficients. Now try to fit an alternative production function to the same time series. Consider the following:

(13)
$$X = \text{Min}\left(\frac{K}{k}, \left(\frac{L}{A}\right)^{\frac{1}{\beta}}\right)$$

or in other words:

$$K \geq kX$$

$$L \geq AX^\beta \text{ where } 0 < \beta < 1$$

This includes no time trend and instead assumes labor per unit of output to be a function of the level of output. Put differently this means that the rate of growth of labor productivity is a positive function of the rate of growth of output.[15]

In any time-series regression of X on K and X on L it will be practically impossible to distinguish between the two alternative hypotheses represented by (12) and (13). In the same way they might work equally well, for prediction purposes. However, the pricing (i.e., marginal productivity) implications might be very different indeed. This is best seen if we consider the effect of marginal increments of labor in both situations, assuming capital to adjust automatically.

In the time-trend case (12) we get:

$$\frac{\Delta X}{\Delta L} = \frac{X}{L}$$

In the second case (13) we have:

$$\frac{\Delta X}{\Delta L} = \frac{1}{\beta} \frac{X}{L}$$

Now suppose we employ a linear tangential approximation to the function (13), i.e., we assume the *marginal* labor-output ratio to be fixed

15 This has been used, for example, by Verdoorn [12].

around some reference values, $\bar{X}$ and $\bar{L}$. Now, we take the marginal labor-input coefficient as $l \, \bar{K}/\beta\bar{L}$ instead of $\bar{X}/\bar{L}$, adding a constant intercept to the demand for labor so as to have labor requirements at the level $\bar{X}$ the same for both models.

Suppose we do that for the labor-input coefficients of all industries in the economy for which this procedure is relevant. Let us go back to one of our previous trade models, say the Ricardian model (incorporating capital—see Section IIB). The formal structure of our model will remain the same, except that the labor coefficients l_i will now be *marginal* instead of average coefficients, and the constant L on the right of constraint (3) has to be reinterpreted as the supply of labor less all the constant intercepts.

Obviously the pattern of comparative advantage may now be different. An export industry for which labor productivity (in the direct and indirect sense) grows very fast will have a high β factor and therefore a correspondingly lower marginal labor coefficient.

Table 1 below provides the results of a very rough experiment of this kind performed on Israeli data. The columns in the table give the computed total labor coefficients under the two hypotheses and also the resulting comparative advantage rankings.

There are five activities which move by five ranks or more in the direction of higher comparative advantage. These are the three agricultural activities—livestock, field crops, and miscellaneous agriculture—and two in manufacturing—meat and dairy products and chemicals. There are two activities which move at least five steps in the opposite direction—rubber and plastics and leather goods.

The results of Table 1 should be taken with some very large grains of salt as they are based on very rough time-series estimates. Besides, the alternative method was applied to all sectors although there are certainly some activities to which it is less relevant than to others. These results should only serve to make the general point that ranking may be sensitive to the kind of assumption underlying our linear approximations. More work on the estimation of production relations would be needed to get more robust results.

We are not aware of any attempt to use some such alternative formulation in the literature connected with the Leontief paradox. It should be a worthwhile experiment to perform some calculations of

TABLE 1

Labor Productivity Measured by Trade Activity

Trade Activity (1)	Total Labor Productivity ($1,000 per man-year) Average (2)	Marginal (3)	Ranking Average (4)	Marginal (5)
Fuel	6.1	19.6	1	2
Services and tourism	4.0	8.7	2	5
Metal products	3.9	6.5	3	7
Mining	3.2	7.5	4	6
Cement	3.2	6.5	5	8
Basic metals	2.9	5.9	6	9
Machinery	2.6	4.5	7	11
Shipping and aviation	2.5	5.8	8	10
Rubber and plastics	2.4	3.6	9	14
Paper and printing	2.3	3.7	10	13
Polished diamonds	2.2	3.5	11	15
Equipment	1.9	3.5	12	16
Leather goods	1.9	2.0	13	21
Livestock	1.8	12.4	14	4
Textiles	1.7	2.1	15	19
Field crops	1.6	12.9	16	3
Vehicles	1.6	2.0	17	20
Miscellaneous agriculture	1.6	25.4	18	1
Food products	1.5	2.6	19	18
Meat and dairy products	1.4	4.4	20	12
Miscellaneous transport and communication	1.2	3.4	21	17
Wood products	1.0	1.6	22	24
Chemicals	1.0	2.4	23	18

[a]Labor productivity (columns 2 and 3) is $v_i/1_i$ (in $1,000 per man-year) i.e., the foreign exchange revenue per unit of total labor (direct plus indirect plus allowance for capital growth). Column 2 gives the estimates under the simple time trend assumption and column 3 under the alternative hypothesis. In both cases the estimates are projections for 1970. Sector definitions are as in my paper [5], but data for column 2 should not be compared with that study as they were based on earlier and now outdated estimates. They are only used for consistent comparison with column 3. Citrus is not included in the present comparison.

the total labor (and capital) content of $1 million incremental exports or import substitutes using *marginal* rather than average coefficients.

The use of marginal coefficients within a static framework would be an indirect way of bringing in dynamic considerations. We now turn to a model in which time appears in a much more explicit form.

IV. AN INTERTEMPORAL ANALYSIS OF TRADE AND GROWTH

So far we have only dealt with one-period maximization problems. With the tools at hand one could tackle multiperiod planning by looking at each period as a separate optimization problem, i.e., we would set up for each period, separately, all the required information on the spectrum of trade activities relevant to that period, with the corresponding information on the supply of the various exogenous factors of production, etc. This, however, would at best give us comparisons of stationary or steady states. Both growth and foreign trade planning involve time in an essential way—the correct way of looking at the problem requires the simultaneous analysis of the key variables over all time phases of the planning horizon taking into account the intertemporal relations on both the supply and demand side.[16]

Clearly there are many ways in which a dynamic trade and development model could be set up. We choose to concentrate on a number of relations that seem to us to be of major importance and at the same time can, in principle, be empirically applied.

Just as in the static model, we limit ourselves to a model in which an aggregate consumption good (C) is produced, as well as an investment good (I), and in which there are m trade activities, which for simplicity we shall assume to consist only of different export goods (denoted by E_i, $i = 1, 2, \ldots, m$).[17] We shall use superscripts to date variables

---

[16] This is not to argue that a multiperiod model cannot be decomposed into a sequence of single period optimization problems. However, as indicated later in the text, this must be done in a way that is consistent with the underlying dynamic structure.

[17] The empirical illustration to be given in the next section involves a model by Dougherty, Fraenkel and myself [6] that is slightly more general, because it has a greater number of factors and also involves import substitutes. The present analysis will be slightly simplified in order not to obscure the main issues.

over a planning horizon of T periods (i.e., E_i^t = the quantity of the ith export in period t, where $t = 1, 2, \ldots, T$).

The technology will consist of the generalization over time of the single-period activity model, i.e., for E_i^t we have a marginal revenue coefficient, v_i^t, and input coefficients, l_i^t and k_i^t, for labor and capital respectively. All of these may, of course, be different for different time periods, t, but will be assumed to be exogenously fixed coefficients. A similar assumption will be made for the input structure in the production of C^t and I^t (l_0^t, k_0^t, m_0^t, and l_k^t, k_k^t, m_k^t respectively). As before, all these coefficients are meant to be interpreted as *total* (direct and indirect) coefficients in the input-output sense.

The supply of the primary factor (labor or some specific skill, say) at each point in time ($L^t, t = 1, 2, \ldots, T$) is given (usually growing over time). Capital, on the other hand, is accumulated by a process of investment and is subject to a fixed depreciation rate, μ, so we have:

$$(14) \qquad l_0^t C^t + l_k^t I^t + \sum_{i=1}^{m} l_i^t E_i^t \leq L^t \qquad \text{(replaces (3c))}$$

$$(15) \qquad k_0^t C^t + k_k^t I^t + \sum_{i=1}^{m} k_i^t E_i^t \leq K^t \qquad \text{(replaces (9))}$$

$$(16) \qquad K^t = K^{t-1}(1 - \mu) + I^{t-1} \qquad t = 1, 2, \ldots, T$$

(K^t is the stock of capital at the beginning of the year t and K^1 is given).

The following are the other main intertemporal ingredients of our model:

FOREIGN AID

We shall assume that foreign exchange can be borrowed and lent at a fixed rate of interest (α) within the planning horizon.[18] The economy starts with an initial endowment of foreign exchange, B, which it can lend or augment by additional borrowing providing that at the end of the planning horizon the economy is left with no more debts than it had

---

[18] More realistic formulations involving upward sloping supply curves of foreign loans can be introduced. This forms the subject of an independent study by M. Fraenkel of the Bank of Israel. Even in the present case, however, as indicated at a later point in this paper, borrowing will be effectively limited.

at the beginning, i.e., all additional debts have to be returned before the planning horizon comes to an end. Instead of having a separate foreign exchange constraint like (2) or (2c) for each period separately, we get one overall intertemporal foreign exchange constraint, as

$$(17) \qquad m_0{}^t C^t + m_k{}^t I^t - \sum_{i=1}^{m} v_i{}^t E_i{}^t - F^t \leq 0 \qquad \text{(replaces (2c))}$$

$$\sum_{t=1}^{\tau} \frac{F^t}{(1 + \alpha)^{(t-1).}} \leq B \ [19]$$

EXPORT CONSTRAINTS

In the static framework we assumed the existence of absolute exogenous bounds on the range of operation of the various trade activities. Here, in coming to deal with a dynamic setting we make a major departure from our previous assumption.

The development of exports is a process that takes time. An export activity involves a certain amount of irreversible investment both in terms of capital goods and manpower. At the same time, the ability to expand exports both on the demand side (penetrating new markets and developing goodwill) and on the supply side (learning to overcome supply bottlenecks) is certainly not independent of the past scale of operation. A simple way of taking into account the irreversibility of the process is to assume that exports in period (t) cannot be smaller than exports in period $(t - 1)$. The second point we express by postulating that it is the *rate* of increase rather than the absolute level of each export, that is constrained in the short run. In other words, to each export activity we attach an exogenous maximal growth factor, $h_i{}^t$, and we have:

$$(18) \qquad E_i{}^{t-1} \leq E_i{}^t \leq (1 + h_i{}^t) E_i{}^{t-1} \qquad (t = 1, 2, \ldots, T)$$
$$E_i{}^0 \text{ is given.}$$

Obviously this is a highly simplified formulation of what may in fact be a much more complex phenomenon, but in our view it does catch at least a certain aspect of increasing returns or external economies

[19] To prevent confusion, whenever we mean a power rather than a superscript we shall add a dot after the power, e.g., $(1 + \alpha)^{t.}$ means the brackets to the power of t.

which one often feels are there but which are difficult to quantify. By learning to export a good now, one is investing for greater future exports, and, even if technical progress is given, it takes time to reap its full benefits. Also this is one, albeit simplified, way of expressing the fact that there are "growth" industries (with high h-factors) and there are more stagnant fields of activity. These differences are not necessarily reflected only in productivity growth rates (e.g., differential changes in l_i^t over time) but may also be evident in the sheer ability to expand sales and production. As we shall see presently, this way of formulating the model has some interesting and highly plausible implications for the price structure of a dynamic trade model.

THE OBJECTIVE FUNCTION

In the static model we had the economy maximizing consumption or GNP at each point in time. Here we take the objective to be the maximization of the discounted flow of consumption over the planning horizon (with a given social discount rate, ρ) plus the imputed value of the post-terminal capital stock (K^{T+1}):

$$(19) \qquad \text{Max} \sum_{t=1}^{T} \frac{C^t}{(1 + \rho)^{(t-1)}} + \frac{p_k^T K^{T+1}}{(1 + \rho)^{(T-1)}}.$$

The maximization of discounted consumption is consistent with the procedure adopted in Ramsey-type optimal growth models. It can also be shown (by using modern control theory) that this maximand is consistent with a period by period GNP maximization, subject to the various single period constraints and choosing the right price for investment (see below). Our treatment of terminal capital is analogous to an alternative procedure often used—the assumption that the terminal *quantity* of capital is given.[20]

To sum up—formally we have a multiperiod linear programming problem which involves maximizing (19) subject to constraints (14)–(18). Again, from a formal point of view we have $[2(m + 2)T + 1]$ constraints [21] to determine $(4 + m)T$ variables E_i^t, C^t, I^t, F^t. At first

[20] A proper choice of p_k^T will make the two methods identical. In practice, clearly, some guesswork or successive approximation must be employed, or else we can use the steady state estimate.

[21] We have: $T(14)$, $T(15)$, $T(16)$, $(T + 1)$ (17), $2mT(18) = [2(m + 2) T + 1]$ in all.

sight it seems that a numerical solution would be required to see what happens in a model like this. A closer inspection of the structure of the model and in particular its associated price system, however, reveals the general characteristics of the optimal solution. As before, we proceed by considering simple cases first and then generalizing from them. It turns out that the essence of dynamic comparative advantage in this model can be learned from inspection of a truncated version of this model in which $m = 2$, $T = 2$ and capital does not appear (at least not explicitly). This we proceed to do first.

A. The dynamic Ricardian system

We start with a simplified version of the equations in which I^t and K^t do not appear explicitly.[22] This means that we leave out constraints (15) and (16) and delete I^t from constraints (14) and (17), K^{T+1} from (19). Suppose we write down our truncated system for the case $m = 2$, $T = 2$, and consider the associated ("dual") price system.

Let us use the following notation for the *undiscounted* [23] prices:

w^t = the real wage at time t (associated with (14))

q^t = the exchange rate at time t (associated with the first part of (17))

$\bar{q}$ = the overall shadow rate of exchange (associated with the B constraint in (17))

$\bar{p}_i{}^t$ = the shadow price attached to the maximum bound in (18)

$p_i{}^t$ = the shadow price attached to the minimum bound in (18).

As before we confine ourselves to the case in which C^t is always produced in positive amounts [24] so that the costs of production in

[22] When we say that investment and capital do not appear explicitly, we mean that they might still appear implicitly in the very special "Ricardian" form discussed in Section IIB. In that case all that is required is a modified interpretation of the various labor and import coefficients in (14) and (17) to take account of exogenously fixed growth rates of the capital stocks.

[23] The way the model is written the shadow prices for the various periods would be *discounted* prices (because the price attached to a unit of consumption in time t is $[1/(1 + \rho)^{(t-1)}.])$. To obtain *undiscounted* prices these have to be multiplied by the discount factor. Our notation here is for convenience related to the prices after this correction, so they are the actual (undiscounted) prices relevant to each period in time.

[24] This can be shown to depend on a minimum L^t and the coefficient matrix. These conditions are met in our empirical investigation [6].

consumer goods will always add up to one. In the 2×2 case we obtain the following equations.

For the *first period* $(t = 1)$:

(20.1) Equation for C^1: $l_0^1 w^1 + m_0^1 q^1 = 1$

(20.2) Equation for E_1^1: $l_1^1 w^1 - v_1^1 q^1 + \bar{p}_1^1 - \underline{p}_1^1$

$$-\left[\frac{1 + h_1^2}{1 + \rho}\right]\bar{p}_1^2 + \frac{1}{1 + \rho}\underline{p}_1^2 = 0$$

(20.3) Equation for E_2^1: $l_2^1 w^1 - v_2^1 q^1 + \bar{p}_2^1 - \underline{p}_2^1$

$$-\left[\frac{1 + h_2^2}{1 + \rho}\right]\bar{p}_2^2 + \frac{1}{1 + \rho}\underline{p}_2^2 = 0$$

(20.4) Equation for F^1: $-q^1 + \bar{q} = 0$

For the *second period* $(t = 2)$

(21.1) Equation for C^2: $l_0^2 w^2 + m_0^2 q^2 = 1$

(21.2) Equation for E_1^2: $l_1^2 w^2 - v_1^2 q^2 + \bar{p}_1^2 - \underline{p}_1^2 = 0$

(21.3) Equation for E_2^2: $l_2^2 w^2 - v_2^2 q^2 + \bar{p}_2^2 - \underline{p}_2^2 = 0$

(21.4) Equation for F^2: $-\dfrac{q^2}{1 + \rho} + \dfrac{\bar{q}}{1 + \alpha} = 0$

On the basis of a priori reasoning we may assume that (20) and (21) can properly be written as equations, i.e., *exactly* satisfied. We can further assume (cf., also footnote 5) that for each i and t either $\bar{p}$ or $\underline{p}$ will be zero and for *one* of them *both* $\bar{p}$ and $\underline{p}$ will be zero ("just" profitability). This leaves us with eight equations to determine eight variables. We shall presently see how we can determine which variables to equate to zero and thus establish the relevant rule of comparative advantage for this case. Before we do that, however, there is one simple rule that follows from inspection of the equations for F^1 (20.4) and F^2 (21.4).

$$q^1 = \bar{q}$$

(22) $$q^2 = \bar{q}\left[\frac{1 + \rho}{1 + \alpha}\right] = q^1(1 + r), \text{ say}$$

where we have approximately: $r = \rho - \alpha$

This expresses a simple and intuitively plausible rule for the intertemporal relationships of the forward foreign exchange rates which is completely analogous to corresponding rules in other fields of capital theory: The own rate of return in the use of real balances of foreign exchange must approximately (and in the continuous case, exactly) equal the difference between the own rate on consumption goods (i.e. the social rate of discount) and the rate of intertemporal borrowing or lending of foreign exchange.[25]

In the general case $(T > 2)$ we get, by induction,

$$q^{t+1} = q^t(1 + r) = q^1(1 + r)^t.$$

If the social internal rate of return is $\rho = 10$ per cent, say, and the rate of interest on intertemporal borrowing $\alpha = 6$ per cent, arbitrage or proper planning must see to it that the real rate of exchange in relation to the domestic (consumer goods) price level will grow at approximately 4 per cent per annum. In the case of Israel, for example, there is empirical evidence that, at least in the 1950–60 decade, some such increase had in fact taken place. The empirical fact (without theoretical explanation) has been established by Michaely [11]. In the context of our model, a positive r implies that it pays to borrow foreign exchange now and return debts later providing, of course, that such foreign exchange can be productively used, or alternatively, that the productivity growth in exports makes such deferment profitable.[26] The special formulation of our trade constraints reduces our ability to postpone abrupt export expansion, a point to which we shall return later. Thus, the productivity argument and the existence of a limiting primary factor also see to it that we do not go to excesses in borrowing at the expense of the future.

It should be clear from the structure of the model that one could introduce more complicated assumptions about increasing marginal costs of foreign borrowing (i.e., increasing α), or decreasing marginal utility of consumption (making for an effectively falling ρ), thus retaining the intertemporal relations between the q^t's but making them variable.

---

[25] A more detailed analysis of this relationship, in particular when there are varying borrowing rates, has been undertaken by M. Fraenkel [8].

[26] A positive r (in other words, q^t growing over time) also means that with time as F^t being decreased (to keep a total B constant), the economy has to go into less and less productive export industries.

Alternatively, one could take an extreme view that the various F^t's are exogenously and independently given so that no intertemporal borrowing or lending is possible and q^t becomes independent (closer to a static model).[27] Here we confine ourselves to the present simple but plausible case.

Let us now turn to our main subject—the pattern of choice of foreign trade activities. It will make things easier if we start by hypothesizing a specific optimal solution and then go on from there to find the conditions under which it will be valid. Consider the following specific choice of activities in the "optimal base": We produce (fully) both exports in period 2, i.e., E_1^2 and E_2^2 are at their relative maxima. In period 1, E_1^1 is just profitable and E_2^1 is not produced beyond its minimum bound. In terms of the p-variables in equations (20) and (21) this implies:

$$\bar{p}_1^1 = \underline{p}_1^1 = \underline{p}_1^2 = \bar{p}_2^1 = \underline{p}_2^2 = 0; \underline{p}_2^1 > 0, \bar{p}_2^2 > 0, \bar{p}_1^2 > 0.$$

Substituting from (20.1) into (20.2), we obtain an equation involving only q^1 and $\bar{p}_1^2$. Similarly, using (22) and substituting from (21.1) into (21.2) we obtain another equation involving only the same two variables. From both these resulting equations we extract $\bar{p}_1^2$ and obtain an expression for the shadow rate, $\bar{q} = q^1$, which we shall also denote by Q_1^1:

(23) $Q_1^1 = q^1 = \bar{q} =$

$$\cfrac{\dfrac{l_1^1}{l_0^1} + \left[\dfrac{1 + h_1^2}{1 + \rho}\right]\dfrac{l_1^2}{l_0^2}}{\dfrac{l_1^1}{l_0^1}\left[m_0^1 + \dfrac{v_1^1}{l_1^1}l_0^1\right] + \left[\dfrac{1 + h_1^2}{1 + \rho}\right]\dfrac{l_1^2}{l_0^2}\left[(1 + r)\left(m_0^2 + \dfrac{v_1^2}{l_1^2}l_0^2\right)\right]}$$

Alternatively this can be inverted and written in the form:

(23.1) $$\frac{1}{Q_1^1} = \frac{1}{a_1^1 + a_1^2}\left(a_1^1 \cdot \frac{1}{R_1^1} + a_1^2 \cdot \frac{1}{R_1^2}\right)$$

and, in the general case, we shall define (for a good i that is just profitable at time t_0 and intramarginal in all subsequent periods):

[27] In our empirical study [6], some such formulations have been experimented with.

$$(23.2) \qquad \frac{1}{Q_i^{t_0}} = \left(\sum_{t=t_0}^{T} a_i^t \right)^{-1} \cdot \sum_{t=t_0}^{T} \left(a_i^t \frac{1}{R_i^t} \right)$$

$$\text{where } \frac{1}{R_i^t} = (1 + r)^{(t-1)} \cdot \left[m_0^t + \frac{v_i^t}{l_i^t} l_0^t \right]$$

$$\text{and } a_i^t = \frac{l_i^t}{l_0^t} (1 + \rho)^{(1-t)} \cdot H_i^t \text{ with } H_i^t = \prod_{n=t_0+1}^{n=t} (1 + h_i^n)$$

$$(\text{and } H_i^{t_0} = 1)$$

In our present special example we have: $i = 1$, $t_0 = 1$, $T = 2$. We see that the reciprocal of the shadow rate [28] is a *weighted average* of the reciprocals of the expressions R_i^t (in the special example these are R_1^1 and R_1^2). As one can immediately discover from our discussion in Section II (6), the latter are the *static* exchange costs for the various periods (evaluated per today's unit of foreign exchange). The weights a_i^t are the ratios of the labor unit input in the trade goods divided by the labor unit input in consumption expanded at the cumulated growth factor h, and divided by the relevant rate of discount factor (ρ). These weights may grow with t or fall, depending on the direction of change of l_i^t/l_o^t over the planning periods (t) and the sign of ($h_i^t - \rho$) (more on this below).

Now the individual R_i^t's might again in principle rise or fall with t. R_i^t will fall with t providing ($m_0 + \frac{V_i}{l_i} l_0$) has a rate of change (over different periods t) that is less than r. In our empirical application this happens to be the case,[29] and we therefore assume $R_1^2 < R_1^1$. If we look at (23.1) and remember that the weights a are positive, it follows that Q must lie between the two R's, i.e.,

$$(24.1) \qquad R_1^1 > Q_1^1 > R_1^2$$

In the more general case if R_i^t falls over time one can similarly show that we have $R_i^{t_0} < Q_i^{t_0} < R_i^T$. In the general case it will also

---

[28] The reciprocal of the shadow rate is in the nature of the marginal productivity of foreign exchange in terms of domestic resources.

[29] More on this is found in footnote 37.

follow that $Q_i^{t_0} > Q_i^{t_0+1}$,[30] for any t_0 between 1 and T, a fact of which we shall make use below. So we can write:

(24.2) $$R_i^{t_0} > Q_i^{t_0} > Q_i^{t_0+1} > \ldots > R_i^T$$

$$(t_0 = 1, 2, \ldots, T - 1)$$

Returning to our specific example and (24.1), it follows from the latter that if E_1 is just profitable in the first period it must be intramarginal in the second period and will certainly be produced then, which is exactly what we have assumed in this specific solution. That (24.1) is a necessary condition for this to hold also follows from spelling out the conditions under which $\bar{p}_1^2 > 0$ (using (20) and (21)). Similarly $\bar{p}_2^2 > 0$ implies that we must have $Q_1^1 > R_2^2$ and finally $p_2^1 > 0$ implies $Q_1^1 < Q_2^1$. Now Q_2^1 would be the shadow rate if E_2 would be just profitable in period 1 and E_2 not. Further, we see from (23.2) that $Q_i^2 = R_i^2$ $(i = 1, 2)$, and in general $Q_i^T = R_i^T$.[31] All of this justifies calling the term Q_i^t the *dynamic exchange cost,* since it provides the dynamic analogue of the exchange cost concept, i.e., the measure of *dynamic comparative advantage* ranking.

What this measure means is: If we perform the experiment of changing the quantity B in (17), leaving all other exogenous parameters fixed, we shall get a series of optimal solutions for our dynamic model. The choice of export activities in the optimal solutions will follow the order of the various Q_i^t's $(i = 1, 2, \ldots, m; t = 1, 2, \ldots, T)$.[32] Suppose we fix a certain level for B and obtain a shadow exchange rate $\bar{q}$ at which $\bar{q} = Q_i^t$ for some i and t. This implies that the export activity E_i is just profitable at time t. But not only that, it also means that the process of its expansion is *started* at time t and that it will be produced to the full amount (i.e., at the maximal growth rate based on its level at time t) in all *subsequent* planning periods up to T. All E_i^t for which $Q_i^t < \bar{q}$ will remain at their minimum bounds, and those for which the inequality is reversed will be at their relative maximum.[33] When we say that an export activity is just profitable here, we

[30] This will usually hold if $h_i^{t_0} > \rho$.

[31] I.e., in the last period the shadow rate coincides with the static exchange cost (providing, of course, R_i^t falls with t).

[32] Strictly speaking, we should use t_0 as a running index here instead of t, but we hope this will cause no confusion.

[33] Counter to the static model, maxima here will usually be *relative.* An *absolute* maximum is achieved only when an export is fully produced from the *first* period.

ought to say that it is profitable in the *dynamic* sense. The importance of distinguishing between profitability in a static and a dynamic sense can be illustrated if we return to our 2×2 example. When $E_1{}^1$ is just profitable we have $\bar{q} = q^1 = Q_1{}^1 < R_1{}^1$. This clearly shows that producers or planners acting on the basis of static profitability considerations of the kind discussed in Section II would opt *against* the production of E_1. This can also be seen directly by looking at (20.2):

$$l_1{}^1\, w^1 - v_1{}^1 q^1 = \frac{1 + h_1{}^2}{1 + \rho}\, \bar{p}_1{}^2 > 0$$

i.e., marginal (static) cost is higher than marginal (static) revenue, and yet in a dynamic sense it pays to *expand* production. The economic reason here is the existence of external benefits which accrue only in the future. The externality consists in the ability to expand future exports, which can be achieved only by undertaking present-day export efforts. Clearly this follows only because of our specific choice of maximal export constraint. For suppose we were to postulate that it is the absolute level of exports that is exogenously bounded. In terms of our 2×2 example this would amount to letting $a_1{}^2$ approach zero. From (23.1) we would then get $Q_1{}^1 = R_1{}^1$ and we would be back to a static world.[34]

The main point we would like to make is the following: in the static Ricardian model we saw that one could unambiguously rank activities by factor productivity alone. In a dynamic world this is no longer possible. Ranking involves both goods and time [35] and there is no reason to suppose that goods could still be ranked independently of time.[36] Our measure now incorporates technical coefficients of various periods, "growth" factors, and the discount rates.

Before we turn to the more general model with capital let us go back to look at the various factors determining Q in the present model. The general term $a_i{}^t/R_i{}^t$ appearing in the expression (23.2) can also be written in the form (remembering that $(1 + \alpha)\,(1 + r) = 1 + \rho$):

$$(25) \qquad \frac{a_i{}^t}{R_i{}^t} = H_i{}^t\, (1 + \alpha)^{-(t-1)} \cdot \left(\frac{l_i{}^t}{l_0{}^t}\, m_0{}^t + v_i{}^t \right)$$

[34] The other extreme would be to assume that there is no maximum bound at all, in which case we obtain $a_1{}^2 \to \infty$ and we get $Q_1{}^1 \to R_1{}^2$, i.e., it is only the future performance that matters.

[35] Commodity x at a *different* time being a different commodity.

[36] In Section V we give empirical illustration of this fact.

is dynamic model can be extended in various ways without bringing
t any drastic change in these general findings. First, we could
duce a number of heterogeneous capital goods instead of one.
would involve us with more than one capital intensity (and price
ppearing in the various expressions but would otherwise leave the
ce of the model the same. Also, there is no need to make the
nption that there is a one-to-one correspondence between activities
xport goods.[42] One can allow choice of a number of activities per
nodity, leaving the rate of growth constraint as applying to com-
ties, rather than to the component activities. In that case, the
mula remains the criterion of choice, as before, except that the
idual coefficient entries in each time period may run over a number
ernative sets of data.

in the static case, the introduction of another nonreproducible
ry factor of production does not present any practical difficulty,
ne cannot in that case give the explicit single activity-time formulae
characterized all the other cases that were discussed here.

HER CONSIDERATIONS—LABOR TRAINING EFFECTS

ly one could think of further complications and additional dynamic
ts of trade and development which we have not analyzed here.
ave confined our discussion to a case in which the solution of the
l can be given more or less explicitly without having to solve a
lete numerical model. Also, using a linear framework has con-
ble appeal from a practical point of view but might pose some
tions from the analytical point of view.[43] Of the possible further
ments we shall briefly discuss one form of externality which is
nt to dynamic trade theory and can be incorporated in our linear
l—labor training effects.

m the preceding analysis it should be clear that we could without
lty introduce human capital and investment in education into the
l, by treating human capital of one or more kinds like other capital

---

s already mentioned, there is no problem of adding import substitutes
model; in that case, one applies the same formulation as in the static

or example, the strict, textbook type of increasing returns production
n cannot be incorporated in a simple linear-programming framework.
er, the burden of much of our discussion here is to show that certain
of increasing returns and external effects can be usefully explored within
nfines of a linear model.

Consider the rate of change of this term over the different planning period t. This approximately equals the sum of the rates of change of the individual components of (25). Calculating these we obtain that the rate of change equals approximately $h_i - \alpha - \beta_i d_i$, where β_i denotes the difference between the rate of change of labor productivity in the ith export industry and in the consumption good (i.e., rate of change of l_0/l_i) and $d_i = 1/(1 + v_i l_0/l_i m_0) < 1$. Even for h values that are not very large, this expression is most likely to be positive.[37] When it is positive this means that a_i/R_i rises over time (and not only $1/R_i$) which throws some additional light on the relative importance of the various components of $1/Q_i$ in (23.2).

We now turn back to the more general model in which capital is included as a separate factor of production. This complicates the expressions somewhat but, as we shall see, does not change the findings in any essential way.

B. *The model with explicit capital*

Consider the full model (14) to (19) with capital as an endogenous factor. This now turns out to complicate matters only slightly, for we can make use of some known properties of capital models and the static analysis of Section II to write down the solution for this case. We shall not go through the arduous details of the analysis but consider the main results.

An analysis of the dual price system associated with constraints (14) to (19), or recourse to known results from capital theory, reveal the following intertemporal relation involving the prices and rentals of the capital good:

$$(26) \qquad p_k{}^t(1 + \rho) - s^{t+1} - p_k{}^{t+1}(1 - \mu) = 0$$

$$(t = 1, 2, \ldots, T - 1)$$

---

[37] In our empirical illustrations (for example Section V), h_i is of the order of at least 10 per cent, α is 6 per cent and β_i is not likely to be above 2–3 per cent, say (it can of course also be negative). On a priori grounds one could argue that the first (h_i) and the last (β_i) element in this expression are not entirely independent, as a high growth factor might be expected to appear together with a high relative productivity growth rate. In any case this must be a subject for empirical investigation in each case.

or:
$$\frac{p_k{}^{t+1} - p_k{}^t}{p_k{}^t} = \frac{1}{1-\mu}\left(\rho + \mu - \frac{s^{t+1}}{p_k{}^t}\right)$$

where [38]
$$p_k{}^t = l_k{}^t w^t + k_k{}^t s^t + m_k{}^t q^t$$

and $p_k{}^t$ is given (see 19)). This establishes a recursive relation for $p_k{}^t$ and s^t, going backward from the last period T.

For each period we now obtain a set of price relations like the triple set (4c), (5c), and (10) in Section IIC, with the relevant p variables added as in (20) and (21). Going backward, for period T, in which $p_k{}^T$ is given, we get the same triple set determining among other prices s^T. We then have the recursive relation (26) determining $p_k{}^{T-1}$. We now go to period $(T-1)$ and so on backward in a series of triple price equation sets in each of which $p_k{}^t$ can be treated as if given.[39]

What we have to do now is to write down the modified solution for the case in which capital appears, using what we already know about the modifications required in the static model when passing from the Ricardian to the more general capital model. If we do this, following the same kind of steps as in the Ricardian model, we obtain an expression for dynamic comparative advantage, $O_i{}^{t_0}$, which is analogous to (23.2). The $R_i{}^t$'s are the ones relevant to the static capital model (see (6c)) involving both the capital intensities (x_i) and labor productivities (y_i) and $a_i{}^t$ are generalized weights:

(27)
$$\frac{1}{Q_i{}^{t_0}} = \left(\sum_{t=t_0}^{T} a_i{}^t\right)^{-1} \cdot \sum_{t=t_0}^{T}\left(a_i{}^t \cdot \frac{1}{R_i{}^t}\right)$$

where $R_i{}^t = (1+r)^{(t-1)} \cdot$
$$\times (R_i \text{ of (6c) evaluated at time } t)$$

and $\quad a_i{}^t = H_i{}^t(1+\rho)^{(1-t)} \cdot \left(\frac{l_i{}^t}{l_0{}^t}\right)\left[\frac{(k_k - k_0 p_k) - x_i(l_k - l_0 p_k)}{k_k - l_k k_0/l_0}\right]^t$$

$(H_i{}^t$ defined as in (23.2))

[38] We are only considering the case in which investment is produced at all times, and we obtain (26) by looking along the column-vectors I^t and I^{t+1} (multiplied by $(1-\mu)$) and then subtracting the two expressions.

[39] As is known from optimal growth theory, a Ramsey model of this kind is, in fact, equivalent to a series of single period GNP maximizations plus the system of dynamic relations combining the p_k's and p's and q's of the various periods.

Next, as in the previous case, we write out the e term a/R and obtain, after some manipulation:

(28)
$$\frac{a_i{}^t}{R_i{}^t} = H_i{}^t(1+\alpha)^{-(t-1)} \cdot \left[\frac{l_i}{l_0}\frac{\left(k_0\dfrac{m_k}{l_k} - m_0\dfrac{k_k}{l_k}\right)}{\left(\dfrac{k_0}{l_0} - \dfrac{k_k}{l_k}\right)}\right.$$

First of all, we check and find that in the s all the expressions in (27) and (28) become found in (23.2) and (25). Next let us specific: (25) to see what we can say about the expect time in the more general case. Consider the case in which the m and k coefficients are mor time and labor productivity in the consumption rises at an approximately even pace (i.e., l_0 at that case the expression in square brackets can $((l_i{}^t/l_0{}^t)b_1 + b_2)$ where b_1 and b_2 are constants (28) with (25), we can also apply all the previo rate of change of a/R in this case, and the previc ing the one about the decrease of $R_i{}^t$ over time the case in which capital appears explicitly.

We have thus found that the main character parative advantage determination in the model a ent in the more general model. Ranking involves time. Dynamic exchange costs are a weighted ave costs (or rather the reciprocals thereof are), i factors also enter. Finally we still have a rule applied without having to measure factor rentals.

[40] Constant capital coefficients is an assumption tha usually makes good empirical sense. As for the const coefficients m_0 and m_k (and indirectly also m_i throug v_i), we have to remember that in the way we have model import substitution can appear separately in th Constancy of m does not have to imply lack of imp not carried over in the dynamic discussion but can ea fact incorporated in our empirical analysis [6]). How do not need such extreme constancy assumptions to ge

[41] Providing, of course, we know that these rentals a

goods. Suppose, however, there is some specific form of skill (management, say) which can only be acquired through experience in production itself. We would then introduce another separate skilled labor input in the economy and let certain activities in the economy produce as a by-product, and at a time lag, trained labor.[44] Suppose this is the case with certain trade activities. Put formally, in the context of our model, we would introduce another primary factor as in Section IID (11). But now, instead of having an activity only described in terms of a foreign exchange output (v_i) and a list of inputs (l_i, k_i, g_i) all dated at time t, we now assume that it has an additional output at time ($t + n$), say, which consists of λ_i units of trained labor ($- \lambda_i^{t+n} < l_i^t$). $\lambda_i E_i^t$ units of trained labor will appear as an output (or negative input) in the skilled labor constraints of period ($t + n$). Correspondingly we will get, in the price equation corresponding to the ith export good, an additional benefit (or negative cost) element $\lambda_i z^{n+t}$ (where z is the shadow wage of trained labor).[45] Although one can no longer give a simple price-free formula for dynamic comparative advantage ranking (Q) in this general model, it can be seen that optimization may, in this case as in the previous dynamic model, point to a choice of activities which might in the short run look unprofitable. This is after all what the infant-industry argument is all about. Unlike the previous case, however, this type of refinement seems a more difficult one to fill with empirical content. Our present empirical illustration, at least, will be given without this extra refinement.

V. EMPIRICAL ILLUSTRATIONS OF THE DYNAMIC MODEL

In the present section we give a short description of a trial application of the dynamic model to data based on the Israeli economy. A fuller

[44] The micro aspects of this type of on-the-job training have been analyzed by Gary Becker [2]. In the context of development this phenomenon has been used by Hirschman [9] as an argument for promoting capital-intensive lines of production because of the labor training externalities involved (it is not a priori clear, however, why they have to be capital intensive). Finally Arrow's [1] "learning by doing" is not exactly the same thing but is a close relative.

[45] In an unpublished study a few years ago, I analyzed the optimal growth process in a linear model where such training effects occur as a by-product of the production of certain consumption goods, and growth is obtained by gradually switching from unskilled export goods to more productive, high-skill, export production. That model was simple enough to allow for full analytical solution.

description of the actual model and of solutions has been given elsewhere.[46]

The model is structured more or less according to the system described in the previous section with a few modifications. It includes one composite consumption good, three capital goods, and thirty trade activities (four import substitutes and twenty-six export activities), and there are two primary labor constraints—total and "skilled" labor. The model is formulated for six future planning years, spaced at two and one-half year intervals ranging from 1967/68 to 1980.

The first experiment is one in which we maximize an objective function like (19) ($T = 6$) subject to a set of constraints like (14) to (18), modified as above, but assuming for the moment that the skilled labor supply is adjusted automatically.[47] In this case only the total labor supply provides an effective constraint on long-run growth. Maximization is repeated for a wide range of change of B, the supply of foreign exchange transfers. Following the discussion of Section IV, we allow interperiod borrowing of foreign exchange so that the actual import gap at each point in time becomes an endogenous variable and part of the optimization process itself. The resulting optimal time pattern of foreign borrowing is in itself an interesting subject of discussion [6]. Here, however, we confine ourselves to the trade aspects.

Table 2A summarizes the order of profitability (i.e., dynamic comparative advantage) as defined in the previous discussion. The ranking is the over-all ordering of activities and expansion times. As seen in Table 2B, it starts from number 1 at the most abundant foreign exchange endowment (equivalent to an annual F-flow of $1,917 million and a shadow rate of 1.86 IL/\$) and ends with number 124 at an almost zero endowment (annual equivalent flow of $18 million and a shadow rate of 5.15 IL/\$, at 1962 prices).[48]

---

[46] See joint paper with Dougherty and Fraenkel [6].

[47] In the Israeli context this would imply adjustment through the composition of immigration. In general, a more realistic approach would be to bring in the educational system.

[48] For reference purposes one could consider an average expected F-level of $400 million to be a reasonable guess for the future. This would point (see Table 2B) to a shadow rate of 4.20 (at 1962 prices), which amounts to about 5 IL/\$ at 1968 prices. The official market rate now is 3.50, but with export premiums and other subsidies it amounts to an effective rate of about 4.25 IL/\$ on most exports, with a somewhat higher rate for some "progress" industries (the effective protective rate on imports is much higher and runs to about 6–7 IL/\$— see [11]).

TABLE 2A

Trade Activities and Expansion Times
(ranked by order of profitability)

Trade Activities	Period					
	1967/68[a]	1970	1972/73	1975	1977/78	1980
Export Increments						
Livestock	69	58	40	35	28	19
Citrus	83	75	61	46	36	32
Mining	21	14	8	4	1	−
Food products	92	87	82	79	71	68
Textiles	101	98	95	91	89	94
Wood products	110	105	100	96	93	97
Paper and printing	77	70	65	59	52	54
Rubber and plastics	33	30	26	22	16	15
Chemicals	−	123	121	116	109	118
Fuel	25	20	11	7	5	2
Diamond polishing	74	66	57	48	43	47
Basic metals	62	55	45	37	34	31
Metal products	29	27	23	17	13	10
Machinery	63	60	51	44	39	38
Household equipment	67	64	56	49	42	41
Vehicles	86	84	80	78	72	76
Shipping and aviation	120	117	113	106	102	111
Other transport	115	107	99	90	85	81
Services	24	18	12	9	6	3
Import Substitutes						
Livestock	−	−	−	124	108	112
Chemicals	−	−	−	122	104	114
Machinery	119	103	88	73	50	53

Source: Table is based on Table 2, Bruno, Dougherty and Frankel [6].

[a]The model is formulated for six future planning years, spaced at two-and-one-half-year intervals from 1967/68 to 1980.

TABLE 2B

Activity Ranks and Associated Shadow Rates of Exchange

Annual Equivalent of Foreign Aid ($ million)	Ordinal Number Ranking	Period	Shadow Rate of Exchange (I£/$ at 1962 prices)
1,917	1	1977/78	1.86
1,777	10	1980	2.36
1,100	28	1977/78	2.61
997	40	1972/73	3.03
980	50	1977/78	3.14
947	59	1975	3.22
817	71	1977/78	3.43
741	76	1980	3.49
654	86	1967/68	3.83
400	98	1970	4.20
115	114	1980	4.59
18	124	1975	5.15

Source: See Table 2A.

Table 2A conforms to the rule that $Q_i^t > Q_i^{t+1}$ (see Section IV (24.2)). There are a few exceptions in the last period.[49] The table also illustrates our general point that activities and time periods are intermixed in the ranking, and we cannot say that one activity is more profitable than another unless we attach a time subscript to it.[50]

[49] These exceptions come from an aberration in the present solution of the model for the last period. A trial value of unity has been chosen for p_k^T in the objective function (19). This apparently is too high because it abruptly forces construction activity up and consumption down to zero in the last period (in previous periods consumption rises smoothly, as would be expected). Apart from being unrealistic it also violates one of the conditions underlying the analysis in Section IV (namely positive C throughout).

[50] One might note, however, that *within* periods the sector ranking turns out to be quite similar. This comes from the fact that at our level of aggregation the sector differences in productivity change and in "growth" factors are not sufficiently marked to make for considerable variation in this respect. This is consistent with a similar finding for the static model [5] but only so as long as variations in the labor skill constraint are not introduced.

VARIATIONS IN THE SKILL CONTENT OF LABOR

In the first experiment we assumed that no constraint was imposed by labor skills. To see the effect on comparative advantage of relaxing this assumption, we perform the following experiment: We let the foreign exchange endowment be fixed at the equivalent of an *average* discounted annual flow of $400 million. Now we gradually change the share of skilled labor in the total labor supply of all periods from "relatively abundant" (zero price of "skill") to a time pattern consistent with the "naive" forecast of no change in the skill composition of labor. The final state is one in which skilled labor is highly scarce and the basic shadow wage for nonskilled is zero. In this process the optimal trade pattern will change with the variation in the skill composition and will indicate the role of human capital in the analysis of comparative advantage.

The results are recorded in Table 3. All cells enclosed to the right of the *thick* line are occupied by activities which at the $400 million foreign exchange level were profitable in the previous experiment (i.e., all activities numbered 1 to 98 in Table 2B). Now, with the gradual reduction in the supply of skill, new trade activities come in ("+" sign in Table 3), and existing ones go out ("−" sign in Table 3). The order at which they enter and exit is given by the ordinal number in the various cells. In the final state all cells enclosed to the right of the *dotted* line are occupied by activities that are profitable in the scarce-skill situation, given the $400 million foreign exchange endowment.

We note that textiles, wood products, vehicles, and diamond polishing are partially or wholly removed from the optimal trade bundle. For the first three industries this more or less conforms to one's intuitive judgment of the Israeli export industries. These industries enjoy a highly protected domestic market and a relatively high effective exchange rate. "Correct" pricing of their use of skills places them, at least partially, lower down in the list. For diamond polishing this seems intuitively wrong and the explanation here (as in the static analysis [5]) comes from the fact that we have aggregated diamond polishers, who on the whole are semiskilled and have a short training period, with highly skilled labor, which is really scarce.

It is also worth noting that there are several cases in Table 3 in which activities switch in and out several times in the course of the

TABLE 3

The Effect on Trade of Varying Skill Composition of Labor

Trade Activity	Period					
	1967/68[a]	1970	1972/73	1975	1977/78	1980
Export Increments						
Livestock						
Citrus						
Mining						
Food products	15+	24-				
Textiles	18-	26+				25-
		32-				
Wood products			2 -	4 -		22-
			13+	6 +		
			19-	23-		
Paper and printing						
Rubber and plastics						
Chemicals						
Fuel						
Diamond polishing	12-	11-	31-	35-	34-	27-
Basic metals						
Metal products						
Machinery						
Household equipment						
Vehicles	20-	30-	33-			28-
Shipping and aviation						
Other transport	10+	7 +	1 +			
Services						
Import Substitutes						
Livestock				3+		21+
Chemicals				14+/18-		
				26+/30-		
Machinery						

Note: + denotes entry of activity; - denotes exit; number denotes order of entry or exit.

[a]The model is formulated for six future planning years, spaced at two-and-one-half year intervals from 1967/68 to 1980.

analysis. This is consistent with our assertion that in the case of two primary factors one cannot rank activity-time cells independently of relative factor supplies.

This analysis of labor skill variation is, of course, only a very rough indicator of the importance of introducing the quality of the labor force. One additional calculation that could be performed with the present model is to make an actual forecast of the supply of skilled labor, taking into account the expected increased output of the educational system, and then repeat the experiment of changing the supply of foreign exchange (as in Table 2B). Better still would be to give a finer breakdown of the labor force and to explicitly introduce the educational system into the planning model (as for other physical capital goods).[51]

Finally, for an indication of the past change in the quality of labor input in Israeli exports,[52] let us disaggregate the labor force in input-output calculations into four main categories (see below) and compute the change in the direct and indirect labor input in the export of manufactures (excluding diamonds) from 1958 to 1965, using base-year input coefficients and taking into account *only* the change in *composition* of exports. The following figures result:

Ratio of Direct Plus Indirect Man-Year Input, 1965 Over 1958 *

Total labor (*unweighted*):		2.36
unskilled	(5.1)	2.33
semiskilled	(9.7)	2.35
skilled	(11.7)	2.37
academic and technical	(14.7)	2.53

* Figures in parentheses refer to approximate training period in years.

We see that there has been a small but consistent shift toward the use of higher grades of skilled labor in manufacturing exports. One should stress that this calculation has been performed without taking into account the actual increase in the skill content *within* individual

[51] One would introduce a submodel of the educational system of the kind presented by Bowles [4].

[52] I am indebted to M. Hershkovits of the Bank of Israel for performing this computation at my request (this is a by-product of a study that he is presently conducting).

industries. With the upgrading of the labor force during this period, such change had no doubt taken place. This would only strengthen the above finding.

REFERENCES

1. Arrow, K. J., "The Economic Implications of Learning by Doing," *Review of Economic Studies,* June 1962.
2. Becker, G. S., "Investment in Human Capital: A Theoretical Analysis," *Journal of Political Economy* (Supplement), October 1962.
3. Bhagwati, J., "The Pure Theory of International Trade," *The Economic Journal,* March 1964.
4. Bowles, S., "A Planning Model for the Efficient Allocation of Resources in Education," *Quarterly Journal of Economics,* May 1967.
5. Bruno, M., "Optimal Patterns of Trade and Development," *Review of Economics and Statistics,* November 1967.
6. Bruno, M., Dougherty, C., and Fraenkel, M., "Dynamic Input-Output, Trade and Development," in Carter, A. P., and Brody, A. (eds.), *Applications of Input-Output Analysis,* Amsterdam, 1969.
7. Chenery, H. B., "Comparative Advantage and Development Policy," *American Economic Review,* March 1961.
8. Fraenkel, M., "Some Aspects of Planning in an Open Economy," M.A. thesis, Hebrew University, 1968.
9. Hirschman, A. O., *The Strategy of Economic Development,* New Haven, 1958.
10. Leontief, W. W., "Factor Proportions and the Structure of American Trade: Further Theoretical and Empirical Analysis," *Review of Economics and Statistics,* November 1956.
11. Michaely, M., *The System of Effective Exchange Rates in Israel,* Jerusalem, 1968, (in Hebrew, English edition forthcoming.)
12. Verdoorn, P. J., "Complementarity and Long Range Projections," *Econometrica,* October 1956.

COMMENTS

ROBERT Z. ALIBER

University of Chicago

The topic of this session might be, "The Ranking of Economic Models for Analysis of Dynamic Comparative Advantage." Unfortunately, the competition is limited; only one model is available. Were competing models available, the immediate question is the criteria that might be used for ranking.

The difficulty of predicting how dynamic comparative advantage changes is illustrated by the paper in this volume of Professors Ruttan, Houck, and Evenson on the richness and variety of the process of transfer of agricultural technology. Domestic developments in the packaging of bananas, in disease resistant varieties, in the ability to use seeds and techniques developed elsewhere, change comparative advantage; similar developments abroad affect domestic comparative advantage. The implication of this experience is that predicting how world prices may change may be more important than predicting how supply functions may change.

One of the major criteria applicable to a model like Bruno's is usefulness—the test is whether the model facilitates better decisions. In other activities the feedback from a decision is rapid: firms fail, and coaches lose ball games and get sacked. With long-term planning models, the feedback is not nearly as quick. The investment errors of this generation of planners may only become evident to their successors. Economists developing models are also concerned with their usefulness—they want the models to be computational. The question is whether a model which is operational is necessarily better than none.

Professor Bruno's paper on dynamic comparative advantage does an elegant job of highlighting some of the issues in development policy. No term has been invoked more often to explain away the errors of planning and trade policy than *dynamic comparative advantage:* today's errors are defended as tomorrow's bonanzas. A model is desirable to provide a basis for analyzing where the investments should be placed as comparative advantage changes through time. To Professor Bruno, comparative advantage is defined as the set of activities which keeps the set of existing factors employed. A country either has or does not have comparative advantage in a product; it cannot have a comparative advantage for a certain level of output. This is because supply functions are linear—average costs and marginal costs are the same. Changes in comparative advantage involve changes in the mix of industries. In the Bruno model, comparative advantage changes through time in response to changes in external assistance; he demonstrates the interdependence among such assistance, the exchange rates, and the set of productive activities in which a country will have a comparative advantage. The model recognizes that changes in external assistance alter the trade deficit, hence the need to produce exports and substitutes for imports. To satisfy these needs requires a certain configuration of factors. Such changes, therefore, alter the relative supplies of factors available to produce a different set of domestic products and exports. If some industries are more fully subject to labor training skills or export externalities than others, the investment priorities are clearly affected. The model can be used to answer questions about trade-offs between aid level and the exchange rate, between interest rates and the level of foreign borrowing, and the labor training skills or export externalities required if a particular industry is to have comparative advantage at some future date. The model is dynamic in several senses—on its view of intertemporal borrowing and the relationship in a given period among production levels, export externalities, and labor training. The dynamic component in the model involves changes in external assistance and externalities in exports or labor training skills; in their absence, the dynamic element drops out.

To ask whether such a model is useful is to ask whether it facilitates the investment decisions. Since the logic can be assumed to be impeccable, attention should be given to the explicit and implicit assumptions. The model provides a useful way to organize some information not readily available. The limitation of the model is that certain aspects of dynamic comparative advantage—changes in relative prices due to changes in factor endowments, demands, or technologies—are ignored, even though their impact on dynamic comparative advantage may be greater than those of the export externalities. In a conference on trade and technology, the model seems barren in its treatment of technological change.

As the exchange rate changes, certain industries drop out of the domestic comparative advantage set, and others drop into this set. The reason is that the comparative advantage set is determined largely by average labor productivity. Given its stock of capital, labor, and the available technologies, this approach looks at the industry mix which keeps all domestic factors fully employed. If foreign aid to Israel should rise to $2 billion a year, the model suggests there is only one profitable export activity; as the aid level declines, the number of such industries increases. For Bruno, the question is which activities comprise the comparative advantage set; in the real world, the question is how much of each activity. This difference reflects that Bruno's model assumes linear production functions, even though his data shows substantial differences between average and marginal productivity. Perhaps one might decompose various productive activities into a number of tranches, with each tranche a different activity—thus the first million-dollar increment of mining is one activity, the second million-dollar increment is another, and so on. But while this approach might seem helpful for conceptual purposes, it may not be operational. The data for one industry may not be sliced into tranches in this way—the need for the model to be operational and computational is overriding. A suggestion of this approach is implicit in Bruno's data on marginal labor productivity. Ideally, one would like such data for each of the relevant tranches.

Perhaps an approach based on a portfolio balance model might be useful for meeting the problem of dynamic comparative advantage. Such a model would be superior to that of Professor Bruno's in some respects and inferior in others. The portfolio balance model would be no better at predicting changes in relative prices, technologies, and export externalities—attempts to predict change on any basis probably depend more on comparative or cross-sectional analysis. The portfolio balance model would be superior to Bruno's with regard to the intertemporal aspects of development policy, including the choice between adjustment through changes in reserves and adjustment through changes in the comparative advantage set. The portfolio balance model would be superior with regard to assigning probabilities and payoffs to alternative views of the future; the planning minister might offer his president the choice of *n*-development strategies. The portfolio balance model would be inferior in its capacity to identify efficient solutions to the static comparative advantage set—that is, to determine the industrial structures which, given the technology, the trade balance, and the capital stock, would result in full employment of domestic labor. And in the near-term at least, and perhaps forever, the Bruno model has a computational advantage.

NATHAN ROSENBERG
Harvard University

Technological change is, itself, one of the major growth industries in the economics profession. In the last ten or twelve years, beginning with the work of Solow and Abramowitz, growing concern with the impact and consequences of technical change has provided a fruitful basis for a substantial redirection of empirical research. I would like to record my judgment, at the outset, that I think this has been a highly desirable movement, and to say also that I would welcome a similar regrouping of our intellectual forces in the field of international trade. For the role of technical change is as badly neglected in trade theory today as it was in growth theory fifteen years ago. Perhaps in ten years' time we will all have the satisfaction of looking back upon this conference and saying that we participated, in one way or another, in the beginning of this revolution. I have even given some thought to the matter of providing a suitable slogan to this movement of potential revolutionists. Unfortunately, the only slogan I have been able to think of is one which is not well calculated to generate an appropriate sense of revolutionary fervor among international trade economists, although it does express the sense of part of what I have to say to them. It goes: "Trade theorists of the

world arise! You have nothing to lose but your comparative advantage."
I have a nagging intuition that this is likely to have only a very limited
appeal.

I am in the somewhat awkward position of having to comment on
two papers each of which, in its own way, I regard as excellent. This
leaves me with the alternative of either quibbling in a somewhat pedan-
tic and graceless way over small points or addressing myself in a more
general way to the issues raised in the paper by Bruno and that of Evenson, Houck, and Ruttan.[1] Having expressed my alternatives to you in
this fashion, it must be obvious that I have chosen the latter course.

Bruno, in his extremely interesting paper ("Development Policy and
Dynamic Comparative Advantage"), attempts to introduce dynamic considerations into the theory of comparative advantage in a way which
will eventually provide a basis for making decisions concerning trade
and development policies. The model which results is, perhaps inevitably,
somewhat complex. Its main element of novelty is an explicit consideration of intertemporal relations, including the treatment of externalities
in the export process and suggestions concerning an incorporation of
certain labor-training effects. Bruno shows considerable ingenuity in
demonstrating how some kinds of externalities can be considered within
the framework of a linear model. Although such a model has practical
attractions, and Bruno has demonstrated its versatility, it should also be
said that it has some severe analytical limitations, such as the inability
to handle increasing returns to scale in production.

In spite of the fact that Bruno has gone to some pains to cloak his
model in the traditional dress of comparative advantage, the novelty of
his analysis keeps poking through the traditional garb. The question I
want to raise is whether once we have introduced dynamic considerations, of the sort raised by Bruno, we are not in a somewhat different
ballpark, with somewhat different ground rules and goals, from the
one where comparative advantage is typically played. Clearly the question which I am raising does not concern the logic of comparative
advantage (which is impeccable) but its relevance and the extent of
its usefulness. I am suggesting that in a world where rapid technological
change is taking place we may need an analytical apparatus which
focusses in a central way upon the process of technological change

[1] For comment on Evenson, Houck, and Ruttan, see pp. 481–483, below.

itself, rather than treating it simply as an exogenous force which leads to disturbances from equilibrium situations and thereby sets in motion an adjustment process leading to a new equilibrium. If technological change is as important as it now appears to be (since Abramowitz and Solow woke us from our dogmatic slumber), then I suspect that an effective way of understanding the future pattern and prospects of world trade, together with its impact on individual economies, will be by focussing attention more directly than we now do upon the characteristics of a technology, together with its requirements, its opportunities, and its constraints.

Of course, it is possible to say that I am just asking for a shift in relative emphasis, and if, out of some sense of filial piety, the basic framework of comparative advantage is retained, I would not raise strenuous objections. I would then say that when we accord a more prominent role to the effects of a dynamic technology comparative advantage appears in a somewhat different light. It is no longer based upon cost differences which are rooted in immutable forces of climate or geology. Rather, it is the continually changing result of human ingenuity and inventiveness, reflecting the differential capacity of different countries to *develop* techniques which enable them to take advantage of opportunities which are only implicit in their resource endowment. The *primacy* of resource endowments recedes as an explanatory variable in a country's economic activities. Thus the barren stretches of the Negev have produced the barest subsistence under Bedouin nomadism but have a very different response when subjected to the forces of modern technology and water control at the disposal of an Israeli kibbutz. The difference in emphasis, then, is far from trivial. It is the difference between emphasizing an unalterable natural resource endowment as the prime determinant of economic performance and emphasizing the level of technological sophistication and versatility. For the fact is that not only do different countries employ different technologies; countries also vary considerably in their ability to *produce* appropriate technical changes and to adapt and modify the technology of other countries to their own requirements. This differential ability of countries to produce technical change is, it seems to me, of enormous importance, but it is not something which has been incorporated into our theorizing about international trade relations.

I think, then, that we must begin to inquire into the *sources* of technological versatility. If it can be established that certain kinds of economic activities are more successful than others in contributing to the development of inventive abilities and entrepreneurial and organizational talents, such information would have important policy implications. Technological change is not, after all, something which has emerged in a random way from all sectors of the economy. It is the result of a problem-solving skill which, historically, has been heavily concentrated in some specific sectors of the economy. In the early stages of industrialization these skills were heavily concentrated in machine tools and engineering; later, partly as a result of scientific advances, this focus shifted to chemistry-based and more recently to electronics-based industries.

In his paper, Bruno has made some comments on the learning process insofar as it pertains to workers acquiring *existing* skills—labor-training effects. I find these comments useful, but I would like to raise in addition the intriguing question of the process whereby society as a whole acquires new skills: either knowledge which previously did not exist, or applications or modifications of general principles which previously had not been undertaken. If industries differ drastically, as I suspect they do, in their capacity to prepare an economy for these "voyages of discovery," the acquisition of further information about these differences ought to be high on our list of research priorities. If one productive process involves a learning activity which leads to new techniques or products, and another does not, these are externalities of the greatest importance. Somehow we must take account of the fact that, whatever else may be said of the silk industry, it represented a technological "dead end." No amount of messing around with silkworms and mulberry leaves could ever have produced nylon. This innovation was dependent on an elaborate learning experience concerning the molecular structure of materials which would hardly have taken place in the absence of association with a large chemicals industry. Once this learning experience had taken place, it became in turn the basis for a veritable flood of innovations based upon the newly developed capacity to produce synthetic materials with specific characteristics. Similarly, the experience of the successful industrialization of countries in the nineteenth century indicates that the learning experiences involved in the design and production of machinery were vital sources of technological dynamism and flexibility for the country as a whole. Countries which rely upon the importation of foreign technology derive much benefit from doing so, but they are also cut off from what may be a critical learning experience. Generally, then, our theory must deal with the fact that industries have "outputs" other than the final product itself—the production of knowledge, skills, and talent which in turn determine the level of technical competence of the economy in the future. How do we incorporate into our theory the fact that certain kinds of activities may give an economy a comparative advantage in the capacity to *generate* technological change?

The growing awareness of the significance of technological change raises a related point about which we have hardly begun to theorize: Countries possessing a dynamic technology will also be the leaders in the introduction of new products. But we have not yet begun seriously to explore the consequences of this sort of technological leadership. Economic theory has always had a difficult time coming to grips with the problems posed by new products. Our analytical apparatus and our techniques of measurement have been notably deficient in the handling of product innovation as opposed to cost-reducing process innovation. But clearly product innovation has been playing, and will probably continue to play, a major role in the changing pattern of international trade, and it is very important that we develop analytical tools which can handle it. Raymond Vernon's suggestive article "International Investment and International Trade in the Product Cycle" [2] is a useful step in this direction. But clearly we still have a long way to go.

[2] *Quarterly Journal of Economics,* May 1966, pp. 190–207.

The Role of Technology

in the Theory of

International Trade

RONALD W. JONES

UNIVERSITY OF ROCHESTER

"Technology" refers to the way in which resources are converted into commodities. This is such a basic feature of an economic model, whether of a closed or open economy, that any discussion of the "role" of technology in the theory of trade must be arbitrarily incomplete. In what follows I have tried to cast the net widely and deal with several aspects of technology in the theory of international trade.

I. A TWO-COUNTRY, TWO-COMMODITY, TWO-FACTOR MODEL

Some years ago the literature on trade theory was largely concerned with the analysis of the impact of technological change on the equilibrium position in a two-commodity, two-country model of trade. Although the analysis involved in discussing the role of technical change in influencing trade patterns may be in its infancy, the analysis of the impact of *exogenous* changes in techniques is basically complete. It is useful to begin by sketching out the standard trade model in a form that permits a general treatment of the exogenous case. In doing so I shall rely heavily on the procedure I developed several years ago [8].

NOTE: I am indebted to Richard Caves and Trevor Underwood for useful conversations on the topic of this paper. This research is supported in part by The Center for Naval Analyses of the University of Rochester. Such support does not imply endorsement of the content by the Navy.

Consider a competitive trade model in which each of two countries is incompletely specialized in the production of two goods, M (manufactured goods) and F (food). Two factors of production are fully employed, L (labor) and T (land), and no international factor mobility is allowed. For the questions to be discussed in this section, it is easy to consider the general case in which production functions are allowed to differ between countries.

Even in this simple two-country case many conditions are required to describe a world trade equilibrium. It is useful to consider these conditions in smaller groups. First, examine the conditions relating to the production sector in each economy. The prevailing technology in each country can be specified by a set of input-output coefficients and their dependence upon the factor-price (wage-rent) ratio (w/r) ruling in that country at the time (t). These are shown by set (1).[1]

$$(1) \qquad\qquad a_{ij} = a_{ij}\left(\frac{w}{r}, t\right)$$

For any time t the unit isoquant in the jth sector can be traced out by considering the set of a_{ij} that would be chosen over the whole range of factor price ratios. Technical change is shown by a shifting of the unit isoquant (through a change in t). The basic (exogenous) parameters of technical change show the relative reductions in a_{ij} that would take place as of a given factor price ratio.[2]

There remain four other relationships on the production side in each country. The requirement that both factors be fully employed is shown by (2), and the competitive profit conditions, whereby the unit cost of producing each good is equated to its price, are given by the "dual" set (3).

$$(2) \qquad\qquad a_{LM}M + a_{LF}F = L$$

$$a_{TM}M + a_{TF}F = T$$

$$(3) \qquad\qquad a_{LM}w + a_{TM}r = p_M$$

$$a_{LF}w + a_{TF}r = p_F$$

---

[1] Subscripts for each country are omitted where no confusion is apt to arise. Thus there is a different set (1) for each country.

[2] One input-output ratio might increase. In this case the other must be reduced if technical *progress* is to be shown.

Before proceeding to complete the model, consider the impact on the production sector in each country of a change in technology. From set (1) it is clear that the methods of production change directly at the initial factor prices and indirectly through any tendency for the equilibrium set of factor prices to change. Thus the relative change in a_{ij} can be broken down into the two components shown by (1'). $\hat{b}_{ij}$ represents the relative *reduction* in an input requirement at constant factor prices, and $\underline{\hat{a}}_{ij}$ the relative change in the input-output coefficient along a given isoquant.[3] Furthermore, $\underline{\hat{a}}_{ij}$ depends upon the extent

$$(1') \qquad\qquad \hat{a}_{ij} = \underline{\hat{a}}_{ij} - \hat{b}_{ij}$$

of any change in the factor price ratio, and on the elasticity of substitution in sector j. As I have shown elsewhere,[4]

$$\underline{\hat{a}}_{Lj} = - \Theta_{Tj}\sigma_j(\hat{w} - \hat{r})$$
$$\underline{\hat{a}}_{Tj} \quad \Theta_{Lj}\sigma_j(\hat{w} - \hat{r})$$

where Θ_{ij} denotes factor i's distributive share (e.g., wa_{LM}/p_M for labor's share in the M industry) and σ_j the elasticity of substitution in the jth industry.

Whereas the $\hat{b}_{ij}$ reflects the details of technological change, it is only certain aggregates of these parameters that are important in tracing through the impact of technical change on terms of trade, outputs, and real incomes. These aggregates are of two types: (1) the relative extent of the cost reduction in industry j. This is denoted by $\pi_j \equiv \Theta_{Lj}\hat{b}_{Lj} + \Theta_{Tj}\hat{b}_{Tj}$, the distributive-share weighted average of the direct reduction in all input-output coefficients in the jth industry: (2) relative extent of the cost reduction in a particular factor's use in all industries. This is a less familiar concept. Considering labor, the relative reductions in labor use per unit output in the two industries are $\hat{b}_{LM}$ and $\hat{b}_{LF}$. Weight each by the fraction of the labor force used in that industry, λ_{Lj}, and define π_L as $\lambda_{LM}\hat{b}_{LM} + \lambda_{LF}\hat{b}_{LF}$. Now consider the effect of a general tech-

---

[3] In general a " ^ " over a variable denotes a relative change in that variable. Thus $\hat{a}_{ij}$ is da_{ij}/a_{ij}.

[4] For a derivation see Jones, [8]. Consider the M industry. Cost minimization per unit of output is shown graphically by requiring a tangency between the unit isoquant and an isocost line. Algebraically this states that the distributive share weighted average of the changes in input-output coefficients, $\Theta_{LM}\underline{\hat{a}}_{LM} + \Theta_{TM}\underline{\hat{a}}_{TM}$, must be zero. This, together with the definition of σ_M as $-(\underline{\hat{a}}_{LM} - \underline{\hat{a}}_{TM})/(\hat{w} - \hat{r})$, is sufficient to solve separately for $\underline{\hat{a}}_{LM}$ and $\underline{\hat{a}}_{TM}$.

nological change on an economy with given factor endowments by differentiating (logarithmically) the sets (2) and (3) to obtain (2′) and (3′):

(2′) $$\lambda_{LM}\hat{M} + \lambda_{LF}\hat{F} = \pi_L + \delta_L(\hat{w} - \hat{r})$$

$$\lambda_{TM}\hat{M} + \lambda_{TF}\hat{F} = \pi_T - \delta_T(\hat{w} - \hat{r})$$

(3′) $$\Theta_{LM}\hat{w} + \Theta_{TM}\hat{r} = \hat{p}_M + \pi_M$$

$$\Theta_{LF}\hat{w} + \Theta_{TF}\hat{r} = \hat{p}_F + \pi_F$$

where $$\delta_L = \lambda_{LM}(\Theta_{TM}\sigma_M) + \lambda_{LF}(\Theta_{TF}\sigma_F)$$

$$\delta_T = \lambda_{TM}(\Theta_{LM}\sigma_M) + \lambda_{TF}(\Theta_{LF}\sigma_F)$$

If there were no change in technology, (2′) and (3′) would show how any change in commodity prices would disturb factor prices (through (3′)) and how such a change in factor prices would require a change in the composition of outputs in order to maintain full employment (through (2′)). These output changes, of course, could be represented by movements along a transformation curve. Technological progress is seen to complicate matters further in two ways. First, the reduction in factor requirements is seen to act like an increase in the quantity of factors available in (2′). Thus if factor prices were constant and only labor coefficients were reduced ($\pi_L > 0$, $\pi_T = 0$), the transformation schedule would be shifted outward and the output of the labor-intensive commodity would be increased while the output of the land-intensive commodity would be reduced. Although this sounds like the Rybczynski result [16], technical change of this kind also disturbs the relationship between commodity and factor prices through its cost-reducing impact in (3′). Therefore at the new production point the new (outer) transformation schedule need not have the same slope as at the initial point. That is, not only does any technical change act in part like an increase in factor endowments, it also acts in part like a change in commodity prices, or more accurately, like a set of industry subsidies.

With an exception I shall consider below, exogenous technical change disrupts only the production side of the model. However, it is necessary to consider the demand side in order to complete the picture of this two-country trading community. In each country demand functions must be specified. By Walras' law it would only be necessary to specify, say, that the demand for M in each country depends on that country's income and the terms of trade. Then derive a world demand function and require that, as a result of technical progress, commodity prices must adjust so as to clear markets. The relationships shown by (3') would suffice to determine the impact on each country's factor prices.[5]

The exception I noted refers to the possibility that technical change results in an improvement in the quality of commodities instead of (or in addition to) a reduction in input coefficients. To handle this (in an exogenous fashion), introduce "t" as a variable in the demand functions. This would serve to capture the shift in taste patterns that would be triggered off by the quality changes.

Attention in the trade literature has sometimes centered on the impact of technical change on the real incomes of the countries participating in trade. In an extreme form the question raised concerns the possibility of immiserizing growth: Can technical progress in a country so affect the terms of trade that real income in that country is reduced? The answer, of course, is that this is a theoretical possibility. Any deterioration in a country's terms of trade (e.g., through progress in its export sector) reduces real income directly by an amount that is related both to the extent of the deterioration and the extent of the country's *imbalance* between consumption and production patterns. For example, suppose a country exports commodity M; let its real income be denoted by "y" measured in units of commodity F, and its consumption of M by M^*. If Θ_M and Θ_F denote the shares in national income (Y) of the *production* of each commodity, the following expression shows the change in real income.[6] Any deterioration in p_M/p_F would have

$$dy = (M - M^*)\, d\!\left(\frac{p_M}{p_F}\right) + Y[\Theta_M \pi_M + \Theta_F \pi_F]$$

[5] It should be mentioned that this nonmonetary system will not yield a solution for the change in each commodity price. One commodity, say F, could be taken as numeraire. I have retained $\hat{p}_F$ so as not to disturb the symmetry in the expressions.

[6] This expression is derived from the budget constraint (or balance-of-payments constraint), $p_M M^* + p_F F^* = p_M M + p_F F$ and the definition of a real income change (in units of F) as the price-weighted sum of changes in consumption, $(p_M/p_F)\,(dM^*) + dF^*$.

to be set against the directly beneficial effect on real incomes of the improvement in technology.

This is the basic model that has been used to analyze the impact of any kind of technical change on prices, consumption, production, and real incomes of countries in a trading community. It is deficient because it does not come to grips with the *inducement mechanism* whereby the $\hat{b}_{ij}$, and therefore the π's, are linked to changes in other economic variables. I shall comment upon this in more detail in Section III. However, it is worth setting out the model in some detail because whatever inducement mechanism is considered, it is this basic model that can then be used to trace through the consequences of technical change.

II. A MODIFICATION OF THE HECKSCHER-OHLIN THEORY

The preceding section has been devoted to the question of how a *change* in technology used anywhere in the world disturbs a preexisting trading equilibrium. In this section I discuss a closely related but separable aspect of the role of technology in trade theory, namely, how the basic Heckscher-Ohlin model of trade that assumes identical production functions must be modified to take account of *differences* in production functions between countries.

In a sense the Heckscher-Ohlin model represents a step backward from the earlier Ricardian tradition. With Ricardo, international differences in production functions were not only allowed, but served as the basis for explaining positions of comparative advantage. Early work on the Heckscher-Ohlin model concentrated on differences in factor endowments as the source of comparative advantage and found it convenient to ignore differences in technologies between countries (and tended to minimize the influence of differences in taste patterns). This deficiency was repaired in the trade literature of the past decade.[7]

One immediate consequence for the Heckscher-Ohlin theory of allowing countries to differ in their prevailing states of technology can be inferred from equations (3'). The changes in factor and commodity prices exhibited there can be interpreted as reflecting the pretrade differences in these prices between two countries with slightly differing

[7] For a summary statement, see Amano [1].

technologies. Subtract the bottom equation in (3′) from the top and rearrange to obtain (4):

$$(4) \qquad (\hat{p}_M - \hat{p}_F) = |\Theta| (\hat{w} - \hat{r}) - (\pi_M - \pi_F)$$

where

$$|\Theta| \equiv \Theta_{LM} - \Theta_{LF}$$

The sign of $|\Theta|$ indicates which industry is labor intensive. Suppose in both countries M is labor intensive so that $|\Theta|$ is positive. A strong form of the Heckscher-Ohlin theorem states that when two countries have identical technologies, the low-wage country has a comparative advantage in producing the labor-intensive commodity. Equation (4) suggests how easily this proposition can be modified to account for differences in technologies. The labor-intensive commodity could turn out to be relatively expensive in the low-wage country if the other country had a sufficiently strong *relative* technological superiority in producing M. In the spirit of the doctrine of comparative advantage it is only relative differences in productivity that count.

Further analysis is required if the role of technological differences between countries in determining positions of comparative advantage is to be contrasted with the bias imposed by differences in physical factor endowments. The production side of the model needs to be expanded by adding L and T respectively to the right-hand side of equations (2′) to allow for differences in factor endowments as well as technologies. Solve (4) for the difference in factor price ratios and insert into (2′). Then solve this set for the difference in the ratio of goods produced to obtain (5): [8]

$$(5) \quad (\hat{M} - \hat{F}) = \frac{1}{|\lambda|} \{(\hat{L} - \hat{T}) + (\pi_L - \pi_T)\}$$
$$+ \sigma_S \{(\hat{p}_M - \hat{p}_F) + (\pi_M - \pi_F)\}$$

where

$$|\lambda| \equiv \lambda_{LM} - \lambda_{TM}$$

$$\sigma_S \equiv \frac{\delta_L + \delta_T}{|\lambda| \; |\Theta|}$$

For a closed economy, this change in the ratio of outputs produced must be matched by a similar change in the ratio of quantities consumed.

---

[8] $|\lambda|$ is positive if, as assumed, M is labor intensive. σ_S is the elasticity of substitution on the supply side (along the transformation schedule).

To wash out the separate role played by differences in tastes or income levels, I assume that both countries have identical homothetic taste patterns. Equation (6) follows from the definition of the elasticity of

$$(6) \qquad (\hat{M} - \hat{F}) = -\sigma_D(\hat{p}_M - \hat{p}_F)$$

substitution on the demand side. Equating (5) and (6) permits a solution for the difference in the relative commodity price ratio, and this is shown as follows:

$$(7) \quad (\hat{p}_M - \hat{p}_F)$$

$$= -\frac{1}{|\lambda|(\sigma_S + \sigma_D)} \{(\hat{L} - \hat{T}) + (\pi_L - \pi_T) + |\lambda|\sigma_S(\pi_M - \pi_F)\}$$

What the expression given by (7) allows is a comparison of the autarchy price ratios that would rule in two economies slightly different, both in their technologies and in factor endowments. It points out that two general features of the differences in technologies are crucial in influencing positions of comparative advantage. The first, $(\pi_L - \pi_T)$, might be termed the "differential factor effect" and it is seen that this influences commodity prices in exactly the same manner as do differences in factor endowments. The second, $(\pi_M - \pi_F)$, the "differential industry effect," points out that technological differences between countries bias commodity prices directly to the extent that a country's technological superiority over another country is not evenly spread over both industries.[9] Elsewhere I have defined technical change (or, in this case, differences between countries) to be "regular" if a greater aggregate reduction in labor coefficients than in land coefficients corresponds to a differential impact on costs favoring the labor-intensive industry.[10] In such a case $(\pi_L - \pi_T)$ $(\pi_M - \pi_F) \geqq 0$,[11] and both features of the technological differences between countries influence the commodity price ratio in the same direction. The Heckscher-Ohlin theorem, of course, can be reversed by differences in technology. Expression (7) shows how pronounced these differences would have to be.

[9] π_M and π_F are Hicksian measures of technological difference. Later in this section I shall point out how the different Harrod measures may be crucial in explaining comparative advantage positions in a world in which capital is freely mobile.

[10] See Jones [8]. Technical change need not be "regular." Consider a reduction in the labor coefficient only in the land-intensive industry.

[11] This assumes again that M is labor intensive.

Perhaps the most celebrated result of the standard Heckscher-Ohlin model is the factor-price equalization theorem: with identical technologies, incomplete specialization in both countries guarantees that free trade brings about an equality in the real returns to similar factors in both countries.[12] This result disappears if technologies differ between countries.

The fact that factor prices are not equalized in the Heckscher-Ohlin model is the factor-price equalization theorem: with identical techquences for the standard assumption of international factor immobility underlying the body of traditional trade theory. This assumption is tolerable if goods trade is a perfect substitute for factor movements. In what follows I assume that capital and labor replace land and labor as the two explicit factors of production in the model and, for simplicity, assume that only capital is potentially mobile.[13] At initial pretrade stocks of capital, rates of return to capital in the two countries would normally not be brought into line. In such a case there is incentive to develop the theory of trade to incorporate trade in capital goods and foreign investment. For example, recent theoretical work on foreign investment has been concerned with the problem of the interconnections between impediments placed on goods trade and taxes levied on income earned on capital placed abroad, in the context of a model in which technologies in two countries are assumed at the outset to differ [12, 10]. Quite aside from the question of devising optimal tariff and tax strategy is the more general question relating to the properties of trade models in which capital is internationally mobile subject, perhaps, to certain taxes on repatriated earnings. In concluding this section I shall briefly note a few of these.

Consider, first, the question of specialization in production in a two-commodity, two-factor, two-country, competitive, riskless world in which real capital is mobile (through the possibility of foreign investment). In a recent article I claimed it was unlikely, if technologies differed between countries, to find both countries incompletely specialized. As has recently been suggested by Kemp and Inada [13], this is an unwarranted remark. If the technological comparison between coun-

---

[12] I rule out the possibility of factor-intensity reversals.

[13] It would be possible to construct a three-factor model to include land, and require land to be immobile internationally.

FIGURE 1

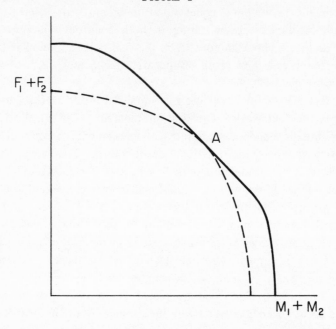

tries is such that at any common commodity price ratio the return to capital is higher in one country than another, unimpeded capital flows will drive at least one country to specialize completely. Kemp and Inada were concerned with another case—that in which there existed some commodity price ratio at which rates of return to capital would be equalized with both countries incompletely specialized. As John Chipman has pointed out, it is possible to derive a world transformation schedule assuming capital is freely mobile [5]. Such a schedule has a "flat"—a portion of the schedule is linear. This transformation schedule is shown by the solid curve in Figure 1. The curved sections of this schedule correspond to price ratios at which at least one country is driven to specialize completely. Thus with capital mobile it is quite possible that a free trade solution occurs along the flat and both countries are incompletely specialized. It is interesting to compare this locus with the world transformation schedule that would obtain if capital were immobile internationally, as in the traditional Heckscher-Ohlin model. This schedule is the dashed one in Figure 1.

In drawing this second locus I have assumed that there exists one commodity price ratio at which rates of return to capital can be equated consistent with incomplete specialization in both countries and with the given stocks of labor and capital in the two countries. This corresponds to point A. For all other points rates of return differ between countries. Free trade in goods will then not suffice to substitute for movements of capital, either to bring about international equality in their returns or to reach the solid world efficiency frontier.[14]

Second, consider the determinants of comparative advantage if trade in capital goods serves to equalize rates of return to capital between countries. Let the two countries differ only slightly in their technologies. Subtract $\hat{r}$ from both sides of (3') to obtain (3'') as the solution for the difference in the factor price ratio between countries

$$(3'') \qquad (\hat{w} - \hat{r}) = - \frac{1}{\Theta_{LM}} (\hat{r} - \hat{p}_M) + \frac{\pi_M}{\Theta_{LM}}$$

To consider equal rates of return to capital, set $(\hat{r} - \hat{p}_M)$ equal to zero in (3'') and substitute into (4) to obtain (4'):

$$(4') \qquad (\hat{p}_M - \hat{p}_F) = \Theta_{LF} \left\{ \frac{\pi_F}{\Theta_{LF}} - \frac{\pi_M}{\Theta_{LM}} \right\}$$

In a world of capital mobility, positions of comparative advantage are determined by the Harrod, as opposed to the Hicks, measures of technical difference.[15] Now suppose that in the capital abundant country more resources have been devoted to improving the technology and that this country has a uniform Hicksian advantage in all lines (i.e., $\pi_M = \pi_F$). In a world of capital mobility, this nonetheless biases comparative advantage in the direction of having the capital abundant country export the capital intensive commodity.[16] Note the sensitivity

---

[14] Of course, with labor assumed immobile and technologies different, there will generally not be any tendency to equate real wages in the two countries. Interesting further work remains in following up Chipman's results in those cases in which taxes (or perhaps considerations of risk) serve to impede capital flows. One preliminary result may be noted: the world transformation curve will lie inside the solid curve of Figure 1, but will also have a linear segment. However, unlike the untaxed case shown in Figure 1, the slope of the transformation curve does *not* correspond to the commodity price ratio despite the fact that no direct impediments exist to commodity movements.

[15] π_j/Θ_{Lj} shows the improvement in output per man at a given capital-output ratio (or, for small changes, at a given rate of profit). See Jones [8, 9].

[16] If M is capital intensive the right-hand side of (4') is negative.

of this result to the crude inducement mechanism whereby it is the more capital abundant country that has devoted more resources to technical improvement. If production functions in the labor abundant country should represent superior technology, of the same Hicksian measure for each industry, and if rates of profit should be equalized between countries, the labor abundant country would tend to have a comparative advantage in the capital intensive commodity.

Of course the entire concept of factor abundance is subject to question if capital is mobile between countries. Equation (4') suggests how differential rates of technical differences between countries come to dominate the determination of comparative advantage. Differences in factor endowments, in the sense of national ownership of capital per man, then get linked to commodity price ratios through the intermediate step of affecting levels of technology through research and development.

To conclude this section consider the way in which the Heckscher-Ohlin model could be applied to Vernon's concept of the "product cycle" [18]. Vernon argues that advanced countries tend to have a comparative advantage in producing those commodities that are newly being developed. Whereas special knowledge of the large home market and the prior existence of distribution channels imparts a bias to producing *for* the home market, the question of interest here is why the location of production should also be at home.[17] Vernon suggests that high labor costs at home may nonetheless be outweighed by the advantage of having a location in which a variety of factors of production (or special skills) is readily accessible. The role of technology is important, for what is being suggested is that the input mix at the early stages of the development of the product is different from the input mix later, when production becomes standardized. That is, in the course of the product cycle there is a systematic bias in the change in the production function required to produce the commodity.

In simplified terms, this suggests a three factor model: capital, "ordinary" labor, and a third factor that comprises a host of special skills on the part of labor or of capital equipment. The uncertainty associated with early stages of production, whereby the actual production process that will be required at a later stage is still not known, is thus

---

[17] Significant transport costs could heavily influence this decision.

translated into a third factor of production. Advanced countries, such as the United States, have a relative abundance of this third factor and hence a comparative advantage in producing new commodities at early stages of production. Later stages are associated with a shift in factor intensities toward a relatively greater role played by capital and labor.

To the extent that foreign production of commodities is undertaken as a form of foreign investment by firms in advanced countries, the previous remarks about trade theory in a world of capital mobility are relevant. If the rates that must be paid for the use of capital are brought into line for certain industrial activities between advanced and less advanced areas, the role of returns to capital as an explanation of comparative advantage tends to be neutralized, making it easier to conceptualize Vernon's product cycle in terms of two factors—labor and this third bundle representing various skills and amenities. That is, a comparison of labor shares with third-factor shares would be crucial in depicting a ranking of industries by comparative advantage.

One special feature of a trading world in which foreign investment is important should be noted. Capital markets within less developed countries tend to be fragmented in the sense that some industrial activities—particularly if foreign owned—yield rates on capital in line with generally low rates in the advanced countries, whereas local entrepreneurs might have to pay higher returns for the use of capital. The standard idealization in the theory of trade, whereby factor prices are equated within, but not necessarily between, countries (especially if technologies differ), needs to be revised to take account of differences within and similarities between countries with reference to returns to factors that may be more mobile internationally than nationally.[18]

III. INDUCEMENT MECHANISMS

What determines technical change? This basic question is not specific to trade theory, but any theory of the inducement mechanism has consequences for the kind of trade model discussed in the preceding sections.

[18] This brings up the old concept of noncompeting groups and the stimulating challenge to traditional trade theory given by J. H. Williams [19].

A crude sort of inducement mechanism was given in Section II. It was suggested there that the rate of technical progress in any industry would increase as the economy's relative stock of owned capital (or wealth) increased. That is, wealthy countries put more resources into improving technology. Although this assumption had consequences for positions of comparative advantage in a model in which capital is mobile, it nonetheless gave no clue as to which industries would be especially favored by the input of resources to improve technology.

There is a simple inducement mechanism that discriminates between industries and is formally similar to the existence of external economies. The state of technology in any industry is linked to the level of that industry's output. In a recent article I have explored some of the ties between the Rybczynski theorem linking factor growth with the composition of outputs, the Stolper-Samuelson theorem linking commodity and factor prices, and the question of the shape of the transformation schedule, demonstrating how standard results in trade theory are altered when each a_{ij} is dependent not only upon factor prices but also upon the level of output in industry j.[19] The existence of economies of scale acts like a shift in the production function facing firms if these economies are external to the operation of the firm. If the resources devoted to R&D tend to increase with the scale of operations, further support is lent to treating each a_{ij} as a function of the output of j. Instead of pursuing the formal analysis here, I only note that the model described in Sections I and II can be used with proper modification of (1).

Although the effects of economies of scale on the model may be similar to those of having knowledge improved with greater use of resources for research as output expands, they are not identical in that economies of scale may be reversible whereas genuine technical progress is presumably permanent. That is, it may be useful in modifying (1) to introduce a "ratchet" effect whereby each a_{ij} depends upon the previously attained highest level of output. A more complicated adjustment would entail having the inducement to technical change be represented by the past integral of output. In this way, the unit isoquant would still be shifting inward, even if the level of output were to remain constant.

---

[19] See Jones [11]. A variation on this type of external economy is to have each a_{ij} linked to the quantity of capital employed in industry j.

An even better procedure might entail setting up a distinction between the use of resources to produce the commodity and the use of resources to produce new technical knowledge. That is, the $\hat{b}_{ij}$ could be considered to be outputs of a separate production process.

Any of the above alternatives falls short of capturing a realistic mechanism to explain rates of technical change. Expectations as to future sales must affect the quantity of resources devoted to improving the technology. To highlight this distinction consider, again, Vernon's model of the product cycle. It is at the early stages, where new products are being introduced, that relatively heavy use is made of resources in R&D. Reliance on current output levels as an explanation of the level of technology would fail to incorporate this phenomenon.

All these remarks deal primarily with the determinants of the *rates* of technical progress by industry and with the scale of resources devoted to shifting the production function. A small literature over the past few years has been devoted to the question of the determinants of *bias* in technical progress, *given* the inputs of resources used to improve technology [14, 17, 6, 2]. This literature derives its motivation from models of growth rather than models of trade and, in particular, attempts to demonstrate a tendency toward Harrod neutrality. Nonetheless, any inducement mechanism that serves to explain why labor coefficients are altered by different relative amounts than are capital coefficients has implications for the model set out in Sections I and II.

The basic concept in the literature on induced bias is that of a convex technological improvement frontier representing the maximum possible saving in the use of one factor for various prescribed levels of saving in the other factor (and given a fixed research budget). However, there are several interpretations of this frontier, depending upon which parameters are chosen to represent "saving" for a factor of production. For example, augmenting coefficients could be used, or improvements in marginal products at given capital/labor ratios, or reductions in input-output coefficients at constant factor prices (the $\hat{b}_{ij}$ of this paper) or at a constant rate of profit. Basic to the theory in its present state is the assumption that the frontier is exogenously positioned in time.[20] This

---

[20] This rules out the possibility of diminishing returns to research effort, which would cause the frontier to shrink over time, especially perhaps in the neighborhood of points previously chosen.

represents little advance over a completely exogenous treatment of technical change. In addition, the assumption that a frontier specified in terms of one set of parameters is fixed in position over time in general negates the possibility that a frontier specified in terms of another set of parameters is also stationary. Furthermore, the conditions for convergence to "neutrality" depend crucially upon which representation is chosen.

For these reasons I suspect that this literature is not now directly useful to trade theory. However, it does throw out the notion that a factor's distributive share may be a key inducement variable. That is, at the optimal point along the innovation possibility frontier, the absolute value of the slope of the frontier is equated to the ratio of distributive shares. In the language of the model in Section I, the object is to pick $\hat{b}_{ij}$ in such a way that π_i, equal to $\Theta_{Lj}\hat{b}_{Lj} + \Theta_{Kj}\hat{b}_{Ki}$, is a maximum.[21] Given any disturbance to a trading world (such as the imposition of tariffs or the adjustment required in the face of growth and capital accumulation), distributive shares as well as factor prices are affected, and thus indirectly the choice of new technologies. The novel element is that the question of whether the elasticity of substitution between factors is greater or less than unity becomes important because the behavior of the Θ's depends upon this. Thus it might be possible that through trade there is a tendency for factor prices to get equilibrated but at the same time for factor shares to move further apart, thus stimulating more diverse developments in the technologies of the two countries.

The view that technology is improved because there is "learning by doing" is a statement both about the inducement mechanisms for rates of change and about bias.[22] According to this concept the higher the level of production (or, in some models, the integral of past production or investment) or the more "experience" about techniques gained by using them, the greater is the rate at which these techniques become more productive. This is similar to the external economy effect discussed earlier. But there is an important difference: the learning-by-doing hypothesis suggests that the unit isoquant gets pushed in primarily in

[21] Implicitly it may be assumed that Section I's model has a right-angled innovation possibility frontier.

[22] The basic paper is K. J. Arrow, [3]. See also the interesting paper by A. B. Atkinson, and J. E. Stiglitz [4].

the region where production is taking place. In the words of Atkinson and Stiglitz, technical progress is "localized." Although nothing is hypothesized about a "local" tendency to "bias" (i.e., whether learning by doing makes the production process more or less labor intensive), there is bias in a "global" sense—that rates of change are higher near the prevailing factor proportions.

The "localization" feature of learning by doing is of interest to trade theory because it raises the question of how transmittable technical change is from one country to another.

IV. TRANSMISSION OF TECHNOLOGY

Is the technical progress of one country readily transmittable to other countries? The discussion in Section I presumed that it was not, but underlying the traditional Heckscher-Ohlin model is the notion that it is difficult to keep secret new techniques of production.

For some types of technical knowledge patents or licensing arrangements would allow new techniques to be sold internationally as are other commodities. The traditional view is that basic knowledge cannot be appropriated in this way, that technical knowledge takes on more the form of a public good. In this sense technical progress is freely transferable.

Even in this limiting case, however, technical progress in one country may not spill over to actually affect techniques used in other countries. Consider Figure 2 in which a common (solid) isoquant for two countries is shifted to the dashed isoquant again commonly available to two countries. If the high wage advanced country is producing at *A,* and if the low wage country is using techniques shown by *B,* the improvement in techniques shown by the dashed curve does not serve to lower costs in the low wage country.

Two features of this example are crucial in limiting the transference of technical improvements: (1) Factor prices differ between countries, so that different actual techniques are used along the same isoquant, and (2) technical progress in one country tends to be "localized" in the region of existing techniques. The learning-by-doing hypothesis fits the latter category and thus serves as one basis for explaining why it is that all countries need not benefit from improvements made in one of

FIGURE 2

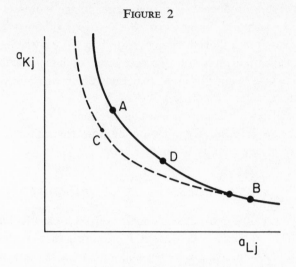

them, even though no secrets are kept. But the argument against the effective transmittal of new knowledge is even stronger than this. The movement from A to C in Figure 2 may have been the result of a technical improvement that was discovered as a consequence of time spent using the technique at A. On the other hand, what may be represented is that labor needs the experience of working with capital before point C can be reached. In this latter instance even if the low wage country is at point D it may not be able to benefit until its factors can adapt to the techniques at A.

The picture that emerges from this is that production functions may in some sense be the same between countries, but factor prices are different, and in their research efforts countries are really "chipping away" at different points on a common production surface.

If technical progress is embodied, clearly the transmission of technical knowledge depends upon allowing trade in capital goods. The same feature also obtains with labor and the possibility of moving trained managers and special skills, perhaps through foreign investment. The view that much of the change or difference that is observed in input-output coefficients is a reflection of changes in factor skills rather than in technical knowledge leads to the position that a critical bottleneck to the international transmission of technology resides in international factor immobilities. Trade in factors is synonymous with exporting the technology.

In concluding this paper I would like to suggest how a mixture of these views could be fitted together into the framework of a model developed recently by Peter Kenen [15]. Kenen views capital as a resource which is used to improve the quality of uneducated labor and infertile land. That is, resources (capital) are used to raise the quality of the basic factors of production, which are then used to produce commodities that enter into trade (as well as capital). By analogy think of techniques newly developed in an advanced country. Before these can be utilized in a less developed country, resources must be devoted to the learning process. In this way, technical knowledge is not kept "secret," but transmission is nonetheless not without cost.

With foreign-produced technology not adaptable without the use of a country's own resources, the question arises as to the proper allocation of local capital and labor to improve "technology." Two uses are suggested, each perhaps subject to diminishing returns: (1) adapt the foreign technology as suggested above, or (2) devote resources, partly through learning by doing, to improve local techniques that are dictated by local factor prices. These uses for resources must compete with the alternatives of raising labor productivity through capital accumulation or working directly, through education, to improve factor skills. It is not difficult to envisage a model in which the productivity of all four uses for resources gets equated at the margin.

REFERENCES

1. Amano, A., "Determinants of Comparative Costs: A Theoretical Approach," *Oxford Economic Papers*, November 1964, pp. 389–400.

2. Amano, A., "Induced Bias in Technological Progress and Economic Growth," *The Economic Studies Quarterly*, March 1967, pp. 1–17.

3. Arrow, K. J., "The Economic Implication of Learning by Doing," *Review of Economic Studies*, 1962, pp. 155–73.

4. Atkinson, A. B., and Stiglitz, J. E., "A New View of Technological Change," unpublished.

92   *Models Incorporating Technology Factor*

5. Chipman, J., "International Trade with Capital Mobility: A Substitution Theorem," unpublished.

6. Drandakis, E., and Phelps, E., "A Model of Induced Invention, Growth and Distribution," *Economic Journal,* December 1966, pp. 823–40.

7. Jones, R. W., " 'Neutral' Technological Change and the Isoquant Map," *American Economic Review,* September 1965, pp. 848–55.

8. ———, "The Structure of Simple General Equilibrium Models," *Journal of Political Economy,* December 1965, pp. 557–72.

9. ———, "Comments on Technical Progress," *The Philippine Economic Journal,* Second Semester, 1966, pp. 313–32.

10. ———, "International Capital Movements and the Theory of Tariffs and Trade," *Quarterly Journal of Economics,* February 1967, pp. 1–38.

11. ———, "Variable Returns to Scale in General Equilibrium Theory," *International Economic Review,* October 1968, pp. 261–72.

12. Kemp, M. C., "The Gain from International Trade and Investment: A Neo-Heckscher-Ohlin Approach," *American Economic Review,* September 1966, pp. 788–809.

13. Kemp, M. C., and Inada, K., "International Capital Movements and the Theory of International Trade," *Quarterly Journal of Economics,* August 1969.

14. Kennedy, C., "Induced Bias in Innovation and the Theory of Distribution," *Economic Journal,* September 1964, pp. 541–47.

15. Kenen, P. B., "Nature, Capital and Trade," *Journal of Political Economy,* October 1965, pp. 437–60.

16. Rybczynski, T. M., "Factor Endowments and Relative Commodity Prices," *Economica,* November 1955, pp. 336–41.

17. Samuelson, P. A., "A Theory of Induced Innovation along Kennedy-Weizsacker Lines," *Review of Economics and Statistics,* November 1965, pp. 343–56.

18. Vernon, R., "International Investment and International Trade in the Product Cycle," *Quarterly Journal of Economics,* May 1966, pp. 190–207.

19. Williams, J. H., "The Theory of International Trade Reconsidered," reprinted as Chap. 2 in *Postwar Monetary Plans and Other Essays,* Oxford, 1947.

COMMENT

JAGDISH N. BHAGWATI
Massachusetts Institute of Technology

The papers of Harry Johnson and Ronald Jones concur in the theme that trade theory has been somewhat left behind by the real world, especially in relation to the phenomenon of technological progress.[1] While Jones essentially tries to develop the traditional Heckscher-Ohlin-Samuelson model of trade theory (which is basically a simplified general equilibrium model of the Hicksian variety) in directions implied by the consideration of technical change, the Johnson paper attempts to develop themes which are on a more "imaginative" scale but which seem to have no theoretical foundations as of the present moment.

In the case of technological progress, trade theory's lag behind non-trade theory is only nominal, as John Chipman's introductory survey to his theoretical exercise incisively indicates. We still have very little theoretical work on the causes of technical change, either in terms of its origins or its spread. In this respect, I find Ronald Jones' review of the existing literature on technical change in trade theory excellent. He has elegantly restated an important body of literature starting with the work of Findlay-Grubert and Johnson. This line of investigation explores the effects of Hicks-neutral and Hicks-biased technical change, *exogenously* introduced, on the output-elasticity of supply at constant commodity prices, embodied in the Heckscher-Ohlin-Samuelson model. Jones has also extended the analysis to the case explored by Minhas, Bhagwati, and Bardhan where Hicks-neutral efficiency differences are introduced between countries, so that we have what I described in my *Economic Journal* survey (1964) as a Ricardo-Heckscher-Ohlin theory.

[1] For Johnson comment, see page 22 above.

Of considerably greater interest is his review of the recent literature which introduces the international mobility of one of the factors in a world of such technological differences.

I also find interesting Jones' review of different suggestions concerning the origin and dissemination of technical change, on which there is practically no theoretical work in trade yet. As soon as we bring in these types of possibilities, I can think of several interesting questions, particularly in welfare analysis. Think, for example, of technical change being determined by any specified form of technical-progress function (e.g., a Kennedy function). If we can then introduce into such a system the possibility of dissemination of technical change abroad, distinguishing between different rates of dissemination on different types of technical change (either by the nature of the bias or by the activity in which the change occurs), then there could well be a case of externalities requiring governmental intervention, because the market could well lead to allocation of resources to technical change which are socially less productive via the spread effects abroad.

Furthermore, among the interesting, dynamic models that could be built around the notion of dissemination of technical change would be one in which an Atkinson-Stiglitz type of "localized," learning-by-doing technical change were introduced and combined with international mobility of one of the factors (say, labor) with a constraint on the magnitude of factor mobility permitted per unit period. Such analyses would permit the examination of welfare questions in a dynamic context. Thus, once we have begun to introduce technical change as an *endogenously* produced and disseminated factor, there are numerous possibilities of pushing economic analysis ahead to yield interesting insights and results in both positive and welfare theory.

Induced Technical

Change and Patterns

of International Trade

JOHN S. CHIPMAN

UNIVERSITY OF MINNESOTA

1. INTRODUCTION

What largely distinguishes the modern from the classical theory of international trade is its exploitation of and dependence on the concept of a production function in its narrow conception as a relation between a constant stream of output on the one hand and constant streams or constant stocks of inputs on the other. More narrowly still, production functions are usually assumed to be concave and homogeneous of the first degree.

Differences observed in these input-output relations between countries at a given time, or within a country at different times, are termed technological. Within the neoclassical tradition (as opposed to that of Marx and Schumpeter), these differences have been generally regarded as exogenous to economic science. But empirical studies increasingly indicate that such differences "account for" a large fraction of both trade and growth. The growth studies are extremely well known and need not be mentioned here; among empirical investigations suggesting the importance of technical differences (and especially, technical lags) in the explanation of trade patterns, are the celebrated researches of Leontief [35, 36] as well as the studies of Kindleberger [32, 33], Kravis [34],

NOTE: This paper is dedicated to the memory of my late colleague Jacob Schmookler.

MacDougall [38], Hoffmeyer [24], Freeman [16, 17], Hufbauer [25], Brechling and Surrey [7], Vernon [64], and Gruber, Mehta, and Vernon [18]. Some of these studies also tend to suggest, as have empirical studies of economic growth, that "technology" is an economic activity responsive to economic forces, although not very much is known as yet concerning the precise form of such responsiveness. A highly suggestive, though admittedly speculative, study by Habbakuk [19] lays great emphasis on induced biases in the direction of technical change among countries.

A theorist could approach this problem in two ways. One is to "fix up" or supplement the conventional concept of a static production function by providing a recipe for changing it. Another is to abandon the static production function altogether and replace it with a dynamic function of a particular kind. Both procedures are scientifically respectable. If by postulating the existence of an extra planet an astronomer can reconcile Newtonian theory with observations, his procedure is justified even if the planet is not independently "observed"—provided, of course, that he does not have to keep inventing new planets to explain fresh sets of observations. On the other hand, the ill-fated concept of "ether," which the physicists were obliged eventually to abandon, illustrates the case in which it is better to do away with the old concepts altogether.

The two approaches just mentioned need not be mutually exclusive. Starting from a definite recipe for changing a static production function, one can define a dynamic one. Conversely, it is possible in some cases (cf. Arrow [3]) to define a concept similar to a static production function starting from a dynamic progress function. (A large part of the early controversies in capital theory dealing with the problem of "maintaining capital intact" may be interpreted as being addressed to this type of problem.) The important thing—whichever approach is used—is to be left with some structure and therefore some possibility of prediction.

In the present paper I shall adopt the first of the above approaches. This is not because I consider the concept of the static production function sacrosanct; rather, the approach seems to be a convenient one in the circumstances. A distinct advantage in retaining the static production function concept, at least for the present, is that the modern Heckscher-Ohlin-Lerner-Samuelson theory of international trade, with given or exogenously changing production functions, has been fairly well worked out. From the development that followed Hicks' Inaugural Lecture [23], on the part of Corden [9], Johnson [26, 27], Findlay and Grubert [15], Bhagwati [6], Takayama [58], Bardhan [5], Jones [28], and others, we have a catalog of possible outcomes according to whether technical progress is capital-saving or labor-saving, or is concentrated in export industries or import-competing industries. What is lacking as yet is a systematic theory leading to a presumption as to which among the great variety of possible "technical changes" can be expected to take place.

Three approaches to the "endogenization" of technical change have achieved prominence in the theoretical literature. One is that of Arrow [3], followed up by Levhari [37], Sheshinski [56], and others, which stresses experience or "learning by doing." A second is that of Hicks [22], Kennedy [30, 31], Samuelson [48, 49], and Drandakis and Phelps [10], with related developments by Fellner [13, 14], Amano [2], Kamien and Schwartz [29], and others; this approach stresses induced direction of technical change. A third is that of Uzawa [61] stressing induced intensity of technical change; this has been synthesized with the previous group of developments by Nordhaus [42] and Drandakis and Hu [11]. The present paper builds on and extends the second and third approaches.

A few remarks may be in order to justify this choice. In explaining "imitation lags" among countries, it is natural to appeal to concepts such as experience and "learning by doing," as has been done, for instance, by Hufbauer [25]; however, the mathematical content of Arrow's model is that labor productivity is an increasing function of cumulated gross investment, which for practical purposes can be identified with the stock of capital. The identification of this cumulated stock with "experience" is a possible but not necessary interpretation of the model [cf. 44], and a direct translation of these concepts to international trade—equating transfers of capital with transfer of experience—might be questionable or would at least require some reformulation in view of the problems of capital absorption. The intuitive concept of "experience" is as difficult to isolate as that of "technical change" itself—both tend to be defined as residuals—and in using the notion of "learning by doing" to explain "technical progress" one runs the risk of employing one ill-defined concept to explain another.[1]

Induced technical change

The approach I shall use is to adopt a neoclassical production function $F(AL, BK, CN)$ relating a constant flow of capacity output to constant stocks of labor, L, and capital, K, and constant flows of raw material inputs, N. These factors are to be considered as aggregates or surrogates; in particular, natural resources, N, should be thought of as a variable taking the place of raw materials of all kinds, so that an increase in it may represent recourse to further kinds of primary products. In other words, it replaces the actual extensive margin by a fictitious intensive margin. Inclusion of raw materials follows Meade [40] and certainly seems appropriate in dealing with international trade.

Technical change will be assumed to be of the factor-augmenting type, involving changes in the coefficients A, B, C; in the case of fixed technical coefficients, any technical change can be decomposed uniquely into factor-augmenting technical changes, so the factor-augmentation hypothesis seems reasonable as long as the elasticities of substitution between any pairs of inputs are small. It will be assumed for the most part that they are bounded below unity.[2] Following tradition, and so as not to compound problems, F will be assumed to be homogeneous of the first degree.[3]

[1] Arrow cites as an example [3, p. 156] the case of the Horndal iron works in Sweden which "had no new investment (and therefore presumably no significant change in its methods of production) for a period of fifteen years, yet productivity (output per man-hour) rose on the average close to 2 per cent per annum. We find again steadily increasing performance which can only [sic] be imputed to learning from experience." A number of alternative explanations might present themselves, however: (1) disembodied technical change due either to internal R&D or to knowledge acquired from trade journals, etc.; (2) improved quality of the labor force; (3) improved quality of raw material inputs; (4) errors of measurement. Moreover, in terms of the specific model, without new investment there would have been no learning from experience; one would presumably want to use cumulated output here rather than cumulated investment as an index of experience.

[2] It is well known [cf. 59] that the factor-augmenting coefficients cannot be identified if the elasticity of substitution is unitary. In the formal analysis to follow it can equally well be assumed that elasticities of substitution are bounded above unity, but the factor-augmentation hypothesis is difficult to justify in this case [cf. 1].

[3] Elsewhere [8] I have suggested a method for handling increasing returns to scale. For the difficulties that would be involved in introducing them here, see footnote 10 below.

The crucial additional assumption is that the rates of factor augmentation $\alpha(t) = \dot{A}(t)/A(t)$, $\beta(t) = \dot{B}(t)/B(t)$, $\gamma(t) = \dot{C}(t)/C(t)$, are related by a "Kennedy function" of the form $\alpha = \phi(\beta, \gamma; r)$ where ϕ is strictly concave, decreasing in β and γ and increasing in r, where r is the proportion of capacity output devoted to the process of factor-augmenting technical change. Actual output is then given by $(1 - r)F(AL, BK, CN)$. A degenerate limiting case of the above would be that in which $\alpha = \beta = \gamma =$ constant, independently of r, leading to Hicks-neutral technical change.

While r could be interpreted as the proportion of capacity output devoted to research and development (R&D), it need not be interpreted quite so narrowly, or equivalently R&D may be broadly interpreted as any activity leading to an increase in A, B, or C. In particular, it need not be limited to "inventions" and their developments. For example, it could include maintenance, repair, and adjustment of equipment, leading to better future performance, or to on-the-job training of personnel.[4] Neither of these necessarily involves production of new information in Arrow's sense [cf. 4, p. 616]. Even in the case of inventions, it has been stressed by Schmookler [52] and others that most inventions make use of relatively old basic knowledge: Schmookler has also argued [cf. 50, 51, 52] that invention is strongly subject to economic forces. Even if individual inventions are not predictable, inventive activity in general may have predictable consequences; this hypothesis lies at the basis of the Kennedy function or similar formulations.

The present model is, of course, open to a number of a priori objections. It can be argued that one cannot expect such a Kennedy function to remain invariant over time or that it is unreasonable to suppose that the alternative growth rates of factor augmentation coefficients should have a constant exponential form. If objection is made to *any* form of time invariance in the creation of technical change, this is tantamount to renouncing any attempt to explain the major components of economic growth, as well as one of the main bases for international trade. While

---

[4] The usual definition of a production function describes the maximum flow of output obtainable from given flows (or stocks, as the case may be) of inputs, in a given state of knowledge. As the illustrations just given indicate, an *ultimately* larger steady flow of output can in general be obtained from the given inputs by means of an initial investment, and a maximal flow of this sort (if it exists at all) would only be achieved with a zero rate of interest. Differences in production functions among countries could therefore be simply a reflection of differences in the rate of interest.

the Kennedy function may not provide the most suitable expression for what time invariance there is, it should be kept in mind that objections to it apply equally well to customary formulations in terms of exogenous exponential technical change which—as noted above—can be considered as degenerate limiting cases of the present model. It should also be kept in mind that the entities we are dealing with are aggregates, so that while particular methods of factor augmentation become exhausted, others take their places; e.g., silk gives way to rayon, and rayon to nylon. To subsume such complex processes in a single function is admittedly heroic, but perhaps no less so than to adopt the usual aggregative production function. Economists are very familiar with the latter concept, but it is sometimes forgotten that when the linear homogeneous production function was first introduced into English economic thought by Wicksteed, Edgeworth [12] greeted the concept with nothing less than derision.

A theory of induced technical change is not obliged to account for every technical change that takes place, nor to explain the entire sweep of history. If it can help explain a fair proportion of the rate and direction of technical progress over a relatively brief period, say ten to twenty years, this might be the best one could expect.

There are two limitations in the present model which should be pointed out. One is the representation of all technical change as disembodied; this is particularly limiting inasmuch as the international transmission of technical change often is effected by means of the export of new types of equipment. The other is the assumption that the *proportion* of capacity output devoted to R&D is the relevant variable, thus abstracting from the type of scale economies that result from the fact that a given *amount* of inventive activity could lead to improved techniques (higher factor augmentation coefficients) regardless of the scale of operations.[5]

When one introduces the possibility of dynamic variations in productive techniques, one has to introduce some kind of behavior assumptions governing their introduction. The formal model presented in the following section is set up as a social optimization problem; nevertheless I shall interpret the model as a descriptive one. To justify this, the follow-

[5] For alternative formulations of the treatment of investment in research, see Phelps [45].

ing interpretation will be suggested. Let us assume that all technical change is carried out by "firms," broadly interpreted to include governmental agencies involved in research activities, and that these entities choose the parameters of the appropriate Kennedy function so as to maximize the present value of their future profits given certain assumptions concerning the future. The simplest assumption to make is the usual one of static expectations: constant product and factor prices, constant factor proportions, and constant rates of factor augmentation. Under these conditions the problem reduces to maximizing the present value of output per head:

$$(1.1) \quad \int_0^\infty e^{-\delta t}(1 - r) \, A(0)e^{\phi(\beta,\gamma;r)t} f[\kappa(0)e^{[\beta - \phi(\beta,\gamma;r)]t}, \nu(0)e^{[\gamma - \phi(\beta,\gamma;r)]t}] \, dt$$

where $f = F/AL$, $\kappa = BK/AL$; $\nu = CN/AL$, $L(0) = 1$, and $\delta = \rho - \lambda$ where ρ is the rate of discount and λ the rate of increase of the labor force employed. When (1.1) is maximized with respect to β and γ one obtains the conditions [6]

$$(1.2) \quad -\frac{\partial \phi}{\partial \beta} = \frac{\kappa f_\kappa(\kappa, \nu)}{f(\kappa, \nu) - \kappa f_\kappa(\kappa, \nu) - \nu f_\nu(\kappa, \nu)},$$

$$-\frac{\partial \phi}{\partial \gamma} = \frac{\nu f_\nu(\kappa, \nu)}{f(\kappa, \nu) - \kappa f_\kappa(\kappa, \nu) - \nu f_\nu(\kappa, \nu)}$$

as in Samuelson [48] and Drandakis and Phelps [10]. This states that the slopes of the Kennedy function should be equal to the imputed relative shares of capital and labor and of resources and labor, respectively. Likewise, maximization of (1.1) with respect to r yields, after some computations,

$$(1.3) \quad \frac{\partial \phi}{\partial r} = \frac{\delta - \phi(\beta, \gamma; r)}{1 - r} \cdot \frac{f(\kappa, \nu)}{f(\kappa, \nu) - \kappa f_\kappa(\kappa, \nu) - \nu f_\nu(\kappa, \nu)}.$$

The second factor on the right is the reciprocal of the imputed relative share of labor in total output.

The criteria (1.2) and (1.3) appear in (2.31) below and correspond to the optimality conditions in a situation of balanced growth. The more

---

[6] It is necessary to assume that δ is sufficiently large so that the integral converges; a sufficient condition for this is that $\delta > \phi\ (0, 0; 1)$ (see (2.18) below). It is further assumed that f is sufficiently regular to permit differentiation under the integral sign in (1.1).

general optimality conditions (2.21) and (2.22) given below could be interpreted as defining "rational expectations" on the part of firms. They might be considered, to that extent, as accounting for some of the expectational considerations stressed by Fellner [13, 14], though these considerations do not alter the basic long-run result.

If investment in technical change involves no production of new "knowledge," the above formulation presents no fundamental difficulties. Trouble occurs [cf. 4] when and to the extent that the research outlays of one firm result in knowledge useful to others. If the industry's R&D activities are completely monopolized, and if the benefits of research do not extend to other industries and cannot be absorbed by the corresponding industry in other countries, and if product and factor markets remain perfectly competitive—in these limited circumstances an optimal allocation of resources could be achieved. Although optimality is not to be expected in general, it is at least arguable that the quantitative distortions are not too great and that alternative and more realistic assumptions would not lead to radically different conclusions. For instance, the first innovator in the field must make allowance for being followed by imitators and may therefore fall short of the optimal r; on the other hand, imitators might crowd the field and collectively push beyond the optimal r. Since the error could go in either direction, the optimality assumption at least seems neutral, even if it is not very accurate.

Imports of primary products

One of the controversial topics of the past few decades has been that of the role and prospects of natural resources in international trade. The thesis set forth by Prebisch [47] and Singer [57] that there is a tendency towards a deterioration in the terms of trade of raw material producing countries has been challenged factually and has also given rise to theoretical discussion [cf. 65, 20, 21]. The analysis of Schultz [55] has the great virtue of focusing not on the terms of trade but rather on the ratio of expenditures on raw materials to gross national product; his figures show a clearly declining tendency since the early 1900's.

Nurkse [43] has described how industrial expansion in the nineteenth century was accompanied by a more than proportionate expansion in imports of raw materials, whereas in the twentieth century these imports have been much less than proportionate. The two explanations that received the greatest emphasis by Nurkse [43, p. 23] are low income elasticities of demand and technical progress in the use of natural materials as exemplified by the rise of synthetics industries. Nurkse recognized the existence of an "identification problem" in this analysis [43, p. 26]; this was also perceived by Schultz [55] who concluded that low income elasticities provided the correct explanation.[7] Schultz's conclusion was based on the proposition that consumer demand functions are empirically stable, whereas production functions are not; in his words [55, pp. 316–317]:

> The production function is . . . a venerable concept, based on received theory of long standing. It has not been a useful concept, however, in organizing data and gaining from them dependable insights about supply. . . . For a function to be useful it must either be fairly stable, or we must be able to predict how it will change. The stability of demand functions . . . is dependent upon what happens to tastes, while the stability of the supply function rests upon technology. Fortunately for demand analysis, tastes remain fairly stable. Technology, on the other hand, does not. Therefore . . . unless we can predict the changes in technology, estimates of production functions are comparatively useless in a logical positivistic sense.

Although it is not claimed that the model used here can predict changes in technology with any accuracy, it nevertheless supports Schultz's thesis in the weak sense that the declining share of raw materials expenditure in national income cannot be accounted for on the basis of the hypothesis of induced resource-augmenting technical progress alone. On the contrary, with consumer goods being represented in our model by a single aggregate commodity (implying unitary income elasticity), an ultimately constant share of raw material expenditure is predicted. The same conclusion is obtained if part of the primary product is assumed to be consumed directly and a constant proportion of income is devoted to it; on the other hand, a declining proportion of direct expenditures on primary products is shown to lead, under certain reasonable conditions, to a declining share of resource income to total income.

If foodstuffs are omitted from the list of raw materials, as well as forest products (other than pulpwood), Schultz's figures indicate only a slightly declining trend. Considering that certain services from natural resources, such as hydroelectric power, tourism, and unpriced or hard-

[7] Schultz's thesis is further elaborated in two other papers [53, 54].

to-price uses of land, water, and air for travel and communication, are omitted from the list, a case might be made for the proposition that except for foodstuffs (to which Engel's law applies) and rents imputed to them, the share of natural resources is relatively constant. This share is in any case small.[8]

The main result of the formal model in the next section can be summarized as follows. If the home country produces a single consumer good, using up labor, capital, and imported raw material, then an equilibrium growth path will be approached in which technical change is Harrod neutral as far as capital is concerned (that is, there will be no capital-augmenting technical change), whereas the rate of augmentation of natural resources will be determined by the formula $\gamma = (\lambda + \alpha)/(1 + \eta)$, where λ is the rate of growth of population, α the rate of labor-augmenting technical change, and η the elasticity of the foreign offer curve. Thus, if resources are in perfectly elastic supply ($\eta = \infty$), there will be no resource-augmenting technical improvement, whereas at the opposite extreme of perfectly inelastic supply ($\eta = 0$), resource-augmenting technical change will proceed at the rate $\lambda + \alpha$. The volume of primary products grows at the rate $(\lambda + \alpha)\eta/(1 + \eta)$, and the foreign terms of trade improve at the rate $(\lambda + \alpha)/(1 + \eta)$.[9]

These results must, of course, be interpreted with caution. The model does not distinguish the particular types of raw materials that enter into the production of synthetics from those they displace or supplement, nor does it distinguish whether they will be obtained from imported or domestic sources. If the foreign supply of natural rubber, cotton, wool, hides, etc., becomes inelastic while the domestic supply of petroleum, natural gas, pulpwood, etc., remains relatively elastic, and, if these latter items are technologically more suitable for resource-augmenting improvement, then a declining share of foreign primary products in national expenditure could be explained on this basis.

The question naturally arises as to how this type of analysis would extend to the standard Heckscher-Ohlin model of international trade, in which factor supplies in the several countries are given. It is well

---

[8] Vanek [62, 63] in his analysis of the resource content of traded products has made use of the a priori assumption of constancy of the relative share of resource income. He has not tested this hypothesis directly, however.

[9] These are asymptotic results. The speed with which the balanced growth solution is achieved depends on the magnitude of $\delta - \alpha$, and the solution can therefore be taken as approximating actual events only if the discount rate is not too small.

known that a uniform expansion in the home country would, in general, worsen the expanding country's terms of trade. This will lead to a relative decline in the price of the factor intensive in the export industry; for instance, if the country's exports are capital intensive, it will lead to a relative rise in wages. On the basis of the theory of induced technical change one would then expect that technical improvement should take place in the export industry, thus bringing down the wage-rental ratio and thereby restoring the relative share of labor and capital to its former level. On this basis, one would expect induced technical change to be "ultra-pro-trade biased" in Johnson's [26] terminology; this would also conform to the results of Gruber, Mehta, and Vernon [18] to the effect that R&D effort tends to be strongest in the export industries. The following definite results can be shown, however: If factor-augmenting technical change is obtainable by a Kennedy function in each industry, and if it is not transferable (via factor movement) to other industries, then balanced growth in rates of factor augmentation is possible only in the special case of "Cobb-Douglas" utility functions (unitary elasticity of substitution in consumption) and exactly matched expansion in the foreign offer function; in other words, balanced growth and constant relative shares are no longer to be expected. A detailed analysis of this extended model is postponed to another occasion.

2. ON INDUCED TECHNICAL CHANGE IN THE FACE OF SCARCE NATURAL RESOURCES

This section is devoted to analyzing a very simple model which may be conceived of as depicting in a crude fashion some of the long-run trade patterns between developed industrial nations on the one hand and underdeveloped suppliers of raw materials on the other.

Let the developed country produce a single consumer good which it exports in exchange for raw material inputs which are used together with labor and capital to produce the consumer good. Output of this consumer good is assumed to be given by

(2.1)
$$Y(t) = (1 - s(t) - r(t))F[A(t)L(t), B(t)K(t), C(t)N(t)]$$

where $L(t)$, $K(t)$, $N(t)$ are the quantities of labor, capital, and natural resources (raw material) used at time t, $A(t)$, $B(t)$, $C(t)$ are the respective factor augmenting coefficients of (disembodied) technical progress, and $s(t)$, $r(t)$ are the proportions of capacity output used for capital accumulation and for research and development, respectively [cf. 11]. Assuming capital to depreciate of the constant rate μ, net investment is then determined according to

(2.2) $\dot{K}(t) = s(t)F[A(t)L(t), B(t)K(t), C(t)N(t)] - \mu K(t), \quad (\mu \geqq 0).$

Labor is assumed to grow at the constant rate λ:

(2.3) $$L(t) = L(0)e^{\lambda t}, \quad (\lambda \geqq 0).$$

Denoting

(2.4) $\alpha(t) = \dot{A}(t)/A(t), \; \beta(t) = \dot{B}(t)/B(t), \; \gamma(t) = \dot{C}(t)/C(t),$

I assume that technical progress is determined according to a Kennedy function of the form

(2.5) $$\alpha(t) = \phi[\beta(t), \gamma(t); r(t)]$$

where ϕ is strictly concave, decreasing in β and γ and increasing in r. Further assumptions concerning ϕ will be specified when needed below; see Kennedy [30], Samuelson [48, 49], Drandakis and Phelps [10], Nordhaus [42], Kamien and Schwartz [29], and Drandakis and Hu [11].

Domestic consumption (in the industrial country) of the consumer good is given by

(2.6) $$X(t) = Y(t) + Z(t)$$

where $Z(t)$ is the amount imported (if positive) or exported (if negative); in the present case $Z(t)$ will be negative. The imported good will be assumed to have a price of $p(t)$ relative to that of the exported good; thus, $p(t)$ is the foreign (underdeveloped) country's terms of trade. The home (developed) country faces the budget constraint

(2.7) $$p(t)N(t) + Z(t) = 0.$$

The foreign offer function will be of the general form

(2.8) $$N(t) = h[p(t), t]$$

of which we will consider below the special cases of perfectly elastic supply (constant p and unlimited supplies N) and perfectly inelastic supply (constant N).

Since the possibility of investment in technical progress in general precludes untrammeled perfect competition—requiring some form of monopoly control, licensing, or secrecy—our model will be cast in terms of an optimization problem. However, problems of commercial policy are beyond the scope of this study, and the terms of trade $p(t)$ will be assumed to be regarded as a parameter by optimizing firms and individuals. Thus, the offer function (2.8) will not figure as a constraint in the optimization problem, but will be substituted into the solution of the optimization problem which has (2.7) as the corresponding constraint. The problem is then to

$$(2.9) \qquad \text{Maximize } \int_0^\infty e^{-\rho t} X(t) dt$$

subject to the above constraints, other than (2.8).

I shall assume constant returns to scale,[10] so that

$$(2.10) \quad F[A(t)L(t), B(t)K(t), C(t)N(t)] = A(t)L(t)f\left[\frac{B(t)}{A(t)} k(t), \frac{C(t)}{A(t)} n(t)\right]$$

where

$$(2.11) \qquad k(t) = \frac{K(t)}{L(t)}, n(t) = \frac{N(t)}{L(t)}$$

and f (assumed increasing in both arguments and strictly concave) is defined by

$$(2.12) \quad f\left[\frac{B(t)}{A(t)} k(t), \frac{C(t)}{A(t)} n(t)\right] = F\left[1, \frac{B(t)}{A(t)} k(t), \frac{C(t)}{A(t)} n(t)\right].$$

It will also be convenient to define the capital-labor and nature-labor ratios in terms of efficiency units:

$$(2.13) \qquad \kappa(t) = \frac{B(t)}{A(t)} k(t), v(t) = \frac{C(t)}{A(t)} n(t).$$

Finally, define

$$(2.14) \qquad x(t) = \frac{X(t)}{L(t)}, y(t) = \frac{Y(t)}{L(t)}, z(t) = \frac{Z(t)}{L(t)}.$$

[10] Introduction of scale economies in models such as these tends to give rise to problems of convergence of the integral (2.9). For instance, if r were to be replaced by Y in the argument of (2.5), representing a scale economy in the Kennedy function rather than the production function, one would obtain a divergent integral unless ϕ was bounded with respect to Y.

In view of (2.10) and (2.11), the investment equation (2.2) may be transformed to

$$(2.15) \qquad \dot{k}(t) = s(t)A(t)f\left[\frac{B(t)}{A(t)}k(t), \frac{C(t)}{A(t)}n(t)\right] - (\mu + \lambda)k(t)$$

and the maximand (2.9) becomes

(2.16)

$$L(0)\int_0^\infty e^{-(\rho-\lambda)t}\left\{[1 - s(t) - r(t)]A(t)f\left[\frac{B(t)}{A(t)}k(t), \frac{C(t)}{A(t)}n(t)\right] - p(t)n(t)\right\}dt.$$

For convenience, denote

$$(2.17) \qquad\qquad \delta = \rho - \lambda.$$

It will be assumed that

$$(2.18) \qquad\qquad \delta > \phi(0, 0; 1),$$

and that the elasticity of substitution between any two of the factors is bounded below 1.

The appropriate Hamiltonian expression for this problem [cf. 46] is

$$(2.19) \quad H(q, a, b, c; k, A, B, C; r, s, \beta, \gamma, n; p) = (1 - r - s + qs)$$

$$Af\left(\frac{B}{A}k, \frac{C}{A}n\right) - pn - q(\mu + \lambda)k + aA\phi(\beta, \gamma; r) + bB\beta + cC\gamma,$$

where the time variable has been dropped for notational convenience. The state variables are k, A, B, C, the controls or instrument variables are r, s, β, γ, n, and the auxiliary variables q, a, b, c satisfy the differential equations

$$\dot{q} = \delta q - \frac{\partial H}{\partial k} = (\rho + \mu)q - (1 - r - s + qs)Bf_\kappa(\kappa, \nu)$$

$$\dot{a} = \delta a - \frac{\partial H}{\partial A} = [\delta - \phi(\beta, \gamma; r)]a$$

$$(2.20) \qquad\qquad - (1 - r - s + qs)[f(\kappa, \nu) - \kappa f_\kappa(\kappa, \nu) - \nu f_\nu(\kappa, \nu)]$$

$$\dot{b} = \delta b - \frac{\partial H}{\partial B} = (\delta - \beta)b - (1 - r - s + qs)kf_\kappa(\kappa, \nu)$$

$$\dot{c} = \delta c - \frac{\partial H}{\partial C} = (\delta - \gamma)c - (1 - r - s + qs)nf_\nu(\kappa, \nu)$$

where f_κ, f_ν are the partial derivatives of f with respect to κ, ν, the latter being defined by (2.13). q may be interpreted as the imputed value of the activity of capital accumulation, expressed in relation to the value of the foregone production of current consumer goods. Likewise, *a*, *b*, *c* may be interpreted as imputed values, in terms of foregone current output of consumer goods, of the activities of investing in labor-augmenting, capital-augmenting, and resource-augmenting technical progress respectively.

In accordance with the Pontryagin maximum principle, the variables $s(t), r(t), \beta(t), \gamma(t), n(t)$ must be chosen so as to maximize H at each instant of time, t. Maximization with respect to $s(t)$ requires maximization of $1 - r(t) + [q(t) - 1]s(t)$ with respect to to $s(t)$, hence $s(t) =$ 1, [0, 1 − r], or 0 according as $q(t) >, =,$ or < 1. This is intuitively obvious; since the capital good and consumer good are physically identified (a unit of one can be transformed into a unit of the other in accordance with (2.2)), if the capital good has a higher imputed value than the consumer good then all output should be accumulated, and in the converse case none of it should be. The cases of interest will clearly be those in which $q(t) = 1$.

Maximization of H with respect to $r(t)$ requires maximization of $a(t)\phi[\beta(t), \gamma(t); \ r(t)] - r(t)f[\kappa(t), \nu(t)]$ with respect to $r(t)$. If $a(t)\partial\phi[\beta(t), \gamma(t); \ r(t)]/\partial r - f[\kappa(t), \nu(t)]$ is always positive, then $r(t) = 1$, or if always negative then $r(t) = 0$. We shall naturally be interested mainly in conditions leading to an interior maximum for which

$$(2.21) \qquad \frac{\partial\phi[\beta(t), \gamma(t); r(t)]}{\partial r} = \frac{f[\kappa(t), \nu(t)]}{a(t)},$$

and similarly in conditions under which H is maximized with respect to $\beta(t)$ and $\gamma(t)$ when

$$(2.22) \qquad \frac{\partial\phi[\beta(t), \gamma(t); r(t)]}{\partial\beta} = -\frac{b(t)B(t)}{a(t)A(t)}; \quad \frac{\partial\phi[\beta(t), \gamma(t); r(t)]}{\partial\gamma} = -\frac{c(t)C(t)}{a(t)A(t)}.$$

Finally, assuming f to be strictly concave with $f_\nu(\kappa, 0) = \infty$ and $f_\nu(\kappa, \infty) = 0$, maximization of H with respect to $n(t)$ entails

$$(2.23) \qquad [1 - r(t) - s(t) + q(t)s(t)]C(t)f_\nu[\kappa(t), \nu(t)] = p(t),$$

which simply states that the value of the marginal productivity of the raw material should be equated to its world price.

Following Drandakis and Hu [11] it is convenient to deal directly with the variables appearing in (2.22). Let these be denoted

$$(2.24) \qquad u(t) = \frac{b(t)B(t)}{a(t)A(t)}, \quad v(t) = \frac{c(t)C(t)}{a(t)A(t)}.$$

From (2.20), (2.4), (2.13) and (2.24) one verifies that

$$\dot{u}(t) = [1 - r(t) - s(t) + q(t)s(t)]\frac{m[\kappa(t), v(t)]}{a(t)}\left\{u(t) - \frac{\kappa(t)f_\kappa[\kappa(t), v(t)]}{m[\kappa(t), v(t)]}\right\}$$

$$(2.25)$$

$$\dot{v}(t) = [1 - r(t) - s(t) + q(t)s(t)]\frac{m[\kappa(t), v(t)]}{a(t)}\left\{v(t) - \frac{v(t)f_v[\kappa(t), v(t)]}{m[\kappa(t), v(t)]}\right\}$$

where

$$(2.26) \qquad m(\kappa, v) = f(\kappa, v) - \kappa f_\kappa(\kappa, v) - v f_v(\kappa, v),$$

this being $\partial F/\partial(AL)$, i.e., the marginal product of labor in terms of efficiency units.

It is also convenient to obtain the corresponding differential equations for $\kappa(t)$ and $v(t)$. From (2.13) and (2.15) these are

$$\dot{\kappa}(t) = [\beta(t) - \phi[\beta(t), \gamma(t); r(t)] - \lambda - \mu]\kappa(t) + s(t)B(t)f[\kappa(t), v(t)]$$

$$(2.27)$$

$$\dot{v}(t) = [\gamma(t) - \phi[\beta(t), \gamma(t); r(t)] - \lambda]v(t) + \frac{C(t)}{A(t)L(t)}\dot{N}(t).$$

Let the offer function (2.8) be assumed to have the constant-elasticity static form

$$(2.28a) \qquad N(t) = \bar{N}^{1+\eta}p(t)^\eta \quad (0 \leqq \eta < \infty).$$

For $\eta = 0$ this reduces to $N(t) = \bar{N}$. As $\eta \to \infty$ we obtain the limiting form

$$(2.28b) \qquad p(t) = 1/\bar{N}.$$

If (2.28b) holds, $p(t)$ is constant in (2.23). If (2.28a) holds, the second equation of (2.27) becomes

$$(2.29) \quad \dot{v}(t) = [\eta\dot{\pi}(t)/\pi(t) + (1 + \eta)\gamma(t) - \phi[\beta(t), \gamma(t); r(t)] - \lambda]v(t)$$

where

$$(2.30) \qquad \pi(t) = \frac{p(t)}{C(t)};$$

$\pi(t)$ is the price of the raw material (the foreign terms of trade) expressed in efficiency units.

Balanced growth solution

In solving our system of differential equations, it is natural to look first for a singular solution. Suppose an "equilibrium" or balanced-growth solution exists with constant $u(t)$, $v(t)$, $\kappa(t)$, $v(t)$, $a(t) \neq 0$, $q(t)$, $r(t)$, $s(t)$. Denoting equilibrium values of variables by daggers, we obtain from (2.21), (2.22), (2.24), (2.25,), and the first two equations of (2.20), the system

(2.31)

$$- \frac{\partial \phi(0, \gamma^\dagger; r^\dagger)}{\partial \beta} = \frac{\kappa^\dagger f_\kappa(\kappa^\dagger, v^\dagger)}{m(\kappa^\dagger, v^\dagger)}$$

$$- \frac{\partial \phi(0, \gamma^\dagger; r^\dagger)}{\partial \gamma} = \frac{v^\dagger f_v(\kappa^\dagger, v^\dagger)}{m(\kappa^\dagger, v^\dagger)}$$

$$\frac{1 - r^\dagger}{\partial - \phi(0, \gamma^\dagger; r^\dagger)} \frac{\partial \phi(0, \gamma^\dagger; r^\dagger)}{\partial r} = \frac{f(\kappa^\dagger, v^\dagger)}{m(\kappa^\dagger, v^\dagger)}.$$

If a solution to these equations exists, they may be combined in view of (2.26) into the single equation

(2.32)

$$\frac{\partial \phi(0, \gamma^\dagger; r^\dagger)}{\partial \beta} + \frac{\partial \phi(0, \gamma^\dagger; r^\dagger)}{\partial \gamma} + \frac{1 - r^\dagger}{\delta - \phi(0, \gamma^\dagger; r^\dagger)} \frac{\partial \phi(0, \gamma^\dagger; r^\dagger)}{\partial r} = 1,$$

which defines an implicit relation between γ and r.

Now from (2.23) and (2.30) we have $\dot{\pi}(t) = 0$ whence (2.29) yields

(2.33)
$$\gamma^\dagger = \frac{\lambda + \phi(0, \gamma^\dagger; r^\dagger)}{1 + \eta}$$

for $0 \leq \eta < \infty$. This defines another implicit relation between γ and r. In the limiting case $\eta = \infty$ when (2.28b) holds, we have $\gamma^\dagger = 0$ from (2.23), and thus (2.33) remains valid upon substituting $\eta = \infty$. Together, (2.32) and (2.33) enable us to solve for $\gamma^\dagger$ and $r^\dagger$; some sufficient conditions for a unique solution will be specified below.

If the initial conditions are such that the system is in a state of balanced growth, then (2.33) and (2.23) imply that

(2.34)
$$C(t) = C(0)e^{\frac{\lambda+\alpha}{1+\eta}t}, \quad p(t) = p(0)e^{\frac{\lambda+\alpha}{1+\eta}t}$$

and consequently, from (2.28), imports of raw materials satisfy

$$(2.35) \qquad N(t) = N(0) \exp\left\{(\lambda + \alpha)\frac{\eta}{1 + \eta}t\right\}.$$

The term $p(t)n(t)$ of (2.16) therefore grows at the rate α and the integral converges in view of (2.18).

The above equations (2.34) and (2.35) are valid for $0 \leqq \eta \leqq \infty$. Thus, in the limiting case $\eta = \infty$ of unlimited supplies of natural resources, there will be no resource-augmenting technical progress, but instead the quantity of raw materials imported will grow at a rate $\lambda + \alpha$ equal to the rate of increase of the domestic labor force measured in efficiency units. At the opposite extreme $\eta = 0$ of fixed supplies of natural resources, resource-augmenting technical improvement will proceed at the rate $\lambda + \alpha$.

In either case, as well as in the cases in between, we have what may properly be called an economic rather than historical law of constant returns.

The remainder of this section will be devoted to providing a set of sufficient conditions for the existence of a unique solution to equations (2.31) and (2.33) in the variables $\gamma^\dagger$, $r^\dagger$, $\kappa^\dagger$, $\nu^\dagger$, enabling one to solve for the remaining variables; then we shall justify the attention paid to this equilibrium solution by sketching an argument to show that it is approached asymptotically by the optimal path.

Let the production function F be of the constant-elasticity-of-substitution type [cf. 60], with elasticity of substitution $\sigma < 1$, so that

$$(2.36) \qquad f(\kappa, \nu) = (\mu_0 + \mu_1\kappa^{1-1/\sigma} + \mu_2\nu^{1-1/\sigma})^{\sigma/(\sigma-1)} \quad (\sigma < 1).$$

Then, denoting $\mu_1' = \mu_1/\mu_0$, $\mu_2' = \mu_2/\mu_0$, equations (2.31) reduce to

$$-\frac{\partial\phi(0, \gamma^\dagger; r^\dagger)}{\partial\beta} = \mu_1'\kappa^{1-1/\sigma}; \quad -\frac{\partial\phi(0, \gamma^\dagger; r^\dagger)}{\partial\gamma} = \mu_2'\nu^{1-1/\sigma};$$

$$(2.37)$$

$$\frac{1 - r^\dagger}{\delta - \phi(0, \gamma^\dagger; r^\dagger)}\frac{\partial\phi(0, \gamma^\dagger; r^\dagger)}{\partial r} = 1 + \mu_1'\kappa^{1-1/\sigma} + \mu_2'\nu^{1-1/\sigma}.$$

The terms $\mu_1'\kappa^{1-1/\sigma}$ and $\mu_2'\nu^{1-1/\sigma}$, which are respectively the ratio of capital outlays to labor outlays and of raw material outlays to labor outlays when factors receive the value of their marginal product, are monotone decreasing from ∞ to 0 as κ and ν respectively increase from

0 to ∞. Thus, if a solution $\gamma^\dagger$, $r^\dagger$ exists to (2.32) and (2.33), then a unique positive solution $\kappa^\dagger$, $\nu^\dagger$ exists to (2.37).

First, let us obtain sufficient conditions for the existence of a solution to (2.32) and (2.33). As the conditions are intricate, I shall not attempt to obtain general conditions, especially for uniqueness (which is not to be expected in general); it will suffice to display an example that meets our requirements, in order to ensure that the method of analysis is meaningful and the required assumptions plausible.

Denote

$$(2.38) \qquad \alpha_1 = \alpha, \ \alpha_2 = \beta, \ \alpha_3 = \gamma$$

and let the function ϕ of (2.5) be defined implicitly by

$$(2.39) \quad \Phi(\alpha_1, \alpha_2, \alpha_3; r) = \sum_{i=1}^{3} \sum_{j=1}^{3} c_{ij}\alpha_i\alpha_j - (\delta_1^2 - \delta_0^2)r^\epsilon - \delta_0^2 = 0$$

for values of α_1, α_2, α_3 not all ≤ 0, where $c_{ij} > 0$ and the matrix $[c_{ij}]$ is symmetric positive definite, and where the following conditions also hold:

$$(2.40) \qquad c_{11} \geq 1; 0 < \epsilon < 1; \sqrt{c_{33}} \lambda < \delta_0 < \delta_1 < \delta < 1.$$

Then (2.32) and (2.33) have a solution satisfying (2.18), and such that $0 < r < 1$. This is shown by the following argument:

Define $\psi(r)$ implicitly by the identity

$$(2.41) \qquad \Phi\left(\psi(r), 0, \frac{\lambda + \psi(r)}{1 + \eta}; r\right) \equiv_r 0.$$

Then the conditions $\delta_0 > \sqrt{c_{33}} \lambda$ and $c_{11} \geq 1$ of (2.40) imply that

$$(2.42) \qquad 0 < \frac{\delta_0^2 - c_{33}\lambda^2}{c_{11} + c_{33} + 2c_{13} + 2\lambda(c_{13} + c_{33})} \leq \psi(r) \leq \delta_1,$$

for all $\eta \geq 0$. Thus (2.18) is satisfied.

Defining $\chi(r)$ by

$$(2.43) \qquad \chi(r) = \frac{1 - r}{\delta - \psi(r)} \frac{\partial\phi\left(0, \dfrac{\lambda + \psi(r)}{1 + \eta}; r\right)}{\partial r}$$

it follows from (2.42) that $0 < \chi(r) < \infty$ for $0 < r < 1$, $\chi(0) = \infty$, and $\chi(1) = 0$. On the other hand, (2.42) implies that the functions

$$(2.44) \quad -\frac{\partial\phi\left(0, \dfrac{\lambda + \psi(r)}{1 + \eta}; r\right)}{\partial\alpha_2} = \frac{\left(c_{21} + \dfrac{c_{23}}{1 + \eta}\right)\psi(r) + c_{23}\lambda}{\left(c_{11} + \dfrac{c_{13}}{1 + \eta}\right)\psi(r) + c_{13}\lambda}$$

$$(2.45) \quad -\frac{\partial\phi\left(0, \dfrac{\lambda + \psi(r)}{1 + \eta}; r\right)}{\partial\alpha_3} = \frac{\left(c_{31} + \dfrac{c_{33}}{1 + \eta}\right)\psi(r) + c_{33}\lambda}{\left(c_{11} + \dfrac{c_{13}}{1 + \eta}\right)\psi(r) + c_{13}\lambda}$$

are uniformly bounded above zero and below infinity throughout the interval $0 \leqq r \leqq 1$. The graph of

$$(2.46) \quad 1 - \frac{\partial\phi\left(0, \dfrac{\lambda + \psi(r)}{1 + \eta}; r\right)}{\partial\alpha_2} - \frac{\partial\phi\left(0, \dfrac{\lambda + \psi(r)}{1 + \eta}; r\right)}{\partial\alpha_3}$$

must therefore cross that of $\chi(r)$ inside the open interval $0 < r < r_1 < 1$, where r_1 is the largest root of $\chi(r) = 1$. This proves that (2.32) and (2.33) have a solution with $0 < r < 1$.

The solution need not be unique. However, if the condition

$$(2.47) \quad \delta_1 < \frac{\delta}{2} - \frac{c_{13}\lambda}{2(c_{11} + c_{13})}$$

is imposed, it may be verified that $\chi(r)$ is monotone decreasing (hence the root r_1 of $\chi(r) = 1$ is unique), and if $c_{11}c_{23} \geqq c_{21}c_{13}$ then (2.44) is monotone increasing. However, positive definiteness of the matrix $[c_{ij}]$ implies that $c_{11}c_{33} > c_{31}c_{13}$ hence (2.45) is monotone nonincreasing; nevertheless, if $c_{11}c_{33} - c_{13}^2$ or λ is sufficiently small (and certainly if $\lambda = 0$) the solution will be unique.

An example satisfying (2.40) and (2.47) is given by

$$\begin{bmatrix} c_{11} & c_{12} & c_{13} \\ \\ c_{21} & c_{22} & c_{23} \\ \\ c_{31} & c_{32} & c_{33} \end{bmatrix} = \begin{bmatrix} 1 & \dfrac{1}{3} & \dfrac{1}{4} \\ \dfrac{1}{3} & \dfrac{1}{2} & \dfrac{1}{5} \\ \dfrac{1}{4} & \dfrac{1}{5} & \dfrac{1}{9} \end{bmatrix}, \quad \begin{array}{l} \lambda = .03, \ \delta = .10, \\ \\ \delta_0 = .02, \ \delta_1 = .04. \end{array}$$

Returning to the solution of the equilibrium system, recall that $s(t)$ maximizes $1 - r(t) + [q(t) - 1]s(t)$ subject to

(2.48) $$r(t) \geqq 0, \quad s(t) \geqq 0, \quad r(t) + s(t) \leqq 1,$$

hence $q(t) > 1$ implies $s(t) = 1 - r(t)$ and $q(t) < 1$ implies $s(t) = 0$.

To solve for $q^\dagger$, eliminate $B^\dagger$ from the equilibrium solutions of the first equations of (2.20) and (2.27) respectively to get

(2.49) $$\frac{s^\dagger q^\dagger}{1 - r^\dagger - s^\dagger + s^\dagger q^\dagger} = \frac{\alpha^\dagger + \lambda + \mu}{\delta + \lambda + \mu} \cdot \frac{\kappa^\dagger f_\kappa(\kappa^\dagger, \nu^\dagger)}{f(\kappa^\dagger, \nu^\dagger)}.$$

If $q^\dagger > 1$ then $s^\dagger = 1 - r$ implying that the left side of (2.49) is $= 1$ which is impossible, since the right side is < 1. Conversely if $q^\dagger < 1$ then $s^\dagger = 0$ and the left side of (2.49) would vanish, which is also ruled out since the right side is positive. Thus, $q^\dagger = 1$ [cf. 61, 11]. The solution for $s^\dagger$ follows immediately from (2.49). $B^\dagger$ is then obtained from the first equation of (2.20), and $a^\dagger$ from the second.

$A(t)$, $b(t)$, $k(t)$ will all grow at the rate α, and $c(t)$, $n(t)$ at the rate $(\alpha\eta - \lambda)/(1 + \eta)$. The latter expression can be either positive or negative; if $\eta = 0$ it is equal to $-\lambda$, and as $\eta \to \infty$ it becomes $+\alpha$. Thus if raw materials are in fixed supply, they obviously decline in proportion to the growing labor force; but if they are in perfectly elastic supply they will actually grow in proportion to the labor force in order to keep up with its increasing efficiency.

Dynamic analysis

It remains to undertake the qualitative analysis of the system of differential equations (2.4), (2.15), and (2.20). These are eight equations in all, in the four state variables $A(t)$, $B(t)$, $C(t)$, $k(t)$ and four auxiliary variables $a(t)$, $b(t)$, $c(t)$, $q(t)$. Together they may be described as the system variables. The remaining variables that appear in those equations are the control variables $r(t)$, $s(t)$, $\beta(t)$, $\gamma(t)$, $n(t)$ which are functions of the eight system variables, as determined by solving (2.21), (2.22), (2.23), (2.28) simultaneously in conjunction with the criterion for determining $s(t)$. The latter problem is handled as in Uzawa [61] and Drandakis and Hu [11] by considering three phases: phase I in which $q(t) > 1$ hence $s(t) = 1$, phase II in which $q(t) = 1$ and $s(t) \in [0, 1]$, and phase III in which $q(t) < 1$ hence $s(t) = 0$.

In the following analysis, I shall limit attention to phase II.[11] If the economy is in phase II for a finite interval of time, then $\dot\kappa$ is determined not from (2.27) but with the help of the first equation of (2.20) which becomes

$$(2.50) \qquad (1 - r)\, Bf_\kappa(\kappa, \nu) = \rho + \mu = \delta + \lambda + \mu.$$

This states that the marginal net productivity of capital is equated to the rate of discount, ρ. Likewise, (2.23) reduces to

$$(2.51) \qquad (1 - r)\, Cf_\nu(\kappa, \nu) = p.$$

From (2.28) and the definition of ν in (2.13) and (2.11), we have

$$(2.52) \qquad \frac{\dot p}{p} = \frac{1}{\eta}\left[\frac{\dot\nu}{\nu} - \gamma + \phi(\beta, \gamma; r) + \lambda\right] \text{ if } \eta > 0;$$

$$\frac{\dot\nu}{\nu} = \gamma - \phi(\beta, \gamma; r) - \lambda \text{ if } \eta = 0.$$

Differentiating (2.50) and (2.51) logarithmically, and substituting (2.52), we obtain for $\eta > 0$:

$$(2.53)$$
$$\frac{-\dot r}{1 - r} + \beta + \frac{f_{\kappa\kappa}(\kappa, \nu)}{f_\kappa(\kappa, \nu)}\,\dot\kappa + \frac{f_{\kappa\nu}(\kappa, \nu)}{f_\kappa(\kappa, \nu)}\,\dot\nu = 0$$

$$\frac{-\dot r}{1 - r} + \gamma + \frac{f_{\nu\kappa}(\kappa, \nu)}{f_\nu(\kappa, \nu)}\,\dot\kappa + \frac{f_{\nu\nu}(\kappa, \nu)}{f_\nu(\kappa, \nu)}\,\dot\nu = \frac{1}{\eta}\left[\frac{\dot\nu}{\nu} - \gamma + \phi(\beta, \gamma; r) + \lambda\right].$$

If $\eta = 0$, the second equation of (2.53) is replaced by the second equation of (2.52).

Since r is a function of κ, ν, u, v, a from (2.21) and (2.22), $\dot r$ will involve derivatives of these variables. Assuming $\partial^2\phi/\partial\beta\partial r = \partial^2\phi/\partial\gamma\partial r = 0$ as in (2.39), we obtain $\partial r/\partial u = \partial r/\partial v = 0$ and

$$(2.54) \qquad \frac{\partial r}{\partial \kappa} = \frac{f_\kappa(\kappa, \nu)}{a\dfrac{\partial^2\phi}{\partial r^2}} < 0, \quad \frac{\partial r}{\partial \nu} = \frac{f_\nu(\kappa, \nu)}{a\dfrac{\partial^2\phi}{\partial r^2}} < 0, \quad \frac{\partial r}{\partial a} = -\frac{f(\kappa, \nu)}{a^2\dfrac{\partial^2\phi}{\partial r^2}} > 0.$$

[11] All the analysis that follows is based on the presumption that the optimal path will be such as to reach the singular point with constant q. However, from the first equation of (2.20) one could have $s = 0$, $\dot q/q = \beta^\dagger$, leading to the possibility of a balanced growth solution in which investment in capital augmenting technical change takes the place of investment in capital accumulation. It is an interesting question, which I cannot go into here, as to what are the exact conditions for optimality of a path leading to one or the other of these points.

Thus,

(2.55)
$$\dot{r} = \frac{\partial r}{\partial \kappa} \dot{\kappa} + \frac{\partial r}{\partial \nu} + \dot{\nu} \frac{\partial r}{\partial a} \dot{a}.$$

Substituting this in (2.53), as well as the differential equation for $\dot{a}$, we obtain the desired system of differential equations. The first equation of (2.27) is then used together with (2.50) to solve for $s(t)$.

The procedure just outlined evidently involves some cumbersome substitutions. The dynamic properties also depend on the magnitude of $\partial^2 \phi / \partial r^2$ in the denominators of (2.54). In what follows I shall therefore confine myself to detailed analysis of a limiting case in which $\partial^2 \phi / \partial r^2 \to -\infty$ and r is fixed. This would correspond to the case in which δ_0 approaches δ_1 in (2.39).

Corresponding to (2.54) we have, from (2.21) and (2.22),

(2.56)
$$\frac{\partial \beta}{\partial u} = -\frac{\partial^2 \phi / \partial \gamma^2}{D} > 0; \quad \frac{\partial \beta}{\partial v} = \frac{\partial^2 \phi / \partial \beta \partial \gamma}{D}$$

$$\frac{\partial \gamma}{\partial u} = \frac{\partial^2 \phi / \partial \gamma \partial \beta}{D}; \quad \frac{\partial \gamma}{\partial v} = -\frac{\partial^2 \phi / \partial \beta^2}{D} > 0$$

where

(2.57)
$$D = \begin{vmatrix} \partial^2 \phi / \partial \beta^2 & \partial^2 \phi / \partial \beta \partial \gamma \\ \partial^2 \phi / \partial \gamma \partial \beta & \partial^2 \phi / \partial \gamma^2 \end{vmatrix}$$

and D as well as $\partial(\beta, \gamma) / \partial(u, v)$ is positive definite. The partial derivatives of β and γ with respect to κ, ν and a all vanish. The above holds with variable as well as fixed r, if $\partial^2 \phi / \partial \beta \partial r = \partial^2 \phi / \partial \gamma \partial r = 0$. From now on I consider the case of fixed r.

With r fixed we obtain from (2.53)

(2.58a)

$$\begin{bmatrix} \dot{\kappa} \\ \dot{\nu} \end{bmatrix} = \begin{bmatrix} -\dfrac{f_{\kappa\kappa}(\kappa, \nu)}{f_\kappa(\kappa, \nu)} & -\dfrac{f_{\kappa\nu}(\kappa, \nu)}{f_\kappa(\kappa, \nu)} \\ -\dfrac{f_{\nu\kappa}(\kappa, \nu)}{f_\nu(\kappa, \nu)} & \dfrac{1}{\eta\nu} - \dfrac{f_{\nu\nu}(\kappa, \nu)}{f_\nu(\kappa, \nu)} \end{bmatrix}^{-1} \begin{bmatrix} \beta \\ \left(1 + \dfrac{1}{\eta}\right)\gamma - \dfrac{1}{\eta}[\phi(\beta, \gamma) + \lambda] \end{bmatrix},$$

an equation which remains valid when $\eta = \infty$. It may also be written

(2.58b)

$$\begin{bmatrix} \dot{\kappa} \\ \dot{\nu} \end{bmatrix} = \begin{bmatrix} -\dfrac{f_{\kappa\kappa}(\kappa,\,\nu)}{f_\kappa(\kappa,\,\nu)} & -\dfrac{f_{\kappa\nu}(\kappa,\,\nu)}{f_\kappa(\kappa,\,\nu)} \\[2ex] -\dfrac{\eta f_{\nu\kappa}(\kappa,\,\nu)}{f_\nu(\kappa,\,\nu)} & \dfrac{1}{\nu} - \dfrac{\eta f_{\nu\nu}(\kappa,\,\nu)}{f_\nu(\kappa,\,\nu)} \end{bmatrix}^{-1} \begin{bmatrix} \beta \\[2ex] (\eta + 1)\gamma - \phi(\beta,\,\gamma) - \lambda \end{bmatrix}$$

which is valid for $\eta = 0$.

We shall write the expressions on the right of (2.58) in the form

(2.59a)
$$\dot{\kappa} = \mathcal{K}(\kappa,\,\nu,\,u,\,v,\,a)$$
$$\dot{\nu} = \mathfrak{N}(\kappa,\,\nu,\,u,\,v,\,a).$$

To complete this system we have

$$\dot{u} = \mathcal{U}(\kappa,\,\nu,\,u,\,v,\,a) = (1 - r)\frac{m(\kappa,\,\nu)}{a}\left\{ u - \frac{\kappa f_\kappa(\kappa,\,\nu)}{m(\kappa,\,\nu)}\right\}$$

(2.59b) $\quad \dot{v} = \mathcal{V}(\kappa,\,\nu,\,u,\,v,\,a) = (1 - r)\dfrac{m(\kappa,\,\nu)}{a}\left\{ v - \dfrac{v f_\nu(\kappa,\,\nu)}{m(\kappa,\,\nu)}\right\}$

$$\dot{a} = \mathcal{A}(\kappa,\,\nu,\,u,\,v,\,a) = [\delta - \phi(\beta,\,\gamma)]a - (1 - r)m(\kappa,\,\nu).$$

Equations (2.59) form a self-contained system of five differential equations.

The Jacobian matrix $J = \partial(\mathcal{K},\,\mathfrak{N},\,\mathcal{U},\,\mathcal{V},\,\mathcal{A})/\partial(\kappa,\,\nu,\,u,\,v,\,a)$ evaluated at the equilibrium point $(\kappa^\dagger,\,\nu^\dagger,\,u^\dagger,\,v^\dagger,\,a^\dagger)$ has a structure partially displayed as follows:

(2.60) $\quad J = \begin{bmatrix} 0 & 0 & \partial\mathcal{K}^\dagger/\partial u & \partial\mathcal{K}^\dagger/\partial v & 0 \\ 0 & 0 & \partial\mathfrak{N}^\dagger/\partial u & \partial\mathfrak{N}^\dagger/\partial v & 0 \\ \partial\mathcal{U}^\dagger/\partial\kappa & \partial\mathcal{U}^\dagger/\partial\nu & \delta^* & 0 & 0 \\ \partial\mathcal{V}^\dagger/\partial\kappa & \partial\mathcal{V}^\dagger/\partial\nu & 0 & \delta^* & 0 \\ \partial\mathcal{A}^\dagger/\partial\kappa & \partial\mathcal{A}^\dagger/\partial\nu & \partial\mathcal{A}^\dagger/\partial u & \partial\mathcal{A}^\dagger/\partial v & \delta^* \end{bmatrix}$

where

(2.61) $\qquad\qquad \delta^* = \delta - \phi(0,\,\gamma^\dagger) = (1 - r^\dagger)\dfrac{m(\kappa^\dagger,\,\nu^\dagger)}{a^\dagger}.$

Denote

(2.62) $\quad J_1 = \begin{bmatrix} \partial\mathcal{U}^\dagger/\partial\kappa & \partial\mathcal{U}^\dagger/\partial\nu \\ \partial\mathcal{V}^\dagger/\partial\kappa & \partial\mathcal{V}^\dagger/\partial\nu \end{bmatrix}, \quad J_2 = \begin{bmatrix} \partial\mathcal{K}^\dagger/\partial u & \partial\mathcal{K}^\dagger/\partial v \\ \partial\mathfrak{N}^\dagger/\partial u & \partial\mathfrak{N}^\dagger/\partial v \end{bmatrix}.$

Then the characteristic polynomial of J is

(2.63) $(\xi - \delta^*)\{[\xi(\xi - \delta^*)]^2 - \text{tr}\,(J_1J_2)\,\xi(\xi - \delta^*) + \det\,(J_1J_2)\}.$

Thus J has one positive characteristic root $\xi_1 = \delta^*$. Denoting

(2.64) $\zeta = \xi\,(\xi - \delta^*),$

the remaining four roots are found by first obtaining the roots ζ_1, ζ_2 of

(2.65) $\zeta^2 - \text{tr}\,(J_1J_2)\zeta + \det\,(J_1J_2) = 0$

and then for each ζ_i solving the quadratic equation

(2.66) $\xi^2 - \delta^*\xi - \zeta_i = 0$ $(i = 1, 2).$

In order that there be a path satisfying (2.59) which approaches the point $(\kappa^\dagger, \nu^\dagger, u^\dagger, v^\dagger, a^\dagger)$ asymptotically, it is necessary and sufficient that at least one root ξ_i of (2.63) have a negative real part. If one of the roots of (2.65), say ζ_1, has a positive real part, then one of the two roots of (2.66), for $i = 1$, will have a negative real part. If $\det\,(J_1J_2) < 0$, (2.65) will have one positive and one negative root. If $\det\,(J_1J_2) > 0$, one of the roots of (2.65) will have a positive real part provided $\text{tr}\,(J_1J_2) > 0$. A sufficient condition for the desired result is therefore that $\text{tr}\,(J_1J_2) > 0$.

Let elasticities of substitution be constant as in (2.36). Then

(2.67) $J_1 = \dfrac{1 - \sigma}{\sigma}\,\delta^*\begin{bmatrix} \mu_1'\kappa^{-1/\sigma} & 0 \\ 0 & \mu_2'\nu^{-1/\sigma} \end{bmatrix}.$

From (2.62) it follows that

(2.68) $\text{tr}\,(J_1J_2) = \dfrac{1 - \sigma}{\sigma}\,\delta^*\left[\mu_1'\,\kappa^{-1/\sigma}\dfrac{\partial \mathcal{K}^\dagger}{\partial u} + \mu_2'\,\nu^{-1/\sigma}\dfrac{\partial \mathfrak{N}^\dagger}{\partial v}\right].$

From (2.56), (2.57), (2.58) it may be seen that $\partial \mathcal{K}^\dagger/\partial u > 0$ and $\partial \mathfrak{N}^\dagger/\partial v > 0$ as long as

(2.69) $\dfrac{\partial^2\phi(\beta,\,\gamma;\,r)}{\partial\beta\partial\gamma} > 0.$

Now $\delta^* > 0$ in view of (2.18) and the existence of a solution to (2.32), (2.33), (2.37); therefore $a^\dagger > 0$ in (2.61). Together with (2.69), a sufficient condition that $\text{tr}\,(J_1J_2) > 0$ is therefore that $\sigma < 1$ in (2.68).

Taking account of (2.58) as well as the strict concavity of f and ϕ, it may be verified that

(2.70)
$$|J_2| = \frac{1 + \eta - \partial\phi/\partial\gamma}{\eta\Delta} > 0$$

where

(2.71)
$$\Delta = \begin{vmatrix} -\dfrac{f_{\kappa\kappa}(\kappa, \nu)}{f_\kappa(\kappa, \nu)} & -\dfrac{f_{\kappa\nu}(\kappa, \nu)}{f_\kappa(\kappa, \nu)} \\[3mm] -\dfrac{f_{\nu\kappa}(\kappa, \nu)}{f_\nu(\kappa, \nu)} & 1 \quad \dfrac{f_{\nu\nu}(\kappa, \nu)}{f_\nu(\kappa, \nu)} \\ & \eta\nu \end{vmatrix} > 0.$$

Consequently, det $(J_1 J_2) = |J_1| \, |J_2|$ has the same sign as $|J_1|$.

The situation may be summarized as follows. If $\sigma > 1$ then det $(J_1 J_2) < 0$ and (2.65) has one positive and one negative root. Consequently, (2.63) will have two positive, one negative, and two imaginary roots. If $\sigma < 1$ and if (2.69) is assumed, then det $(J_1 J_2) > 0$ and tr $(J_1 J_2) > 0$, which guarantees that (2.65) will have two roots with positive real parts. Then (2.63) will have either (a) three positive and two negative roots, or (b) one positive root, two complex roots with positive real parts, and two complex roots with negative real parts. In all of these cases, $(\kappa^\dagger, \nu^\dagger, u^\dagger, v^\dagger, a^\dagger)$ will be either a generalized saddle point or generalized focal point [cf. 41, pp. 187–88]. In the case $\sigma > 1$ there will be a path approaching the equilibrium point monotonically. In the case $\sigma < 1$, there will be either (a) a manifold of such paths, or (b) a path with a corkscrew-like approach to the equilibrium point.

The above local analysis does not, of course, prove the optimality of a path leading to the singular point. Such optimality appears very plausible on geometric grounds, but a formal proof will not be attempted here.

A generalization

The above analysis can be generalized in the following way. Suppose that part of the imported raw material is directly consumed and the rest used as input into the production of the export good. $X_i(t)$, $Y_i(t)$, $Z_i(t)$ will now denote consumption, net production, and import respectively of the ith good ($i = 1, 2$), the first being the export good (whence $Z_1 < 0$) and the second the raw material ($Z_2 > 0$, where

$-Y_2 = N = Z_2 - X_2$ is the amount used as input in the production of commodity 1). We denote

$$(2.72) \qquad x_i(t) = \frac{X_i(t)}{L(t)}, \, y_i(t) = \frac{Y_i(t)}{L(t)}, \, z_i(t) = \frac{Z_i(t)}{L(t)} \quad (i = 1, 2)$$

and $n(t) = N(t)/L(t) = -y_2(t)$ as in (2.14) and (2.11).

Assume that the utility function has the form

$$(2.73) \qquad \int_0^\infty e^{-\rho t} L(t) U[x_1(t), x_2(t)] dt = \int_0^\infty e^{-\delta t} U[x_1(t), x_2(t)] dt$$

where $L(0) = 1$, and suppose further that

$$(2.74) \qquad U(x_1, x_2) = x_1^{\theta_1} x_2^{\theta_2} \quad (\theta_i > 0, \, \theta_1 + \theta_2 = 1).$$

This implies unitary elasticity of substitution in consumption; more important, homogeneity of U implies a unitary income elasticity of demand, contrary to Engel's law.[12]

In place of (2.7), (2.28), the foreign offer function will be assumed to have the form

$$(2.75) \quad Z_2(t) = \bar{N}^{1+\eta} p(t)^\eta e^{\lambda^* t}, \, Z_1(t) + p(t) Z_2(t) = 0 \quad (0 \leqq \eta < \infty)$$

with the limiting form $p(t) = 1/\bar{N}$ as $\eta \to \infty$. λ^* is a shift parameter representing the growth rate of the foreign country.

The four equations (2.20) become slightly modified: In each equation, the second term on the right is multiplied by $U_1 = \partial U / \partial x_1$. The extra condition $p = U_2/U_1$ is added, where $U_i = \partial U / \partial x_i$, and the remaining equations hold as before. Since $p = U_2/U_1 = (\theta_2/\theta_1) (x_1/x_2)$ from (2.74), it follows that

$$(2.76) \qquad \qquad \hat{U}_1 = -\theta_2 \hat{p},$$

where the symbol $\wedge$ denotes logarithmic differentiation with respect to time, i.e., $\hat{p} = \dot{p}/p$, etc. From (2.75) we also obtain

$$(2.77) \qquad \qquad \hat{Z}_2 = \eta \hat{p} + \lambda^*.$$

If there is a singular solution in which Z_2, X_2, and $N = -Y_2$ grow at constant rates, and in which $v^\dagger = CN/AL$ is constant, then with constant $\alpha^\dagger$, $\beta^\dagger$, $\gamma^\dagger$ we have

[12] This is to be taken as a null hypothesis. The consequences of changing θ_i's are discussed below.

$$(2.78) \qquad \hat{X}_2 = \hat{Z}_2 = \hat{N} = \alpha^\dagger + \lambda - \gamma^\dagger.$$

If $r^\dagger, s^\dagger, q^\dagger, \kappa^\dagger, \nu^\dagger$ are constant, then (2.23) yields

$$(2.79) \qquad \hat{p} = \gamma^\dagger.$$

Thus from equations (2.77), (2.78), (2.79), we obtain

$$(2.80) \qquad \gamma^\dagger = \frac{\alpha^\dagger + \lambda - \lambda^*}{1 + \eta}.$$

From the first (modified) equation of (2.20) we obtain, for $\dot{q} = 0$,

$$(2.81) \qquad \hat{U}_1 = \beta^\dagger.$$

Together, (2.76), (2.79) and (2.81) yield

$$(2.82) \qquad \beta^\dagger = -\theta_2 \gamma^\dagger.$$

Consequently, (2.32) and (2.33) are modified by replacing $\beta^\dagger = 0$ by (2.82). As long as $\gamma^\dagger > 0$ in (2.80), it follows from (2.82) that technical progress is strongly capital deepening, i.e., capital increases relative to output.

The dynamic properties of this singular solution may be briefly outlined. Define

$$(2.83) \qquad w(t) = U_1(t)/a(t)$$

where $U_1 = \partial U/\partial x_1$. Recalling that the right side of (2.21) is now to be multiplied by U_1, it may be written $w(t)f[\kappa(t), \nu(t)]$, and taking account of (2.24), it follows from (2.21) and (2.22) that β, γ, and r are functions of κ, ν, u, v, w.

In equation (2.52), λ is now replaced by $\lambda - \lambda^*$, as in the second equation of (2.53). The term on the right of the first equation of (2.53) becomes $(\theta_2/\eta) [\hat{r} - \gamma + \phi(\beta, \gamma; r) + \lambda - \lambda^*]$. As in the development following (2.53), only the case of constant r will be taken up; then (2.58a) is replaced by

$$(2.84)$$

$$
\begin{bmatrix} \dot{\kappa} \\ \dot{\nu} \end{bmatrix} =
\begin{bmatrix} -\dfrac{f_{\kappa\kappa}(\kappa,\nu)}{f_\kappa(\kappa,\nu)} & \dfrac{\theta_2}{\eta\nu} - \dfrac{f_{\kappa\nu}(\kappa,\nu)}{f_\kappa(\kappa,\nu)} \\[2ex] -\dfrac{f_{\nu\kappa}(\kappa,\nu)}{f_\nu(\kappa,\nu)} & \dfrac{1}{\eta\nu} - \dfrac{f_{\nu\nu}(\kappa,\nu)}{f_\nu(\kappa,\nu)} \end{bmatrix}^{-1}
\begin{bmatrix} \beta + \dfrac{\theta_2}{\eta} - \dfrac{\theta_2}{\eta}[\phi(\beta,\gamma) + \lambda - \lambda^*] \\[2ex] \left(1 + \dfrac{1}{\eta}\right)\gamma - \dfrac{1}{\eta}[\phi(\beta,\gamma) + \lambda - \lambda^*] \end{bmatrix}.
$$

If, in addition to strict concavity of f, it is assumed that $f_{\kappa\nu} > 0$ (a condition satisfied by C.E.S. production functions), the matrix in (2.84) will have a positive determinant. Now in equations (2.59), the variable a in the arguments of the functions $\mathcal{K}$, $\mathfrak{N}$, $\mathfrak{U}$, $\mathcal{V}$ is replaced by w, and in the first two equations of (2.59b), $m(\kappa, \nu)/a$ is replaced by $wm(\kappa, \nu)$. Finally, the third equation of (2.59b) is replaced by

$$(2.85) \qquad \dot{w} = \mathcal{W}(\kappa, \nu, u, v, w) = (\hat{U}_1 - \hat{a})w$$

where

$$(2.86) \quad \hat{U}_1 - \hat{a} = - \frac{\theta_2}{\eta\nu} \mathfrak{N}(\kappa, \nu, u, v, w) +$$

$$\frac{\theta_2}{\eta} [\gamma - \phi(\beta, \gamma) - \lambda + \lambda^*] - [\delta - \phi(\beta, \gamma)] + (1 - r)m(u, v)w.$$

The structure of the Jacobian matrix (2.60) remains unchanged. The expression for $|J_2|$ in (2.70) must now be multiplied by $1 - (\theta_2/\eta)$ $\partial\phi/\partial\beta$, and Δ in (2.71) must be replaced by the determinant of the matrix of (2.84). The analysis goes through just as before.

Returning to the singular solution, it will now be shown for the case of fixed r that under certain conditions a decline in θ_2 (hence a decline in the proportion of consumers' income devoted to the primary product) will lead to a decline in the share $\nu^{\dagger}f_{\nu}(\kappa^{\dagger}, \nu^{\dagger})/f(\kappa^{\dagger}, \nu^{\dagger})$ of natural resources in the national income. If r is fixed, $\gamma^{\dagger}$ is determined from

$$(2.87) \qquad \gamma^{\dagger} = \frac{\phi(-\theta_2\gamma^{\dagger}, \gamma^{\dagger}; r) + \lambda - \lambda^*}{1 + \eta}$$

(see equations (2.80), (2.82)). As long as $1 + \eta - ((\partial\phi/\partial\gamma) - \theta_2(\partial\phi/\partial\beta)) > 0$, $\gamma^{\dagger}$ will increase when θ_2 increases. Under these conditions, and assuming (2.69) to hold, we find that a fall in θ_2 leads to a decline in $-\partial\phi/\partial\gamma$ (hence a decline in the share of resources relative to labor's share) and to a rise in $-\partial\phi/\partial\beta$ (hence a rise in capital's share relative to labor's). Similarly a fall in θ_2 leads to a rise in the share of capital relative to resources. Consequently, as the proportion of income devoted to the primary product falls, so does the share of resources in national income, in accordance with Schultz's result.

REFERENCES

1. Ahmad, S., "On the Theory of Induced Invention," *Economic Journal*, June 1966, pp. 344–57.

2. Amano, A., "Induced Bias in Technological Progress and Economic Growth," *Economic Studies Quarterly*, March 1967, pp. 1–17.

3. Arrow, K. J., "The Economic Implications of Learning by Doing," *Review of Economic Studies*, June 1962, pp. 155–73.

4. ———, "Economic Welfare and the Allocation of Resources for Invention," in *The Rate and Direction of Inventive Activity: Economic and Social Factors*, Princeton for NBER, 1962, pp. 609–26.

5. Bardhan, P. K., "On Factor-Biased Technical Progress and International Trade," *Journal of Political Economy*, August 1965, pp. 396–98.

6. Bhagwati, J., "Growth, Terms of Trade, and Comparative Advantage," *Economia Internazionale*, August 1959, pp. 393–414.

7. Brechling, F. P. R., and Surrey, A. J., "An International Comparison of Production Techniques: The Coal-Fired Electricity Generating Industry," *National Institute Economic Review*, May 1966, pp. 30–42.

8. Chipman, J. S., "Parametric External Economies of Scale, Ideal Output, and Competitive Equilibrium," Department of Economics, Harvard University, January 1967 (azographed). To appear in *Quarterly Journal of Economics*, August 1970.

9. Corden, W. M., "Economic Expansion and International Trade: A Geometric Approach," *Oxford Economic Papers*, September 1956, pp. 223–28.

10. Drandakis, E. M., and Phelps, E. S., "A Model of Induced Invention, Growth and Distribution," *Economic Journal*, December 1966, pp. 823–40.

11. Drandakis, E. M., and Hu, S. C., "On Optimal Induced Technical Progress," University of Rochester, January 1968 (mimeographed).

12. Edgeworth, F. Y., "The Theory of Distribution," *Quarterly Journal of Economics*, February 1904, pp. 159–219. Reproduced in F. Y. Edgeworth, *Papers Relating to Political Economy*, I, London, 1925, 13–60.

13. Fellner, W., "Two Propositions in the Theory of Induced Innovations," *Economic Journal*, June 1961, pp. 305–08.

14. ———, "Does the Market Direct the Relative Factor-Saving Effects of Technological Progress?" in *The Rate and Direction of Inventive Activity: Economic and Social Factors*, Princeton for NBER, 1962, pp. 171–94.

15. Findlay, R., and Grubert, H., "Factor Intensities, Technological Progress, and the Terms of Trade," *Oxford Economic Papers*, February 1959, pp. 111–21.

16. Freeman, C., "The Plastics Industry: A Comparative Study of Research and Innovation," *National Institute Economic Review*, November 1963, pp. 22–62.

17. ———, "Research and Development in Electronic Capital Goods," *National Institute Economic Review*, November 1965, pp. 40–91.

18. Gruber, W., Mehta, D., and Vernon, R., "The R&D Factor in International Trade and International Investment of United States Industries," *Journal of Political Economy*, February 1967, pp. 20–37.

19. Habakkuk, H. J., *American and British Technology in the Nineteenth Century: The Search for Labour-Saving Inventions*, Cambridge, 1962.

20. Haberler, G., *International Trade and Economic Development*, Cairo, 1959.

21. ———, "Terms of Trade and Economic Development," in *Economic Development for Latin America*, Ellis, H. S., ed., London, 1962, pp. 275–97.

22. Hicks, J. R., *The Theory of Wages*, New York, 1932. Reprinted, Gloucester, Mass., 1957.

23. ———, "An Inaugural Lecture," *Oxford Economic Papers*, June 1953, pp. 117–35.

24. Hoffmeyer, E., *Dollar Shortage*, Copenhagen, 1958.

25. Hufbauer, G. C., *Synthetic Materials and the Theory of International Trade*, London, 1966.

26. Johnson, H. G., "Economic Expansion and International Trade," *The Manchester School of Economic and Social Studies*, May 1955, pp. 95–112. Reprinted in Johnson, H. G., *International Trade and Economic Growth*, London, 1958, pp. 65–93.

27. ———, "Economic Development and International Trade," *National økonomisk Tidsskrift*, Haefte 5–6, 1959, pp. 253–72. Reprinted in Johnson, H. G., *Money, Trade and Economic Growth*, Cambridge, Mass., 1962, pp. 75–98.

28. Jones, R. W., "Comments on Technical Progress," *The Philippine Economic Journal*, Second Semester, 1966, pp. 313–32.

29. Kamien, M. I., and Schwartz, N. L., "Optimal 'Induced' Technical Change," *Econometrica*, January 1968, pp. 1–17.

30. Kennedy, C., "Induced Bias in Innovation and the Theory of Distribution," *Economic Journal*, September 1964, pp. 541–47.

31. ———, "Samuelson on Induced Innovation," *Review of Economics and Statistics*, November 1966, pp. 442–44.

32. Kindleberger, C. P., *The Dollar Shortage*. Cambridge, Mass. and New York, 1950.

33. ———, *Foreign Trade and the National Economy.* New Haven, Conn., 1962.

34. Kravis, I. B., " 'Availability' and Other Influences on the Commodity Composition of Trade," *Journal of Political Economy,* April 1956, pp. 143–55.

35. Leontief, W., "Domestic Production and Foreign Trade: The American Capital Position Re-examined," *Proceedings of the American Philosophical Society,* September 1953, pp. 332–49. Reprinted in Leontief, W., *Input-Output Economics,* New York, 1966, pp. 68–99.

36. ———, "Factor Proportions and the Structure of American Trade: Further Theoretical and Empirical Analysis," *Review of Economics and Statistics,* November 1956, pp. 386–407. Reprinted in Leontief, W., *Input-Output Economics,* New York, 1966, pp. 100–33.

37. Levhari, D., "Extensions of Arrow's 'Learning by Doing,' " *Review of Economic Studies,* April 1966, pp. 117–31.

38. MacDougall, Sir Donald, *The World Dollar Problem.* London, 1957.

39. Maddala, G. S., and Knight, P. T., "International Diffusion of Technical Change—A Case Study of the Oxygen Steel Making Process," *Economic Journal,* September 1967, pp. 531–58.

40. Meade, J. E., *A Neo-Classical Theory of Economic Growth,* rev. ed., London, 1962.

41. Nemytskii, V. V., and Stepanov, V. V., *Qualitative Theory of Differential Equations,* Princeton, 1960.

42. Nordhaus, W. D., "The Optimal Rate and Direction of Technical Change," in *Essays on the Theory of Optimal Economic Growth,* Shell, K., ed., Cambridge, Mass., 1967, pp. 53–66.

43. Nurkse, R., *Patterns of Trade and Development,* Stockholm, 1959, and Oxford, 1961. Reprinted in Nurkse, R., *Equilibrium and Growth in the World Ecomony,* Cambridge, Mass., 1962, pp. 282–336.

44. Oi, W. Y., "The Neoclassical Foundations of Progress Functions," *Economic Journal,* September 1967, pp. 579–94.

45. Phelps, E. S., "Models of Technical Progress and the Golden Rule of Research," *Review of Economic Studies,* April 1966, pp. 133–45.

46. Pontryagin, L. S., Boltyanskii, V. G., Gamkrelidze, R. S., and Mischenko, E. F., *The Mathematical Theory of Optimal Processes,* New York, 1962.

47. Prebisch, R., *The Economic Development of Latin America and Its Principal Problems,* New York, 1950. Reprinted in *Economic Bulletin for Latin America,* February 1962, pp. 1–22.

48. Samuelson, P. A., "A Theory of Induced Innovation along Kennedy-Weizsäcker Lines," *Review of Economics and Statistics,* November 1965, pp. 343–56.

49. ———, "Rejoinder: Agreements, Disagreements, Doubts, and the Case of Induced Harrod-Neutral Technical Change," *Review of Economics and Statistics,* November 1966, pp. 444–48.

50. Schmookler, J., "Economic Sources of Inventive Activity," *Journal of Economic History,* March 1962, pp. 1–20.

51. ———, "Changes in Industry and in the State of Knowledge as Determinants of Industrial Invention," in *The Rate and Direction of Inventive Activity: Economic and Social Factors,* Princeton for NBER, 1962, pp. 195–232.

52. ———, *Invention and Economic Growth,* Cambridge Mass., 1966.

53. Schultz, T. W., "The Declining Economic Importance of Agricultural Land," *Economic Journal,* December 1951, pp. 725–40.

54. ———, "Connections between Natural Resources and Economic Growth," in *Natural Resources and Economic Growth,* Spengler, J. J., ed., Washington, 1961, pp. 1–9. "Comment" by Abramovitz, M., pp. 9–16.

55. ———, "Economic Prospects of Primary Products," in *Economic Development for Latin America,* Ellis, H. S., ed., New York, 1962, pp. 308–41.

56. Sheshinski, E., "Optimal Accumulation with Learning by Doing," in *Essays on the Theory of Optimal Economic Growth,* Shell, K., ed., Cambridge, Mass., 1967, pp. 31–52.

57. Singer, H. W., "The Distribution of Gains between Investing and Borrowing Countries," *American Economic Review, Papers and Proceedings,* May 1950, pp. 473–85.

58. Takayama, A., "Economic Growth and International Trade," *Review of Economic Studies,* June 1964, pp. 207–20.

59. Uzawa, H., "Neutral Inventions and the Stability of Growth Equilibrium," *Review of Economic Studies,* February 1961, pp. 117–24.

60. ———, "Production Functions with Constant Elasticity of Substitution," *Review of Economic Studies,* October 1962, pp. 291–99.

61. ———, "Optimum Technical Change in an Aggregative Model of Economic Growth," *International Economic Review,* January 1965, pp. 18–31.

62. Vanek, J., "The Natural Resource Content of Foreign Trade, 1870–1955, and the Relative Abundance of Natural Resources in the United States," *Review of Economics and Statistics,* May 1959, pp. 146–53.

63. ———, *The Natural Resource Content of U.S. Foreign Trade, 1870–1955,* Cambridge, Mass., 1963.

64. Vernon, R., "International Investment and International Trade in the Product Cycle," *Quarterly Journal of Economics,* May 1966, pp. 190–207.

65. Viner, J., *International Trade and Economic Development,* Glencoe, Ill., 1952.

COMMENTS

KENNETH J. ARROW
Harvard University

My comments will be addressed for the most part to questions raised by Professor Chipman's characteristically skillful employment of advanced mathematical techniques to deepen significantly our theoretical understanding of economic phenomena; at the end I will make a few remarks concerning the paper presented by Professor Jones at this session.

It may be useful to remark that Chipman's theory of optimal induced technological change is an example of the "dynamic comparative advantage," the subject of Professor Bruno's paper. Whenever there is capital accumulation relative to the growth of original factors, comparative advantage will change over time. But the full flavor of dynamic comparative advantage occurs when there is an element of irreversibility involved in the investment. Then indeed the justification for investment must involve the whole future course of effects on the marginal productivities. This effect appears in Bruno's paper in the rather simple sense that investment today in a given industry increases *its* absorptive capacity for future investment. In Chipman's model, the irreversible investment is the expenditure on research; accumulated research knowledge can neither be transferred to other industries nor undone to provide additional consumption. The justification for an irreversible investment is based on the sum of discounted marginal productivities over the future and not merely the current marginal productivity. (In this context it is misleading to state in equation (2.50) ff. that the product of capital is equated to the rate of discount; in fact the rate of discount is rated to the marginal net product of capital less an excise tax to pay for research expenditures.)

The Pontryagin principle is the natural mathematical tool for any type of model involving allocation of a current flow of resources among a number of activities when some of the activities are forms of capital accumulation. The principle can be given an economic interpretation: assign prices to stocks of different forms of capital to make them commensurate with current consumption. In the short run, resources are allocated so as to maximize income at these prices. The prices themselves must change over time in such a way as to make individuals just willing to hold the stocks, with income including capital gains from changing prices just equal to a rate of discount. Finally, the whole system—prices and quantities—has to tend to a stationary equilibrium. The Pontryagin principle is closely related to recursive optimization, which has been called dynamic programming, where the values of accumulation are imputed from the future. Professor Chipman has used the Pontryagin methods with great skill and economic tact.

The questions one might raise relate mainly to the economics of his model, though one technical problem will be mentioned below. In the first place, as he makes clear, his model is one of central planning; the entire benefit of research expenditures is internalized. Thus, there is no direct reason to argue that it is in any way descriptive; it may be true nevertheless that a perfectly optimizing model, such as Chipman's, may give an accurate qualitative, though not quantitative, picture of the workings of a more realistic model. One can easily imagine models, such as Professor Jones suggests in his paper, where research is carried out by firms who can appropriate part but not all of its benefits. The research done by other firms may be taken as parametric by any given firm, so that the complexities of oligopolistic interdependence may be avoided, and each firm is supposed to carry out an optimization of research over time. Such an analysis is probably only mildly more difficult than the one Professor Chipman has offered us.

In the second place, the assumptions about the relation between research and production function shifts are subject to serious question. These assumptions have become common in recent theoretical literature, and Professor Chipman has distinguished authority for them, but they are nevertheless both theoretically arbitrary and empirically unrealistic. In the Kennedy-Weizsäcker model, there is one kind of technological progress for each factor, namely, a rate of augmentation, and a stable function describing the trade-offs among these rates and some measure of research input. (Professor Chipman's measure, the *proportion* of total output devoted to research, seems especially arbitrary; it seems to imply that knowledge cannot be transmitted at all but must be re-created where needed.) Now there are two main problems in accepting this thesis: (1) is it reasonable to assume that rates of factor augmentation are stably related to research inputs? (2) is there any reason to assume a stable trade-off among rates of augmentation of different factors?

(1) The first point can be discussed most clearly in a one-factor model; suppose labor is the only factor. Then the model becomes, in Chipman's notation,

(1) $$Y(t) = [1 - r(t)] A(t)L(t),$$

(2) $$\dot{A}(t)/A(t) = \phi[r(t)].$$

Equation (2) is supposed to be a specification of the knowledge-producing activity, where knowledge is measured by labor productivity. Clearly, it is reasonable to assume that the rate of production of new knowledge depends both on the resources devoted to it and on the amount of knowledge already accumulated. But why in the world should new knowledge display constant returns to accumulated knowledge at a fixed level of research input? By analogy with the usual economic analysis of more palpable branches of production one might argue for diminishing returns; the easier types of knowledge have been acquired first, and it becomes increasingly difficult (requires more resources) to make new discoveries. To put it another way, is it really credible that, if research inputs are held constant (even if measured proportionately rather than absolutely), then output will grow exponentially while material inputs remain constant. The laws of conservation of matter and energy alone seem to prohibit this.

(2) Analyzing technological progress into rates of factor augmentation is merely one possibility among many and has no very distinguished position either in terms of empirical evidence or analytic convenience. Professor Jones has dealt penetratingly, if briefly, with this point. But in addition the stability of the invention possibility frontier in any form has neither rationale nor empirical support. A gross reading of history suggests the bias is apt to vary from time to time due much more to changes in the state of knowledge than to changes in capital-labor ratios.

An analogy may help. Exploration, especially in the great days from

1492 to 1880 or so, was very analogous to research; resources were invested to produce knowledge about new places and resources. I suggest that which factors were in fact augmented depended primarily on what was in the explored countries and very little on factor ratios in the exploring countries. Columbus may have been impelled by a desire for spices, but it was the supply of corn which was increased.

I do not wish to decry the proposition that the magnitude of technological progress may be responsive to economic motivation, but I have grave doubts that its bias can be explained in any other than accidental and historical terms.

I conclude the discussion of Professor Chipman's paper with two less fundamental remarks. First, Professor Chipman's production function for research, which generalizes equation (2) above, is not a concave function of its arguments, since there are increasing returns to all factors (including both accumulated knowledge and current research expenditures). Just as in ordinary (finite-dimensional) maximization problems, it is then possible that the necessary conditions for a maximum may be satisfied by several policies, some of which indeed may not be even locally maximum. A study of this problem in a somewhat simpler but analogous model will be found in an unpublished dissertation by Larry Ruff.[1]

Second, Professor Chipman minimizes the importance of learning by doing as a cause of technological progress. But the notion of the "product cycle," so much emphasized at this conference, is certainly an example of learning by doing; it is assumed that the requirements for certain skill factors decline with experience in production.

Professor Jones has given, as expected, a beautifully lucid account of a two-factor economy. But with the growing emphasis on skill as a factor of production, we are at least in a three-factor world, and it is only sober sense to recognize that more factors should be distinguished and would be if we had the analytic tools and empirical evidence to do so. Now it is pretty clear that we are unlikely to be able to derive any theorems in the multifactor case comparable to those which hold in a two-factor world. We shall have to switch our emphasis in model-building from derivation of theorems to computation of implications.

[1] Ruff, "Optimal Growth and Technological Progress in a Cournot Economy," Institute for Mathematical Studies in the Social Sciences, Stanford University, 1968, Technical Report 11.

The algorithms by H. Scarf [2] for computation of equilibrium levels, prices, and quantities in a general competitive model, seem to be ideally suited for testing out the implications of alternative foreign trade models.

WASSILY LEONTIEF

Harvard University

Four years ago I had an opportunity to discuss, in this very room, the then relatively new aggregative dynamic models with built in, endogenous technological change. I argued that despite or rather because of their formal elegance this type of theoretical approach could contribute very little to the understanding of real processes of economic growth. Much mathematical ingenuity has been invested since then in further elaboration of such models; Professor Chipman quotes and lists some twenty articles published on that special subject in the last three years. The formulation has become more elaborate and its mathematics higher. In the paper prepared by Chipman for this conference, he applies the full power of the perfected analytical tool to the solution of an important and well-defined problem: What effects can technological change have on imports of raw materials by advanced industrialized economies from the so-called less developed countries?

A study of Chipman's twenty typewritten pages of concise mathematical argument confirms me in my original contention: Elaborate aggregative growth models can contribute very little to the understanding of processes of economic growth, and they cannot provide a useful theoretical basis for systematic empirical analysis.

Taking for granted the internal consistency of Chipman's model, I propose to question the relevance of his conclusions and the validity of the factual assumption on which he builds his argument.

These conclusions are summarized on page 104; "If the home country produces a single consumer good, using up labor, capital, and imported

[2] H. Scarf, "On the Computation of Equilibrium Prices." W. Fellner *et al. Ten Economic Studies in the Tradition of Irving Fisher,* New York, 1967, pp. 207–30.

raw material, then an equilibrium growth path will be approached in which technical change is Harrod neutral as far as capital is concerned (that is, there will be no capital-augmenting technical change), whereas the rate of augmentation of natural resources will be determined by the formula $\gamma = (\lambda + \alpha)/(1 + \eta)$, where λ is the rate of growth of population, α the rate of labor-augmenting technical change, and η the elasticity of the foreign offer curve. Thus, if resources are in perfectly elastic supply ($\eta = \infty$), there will be no resource-augmenting technical improvement, whereas at the opposite extreme of perfectly inelastic supply ($\eta = 0$), resource-augmenting technical change will proceed at the rate $\lambda + \alpha$. The volume of primary products grows at the rate $(\lambda + \alpha)\eta/(1 + \eta)$, and the foreign terms of trade improve at the rate $(\lambda + \alpha)/(1 + \eta)$."

Addressing himself in the light of these conclusions to the "controversial topic of the past few decades"—the thesis set forth by Prebisch and Singer that there is a tendency toward a deterioration in the terms of trade of raw material producing countries—Chipman—on page 103—explains that:

"Although it is not claimed that the model used here can predict changes in technology with any accuracy, it nevertheless supports Schultz's thesis in the weak sense that the declining share of raw materials expenditure in national income cannot be accounted for on the basis of the hypothesis of induced resource-augmenting technical progress alone."

I submit that conclusions drawn from analysis of the properties of that particular model do not add to the understanding of the phenomena it is intended to explain, even if—heeding Chipman's advice—one interprets them with caution. They are wrong in the sense that they are derived from empirically unjustifiable assumptions. The fact that these assumptions conform strictly to the, by now well-standardized, theoretical construction code of the model-building industry lends additional justification to the following critical inquiry.

Trade statistics show that the amounts of raw silk, quebracho bark, or, say, vegetable dyes moving in international trade, attained their highest level many years ago and have been falling steadily since. They may eventually disappear from the list of internationally traded goods. Would it not be reasonable to ask whether the decline in the demand for these raw materials might not have been brought about by changes in some methods of production which, in their turn, could have been based on the acquisition of new technical knowledge brought about by investment in research?

Confronted with Chipman's elaborate refutation of so plausible an explanation, one naturally becomes suspicious of the factual assumptions on which he chooses to base his theoretical argument. The task of tracing these assumptions is complicated by the fact that instead of being presented all at once, additional assumptions are introduced "when needed," that is, in any intermediate stage of the argument at which the going gets too hard. His model contains an aggregative production function, a dynamic utility function and, in addition, the so-called Kennedy function—the *deus ex machina* of the modern pure theory of economic growth that permits the utility maximizing agent to control and, consequently, to predict in advance the future course of all technological change.

I propose to show that among all the structural assumptions built into Chipman's model the one pertaining to the effects of technological change on the shape of his new classical aggregative production function is solely responsible for the theoretical conclusion that I find difficult to accept.

Specifically, this is the assumption that all technological change is "factor-augmenting." The exclusion of all other kinds of structural change implies that the input-output relationships corresponding to all possible past, present, and future methods of producing any given good can be depicted on a single graph showing one set of conventionally shaped and properly numbered "isoquants." The effects of every admissible factor-augmenting innovation can be described simply by a change in the scales showing how many units of the particular factor are represented by each of the equal intervals marked off on that graph along the appropriate axis. With every "augmentation" of an input the number of physical units of the input contained in an inch or centimeter, as the case may be, is increased.

The elasticity of substitution between any two inputs can be said to remain unaffected by this particular kind of technical change in the sense that at any given point of the graph this elasticity remains the same, even after the numerical scales describing the position of that point in terms of input coordinates have been adjusted to reflect factor-augmenting technological change. For good measure Chipman limits the admissible shape of his production function still further by assuming that "the elasticity of substitution between any two factors is bounded below 1," which means that it is less than 1.

Under such conditions technological change cannot possibly eliminate any input from the production process that at any time has been part of the process. Only infinite augmentation in the magnitude of the efficiency coefficient of that factor, as compared to other factors, could conceivably drive the level of its input toward zero.

Following conventional usage and, I suppose, for the sake of casual realism, in addition to raw materials, Chipman's model includes the two primary inputs, labor and capital. Without affecting one way or another the nature or the substantive implication of his mathematical argument, its formulation can be simplified by dropping capital as a separate input. Thus Chipman's (2.1) can be reduced to the following relationships describing the balance between current consumption, production, exports of goods, and imports of raw materials in an economy that produces a single finished good from two inputs, labor and imported raw materials:

(1) $$Y = F(AL, CN)(1 - r) - pN$$

where,

Y is the net output.

$F(\ )$ represents a homogenous production function.

AL is the total labor input measured in "efficiency units"; L represents the number of workers and A, the corresponding technical efficiency (productivity) coefficient.

CN is the total raw material input measured in "efficiency units"; N represents the amount of the raw material measured in natural units; C, the corresponding technical efficiency coefficient.

r is the proportion of gross total output currently allocated to research and development, that in its turn brings about an increase in the magnitude of A or C or of both.

pN represents the amount of the finished good exported in exchange for the imported N units of raw material; p is the price of that raw material expressed in units of the finished good which is being traded for it.

Because it is assumed to be homogeneous (constant returns to scale), the production function $F(\ )$ can be written in the following form:

(2) $$F(AL, CN) \equiv ALF(1, CN/AL) \equiv ALf(CN/AL)$$

If η represents the elasticity of the supply of raw material to the importing country,

(3) $$p = N^{\frac{1}{\eta}} \quad \text{and} \quad pN = N^{\frac{(\eta+1)}{\eta}}$$

Thus,

(4) $$Y = ALf(CN/AL)(1 - r) - N^{\frac{(\eta+1)}{\eta}}$$

The system is dynamic in the sense that each of the variables is considered from the outset to be a function of time. Following all other modern growth theorists Chipman centers his attention on a singular solution for the system better known as the state of the Golden Age, i.e., a state of even, uniform expansion in which the magnitude of each variable either grows (or contracts) exponentially or remains constant. In this particular instance the fraction r of total output allocated to generation of factor-augmenting technological change is assumed to remain constant while the labor force L is taken to be growing at an exogenously fixed annual rate, l.

Each of the other variables is permitted either to grow at some positive constant rate or not to change at all. Thus, under Golden Age conditions, the balance equation (4) acquires the following form,

(5) $$Y_o e^{yt} = A_o e^{at} L_o e^{lt} f(C_o e^{ct} N_o e^{nt} / A_o e^{at} L_o e^{lt})(1 - r) - N_o e^{\frac{\eta+1}{\eta}nt}$$

Moreover, the ratio of the total raw material to the total labor inputs (both measured in "efficiency units") and, consequently, the value of function $f(\ )$ is assumed to be constant too. The capital letters with the subscript o represent the magnitudes of the variables at the time $t = 0$; the small letters in the exponents represent their respective equilibrium (Golden Age) rates of growth. This is a departure from Chipman's own notation which, because of a large number of intermediate variables he has to handle, spills over much further into the Greek alphabet.

Thus, we have one equation with five unknowns: y, a, c, n, and r. Obviously, additional conditions are required for a unique determination of their values. The aforementioned Kennedy function—the assumed functional relationship between r, a, and c—is one of them. The rest are derived from the solution of a maximizing problem in which the values of the four variables are determined in such a way as to maximize, within the limitation imposed by the other conditions, the value of a dynamic social utility function. This does not enter into my reformulation of Chipman's argument at all. I do not have to follow this long path since Chipman's main conclusions concerning the effects of technological change on the demand for raw materials can be derived simply and directly from equation (5).

Consolidating some of the exponents we have,

$$(6) \quad Y_o e^{yt} = A_o L_o e^{(a+l)t} f(C_o N_o e^{(c+n)t} / A_o L_o e^{(a+l)t})(1-r) - N_o e^{\frac{\eta+1}{\eta}nt}$$

The equality between the left-hand and the right-hand side of this equation can be maintained for all values of t only if the coefficients of t in the exponents appearing in its first, second, and third terms are equal, i.e., if

$$(7) \qquad y = a + l = \frac{\eta + 1}{\eta}n$$

The equality between the first and the middle terms means that the net output must increase at a rate equal to the sum of the rate of the factor-augmenting rise in the productivity of labor and the given rate of increase of the total labor force. The second equality describes a simple relationship between the last two magnitudes, the growth rate of the raw material input and the given elasticity of its supply.

The assumed invariance of the ratio of the two exponential expressions entered on the right-hand side of (5), under the function sign, implies,

$$(8) \qquad\qquad c + n = a + l$$

In case $\eta = \infty$, (7) is reduced to:

$$y = a + l = n$$

This is compatible with (8) only if $c = 0$, i.e., no resource augmenting technical change will affect the use of the imported raw materials if their supply happens to be perfectly elastic. In this case, (8) is reduced to:

$$n = a + l.$$

The import of raw material will grow at a rate equal to the growth rate of the labor force plus the augmentation rate of the efficiency of labor.

In case $\eta = 0$, i.e., if the supply of raw material happens to be fixed, the right-hand side of (7) can remain finite only if $n = 0$. According to (8), this implies:

$$c = a + l.$$

These are precisely the results anticipated by Chipman in the first part of his paper and stated concisely in his formulae (2.34) and (2.35). I reached them in a few brief steps using in my argument only his special assumption concerning the effect of technical change on the shape of the production function. After bringing into the argument the Kennedy function and a dynamic social utility function, each carrying with it a number of additional arbitrary assumptions, he obtains these results through an elaborate application of the powerful Pontryagin's "maximum principle."

Thus, we see that it is his special assumption concerning the "factor-augmenting" nature of all technical change that lies at the base of Chipman's refutation of the Prebisch-Singer thesis. In the light of incontrovertible empirical evidence—cited at the beginning of my remarks—I conclude that his theoretical argument simply disproves the validity of his basic factual assumption, an assumption that is incorporated—possibly for reasons of indisputable mathematical convenience—in most of the recently presented aggregative models of economic growth.

REPLY TO PROFESSOR LEONTIEF

JOHN S. CHIPMAN

If under hypothesis A, conclusion C follows if and only if assumption B holds, and if both B and C are empirically observed, I would say that we have an explanation of C. A is the hypothesis of induced factor-augmenting technical change, represented in terms of a Kennedy function, combined with other more traditional assumptions such as constant returns to scale and social behavior represented in terms of optimization. B is Engel's law, and C is the declining share of raw material producing countries in world income. Professor Leontief does not say whether he accepts C, but I shall assume that he does. He states that the assumption "pertaining to the effects of technological change on the . . . production function is solely responsible for the theoretical conclusion . . ." I am not sure whether he means by this to bring into question the validity of Engel's law. For the sake of the argument, however, I shall assume unitary income elasticity of demand and maintain that even under these conditions I do not believe that Professor Leontief has succeeded in establishing his point.

Professor Leontief states: "Trade statistics show that the amounts of raw silk, quebracho bark, [etc.] moving in international trade . . . have been falling steadily. . . . They may eventually disappear from the list of internationally traded goods." While I doubt that trade statistics can provide information about the future, my answer to the ensuing rhetorical question is simple: of course I attribute such a decline to technical change. Far from presenting an "elaborate refutation" of such an explanation, I accepted it as my starting point. Professor Leontief forgets that I stated that "natural resources N should be thought of as a variable taking the place of raw materials of all kinds, so that an increase in it may represent recourse to further kinds of primary products." In fact, I even cited silk myself in stating: "It should . . . be kept in mind that the entities we are dealing with are aggregates, so that while particular methods of factor augmentation become exhausted, others take their places; e.g., silk gives way to rayon, and rayon to nylon." The Prebisch-Singer thesis is not concerned with raw silk and quebracho bark, but with primary products *in general.* The very same trade statistics that show a fall in raw silk show a rise in petroleum and pulpwood—two of the most important ingredients of synthetic materials. But Professor Leontief would have us believe that technological change will allow the miracle fabrics of the future to be produced by labor alone—like the emperor's new clothes in Hans Andersen's fairy tale!

Even granting that we might be heading toward such a resource-free state, I am unable to see what the hypothesis of factor augmentation has to do with the issue. As I pointed out in my paper, under a Leontief fixed-coefficients technology $F(AL, CN) = \min(AL, CN)$, *any* technical change can be uniquely represented as factor augmenting. If my conclusions "are wrong in the sense that they are derived from empirically unjustifiable assumptions," the same must apply to the Leontief input-output system itself.[1] Professor Leontief's objection is that "only infinite augmentation in the magnitude of the efficiency coefficient of [a] factor, as compared to other factors, could conceivably drive the level of its input toward zero." Why should infinite augmentation be excluded? There is nothing in the factor augmentation hypothesis to rule out, say, $A = 1$ and $C = 1/(1 - t)$ if $t \leq 1$, $C = \infty$ if $t > 1$. What *does* rule this out is the Kennedy function. But the Kennedy function does not rule out, say, $A = A_0 e^{\alpha t}$, $C = C_0^{\gamma t}$, $L = L_0 e^{\lambda t}$, with $\gamma > \alpha + \lambda$, entailing an ultimately infinite augmentation in the efficiency coefficient of natural resources as compared with labor. If $\eta > 0$ and $\dot{v}/v < \gamma - \alpha - \lambda$, this would lead to declining and ultimately negligible (if not actually zero) imports of raw materials, as well as of raw material prices. If $\eta = 0$ and $\dot{r} = 0$, one would have from (2.51)

$$\frac{\dot{p}}{p} = \gamma + \frac{vf''(v)}{f'(v)} = \gamma + (\gamma - \alpha - \lambda) \frac{vf''(v)}{f'(v)} =$$

$$\frac{\gamma}{\sigma(v)} \left[\sigma(v) - \left(1 - \frac{\alpha + \lambda}{\gamma} \right) \right] \left[1 - \frac{vf'(v)}{f(v)} \right]$$

(where $f(v) = f(CN/AL) = F(1, CN/AL)$); hence as long as the elasticity of substitution $\sigma(v)$ were less than $1 - (\alpha + \lambda)/\gamma$, and $vf'(v)/f(v) \to 0$ as $v \to \infty$,[2] the terms of trade of the primary producing

---

[1] In his celebrated 1953 article cited in my paper [35], Professor Leontief himself used the criterion of factor augmentation to compare the technologies of different countries, in arriving at his conclusion that "in any combination with a given quantity of capital, one man year of American labor is equivalent to . . . three man years of foreign labor." Amano, in his 1967 article cited in my paper, showed that for C.E.S. production functions with $\sigma < 1$, essentially equivalent results would be obtained with a more general criterion of technological change.

[2] With C.E.S. functions $vf'(v)/f(v) \to 0$ if and only if $\sigma < 1$. With variable elasticity of substitution we must require that for some $\bar{\sigma} < 1$, $\sigma(v) \leq \bar{\sigma}$ for all v. This is *not* the same as assuming that $\sigma(v) < 1$ for all v, as Professor Leontief claims; the boundedness away from unity can be shown to be indispensable.

countries would eventually deteriorate, even if natural resources were in fixed supply. Neither the factor augmentation hypothesis nor the form of the Kennedy function precludes these results; what does preclude them is the asymptotic condition $\gamma = (\alpha + \lambda)/(1 + \eta)$.

The crucial question is therefore whether the differential equations lead asymptotically to the balanced growth solution corresponding to Professor Leontief's equation (5), rather than to a solution such as the above with $\gamma > \alpha + \lambda$. As he points out, the result $\gamma = (\alpha + \lambda)/(1 + \eta)$ follows directly from (5); and this is how it was derived in my paper as well. The whole problem is to justify (5), and this is what requires the heavy mathematical apparatus that Professor Leontief so deplores.

CONCLUDING REMARKS

WASSILY LEONTIEF

In discussing Professor Chipman's paper I commented on two inter-related but nevertheless distinct aspects of his contribution.

First, I endeavored to demonstrate through an elementary mathematical argument that his theoretical conclusion concerning the relationship between the demand for imported raw material and technological changes in an aggregative neoclassical dynamic follow simply and directly from the following assumptions:

1. The input-output relationships within the system can be described by a homogeneous production function admitting only a factor-augmenting type of technological change.

2. The relevant relationship between technological change and demand for imported raw materials are those prevailing when the system finds itself in a state of steady uniform expansion, referred to at times as the Golden Age.

In Chipman's argument, the Kennedy function plays only the auxiliary role of excluding a priori the possibility of negative rates of factor-augmentation, i.e., of either a or c being less than zero. This, incidentally, limits critically the implications of Chipman's observations that "under a Leontief fixed coefficient technology . . . *any* technical change can be uniquely represented as factor augmenting." In describing technological change in terms of changes in the vector of input coefficients, I am prepared to take account of increases as well as of reductions in the magnitudes of individual coefficients. Chipman's Kennedy function, on the other hand, excludes the possibility of an increase in magnitude of any input coefficients under conditions prevailing in the Golden Age: each one of them must either fall or remain constant.

The dynamic aggregative utility function (permitting the application of Pontryagin's maximum principle that makes up the bulk of Chipman's paper) serves—so far as I am able to judge—the sole purpose of justifying the second of the aforementioned assumptions, that is, the reference to the Golden Age. Since the strict and narrow specification of the shape of that utility function seems to be dictated by requirements of mathematical convenience, rather than consideration of empirical relevance, this part of Chipman's argument can contribute very little to an explanation of actual relationships between technological change and the demand for raw materials.

The second point raised in my comments is that of the relationship of Chipman's theoretical constructs to observed facts. He doubts that "trade statistics cannot provide information about the future." What else could? Convenient a priori assumptions?

My reference to instances in which technological change has obviously led to spectacular reduction in the demand for a raw material—without appreciable increase in its supply price—was intended to justify a closer inquiry into the treatment of technological change within the framework of the neoclassical growth model. Since, at least in Chipman's formulation, this theory excludes the possibility of such phenomena, I conclude that it does not provide a viable conceptual framework for empirical inquiry.

Hypotheses and the

Tests of Trade Patterns

The Impact of National Characteristics & Technology

on the Commodity Composition

of Trade in Manufactured Goods

G. C. HUFBAUER

UNIVERSITY OF NEW MEXICO AND

HARVARD DEVELOPMENT ADVISORY SERVICE

It was once fashionable to hear about a "notorious lag" between international trade theory and other branches of economic analysis. The lag may still exist, but in the meantime new theories have surfaced—theories which explain export and import patterns in terms of "technological" variables. These theories often perform well when applied to a single group of commodities or a limited range of countries. But how do they fare when pitted against one another on common commodities and countries? To answer this question is an ambitious task, and the evaluation offered here has several limitations: it deals with the broad sweep of trade theories, often in rashly over-simplified form; it confines itself to manufactured goods; and it examines only the commodity composition of trade. Our principal goal has been to develop empirical measures to test hypotheses in the broadest possible terms, and this goal has been pursued at the expense of theoretical analysis. We are not much interested in the impact of natural resource location on trade

NOTE: I am grateful to the Ford Foundation and the National Science Foundation for support, but neither institution bears responsibility for the views expressed. The data was collected and edited by Melissa Patterson, with the assistance of Frances Bourgeois, Evaldo Cabourrouy, John Barnes, Frances Ray, and Vincent Yegge. With the customary absolution, I want to record my thanks to H. B. Lary and D. B. Keesing for their especially perceptive suggestions, and to F. M. Adler, J. N. Bhagwati, E. Despres, C. P. Kindleberger, and P. T. Knight for criticizing the methods and results.

flows; therefore the analysis has been limited to manufactured goods. The problems of a dual economy are ignored although these problems may significantly affect trade flows. Nor are we concerned with the forces determining the growth and fluctuation of trade. Instead the focus is on commodity composition.[1]

Table 1 outlines the seven trade theories which concern us. All seven have this in common: each views trade as the offspring of an economic marriage between product characteristics and national attributes. The first six theories find in trade a compensating mechanism for international structural differences, but the seventh theory sees an exchange of *similar* goods.

These propositions are illustrated by Figure 1. The vertical axis depicts relative prices.[2] The horizontal axis specifies the national attribute. Goods are distinguished by the presence of the connecting characteristic. For example, the characteristic might be commodity standardization, and the related national attribute, industrial sophistication. Country A, not very sophisticated, enjoys a comparative advantage in making Good 1, a standardized commodity. This is shown by the price relations which prevail in Country A as opposed to other nations. Country B has a comparative advantage in making Good 2, a moderately sophisticated product, while Country C commands the lead in highly sophisticated Good 3. The commodity composition of exports, according to the six "orthodox" theories, reflects these advantages and disadvantages: Country A sells Good 1 in abundance, Country B sells Good 2, and so forth.

S. B. Linder's theory, the seventh, requires a different interpretation of Figure 1. The nonhomogeneity of manufactures is emphasized: goods

---

[1] Kuznets and Linnemann have quantified the forces determining the growth of trade and the size of bilateral trade flows. These topics are accordingly avoided [cf. 38 and 45]. The literature on trade fluctuations is too abundant for citation here. However, I. B. Kravis and R. E. Lipsey have some work under way at the National Bureau of Economic Research which indicates that cyclical fluctuations can sometimes change the composition of national exports. For example, during the Suez crisis, American shipyards received substantial foreign orders on the basis of quick delivery, despite very disadvantageous prices.

[2] The concept of "price," as used here, means more than warehouse price. One nation may offer lower warehouse prices than another, but for lack of quality control, marketing facilities, or ability to meet delivery schedules, its effective prices may be higher. In this paper we assume that abundant exports are the necessary and sufficient indicator of low prices.

TABLE 1

Synopsis of Theories of International Trade

Basic Composition of Trade Theory	Selected Proponents	Essential Commodity Characteristics	National Attributes Pertinent to Exports of Manufactured Goods
1. Factor proportions	Heckscher, Ohlin[a]	Capital = labor ratios	Relative abundance of physical capital leads to export of capital-intensive goods; abundance of labor leads to export of labor-intensive goods.
2. Human skills	Leontief, Bhagwati, Kenen, Kravis, Keesing, Waehrer, Kenen-Yudin, Roskamp-McMeekin, Bharadwaj-Bhagwati, Lary[b]	Skill requirements of production and distribution	Relative abundance of professional personnel and highly trained labor leads to export of skill-intensive goods; abundance of unskilled labor promotes export of goods requiring few skills.
3. Scale economy	Ohlin, Dreze, Hufbauer, Keesing[c]	Extent of scale economies in production and distribution	Large home market is conducive to export of goods produced under increasing returns to scale; small home market is conducive to export of goods produced under constant returns to scale.
4. Stage of production	Import Substitution School[d]	Economic "distance" from the final consumer	Sophistication abets producers' goods exports; simplicity abets consumer goods exports, especially "light" consumer goods.

(continued)

TABLE 1 (concluded)

Basic Composition of Trade Theory	Selected Proponents	Essential Commodity Characteristics	National Attributes Pertinent to Exports of Manufactured Goods
5. Technological gap	Tucker, Kravis, Posner, Hufbauer, Douglass, Egendorf, Gruber-Mehta-Vernon, Keesing[e]	Sequential national entry to production	Early manufacture of new goods confers an export advantage; later producers must rely on lower wages or other static features to promote exports.
6. Product cycle	Hirsch, Vernon, Wells, Stobaugh[f]	Differentiation of commodities	Sophistication and early manufacture leads to export of differentiated goods; lack of sophistication leads to export of standardized goods.
7. Preference similarity	Linder[g]	Similarity between imports, exports, and production for the home market.	Trade is most intensive between countries of highly similar economic structure, least intensive between countries of very different economic structure.

Notes to Table 1

[a]E. F. Heckscher [18]. For a modern restatement, see S. Mookerjee [48a].

[b]On a theoretical plane, the skill approach·was suggested as a possible resolution of the Leontief paradox by W. W. Leontief himself (albeit in "labor efficiency" form) [41]. The same suggestion was made along more definite lines by J. Bhagwati [5]. Similar theoretical suggestions appear in P. B. Kenen [31, 32]. For the empirical thread of analysis, see: I. B. Kravis [36], D. B. Keesing [25, 26], H. Y. Waehrer [78], P. B. Kenen and E. Yudin [33], R. Bharadwaj and J. Bhagwati [6], and K. W. Roskamp and G. C. McMeekin [54], and H. B. Lary [39].

[c]The scale economy theory was mentioned by Ohlin [51, Chap. 3]. J. Dreze skillfully blends the scale economy theory with a commodity-standardization argument to explain Belgium's specialization in semifabricated industrial goods [11]. The statistical support for this argument appears in [12]. Cf. also G. C. Hufbauer [21] and D. B. Keesing [29].

[d]The stage of production thesis typically finds a place in the unspoken assumptions underlying an import substitution strategy, through the thesis is seldom endorsed openly as a normative guide to commercial policy. Cf. [12a, 14, 20, 12].

[e]The distinction between technological gap and product cycle is quite arbitrary. In particular, the R & D analysis has been assigned to technological gap, but it could as easily travel under the product cycle label. [61, 35, 52, 21, 10, 13, 16, 27].

[f]See the introduction to note (e). [19, 76, 81, 57].

change in form and quality to suit the country of manufacture. Figure 1, seen in this light, depicts nine quasidistinct commodities, three in each country, with some qualitative overlap between adjacent countries. Adaptability of domestic production to foreign consumption determines the pattern of trade. The result may be a cross-exchange between B and C of Good 3, between A and B of Good 1, with very little trade between A and C.

The propositions illustrated by Figure 1 suggest two kinds of empirical evaluation, one concerned with nature-of-trade, the other with gains-from-trade. First, to what extent do trade flows reflect economic structure? In other words, how strong are the links between characteristics embodied in trade and national attributes? Second, do imports and exports compensate for structural differences? Or, as Linder argues, do

FIGURE 1

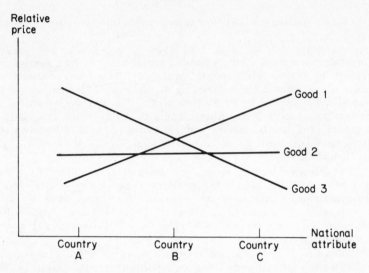

FIGURE 1

they merely extend, in a marginal way, the existing range of consumption alternatives? This paper is based on these inquiries.

THE DATA

Statistical information on trade and economic structure circa 1965 was gathered for a carefully selected group of twenty-four countries, contributing some 90 per cent of the manufactured exports from nonsocialist countries. The twenty-four nations are listed in Table 2. Eliminated in the selection process were nations with relatively small (and hence probably erratic) manufactured exports;[3] nations belonging to the socialist camp (because of closely regulated trade and lack of data);[4] and nations specializing in manufactured exports requiring nontransportable natural resources.[5] Because of this preselection process, the

---

[3] The following countries were excluded because of the small size of their manufactured exports (million dollars of 1965 manufactured exports and percentage of total exports in parentheses): Greece ($44.4; 14 per cent); Brazil ($124.3; 8 per cent); Colombia ($34.8; 6 per cent); Ghana ($3.3; 1 per cent); Iraq ($6.4; 1 per cent).

[4] Although a member of the socialist camp, Yugoslavia is included.

[5] The following nations were excluded because of their specialization in resource-intensive manufactures (product and percentage of country's manufac-

trade theories perform better than if applied to a more haphazard collection of nations.[6] Furthermore, each theory receives, in the alternative, the benefit of one ad hoc exclusion: the one country most at variance with the predictions of each theory is dropped in order to obtain an alternative evaluation of the twenty-three "best" nations.

Commodities were classified both according to the 28 two-digit divisions and the 102 three-digit categories identified in sections 5, 6, 7, and 8 of the revised Standard International Trade Classification (SITC) [63]. (See Appendix Table 2.) The three-digit classification was preferred for analytic purposes. Import and export statistics were generally taken from United Nations sources [64, 80].

SITC sections 5, 6, 7, and 8 exclude many goods, such as processed foods, which are defined as manufactures in the United Nations International Standard Industrial Classification (ISIC). Most such exclusions relate to products with a large, nontransportable, natural resource content.[7]

Table A-2 (Appendix Table 2) presents characteristics for the commodities enumerated in the two-digit and three-digit SITC. Many hazards surround these estimates. Difficulties associated with particular qualities are touched upon later, but certain common problems deserve mention here.

To begin with, the qualities, with the exception of the "consumer goods ratio," were estimated from American experience, an expedient but potentially risky procedure.[8] A frequently mounted theoretical objec-

tured exports are given in parentheses): Finland (wood, paper, 60 per cent); South Africa (assorted metals, minerals, 65 per cent); Turkey (nonferrous metals, 61 per cent); Chile (nonferrous metals, 94 per cent); Malaya-Singapore (nonferrous metals, 67 per cent); Kenya-Uganda-Tanganyika (nonferrous metals, 36 per cent); Nigeria (nonferrous metals, 84 per cent).

[6] This statement mainly applies to evaluation on the basis of Spearman rank correlations. If export-weighted rank correlations are used, then the deviations of the excluded countries become less troublesome, since their role in world manufactures trade is typically much smaller than the included countries.

[7] Even so, the manufactures portion of the SITC includes some highly resource-intensive goods, for example group 68, primary nonferrous metals, while it wrongly excludes both synthetic rubber and man-made fiber. For practical reasons, we have taken the SITC manufactures definition as it stands. The addition of man-made fiber and synthetic rubber and the deletion of nonferrous metals were contemplated too late for incorporation in the calculations.

[8] Furthermore, U.S. 1965 export values were used as weights to convert three-digit characteristics to a two-digit basis. (Two-digit data on skill ratios were estimated directly from United States experience.) However, since two-digit

tion to the use of American coefficients is that widespread "factor intensity reversals" or, more generally, "product characteristic reversals," may mark a world of vastly different factor prices and production circumstances. I happen not to believe this ingenious theoretical objection, but I do not intend to reexamine the controversy here. My skeptical views on capital-labor reversals were stated in 1963,[9] and the work published since then confirms my original suspicion. With regard to the other product characteristics of Table A-2, I am predisposed to an equally skeptical view. Keesing's cross-country analysis of skill coefficients [28; also see 48] and the cross-country examination of wage rates carried out later in this paper both suggest that "skill reversals" are relatively unimportant. Since innovation is a unique event, reversals become theoretically irrelevant in the case of first trade dates; the main difficulty there lies in obtaining the true dates. Japanese-American evidence, mentioned later, indicates that consumer goods ratios are not susceptible to the reversal phenomenon, while, from an a priori standpoint, product differentiation reversals seem most unlikely. A more agnostic attitude is perhaps warranted for scale economies.

The almost total reliance on American coefficients raises, it seems to me, more practical dangers than the reversal threat. Owing to statistical inadequacies and aberrations, some of the characteristics may be improperly measured. Furthermore, the range of values for a particular characteristic may differ somewhat between nations. If coefficients from various nations had been calculated on the three-digit SITC basis, it might be possible to spot the obvious national discrepancies, and also to estimate a set of characteristic coefficients representing the "average" exporting nation.

The dangers of relying on American coefficients are self-evident. Moreover, most characteristics were derived from industry data, not commodity data, even though only an approximate correspondence exists between industrial and commodity classification schemes. A rough-and-ready key developed here for matching the two classification

---

SITC characteristics are barely used in the statistical analysis, and since collateral experiments with Japanese export weights yield much the same two-digit coefficients, this feature seems comparatively unimportant.

[9] See G. C. Hufbauer [21]. The Cambridge University thesis underlying this book was written in 1963, and Appendix B was independently circulated at that time.

TABLE 2

Characteristics Embodied in 1965 Exports

	Capital per Man	Skill Ratio	Wages per Man	Scale Economies	Consumer Goods Ratio[a]	First Trade Date	Product Differentiation
Canada	17,529	.0811	6,583	.0439	.1957	1947.6	.8068
United States	11,441	.1062	6,506	.0596	.2748	1948.4	.9558
Austria	12,423	.0732	5,926	.0372	.2846	1947.1	.8680
Belgium	14,043	.0762	6,202	.0366	.2488	1946.3	.7645
Denmark	8,832	.0932	5,901	.0380	.2993	1948.0	.9849
France	12,480	.0891	6,176	.0455	.2965	1947.2	.8385
Germany	11,734	.1011	6,410	.0430	.2260	1947.8	.9166
Italy	10,379	.0828	5,801	.0333	.3465	1946.8	.8243
Netherlands	11,768	.0969	6,007	.0456	.3327	1947.5	.9116
Norway	16,693	.0860	6,396	.0200	.1665	1946.5	.8593
Sweden	12,873	.0883	6,460	.0463	.2002	1948.3	.9291
United Kingdom	10,868	.0962	6,264	.0435	.2556	1947.9	.8815
Australia	15,181	.0891	6,458	.0242	.1971	1946.8	.7997
Japan	11,006	.0830	5,887	.0313	.3067	1947.4	.8624
Israel	6,317	.0608	4,860	.0282	.3144	1946.6	.7910
Portugal	7,862	.0514	4,777	.0130	.4858	1945.5	.7489
Spain	11,353	.0847	5,735	.0209	.3257	1944.9	.8508
Yugoslavia	10,030	.0826	5,741	.0120	.2799	1945.9	.8498
Mexico	17,926	.0799	6,149	-.0236	.2512	1945.8	.7518
Hong Kong	4,315	.0431	4,049	-.0162	.6624	1946.0	.6701
India	7,339	.0330	4,493	-.0157	.6195	1945.8	.6020
Korea	8,004	.0354	4,761	.0011	.4614	1946.5	.6271
Pakistan	5,725	.0298	4,238	-.0036	.6476	1946.0	.5925
Taiwan	11,697	.0557	5,018	.0200	.4748	1947.2	.6829

Notes to Table 2

Note: Embodied characteristics for 1965 exports were generally found by applying 1965 three-digit SITC export values to the three-digit commodity characteristics in Table A-2. Since three-digit data on skill ratios were not available, two-digit export values were used in that case. For certain countries, 1965 export data was not available in time for the analysis, and 1964 data was used instead. Embodied characteristic j for country i is given as $\sum_{n} c_{jn} \cdot x_{in}$, where c_{in} is is characteristic j as it appears in commodity n, and x_{in} is the percentage of country i's exports accounted for by commodity n.

[a]Calculated with uncorrected values; see note (f) to Table A-2.

schemes is produced in Table A-1 (Appendix Table 1). Another difficulty is that although manufactured goods embody characteristics acquired by purchased supplies drawn from ancillary industries, our analysis runs entirely in terms of "immediate" characteristics.[10]

The qualities enumerated in Table A-2, when applied to each nation's trade composition for 1965, yield the mosaic of embodied characteristics given in Tables 2 and 3.[11] These tables, together with

[10] An input-output distinction divides "immediate," "direct," and "total" characteristics. Immediate characteristics are qualities of the product itself; direct characteristics are qualites of the product plus qualities of its direct inputs. Total characteristics are qualities of the product plus qualities of its direct and indirect inputs. Whether immediate, direct, or total characteristics best suit the needs of trade theory depends on the import content of domestic manufactures. "Domestic" characteristics constitute the ideal analytic tool: all characteristics except those inherited from imported inputs. Domestic characteristics must, of course, fall somewhere between immediate and total characteristics. To the extent domestic characteristics are correlated with immediate characteristics, the use of immediate characteristics is not so bad. High correlations are suggested by the following matrices which show the connection between immediate (I), direct (D), and total (T) capital and wages per man according to 1963 American experience, using the 1958 input-output table; the data are based on the sources enumerated in Table 12.

Rank Correlations

	Capital per man				Wages per man		
	I	*D*	*T*		*I*	*D*	*T*
I	1.000			*I*	1.000		
D	.973	1.000		*D*	.993	1.000	
T	.955	.992	1.000	*T*	.988	.955	1.000

[11] An embodied characteristic is found by multiplying the trade characteristics vector by the export or import percentage composition vector and summing the result.

TABLE 3

Characteristics Embodied in 1965 Imports

	Capital per Man	Skill Ratio	Wages per Man	Scale Economies	Consumer Goods Ratio[a]	First Trade Date	Product Differentiation
Canada	11,051	.0976	6,404	.0464	.2517	1948.2	.8980
United States	13,139	.0771	6,023	.0306	.2913	1946.6	.7995
Austria	11,284	.0937	6,127	.0356	.2758	1947.7	.8684
Belgium	11,462	.0902	6,121	.0345	.2681	1947.2	.8466
Denmark	12,366	.0894	6,155	.0418	.2738	1947.4	.8559
France	13,290	.0930	6,317	.0381	.2404	1947.1	.8825
Germany	13,161	.0779	6,006	.0276	.3074	1946.4	.8061
Italy	13,815	.0982	6,412	.0380	.2584	1947.1	.8985
Netherlands	11,706	.0896	6,057	.0387	.2994	1947.3	.8698
Norway	10,476	.0983	6,199	.0276	.2337	1947.7	.9580
Sweden	11,373	.0923	6,147	.0358	.2795	1947.3	.8674
United Kingdom	12,832	.0832	6,000	.0224	.2739	1946.4	.8591
Australia	11,552	.0951	6,294	.0495	.2803	1948.1	.8763
Japan	14,010	.1033	6,445	.0399	.2589	1946.3	.9148
Israel	10,172	.0886	6,052	.0438	.2228	1948.0	.9107
Portugal	12,039	.0976	6,311	.0467	.2306	1947.7	.8852
Spain	14,162	.0979	6,497	.0418	.1897	1947.6	.9312
Yugoslavia	13,285	.0950	6,451	.0464	.2028	1947.5	.9156
Mexico	12,745	.1119	6,603	.0465	.2105	1948.4	.9729
Hong Kong	10,780	.0770	5,618	.0272	.3625	1947.1	.8442
India	12,019	.1028	6,553	.0513	.1692	1948.1	1.0122
Korea	14,900	.1112	5,887	.0520	.2239	1944.0	.8068
Pakistan	12,371	.0989	6,419	.0448	.1837	1947.1	.9380
Taiwan	13,062	.1066	6,467	.0505	.2102	1947.4	.9175

Notes to Table 3

Note: Embodied characteristics for 1965 imports were generally found by applying 1965 three-digit SITC import values to the three-digit commodity characteristics in Table A-2. The exceptions mentioned in the note to Table 2 pertain here as well. The arithmetic formulation is identical to that given in the note to Table 2, except that import percentages are used instead of export percentages.

[a]Calculated with uncorrected values; see note (f) to Table A-2.

Table 4 on national attributes, furnish the statistical foundation for assessing the first six "orthodox" nature-of-trade theories enumerated in Table 1. In evaluating the product cycle theories, it might have been preferable to use time series data rather than trade for a single year, but this would have required a far more ambitious undertaking. It should be mentioned that certain national attributes—particularly fixed capital per man for several less developed countries and availability of skilled employees in France, Germany, the United Kingdom, and Australia—were "estimated" from "similar" countries. These estimates, marked by note e in Table 4, may be biased in favor of the pertinent theories.

A better procedure, in finding national export characteristics, would have been to use export *value added* (preferably at world prices) for each commodity, rather than export *receipts* for that commodity, as the ingredient of national export composition. As M. Michaely and P. T. Knight observe, export receipts *minus* the world market cost of purchased inputs should ideally serve as the export composition vector. The use of straight export receipts would not be so bad for large countries (which import relatively few inputs), if commodity characteristics had been measured on a "total" rather than an "immediate" basis. Thus, if commodity characteristics had included the characteristics acquired from ancillary industries, both the characteristics of a commodity and the receipts from its sale by big nations would be placed on approximately the same footing. As it happens, the analysis here includes many small countries, and commodity characteristics are measured on an "immediate" basis. The best reconciliation, therefore, would be the employment of export value-added weights in aggregating export characteristics derived from different commodities. To the extent value-added ratios differ between commodities, the use of export receipts in deriving the embodied characteristics of Table 2 produces a distorted image.

TABLE 4

National Attributes

	Fixed Capital per Manufacturing Employee[a]	Skilled Employees as Per Cent of Total[b]	Total Manufacturing Output[c]	GDP per Capita[d]
Canada	8,850	.106	10.55	2,110
United States	7,950	.108	173.04	3,000
Austria	4,000	.068	2.90	1,030
Belgium	4,400	.080	4.11	1,460
Denmark	2,850	.078	2.38	1,680
France	4,900	.083[e]	27.53	1,580
Germany	4,250	.100[e]	40.61	1,770
Italy	2,600	.046	17.40	1,030
Netherlands	4,750	.092	5.55	1,430
Norway	6,100	.080	1.81	1,880
Sweden	5,400	.129	5.62	2,100
United Kingdom	4,000	.095[e]	32.22	1,710
Australia	5,300	.103[e]	5.63	1,810
Japan	3,100	.049	21.56	720
Israel	3,900	.114	0.67	1,090
Portugal	1,500	.027	1.56	420
Spain	1,700	.041	4.44	550
Yugoslavia	2,500	.056	1.95	250
Mexico	2,000	.036	4.75	430
Hong Kong	1,200[e]	.046	0.37[e]	200[e]
India	500[e]	.017	6.84	80
Korea	850	.022	0.51	140
Pakistan	500[e]	.014	0.78	80
Taiwan	1,150	.031	0.32	130

[a]Fixed capital per manufacturing employee, expressed in U.S. dollars of approximately 1958 vintage, was estimated by summing current outlays for gross manufacturing investment between 1953 and 1964 inclusive, and dividing by 1964 manufacturing employment. No explicit allowance was made for depreciation or inflation. Local monetary units were converted to U.S. dollars using mid-period (generally 1958) exchange rates. Among other ad hoc corrections, the United Kingdom figure was arbitrarily increased from an original estimate of $3,150 per man, and the Yugoslavian figure was arbi-

(continued)

158   Hypotheses and Tests of Trade Patterns

Notes to Table 4 (concluded)

trarily decreased from an original estimate of $4,050 per man, both on grounds of "reasonableness." Obviously all estimates must be regarded as crude orders of magnitude. The underlying data was taken from United Nations Statistical Office [66]. Fixed capital per manufacturing employee is used to evaluate the simplistic factor proportions theory.

[b]Skilled employees as a per cent of total employees represent the fraction of the economically active population belonging to Group O of the ILO classification scheme, that is, professional, scientific, and technical personnel. The data come from International Labour Office [22]. (The skilled employee ratio is used to assess the human skills thesis.)

[c]Manufacturing output, expressed in billions of U.S. dollars, was found by applying the United Nations estimates of percentage of gross domestic product originating in the manufacturing sector to the GDP figures. The source for both sets is the United Nations Statistical Office [66]. Total manufacturing output is used to assess the scale economy and stage of production theories.

[d]Gross domestic product figures, expressed in thousands of U.S. dollars, generally apply to the year 1964, but some pertain to 1963. Purchasing power exchange rates, as estimated by the United Nations, were employed for conversion purposes. The data source is [66]. GDP per capita is used to evaluate both the technological gap and product cycle theories.

[e]Values represent arbitrary extrapolation from "similar" countries.

The basic statistical tool employed to assess the impact of structure on trade is the correlation coefficient: the more influence an aspect of economic structure exercises on commerce, the better should be the correlation between the particular national attribute and the trade-embodied characteristic. Both rank and simple correlations are presented. The rank correlation does not depend on the assumptions of normality required for the simple correlation; it avoids high coefficients based solely on a "dumbbell" effect between India and Pakistan at the one extreme, and the United States, Canada, and Sweden at the other. On the other hand, the rank correlation is a less efficient tool; it sacrifices part of the information contained in the underlying data.

The Spearman rank correlation takes no notice of the relative trading importance of different countries, so the danger exists in using this measure that well or badly behaved small countries may contribute

TABLE 5

Rank Correlations Between Commodity Characteristics and Associated National Attributes

| | Commodity Characteristics Embodied in Exports[a] | | | | | | | | | | | | | |
| | Capital per Man | | Skill Ratio | | Wages per Man | | Scale Economies | | Consumer Goods Ratio | | First Trade Date | | Product Differentiation | |
	R	W	R	W	R	W	R	W	R	W	R	W	R	W
Fixed capital:														
24 nations	.704	.736												
23 nations[c]	.814(Mexico)													
Skilled employees:														
24 nations			.695	.822	.784	.960								
23 nations[c]			.796(Israel)		.912(Israel)									
Manufacturing output:														
24 nations							.627	.778						
23 nations[c]							.710(India)							
GDP per capita:														
24 nations									.818	.801	.698	.864	.724	.763
23 nations[c]									.864(Mexico)		.764(Taiwan)		.788(Canada)	

Notes To Table 5

Sources: Tables 2 and 4.

[a]R is the Spearman correlation coefficient:

$$R = 1 - \left(\frac{6 \, \Sigma \, d_i^2}{n^3 - n} \right).$$

W is the weighted rank correlation coefficient:

$$W = 1 - \left(\frac{6 \, \Sigma \, d_i^2 \, w_i}{n^2 - 1} \right).$$

where d_i is the difference in rank orderings for country i; w_i is the percentage of 1965 manufacturing exports contributed by country i; n is the number of countries. When two or more observations were tied, they were assigned an average of the relevant ranks.

[b]The signs of the consumer-goods-ratio rank correlations have been reversed, so a positive correlation indicates agreement with theoretical predictions. The correlations here reflect the uncorrected ratio values; see note (f) to Table A-2.

[c]The country excluded in the twenty-three-nation Spearman rank correlation analysis is named in parenthesis.

more weight to the total impression than they are entitled to do. Therefore, "weighted" rank correlations are also presented, where 1965 national export values furnish the weights.[12]

Spearman and weighted rank correlations between characteristics embodied in exports and the associated national attributes, for the full sample of twenty-four nations and (for Spearman only) allowing each theory "one cut," are given in Table 5. (All the figures are statistically significant at the 1 per cent level, using the Student's t test [49].) Simple correlations between each characteristic and all the national attributes appear in Table 6.

It must be acknowledged that the chosen statistical tools afford little

---

[12] The weighted rank correlation formula is given in the notes to Table 5. The weighted rank correlation, unlike the Spearman coefficient, is not symmetrical about the value zero. If one rank list is reversed, the new coefficient will not necessarily have the same absolute value as the original coefficient. Furthermore, the weighted correlation can take on values less than -1.0.

TABLE 6

Simple Correlations Between Commodity Characteristics and National Attributes of Twenty-Four Nations

	Capital Per Man	Skill Ratio	Wages Per Man	Scale Economies	Consumer Goods Ratio[a]	First Trade Date	Product Differentiation
Commodity Characteristics Embodied in Exports							
Fixed capital	.625	.696	.789	.739	.748	.657	.633
Skilled employees	.396*	.714	.700	.760	.736	.725	.717
Manufacturing output	.067*	.437*	.345*	.457*	.192*	.480*	.392*
GDP per capita	.500*	.777	.799	.809	.727	.765	.749
Commodity Characteristics Embodied in Imports							
Fixed capital	-.353*	-.409*	-.171*	-.383*	-.414*	.166*	-.321*
Skilled employees	-.429*	-.604	-.375*	-.463*	-.535	.139*	-.436*
Manufacturing output	.232*	-.476*	-.193*	-.374	-.274*	-.229*	-.428*
GDP per capita	-.257*	-.552	-.283*	-.516	-.505*	.054*	-.458*

Note: Values in boldface represent the simple correlations comparable to the twenty-four-nation Spearman correlations of Table 5.

Sources: Tables 2, 3, and 4.

[a]The signs of the consumer-goods-ratio simple correlations have been reversed, so a positive correlation indicates agreement with theoretical predictions on the export side, and a negative correlation indicates theoretical agreement on the import side. The correlations here reflect the uncorrected ratio values; see note (f) to Table A-2.

*Not statistically significant at the 1 per cent confidence level, using the Student's *t* test.

more than a crude screen for eliminating unsatisfactory theories. No real attempt can be made, using such measures, to say which of several closely competing theories is "best." Nor can any definitive statements be made about the welfare aspects of trade. These exercises would require rather more sophisticated analysis, possibly cast in terms of Bruno's work on dynamic comparative advantage.[13]

The analysis here focuses on exports because exports are typically less distorted by domestic policies than imports. Even so, as a guide to comparative advantage, exports suffer from at least three difficulties. First, tariffs and quotas severely limit certain international markets, for example, cotton textiles. Textile characteristics are accordingly understated in the exports of nations with a textile advantage. Second, a nation's own import restrictions affect its export composition by drawing resources directly and indirectly from the export industries. If a skill-intensive activity enjoys high domestic protection, that will retard those exports also dependent on skills. Third, Linnemann has shown that geographical and psychological distance adversely affect trade [45]. By implication, Country A will export a different menu of commodities if located in Region I than if located in Region II. Because it would multiply the analytic task many times, location has been ignored in the present statistical work. However, as Bhagwati has rightly stressed, the bilateral dimension can hardly be overlooked in evaluating the nature of trade [5]. Occasional qualitative references are made here to bilateral trade relations on the sound presumption that location affects overall export composition. But it is clear that future scholars should explicitly incorporate the bilateral variable in their analysis.

NATURE OF TRADE

The same elephant?

Table 1 enumerates six supposedly distinct, "orthodox" trade theories. But perhaps these accounts merely provide alternative glimpses of the same elephant. To the extent of intercorrelation between the

---

[13] M. Bruno, "Development Policy and Dynamic Comparative Advantage," this volume.

characteristics listed in Table A-2, the six theories—or at least our presentations of them—differ more in degree than in kind.

Table 7 presents Spearman rank correlations between commodities ordered according to different characteristics. The argument has been suggested that the unimportant groups among the 102 three-digit SITC commodities may, however, unduly influence these Spearman correlations. Therefore, Table 8 presents weighted rank correlations between the commodity characteristics. The weights are 1965 exports, so the weighted correlations give less emphasis to rank differences between small traded commodities than between big ones. As it happens, the Spearman and the weighted rank correlations yield roughly the same impression.

Both Tables 7 and 8 reveal some significant interrelationships between the commodity characteristics. Skill ratios and wages per man show a positive correlation ranging between .579 and .642. The surprising thing, perhaps, is that the relationship is not more robust. Data compiled by Waehrer yield a correlation of about 0.78 between an occupational index and annual earnings by industry [39, pp. 36–37]. A major difference between her results and ours seems to stem from the more comprehensive character of her occupational index. Her index includes professional and technical workers; managers, officials, and proprietors; clerical workers; sales workers; craftsmen and foremen; and service workers—in other words, virtually all high-earning employees. Our skill ratio, by contrast, relates only to professional and technical workers, because Keesing found that the other categories of "skilled employees," with the possible exception of craftsmen and foremen, contribute little to an understanding of trade flows.[14]

Capital per man shows a strong correlation with both indices of "human capital." At the same time, physical and human capital are related to the stage of production. In other words, the consumer-producer goods dichotomy (reflecting "stage of production") overlaps a good deal with the light-heavy industry dichotomy. The overlap applies

[14] Keesing discovered that the proportion of managerial labor embodied in exports changes little between nations, and concluded that professional, technical, and craft labor taken by themselves were better indications of skills embodied in trade [26]. Our analysis likewise excludes managerial labor both from the skill ratio (Table A-2) and the measure of national skill endowments (Table 4).

TABLE 7

Spearman Correlations Between Commodity Characteristics

	Capital per Man	Skill Ratio[a]	Wages per Man	Scale Economies	Consumer Goods Ratio[b]	First Trade Date	Product Differentiation
Capital per man	1.000						
Skill ratio[a]	.590	1.000					
Wages per man	.695	.642	1.000				
Scale economies	-.058*	.165*	.094*	1.000			
Consumer goods ratio[b]	.479	.204*	.418	-.150*	1.000		
First trade date	.105*	.236*	.220*	.157*	.123*	1.000	
Product differentiation	-.119*	.547	.199*	.061*	.039*	.169*	1.000

Note: Commodity characteristics were ranked as follows: capital per man — highest capital-labor ratio to lowest; scale economies — largest increasing returns to scale to smallest; consumer goods ratio — lowest proportion of output going for final consumption to highest; skill ratio — greatest use of technical labor to smallest; wages per man — highest wages to lowest; first trade date — newest products to oldest; product differentiation — most differentiated products to least differentiated products.

The correlations are derived using the Spearman formula. When two or more observations were tied, they were assigned an average of the relevant ranks.

Source: Table A-2.

[a]The correlations between skill ratio and other characteristics are based on the two-digit SITC, since three-digit skill data was not available. All other correlations are based on the three-digit SITC.

[b]See note (f) to Table A-2.

*Not significantly different from zero at the 1 per cent confidence level.

not only to industries light and heavy in machine power, but also to industries light and heavy in brain power. The same trading patterns that confirm or deny the factor proportions theory will thus also tend

TABLE 8

Weighted Rank Correlations Between Commodity Characteristics

	Capital per Man	Skill Ratio[a]	Wages per Man	Scale Economies	Consumer Goods Ratio[b]	First Trade Date	Product Differentiation
Capital per man	1.000						
Skill ratio[a]	.547	1.000					
Wages per man	.655	.579	1.000				
Scale economies	.298	.501	.374	1.000			
Consumer goods ratio[b]	.505	.234*	.513	.191*	1.000		
First trade date	.111*	.377*	.349	.366	.086	1.000	
Product differentiation	-.173*	.686	.018*	.077*	.054*	.011*	1.000

Note: Commodity characteristics were ranked as in Table 7, note. The weighted rank correlation formula is described in note a to Table 5. The weights are total 1965 exports of each three-digit SITC commodity by the twenty-four countries listed in Table 2.

Source: Table A-2.

[a]See Table 7, note a.

[b]See Table A-2, note f.

*Not significantly different from zero at the 1 per cent confidence level, using the same test as for Spearman correlations.

to support or undermine the human skills argument and the stage of production thesis.

Differentiated commodities seem to require skilled labor, so from the outset these two theories have an area of overlap. Scale economies are also linked with skill ratios, judging from the weighted rank correlations. Among the other bilateral characteristic pairs, some correlations are significant, but none is very strong.

Whenever strong intercorrelation appears between two characteristics, the question may arise: does theory X owe its good performance to theory Y, or vice versa? To this question, probably the best answer is: a confluence of theory makes for good results. At any rate, we have not attempted here to resolve such disputes. The question, if it must be answered in "either-or" fashion, demands more than a search for the marginally higher correlation coefficient.

So much for interrelationships between commodity characteristics. What about attributes of economic structure? Table 9 presents a matrix of intercorrelations between the four attributes used here: fixed capital per man in manufacturing industry; skilled employees as a per cent of labor force; total manufacturing output; and gross domestic product

TABLE 9

Spearman and Simple Correlations Between National Attributes

	Fixed Capital per Man in Manufacturing Industry		Skilled Employees as Per Cent of Labor Force		Total Manufacturing Output		Gross GDP per Capita	
	R	S	R	S	R	S	R	S
Fixed capital per man in manufacturing industry	1.000	1.000						
Skilled employees as per cent of labor force	.889	.848	1.000	1.000				
Total manufacturing output	.545	.480*	.469*	.334*	1.000	1.000		
GDP per capita	.947	.914	.892	.879	.579	.581	1.000	1.000

Note: R is the Spearman correlation; S is the simple correlation. All attributes are ordered from largest to smallest. In the rank correlations, when two or more observations were tied, they were assigned an average of the relevant ranks.

Source: Table 4.

*Not significantly different from zero at the 1 per cent confidence level.

per capita. Total manufacturing output presumably influences scale economies in exports. Gross domestic product per capita serves as a catch-all measure of technological sophistication, thereby influencing the age, standardization, and consumer-producer mix of exports. Six trade theories are thus evaluated against four national attributes, one of which does triple duty.

With the exception of total manufacturing output, the attributes show considerable interrelationship, either on a rank or a simple correlation basis. For practical purposes a composite attribute might perform almost as well, or as poorly, in explaining different export characteristics.

Finally, it deserves mention that the commodity export patterns of the largest, richest industrial nations display great similarity. Indeed, as a general proposition, the richer a pair of countries, the greater the coincidence between their export patterns (Table A-4 and the analysis in Table 13 below). Thus, the cosines between U.S., U.K., and German export vectors all exceed 0.9, although these are the extreme cases.[15] The theories that "work" for the United States will "work" for Germany and the United Kingdom, and vice versa. The coincidence of cosine vectors points to the origin of theoretical success at the rich end of the country scale: a similar pattern of commodity exports rather than different patterns embodying the same characteristics.

FACTOR PROPORTIONS

In 1969, the factor proportions account celebrates its fiftieth birthday. The subject of as many scholarly papers since 1919, the theory in its present form can claim an academic parentage resembling a Burke's Peerage of Economists. It deserves special notice that the theory, as enunciated by Ohlin, was a very much more complex and realistic account than the truncated oversimplified two-factor version later employed by its adaptors and critics (including myself). For expositional purposes, nevertheless, we shall consider only the two-factor "parody" and not the more realistic thesis set forth by Ohlin.

Leontief's findings [41, 42] dealt an apparently telling blow to the simplistic two-factor version. Various authorities have sought to repair

---

[15] The cosine analysis of trade vectors is explained in the penultimate section of this paper. The discussion there refers to national import vs. export vectors; the application here is to national export vectors.

the damage; their work in some respects resembles the tortured efforts of pre-Copernican astronomers.[16] "Factor-intensity reversals," for example, are an ingenious but doubtful sort of patching plaster.[17] Other explanations, emphasizing the resource content of American trade [39] and the perverse structure of American tariffs,[18] are a good deal more persuasive.

Leontief's original report was based on the 1947 capital position of U.S. industries, the 1947 U.S. transactions table, and 1947 U.S. trade flows; subsequently he examined 1951 trade flows as well. Conceivably World War II might have distorted the American economy and world trade patterns so as to give unrepresentative results. Before examining the twenty-four-nation data, therefore, I checked Leontief's findings against more recent data, limiting myself, however, to manufactures variously defined.

The confirmation exercise made use of 1963 U.S. fixed capital data, the 1958 U.S. transactions table, and 1963 trade flows. The most questionable statistics are those for fixed capital. To derive these figures, capital outlays between 1947 and 1963 were added to the 1947 Leontief estimates, after correcting for inflation and depreciation. The resulting capital-per-man estimates differ substantially in absolute value from Leontief's figures, and also from the Census Bureau's 1958 "book value" figures [67]. Nevertheless, Spearman rank correlations between the three sets of figures for the industries concerned all exceed 0.88.

Table 10 presents results from the confirmation exercise. The conclusions for 1963 are broadly similar to Leontief's original findings. American imports embody approximately the same quantum of capital

---

[16] Advocates of the Ptolemaic System used epicycles and deferents to square fact with theory. T. S. Kuhn [37].

[17] International empirical evidence against the factor-intensity reversal proposition has been marshalled by H. B. Lary [39]. J. R. Moroney also shows, on interregional evidence, that reversals are something of a red herring [50]. See also the discussion in the addendum to J. Bhagwati's survey [5].

[18] W. P. Travis [60]. B. Balassa found no correlation between effective tariff rates and labor-intensity [3]. However, he used an inappropriate measure of labor-intensity—share of wage payments (direct and indirect) in value of output. This measure confuses skilled labor with crude labor power: an industry may have a large wage proportion owing not to the *numbers* of men employed but rather to the *high* wages per man. If industries are instead ranked according to wages per man, the rank correlation between effective tariffs and wages is −.568. Cf. D. S. Ball [4]. However, for present purposes, a conceptually superior approach would be to rank industries by capital per man.

TABLE 10

Fixed Capital Per Man Embodied in U.S. Manufactures Trade

Year[a]	Definition[b]	Requirements[c]	U.S. Exports[d]	U.S. Imports[d]
1947	para-ISIC	Total	9,048	11,306
1947	para-SITC	Total	10,127	9,287
1951	para-ISIC	Total	9,256	12,412
1951	para-SITC	Total	11,493	10,129
1963	ISIC	Immediate	12,235	14,892
1963	ISIC	Direct	12,292	14,461
1963	ISIC	Total	12,051	13,396
1963	SITC	Immediate	10,632	11,253
1963	SITC	Direct	10,900	11,480
1963	SITC	Total	11,467	11,399

Sources: W. W. Leontief [42, 43]; U.S. Bureau of the Census [69, 74]; H.B. Lary [40].

[a]The date refers to the calendar year for which trade is analyzed, not necessarily the input-output table year or the year for which capital estimates were made.

[b]This column refers to whether manufactures are defined in accordance with the ISIC, Sections 20 through 39, or the more restrictive SITC, Sections 5, 6, 7, and 8. The para-ISIC definition refers to Leontief [42], p. 397, row C4, which encompasses ISIC Sections 20 through 39 plus mining. The para-SITC definition refers to Leontief [42], p. 398, row D, which encompasses SITC sections 5, 6, 7, and 8, plus certain types of mining, food products, and petroleum products. This para-SITC definition consciously excludes certain resource-intensive products that are prominent in imports but not those that are prominent in exports. Hence the comparison is artificially biased toward a high capital figure in exports.

[c]The requirements column indicates whether capital per man is measured only according to what is used in the industry, according to what is used in the industry plus its direct suppliers, or according to what is used in the industry plus its direct and indirect suppliers.

[d]Embodied capital in exports and imports is measured in dollars of 1947 vintage for both 1947 and 1951, and 1963 vintage for 1963.

as American exports. If manufactures are defined according to the SITC, rather than the resource-inclusive ISIC, or if "total" rather than "immediate" requirements are examined, exports take on a more capital-intensive hue. If allowance could be made for the bias of American tariff and quota policy, an orthodox capital intensity differential might even emerge. Nevertheless, it is difficult to believe that variations in fixed capital per man provide the mainspring for American commerce. Many authors have manipulated the figures, but no one has yet shown that U.S. exports enjoy a *pronounced* capital-intensity lead over imports.[19]

In a similar vein, Tatemoto and Ichimura found that 1951 Japanese exports were more capital-intensive than 1951 imports, while Roskamp discovered just the opposite for 1954 West German trade.[20] Given the position of Japan and Germany in any world league of capital endowments, the authors conclude that Leontief's paradox is not confined to U.S. commerce.

To be sure, these single-nation export-versus-import results can be rationalized by introducing new variables. The perverse Japanese findings turn on the difference between exporting "up" and "down"—to Europe and North America and to regions less developed than Japan. "Downward" sales comprised 75 per cent of 1951 Japanese exports, so a capital-intensive bias may be attributed to regional considerations and might disappear if the analysis were conducted in terms of bilateral trade flows.[21] Indeed, Tatemoto and Ichimura found that 1951 Japanese exports to the United States were, in orthodox fashion, more capital-intensive than imports from that country. Germany's Leontief paradox was "resolved" in 1968 by Roskamp and McMeekin through the introduction of a human capital variable, along the lines applied earlier to the Leontief paradox in United States trade.[22] A bilateral dimension, although not introduced in the Roskamp-McMeekin analysis, might shed further light on the German paradox.

---

[19] See the thorough analysis by H. B. Lary [40].

[20] M. Tatemoto and S. Ichimura [59], and K. W. Roskamp [53]. Other single-country studies of the Leontief paradox, not considered here, are: R. Bharadwaj [7, 8] (Leontief paradox refuted for Indian trade); W. Stolper and K. W. Roskamp [58] (Leontief paradox refuted, considering the bilateral direction of East German trade); and D. F. Wahl [79] (Leontief paradox refuted for Canadian-U.K. trade, and confirmed—ignoring the role of natural resources—for Canadian-U.S. trade).

[21] The important distinction between "upward" and "downward" exports, a distinction which needs to be generally incorporated in trade theory, was emphasized by W. P. Travis [60, pp. 194–96].

[22] See K. W. Roskamp and G. C. McMeekin [54] and the work of Kravis, Keesing, and others cited in Table 1.

By contrast with these single-nation results, which require ad hoc explanation, it is interesting that the simplistic factor proportions theory performs surprisingly well when applied to the exports *alone* of the twenty-four-nation sample. The Spearman rank correlation between national fixed capital per man [23] and capital embodied in national exports is .704; the weighted correlation is .736 (Table 5). The simple correlation between fixed capital and capital in exports is .625 (Table 6). Removed from the country sample, of course, have been developing nations with large nonferrous metals exports such as Turkey, Chile, Malaya-Singapore, Kenya-Uganda-Tanganyika, and Nigeria. Nonferrous metals are both highly capital-intensive and closely tied to ore bodies; hence their presence in the exports of capital-poor countries gives an unwarranted impression of capital-intensity.

Indeed, on much the same grounds, Mexico should also be excluded, since nonferrous metal goods comprise 35 per cent of Mexico's manufactured exports. When Mexico is dropped under the "one-cut" rule, the Spearman correlation rises to .814. After Mexico has been excluded, Taiwan, the United States, and Israel deviate most from the predictions of the simple theory. The United States and Israel have much less capital embodied in their exports than the size of their capital stocks would indicate, while Taiwan has much more.

Although the foregoing analysis ignores imports, it might be mentioned that, using United States coefficients, 1965 Japanese exports appear considerably less capital-intensive than imports ($11,006 vs. $14,010 capital per man, cf. Tables 2 and 3). These results, while seemingly contrary to the 1951 Tatemoto-Ichimura results, are nevertheless consistent with their findings: by 1965, more than 50 per cent of Japanese exports were destined "upward" to the advanced nations, compared with only 25 per cent in 1951. On the other hand, Roskamp's 1954 German results (making no allowance for a bilateral dimension)

---

[23] Rank correlations between fixed capital per man in manufactures (F), horsepower per man in manufactures (H), and total capital per capita (T), all circa 1958–63, are as follows:

	F	H	T
F	1.000		
H	.979	1.000	
T	.958	.924	1.000

Horsepower estimates could be made for only sixteen nations, while crude total capital estimates were available for thirty-one countries.

still apply: as with American experience, 1965 German exports are less capital-intensive than her imports ($11,734 vs. $13,161).[24] Furthermore, although Table 6 shows a negative correlation between fixed capital endowments and capital embodied in imports, the relationship is not very strong.

The simplistic theory fares poorly in accounting for the trade composition of the Western world's two largest manufacturing nations, and sheds little light on over-all import patterns. Even so, Heckscher-Ohlin find surprising corroboration when the export patterns of twenty-four nations are examined as a group. The corroboration may partly result from intercorrelation between capital-intensity and skill-intensity on a commodity basis (Tables 7, 8), given the correspondence between national fixed capital endowments and skills embodied in exports (Table 6). But no persuasive theoretical arguments have been advanced for ascribing the good Heckscher-Ohlin performance to the cross-correlation with human skills, rather than vice versa.

HUMAN SKILLS

More than a decade ago Kravis discovered that high-wage industries furnish the bulk of American exports, and that American imports compete with low-wage industries. These findings could have been rationalized in one of two ways. Wages in the import-competing sectors might be temporarily depressed, and wages in the export sectors temporarily inflated, as a disequilibrium result of expanded international commerce. This rationalization cannot be pushed very hard, however, partly because higher export industry wages have persisted since 1899, partly because more impressive evidence has been offered for the alternative explanation.

The second explanation holds that wage differentials are the product of skill differences, and that trade flows reflect the differential application of education and training to human labor. As a matter of fact, in his original article, Leontief proposed a "labor efficiency" resolution of the famous paradox. Somewhat later, Bhagwati suggested that human

[24] Numerous differences of data and methodology separate the Tatemoto-Ichimura and Roskamp-McMeekin analyses from the work presented here. To mention only one example: Roskamp and McMeekin impute the size of factor contributions from the size of income flows. Hence, no exact correspondence can be expected between the various results.

capital should be treated as a factor input, like physical capital, in evaluating trade patterns.[25]

In recent years the skill theme has found able empirical advocates at Columbia University. These advocates have advanced two different "proofs"—Keesing relates trade flows to skill differentials as reflected in inter-industry employment of different kinds of labor; Kenen-Yudin and Waehrer have followed Kravis's lead in relating trade flows to skill differentials as reflected in inter-industry wage differentials. The Kenen-Yudin approach, also employed by Bharadwaj and Bhagwati in evaluating Indian trade,[26] essentially consists of treating the difference between skilled labor wage and unskilled labor wage as an approximate measure of the return to human capital, and capitalizing this rental at appropriate rates to secure estimates of the human capital employed in average exports and imports. A similar method, without the capitalization element, was used by Roskamp and McMeekin in their resolution of the West German Leontief paradox.

The wage-differential school has concentrated on single nation import-export trading patterns, while Keesing has examined the trade of several nations. Both advocates have achieved plausible results. American exports require more skills than American imports, whether skills are measured by wage differentials or occupational categories. The same is true of West German trade. In other words, the presence of human skills appears to compensate for, if not explain, the absence of physical capital in American and German exports. Furthermore, Keesing's rank ordering of the United States and eight other nations according to occupational skills embodied in exports seems eminently plausible,[27] and this ordering is virtually reversed by skills embodied in imports.

Despite the impressive weight of evidence, two loose ends remain in the Columbia School's empirical analysis. First, to what extent are inter-

[25] J. Bhagwati [5]. Bhagwati's addendum reviews the human skill hypothesis at some length.

[26] Bharadwaj and Bhagwati [6] conclude that Indian exports embody marginally more human capital than Indian import-replacing activities. The finding, in contrast to our own orthodox results in Tables 3 and 4, pertains to all trade, not just manufactures, and may turn on the skill intensity of plantation and mineral exports.

[27] The rank ordering is: United States, Sweden, West Germany, United Kingdom, Netherlands, France, Italy, Belgium, and Japan. D. B. Keesing [25]. Keesing also remarks that Hong Kong's exports embody even fewer skills than Japan's.

industry skill differences the same elsewhere as in the United States? Second, what link is there between skill embodied in trade flows and relative national abundance of trained manpower?

To determine whether "skill reversals" loom as an important feature of the economic landscape, I compared the circa 1958 wage rankings of thirteen industry groups in twenty-three nations (data was not available for Hong Kong) [65]. The Kendall coefficient of concordance was .638, easily significant at the 1 per cent level [30]. Of the 253 individual Spearman coefficients, 182 exceeded .500, a value significant at the 1 per cent level. These findings are confirmed by the Arrow-Chenery-Minhas-Solow data [2] on approximately twenty-three industries in eight industrial nations for the early 1950's.[28] The Spearman rank correlation, on an annual earnings basis, between the United States and the seven other countries exceeded in every instance .600, and the average was .724. Keesing's recent work also refutes the skill-reversal hypothesis [28]. Broadly speaking, inter-industry skill differentials are similar the world over, especially as between important manufacturing nations.

In assessing the link between trade flows and skill endowments, the first task was to measure the skill embodied in different manufactured exports. The second task was to measure relative national abundance of trained manpower. Following the Columbia School, Table A-2 gives two indices of skills embodied in traded goods: American wage rates and American professional and technical manpower ratios by industry. Table 4 gives figures on the percentage of national workforces belonging to International Labor Office category O, "professional, technical, and related workers." Unfortunately, the ILO data is not particularly good: the figures are dominated by "service" professionals, a category whose definition is internationally inconsistent and whose presence may be less relevant than professionals directly connected with manufacturing activity.[29]

Despite these limitations, both interpretations yield good results, and the Waehrer-Kenen-Yudin version gives particularly high coefficients. When professional labor force percentages are matched with skill ratios

---

[28] Data analyzed by D. S. Ball [4].

[29] If a country has a disproportionate number of service professionals, certain questions arise. Why has human capital not moved into manufacturing? If human capital is not fungible, what factor is? Where is the explanatory power of a trade theory that must distinguish between types of human capital?

in trade, the Spearman correlation is .695, and the weighted correlation is .822; when the match is with wage rates, the correlations are .784 and .960 respectively. In deriving these correlations, professional labor force percentages for four important countries—France, Germany, the United Kingdom, and Australia—were estimated from the experience of "similar" nations. The estimates may be biased towards a favorable evaluation of the skill theory.

Whether wage rates or skill ratios are used in the analysis of exports, Israel stands out as the deviant country. Israel has the second highest professional labor force percentage, but ranks eighteenth or nineteenth in terms of wages and skills embodied in exports. A similar relationship marks her experience with physical capital. The Israeli phenomenon has attracted explanations from Michaely and others. One line of argument holds that the embodied characteristics of Table 2, derived by using export sales as weights, exaggerate the absence of human and physical capital. If the weights were based, more properly, on export value added at world prices, cut diamonds (a relatively low skill, low capital activity) would be much less prominent. Likewise textiles, a sector particularly favored by the complex system of export incentives, would shrink in importance. Beyond these considerations, however, it could be that Israel has yet to digest the great influx of trained immigrants and the sudden buildup of capital stock. If the "slow digestion" argument has any relevance, it implies that rapid accumulation of skills or capital may take years before "upgrading" the composition of exports.

In any event, weighted correlations between national attributes and embodied export skills give better results than Spearman correlations, primarily because Israeli exports constitute only a small proportion of world manufactures trade; likewise, exclusion of Israel raises the Spearman coefficients to .796 (skills in trade) and .912 (wages in trade).

The physical capital and human skill theories produce enviable results with little ad hoc empirical manipulation or theoretical amplification. Better results might emerge if nonferrous metals were excluded and man-made fibers and synthetic rubbers were included in the definition of manufactured goods. If somehow the biases of commercial policy could be taken into account, the results should further improve. In short, a distressingly simple and orthodox formulation goes a long way to explain trade among manufactured goods.

Since skill-intensive commodities overlap with capital-intensive commodities, while the acquisition of human skills and physical capital both involve acts of saving, there is no reason not to join forces by combining human skills and physical capital into a single measure of man-made resources. Indeed, Bhagwati and Kenen have advocated this approach on a theoretical plane, some of the earlier cited authors have used it in their empirical work, and Lary has put it to fruitful use in examining the export prospects of developing countries [5, 32, 39].[30] The only substantial criticism of this "new" factor proportions explanation of trade is that national acquisition of human skills or physical capital need not necessarily *precede* or *presage* the emergence of these qualities in export sales. Israel illustrates the case in which export composition may lag behind the accumulation of skills and capital; Hong Kong too has rather more human resources than her export composition would indicate. On the other hand, Taiwan's exports lead her manufacturing sector with respect to capital intensity. Apart from this line of criticism, however, the main question is whether any role remains for other explanations of trade.

SCALE ECONOMIES

According to a simplistic version of the scale economy thesis, the large nation, because of an assured home market, will specialize in goods produced with increasing returns to industry size. A small nation might occasionally develop a scale economy industry, relying on export sales to justify production. But geographic and psychological distance, not to mention tariff and quota barriers, restrict that possibility. The presumption is made that large industries are usually the property of large nations. And with specialized production of scale economy goods come certain advantages: easier productivity gains and greater market control.

Jacques Drèze has amplified the scale economy thesis as it applies to small nations [11, 12].[31] In the process, he has modified the ingredients and enriched the final story. The Drèze account, set forth as early as 1960, emphasizes interaction between long production runs and extent

---

[30] Also see Kenen-Yudin [33], Bharadwaj-Bhagwati [6], and Roskamp-Mc-Meekin [54] (notes to Table 1), where, generally speaking, human capital has been superimposed on physical capital.

[31] The work of Drèze was brought to my attention by C. P. Kindleberger in his comments based on the conference version of this paper.

of product differentiation between national markets. In Drèze's framework, industry or firm size is not the key to scale economies so much as number of items turned off a given production line. Furthermore, the differentiation that counts is not so much differentiation *within* a group of goods as differentiation *between* national suppliers. A small industrial power like Belgium can exert little influence over the tastes of its neighbors. For this reason, Belgium is handicapped when exporting goods characterized by "brand" differences between national markets. On the other hand, goods manufactured to international standards, even though manufactured in many varieties, are susceptible to Belgian competition. With these items, Belgium can enjoy long enough production runs to reap the full harvest of scale economies and sell much of the output abroad.

According to Drèze, technical leather goods and plywood are Belgian exports, while domestic leather wares and furniture are not. The plywood industry per se might exhibit greater scale economies than the furniture industry. And, by any objective test, there may exist more varieties of technical leather goods than household leather items. But the interaction between potential production runs and distinctive national tastes renders the technical leather and plywood markets more amenable to Belgian penetration.[32]

The "hypothesis of standardization," as Drèze calls it, may explain not only the concentration of Belgian exports among semifinished industrial goods, but also the export structure of other small European nations. Whether it sheds light generally on the trade of small nations must, in this paper, remain an unexplored issue. For in the analysis here, I attempt to examine scale and standardization as separate rather than interacting influences. Furthermore, my modus operandi is to link characteristics with specific products. Thus, I have not developed a tool to examine Drèze's "assembly line" view of scale economies, nor to evaluate his interesting contentions about differentiation between national markets.[33] In dealing with the scale economy theory here and with the

[32] As a matter of fact, Drèze does not consider intrinsic variations in the scale economy potential of different industries, nor does he much dwell on standardization as a product characteristic apart from the market environment.

[33] Drèze's own statistical work, contained in his second article [12], shows that Belgian industrial exports are concentrated, group by group, in the lower stages

product cycle theory later, I have selected simpler versions than those ingeniously proffered by Drèze.

The simplistic scale economy thesis, taken by itself, depends on size advantages which are internal to the industry, whatever their relationship to the firm or plant. Lacking alternative data, the empirical work here deals only with economies internal to the plant. These economies were estimated from 1963 United States experience.

The 1963 Census of Manufactures, like earlier censuses, gives value-added statistics by size class of establishment for each four-digit industry. The statistics were rearranged according to the three-digit SITC. Value added per man was then compared with establishment size,[34] using the regression equation:

$$(1) \qquad\qquad v = kn^{\alpha}.$$

In this equation, v represents the *ratio* between value added per man for a given size class of plant and the average value added per man for all establishments in the four-digit industry;[35] n represents the average number of men employed per establishment in the given size class; k is a constant; and α represents the scale elasticity parameter. An α value of .06, for example, indicates that a doubling of plant size increases output per man by roughly 6 per cent.

Scale economies are usually measured, not in the manner of (1), but in terms of "plant factors" and "labor factors."[36] These "factors" are exponential expressions of the relationship either between inputs and

of fabrication. Perhaps these products are also standardized according to the unit value coefficient developed later in this paper, even though that coefficient does not measure differentiation between national markets.

[34] Establishments belonging to the smallest size class, 1–4 men, were excluded from the regression analysis. In 70 per cent of the industries, these small establishments had greater output per man than establishments belonging to the next larger size class. Presumably, they carry on specialty trades, quite different from the ordinary plant, and should be excluded on account of product differentiation. Interestingly enough, in about 40 per cent of the industries for which observations were available, for 1,000–2,499 men establishments and those exceeding 2,500 men, the penultimate establishments had larger outputs per man—confirming the familiar phenomenon of inefficient giants.

[35] v was expressed as a ratio because several four-digit industries were pooled to obtain each three-digit SITC parameter. Output per man differs between industries for reasons unrelated to scale; the ratio approach is meant to mitigate these extraneous differences.

[36] There is also the "survival" approach used by G. J. Stigler [56].

output or between inputs and capacity. The typical labor factor formulation is:

(2) $$n = kQ^z, 0 < z < 1,$$

where n represents the number of men, Q represents the physical output or capacity, k is a constant, and z is the labor factor.

If labor and plant factors are identical, it can be shown that the relationship between α of (1) and z of (2) is: [37]

(3) $$\alpha = \frac{1}{z} - 1.$$

Elsewhere I have investigated scale economy conditions in the synthetic materials industry [21]. Alan Manne has recently published scale economy data on aluminum smelting, cement, nitrogenous fertilizer, and caustic soda [46, 17, 77]. These studies, relying on engineering data, come up with plant factors in the 0.6–0.8 range. Labor factors are less certain, but values as low as 0.2 have been suggested for some industries. If both plant and labor factors were 0.8, then alpha would be .25 by virtue of (3). As it happens, scarcely any of the alpha values in the main part of Table A-2 are as large as .25; most are a good deal smaller, and some are even negative.

Of course there is nothing sacrosanct about scale economies estimated from engineering data. Even when available, which is not very often, the engineering estimates are fairly speculative. And they seldom cover

---

[37] Besides the notation in the text, let p represent the proportion (assumed constant) of output required for purchased inputs, and k_1, k_2, etc. represent various constants. Suppose that labor is the only factor of production (it makes no difference if each laborer is joined, regardless of scale of output, by the *same* amount of machinery). Starting with relation (2) in the text:

(i)	$n = kQ^z$	Text equation (2).
(ii)	$v = k_1 \dfrac{Q(1-p)}{n}$	Definition of value added per man. (In the text, v is defined as a ratio, so k_1 represents the inverse of average value added per man for the four-digit industry.)
(iii)	$n^{\frac{1}{z}} = k_2 Q$	From (i).
(iv)	$v = k_3 n^{\frac{1}{z} - 1}$	Substituting (iii) in (ii), remembering that p is a constant.
(v)	$\alpha = \dfrac{1}{z} - 1$	By analogy with text equation (1).

the *range* of plant sizes encompassed by the value added data.[38] Nevertheless, the discrepancy between engineering estimates and Table A-2 estimates provokes at least some mention of potential biases in the present data:

(a) Different factories within a given four-digit industry may make quite distinct products. If products requiring much skilled labor and physical capital are manufactured by large plants, then the alpha coefficients would exaggerate the extent of scale economies; in the opposite case, they would understate the extent of scale economies.

(b) Factories making the same product may nevertheless employ different qualities of labor and different amounts of machinery per man, and these differences may systematically vary with size. A glance at wages by size of establishment for total U.S. industry in fact reveals a monotonically increasing relationship.[39] Part of the statistically estimated scale economies, therefore, probably reflect the use of more highly skilled labor as plant size gets larger. (Note the positive correlation between scale economies and skill ratios, Table 8.) Another part may possibly reflect increasing capital intensity with size.

(c) Competitive forces could serve to concentrate factory sizes around the optimum scale. Under certain circumstances, this might impart a downward bias in estimates of scale economies. On the other hand, some correlation may exist between optimum plant size and plant age. Larger plants may also be newer plants. Alpha would then reflect improved technology as well as larger size, thus overstating the scale element.

(d) Since market power usually accompanies size, alpha could also reflect an element of monopoly profit.

On the whole, these biases point toward alpha estimates which exaggerate the true scope of scale economies. The discrepancy with

[38] For example, the data in G. C. Hufbauer [21], Tables C-21, C-22, and C-23, cover about a tenfold range of plant sizes, a range of unusual magnitude for engineering data. By contrast, the value added data of the present analysis cover establishments of 5 to 2,500 men or more. To be sure, for a given four-digit industry, the range would usually be smaller, but still larger than most available engineering data.

[39] See, for example, U.S. Bureau of the Census [67, p. 767]. Average 1958 wages in establishments of the 1–4 man class were about $3,400; wages increased regularly until, at the 2,500+ man class, they exceeded $6,000. Wage differentials are probably not so great for the typical four-digit industry taken by itself.

engineering estimates thus becomes all the more curious. I bequeath this mystery to future scholars!

With the shortcomings of alpha in mind, Table 5 gives rank correlations between scale economies embodied in exports and national economic size, as measured by national manufacturing output.[40] The Spearman correlation is .627 and rises to .710 when India is eliminated; the weighted correlation is .778. The relevance of the scale economy account is buttressed by Keesing's recent work which found, through cross-country regression analysis, significant size effects for commerce in thirty-six out of forty major groups of manufactured goods [29].

On a simple correlation basis, however, the twenty-four nation correspondence between manufacturing output and export scale economies is only .457, a value not significantly different from zero (Table 6). On the other hand, the simple correlation between GDP per capita and export scale economies is .809. Apparently the benefits of scale economy specialization are distributed not entirely according to the dictates of national economic size, but also with some regard to economic sophistication. Small, rich countries, especially those in Europe with ready access to large markets, sometimes export scale economy products whereas bigger but less affluent countries infrequently specialize in these goods. In part the phenomenon could reflect the connection noted earlier between scale economies and skilled labor. At any rate, the exports of Japan, Mexico, and India show fewer scale economies than sheer size would warrant, while Denmark, the Netherlands, and Sweden specialize more in scale economy goods than their manufacturing output alone would justify.[41]

STAGE OF PRODUCTION

Theories of import substitution often presuppose that a stage of production sequence underlies trade. The newly developing country, so the argument runs, will produce for itself and may even export consumers' goods, while the advanced nation will specialize in exporting

[40] Much the same results emerge if gross domestic product, rather than national manufacturing output, is used to measure economic size. However, GDP per capita gives different findings, as the subsequent text reveals.

[41] As C. P. Kindleberger notes in his comment on this paper, and as I suggested in [21, p. 72], the specialization of Denmark, the Netherlands, and Sweden (possibly also Switzerland) in scale economy goods may also be explained by their role as industrial style-setters, achieving scale economies through exports.

producers' goods. This sequence supposedly results from the "natural" practice of industrializing via backward integration.

The trade implications of import substitution are often pressed no further than to "explain" why poor countries export textiles and import machinery. But this elementary rendition adds nothing to trade accounts which emphasize product sophistication, human skills, and labor intensity. To discover whether the stage of production hypothesis enjoys any independent explanatory power, the backward integration theme must be extended beyond the obvious commodities and reach the whole range of manufactured goods.

In evaluating this extended theme, a quantitative measure is needed which differentiates, by degrees, consumers' goods from producers' goods. Input-output analysis can be of assistance. The measure devised to reflect commodity differences is:

$$
(4) \qquad \text{Consumer Goods Ratio} = \frac{s^{kh} + \sum_n s^{kn} \cdot \dfrac{s^{nh}}{s^n}}{s^k}.
$$

In this statistic, s^{kh} and s^{nh} represent, respectively, sales by industry k and sales by industry n to households and government bodies acting as consumers; s^{kn} represents sales by industry k to industry n on current account; and s^k and s^n represent, respectively, total sales (including imports) of k and n except export and inventory accumulation sales.[42] The ratio thus reflects the percentage of total sales appearing as consumer goods directly and indirectly after the first and second rounds.[43]

Another version of the stage of production argument was peripherally suggested by Jacques Drèze. In his version, the argument is interpreted so that its key variable reflects not how close the item is to the final consumer, but the degree of fabrication. Thus, following tariff practice and the Brussels Tariff Nomenclature, Drèze divides manufactured products into some twenty-eight groups according to the primary material (e.g., wood, copper, inorganic chemicals), and then subdivides

---

[42] Export and inventory accumulation sales are excluded on the grounds that, ultimately, they are distributed between consumer and producer uses in the same ratio as other sales.

[43] A more comprehensive statistic might reflect the number of "rounds" required for sales on consumption account to reach, for example, 95 per cent of total sales. This more comprehensive statistic would require data on the rate of transformation, through depreciation, of capital goods to consumer goods.

each group into six degrees of fabrication. The interpretation of the stage of production as a degree of fabrication thesis was not examined here. But an examination would probably take the same analytic path pursued later, and for different reasons, in looking at the product cycle theory.

The 1960 Japanese input-output table was employed to calculate the concept (4) ratio values appearing in Table A-2. Certain errors crept into the calculations, but they were not large enough to affect the conclusions materially.[44] Despite the errors and statistical peculiarities, the two-digit Japanese ratios show a rank correlation of about 0.8 with their two-digit American counterparts (given in parentheses), derived from the 1958 U.S. input-output table.[45] Nevertheless, the ratio values may occasionally suggest that the theory itself—or at least the version tested here—has little promise. For example, an apparently small portion of pottery sales (SITC 666) goes to final consumers, a partly misleading result because of the importance of industrial ceramics in the particular input-output industry. On the other hand, a seemingly large share of scientific, medical, and optical instruments (SITC 861) is consumed by the public, probably because the group includes cameras. Among these SITC groups, factors beside the stage of production will clearly exert greater influence on the pattern of trade. Generally speaking, since producers' goods have been defined as anything not quickly reaching the consumer, the category embraces semiprecious stones, fertilizer, wood products, paper goods, and other "unlikely" advanced country exports. Thus from the outset the hypothesis may appear none too promising.

The stage of production theory can be tested by comparing statistic (4) either with national manufacturing output or with GDP per capita. The comparison with manufacturing output presumes that sheer indus-

[44] Well after the statistical work was completed, I discovered that the ratio values were calculated neglecting imports and with some classification errors. The Table A-2 values were partially corrected for these errors (which were usually small) but no attempt was made to recompute the embodied characteristics or the various correlation coefficients. See note (f) to Table A-2.

[45] The 1958 input-output table was used to calculate consumer goods ratios on a two-digit SITC basis, but the U.S. table was not sufficiently detailed for three-digit SITC values. The U.S.-Japanese correlation would be better except for (a) the Japanese practice of treating automobile sales as capital formation; and (b) the use of Japanese export weights in calculating the two-digit Japanese values.

trial size determines specialization in consumer or producer goods. The comparison with GDP per capita places more emphasis on sophistication.

As it happens, the comparison with manufacturing output turns out poorly, but the comparison with GDP per capita turns out extremely well. The Spearman and weighted rank correlations for the latter comparison are .818 and .801 respectively, while the simple correlation is .727, despite the sometimes peculiar consumer goods ratios. If backward integration is seen as the concomitant of economic development, rather than sheer size, then trade patterns emerge in quite logical fashion. But it must be remembered that this "logic" overlaps a good deal with the logic of the Heckscher-Ohlin and human skill theories.

TECHNOLOGICAL GAP

The sequence of innovation and imitation vitally affects export patterns, or so I and others have contended. Early producers enjoy easy access to foreign markets, access which is reinforced by technical and managerial leadership; [46] later producers must rely on some factor cost advantage (e.g., low wages) to secure a share of foreign sales. Furthermore, production history may determine whether overseas commitments by leading firms take the form of licensing arrangements, joint ventures, or solely owned corporations.

Technological gap and product cycle analyses of trade have lately enjoyed a certain vogue. It is interesting to note that Reverend Josiah Tucker enunciated the major elements of this theme as early as 1758. In a remarkable essay, "The great Question resolved, Whether a rich Country can stand a Competition with a poor Country (of equal natural Advantages) in raising of Provisions, and Cheapness of Manufacturers?" [61], Tucker opened with the observation:

It has been a Notion universally received, That Trade and Manufactures, if left at full Liberty, will always descend from a richer to a poorer State; somewhat in the same Manner as a Stream of Water falls from higher to lower Grounds; . . . It is likewise inferred, very consistently with this first Principle, that when the poor Country, in Process of Time, and by this Influx of Trade and Manufactures, is become relatively richer, the Course of Traffic will turn again. . . .

[46] J. Diebold contends [9] (without offering any evidence) that the gap is not technological but managerial. What this really means is that alert, technologically oriented managers, with a flair for marketing new products, are as vital as good scientists in the research laboratory—a perfectly unobjectionable contention.

Tucker then posed the great question, apparently a matter of some concern during the mid-eighteenth century:

This being the Case, can it be denied, that every poor Country is the natural and unavoidable Enemy of a rich one; especially if it should happen to be adjoining it? And are not we sure beforehand that it will never cease from draining it of its Trade and Commerce, Industry and Manufactures, 'till it has at least so far reduced it, as to be on a Level and Quality with itself? Therefore the rich Country, if it regards its own Interest, is obliged by a Kind of Self-defence to make War on the poor one, and to endeavour to extirpate all its Inhabitants. . . .

Reverend Tucker, distressed by the apparent conflict between self-interest and Divine Providence, denied this pessimistic outcome, at least for the rich country which had acquired wealth by industrious pursuits rather than gold mines (the distinction between England and Spain). The artisan nation would enjoy, said Tucker, seven advantages over its poorer competitor: (1) a larger stock of direct and infrastructure capital and better organized institutions; (2) superior human skills; (3) bigger capacity for investment; (4) an ability to attract the best talent from the poor country; (5) greater division of labor; (6) more internal competition; (7) lower interest rates. Given these advantages: ". . . it may be laid down as a general Proposition, which very seldom fails, That *operose* or *complicated Manufactures* are cheapest in rich Countries;—and raw *Materials* in poor ones. . . ."

Corn, wheat, and garden-stuff were cited by Tucker as agricultural produce suited to the environs of well-to-do London, while cattle, sheep, and timber were assigned to poorer Scotland. Wooden products, woolen clothes, horn combs, ink-horns, powder-flasks, leather shoes and boots invariably moved from England to Scotland, not vice versa. Even more remarkable was the English import of Swedish raw iron ("and surely Sweden is a country poor enough") and the return export of metal articles to Sweden, despite heavy duties at nearly every border crossing.

In a polemical postcript, addressed to a critic who asked whether ". . . according to this Hypothesis, Improvements, Industry, and Riches, may be advanced and encreased *ad infinitum;* which is a Position too extravagant to be admitted," Tucker dismissed the man with eighteenth century optimism: "No Man can set Bounds to Improvements even in Imagination; and therefore, we may still be allowed to assert, that the richer manufacturing Nation will maintain its Superiority over the poorer one, notwithstanding this latter may be likewise advancing towards Perfection."

Tucker, of course, was forgotten in the Ricardian and neoclassical ascendancy. Today, when continuous technological progress has become an article of faith, no one worries much about the consequences of "spread" for the rich nation. Otherwise, many ingredients of the technology-trade story remain the same.

Several latter day studies of technological gaps and their influence on trade and overseas investment have explored developments among specific high technology products, though at least one investigator promises to look at the low technology end.[47] Another quite different approach, successfully pursued by Gruber, Mehta, and Vernon [16] and Keesing [27], and by Gruber and Vernon in the present volume, is to measure technological sophistication by research expenditure. This approach, by contrast with individual product studies, can quickly encompass a wide range of manufactures trade. But it requires an examination of trade flows on an *industry* basis. In this and the next section, we prefer measures more closely identified with *commodities*. The industry and commodity results are of course reconcilable, and it may well be that, after the reconciliation, R&D offers the statistically superior tool for examining the whole "bundle" of product cycle characteristics.

Nevertheless, in the present section, our preferred tool would be a product date measure readily available for a broad range of commodities. The tentative foundations for this tool are supplied by the U.S. Census Bureau's export classification list, "Schedule B."

Editions of Schedule B were published in 1909, 1915, 1917, 1919, 1921, 1922, 1925, 1928, 1929, 1930, 1931, 1932, 1933, 1938, 1939, 1941, 1944, 1949, 1952, 1955, 1958, and 1965. Each new edition expanded the list of commodity headings, both by subdividing existing

---

[47] Cf. the notes to Table 1: G. C. Hufbauer (plastics, synthetic rubbers, and man-made fibers), G. K. Douglass (motion pictures), R. B. Stobaugh (selected chemicals). J. Tilton of the Brookings Institution has a study underway on diffusion of the semiconductor industry. W. A. Chudson at the Columbia University School of Business is looking at the efficiency with which petrochemical technology is transferred to developing countries. D. R. Sherk of Boston College will examine the postwar Japanese transition from low technology standardized exports to higher technology, more differentiated goods.

groups and by breaking new groups from basket categories. This expansion, which magnified Schedule B from a small pamphlet of one hundred pages in 1909 to a heavy volume of one thousand pages in 1965, provides the basis for dating the arrival of new products to the status of internationally traded goods. The mechanical steps of deriving "first trade dates" from successive editions of Schedule B, and the shortcomings of the data listed in Table A-2, are summarized in the paragraphs that follow.

To begin with, the seven-digit 1965 SITC classification, containing some 2,000 manufactured items, was related to the old six-digit 1964 Schedule B, containing an approximately equal number of headings [71]. Ordinarily, more than one "old" Schedule B group contributed to the commodities under each "new" SITC Schedule B heading. Hence, after obtaining the first trade date for each "old" SITC group (as explained below), an unweighted mean of the contributing groups was used to represent the first trade date for each "new" seven-digit SITC group.

The 1958 edition of Schedule B (reprinted and revised as of January 1, 1962) gave first establishment dates for all six-digit export groups inaugurated after 1939 [68]. The great majority of first trade dates for the old six-digit Schedule B were taken directly from the 1962 volume. For those categories established before 1939, a search was made of earlier Schedule B editions to discover their first appearance. Even so, the first trade dates for certain kinds of six-digit groups could not be determined. For example, basket categories rarely have definitive inception dates. Similarly, groups formed by the combination of two or more groups often had untraceable antecedents. These six-digit Schedule B groups were ignored in finding the first trade date for each seven-digit SITC group.

Commodities which trade in big volume probably get broken out from basket categories sooner than small volume items. First trade dates at a seven-digit level are thus weighted by American export experience, apart from the fact that Schedule B takes no cognizance of new export items shipped from other countries.

Once an unweighted average was obtained for each seven-digit SITC group, two different methods were employed to obtain first trade dates on a three-digit SITC basis. First, the seven-digit values belonging to each three-digit group were weighted according to 1965 United States exports in order to find a value for that three-digit group. Second, an unweighted average of the seven-digit values was taken. In 60 out of 102 cases, the weighted values were more recent than the unweighted values (in 5 cases they were identical), confirming that U.S. exports are concentrated among newer goods. Because of this concentration, it seemed better to use unweighted values in the trade analysis. Unweighted values thus appear in Table A-2.

The dates in Table A-2, ranging from 1927.7 to 1954.6, are not always compatible with a priori expectations. For example, textile yarn and thread (SITC 651) and cotton fabrics (SITC 652) have dates more recent than 1950, although electrical apparatus for medical purposes (SITC 726) has a date of 1944.7. Whether these aberrations reflect mere nuances in the compilation of Schedule B, vagaries in the attempted link between "old" and "new" Schedule B, or in some sense genuine patterns of innovation, we have not investigated. It seems likely that American exports of cotton textiles exhibit an altogether different composition than the bulk of world trade. But even allowing for such ad hoc explanations, the first trade dates very inadequately reflect the commodity characteristic which they purport to measure. These dates surely stand out as the least satisfactory statistic presented in this paper.

Furthermore, as Kindleberger notes in his criticism of the conference version of this paper, an examination of the embodied first trade dates of Table 2 shows that no country has an average composition of 1965 exports dating earlier than 1944, while the latest average comes only to 1948. Kindleberger adds that it is hard to conclude very much about the technological gap theory of trade with data which average out most of the technological differences between countries, and produce sixteen out of twenty-four averages in the two years 1946 and 1947.

To determine whether these (inadequate) first trade dates are linked with economic structure when embodied in exports, some measure of "industrial sophistication" is required. Gross domestic product per capita meets this need in a crude way. As Table 5 shows, the Spearman correlation between first trade dates embodied in exports and GDP per capita is .698, while the weighted correlation is .864. The main deviant nations are Norway and Taiwan—the former with a much older export composition and the latter with a much younger set of exports than their respective levels of per capita GDP would suggest. Both these nations are comparatively small exporters. Hence the weighted correlation is larger than the Spearman coefficient. The exclusion of Taiwan raises the Spearman coefficient to .764.

GDP per capita is highly correlated with both fixed capital per capita and skilled employees as a percentage of the labor force. As we have seen, the resource endowment theories of trade perform quite well. Therefore, it would be reasonable to expect that first trade dates embodied in exports would correspond with GDP per capita only to the extent that commodity first trade dates correspond with commodity physical capital and human skill requirements. But in fact, the weighted rank correspondence between first trade dates and physical capital is only .111, while the correspondence between first trade dates and skill requirements is .377 (Table 8). The successful performance of the first trade date measure is not entirely attributable to the overlap with physical and human capital.

PRODUCT CYCLE

Successive stages of standardization, argues Vernon, characterize the product cycle. Initially a new good is made in small lots, each firm with its own variety. Manufacturing processes are highly experimental; many different techniques are given a try. But as markets grow, changes take place; national and international specifications are agreed upon. Simultaneously, the number of processing technologies decreases as inferior methods are weeded out. The surviving techniques grow more familiar and marketing channels become better established. The expansion of output transforms the items from "sideline" to "mainline" status.

In the early stages, production and export advantages lie with sophisticated firms in advanced nations. As the product cycle unfolds, however, firms and nations with less technical expertise begin making and exporting the item. Standardization aids and abets this migration of industry in two ways—longer production runs and proven production technology bring industry within the technical grasp of more nations; standardized goods are more easily marketed, both because sales channels have been established and because feedback problems are less severe.

The product cycle accounts and the technological gap accounts clearly belong to the same family. Both stress the sequential development of production history. But while technological gap emphasizes *time,* product cycle emphasizes the transition from product *differentiation* to product *standardization.*[48] Hence the two theories merit separate examination.

"Differentiation" and "standardization" convey different meanings in different contexts. For his purposes, Drèze used the six degrees of fabrication distinguished in tariff schedules.[49] For the present context, a measure is needed which compares the homogeneity of a great many products at a given moment in time (assuming that standardized products imply standardized processes).[50] The coefficient of variation in unit export values roughly serves this need:

$$(5) \qquad \text{Product Differentiation} = U_n/V_n.$$

In this expression, U_n denotes the standard deviation of U.S. export unit values for shipments of product n to different countries; V_n denotes the unweighted mean of these unit values. The use of country destination for distinguishing between shipments was dictated by available data. If a product is standardized, presumably the unit values of different shipments will be similar. However, as P. T. Knight points out, cyclical market variations and discriminatory export practices will, to some unknown degree, distort statistic (5) as a measure of differentiation.

The United States Census Bureau, using 1965 export data, computed differentiation coefficients for each seven-digit SITC category on which quantity figures were available. Quantity figures, however, were not

[48] On a somewhat different tack involving the same variable, B. Kit, J. Yurow, and H. Millie [34] have examined the impact of international standards on national exports. Much trade, they claim, turns on the adoption of national specifications for international practice. General Electric, for example, says it has foregone bids on overseas TV equipment amounting to some $11 million during recent years, thanks to the adoption of European rather than American standards ("Case History No. 6," p. 51). When national standards become international practice, the country renders its home market more accessible to foreign imports but at the same time gains broader entry to foreign markets.

[49] For another example, S. A. N. Smith-Gavine [55] develops a statistic suitable for measuring the complexity of a firm's output, with respect to both components and processes.

[50] This assumption is not necessarily correct. There are many goods, such as handicrafts and apparel, which are not themselves standardized but which are made by highly standardized processes. Conversely, new industrial materials may be manufactured in very different fashion by different firms.

available for highly individualistic goods: for example, complex machinery, scientific apparatus, and parts of all description. For purposes of estimating three-digit SITC differentiation coefficients, these "nonquantity" seven-digit groups were treated in two ways. In the first instance, they were ignored. The coefficients given in Table A-2 were estimated following this procedure. In the second instance, the "nonquantity" groups were assigned values equal to the largest coefficients (on a seven-digit basis) directly estimated for the three-digit group. The three-digit coefficients estimated in this way were more widely dispersed than those obtained by the first procedure. But the rank order of commodities was much the same, while the ultimate analytic results were slightly inferior using these assigned value coefficients. The second approach was therefore not pursued.

The three-digit coefficients in Table A-2 represent simple averages of the underlying seven-digit values. Alternatively, the seven-digit values might have been weighted by 1965 U.S. export experience. Weighted coefficients were in fact obtained on a trial basis, but simple averages were preferred for comparability with first trade dates. Interestingly, the weighted coefficients (unlike the weighted first trade dates) were not noticeably biased towards differentiated products. In 51 out of 102 instances, the weighted coefficients were larger than the simple averages (in 4 cases the values were identical), a proportion no greater than random weights would give. As between seven-digit SITC commodities, the United States shows no strong tendency towards differentiated goods.[51]

At a three-digit level, reasonable coefficients seem to emerge, at least in some instances. The SITC categories 652 ("cotton fabrics"), 673 ("iron or steel bars, rods, angles, etc."), and 715 ("metalworking machinery"), for example, yield a plausible sequence of coefficients: .4774, .6916, and 1.3156.

However, it is perhaps surprising that the rank correlation between first trade dates and product differentiation is no higher than .169. But the commodities that detract from a better correspondence are not altogether unexpected. Some goods are intrinsically differentiated, what-

[51] The comparison does not reflect "nonquantity" SITC items. If such items were included, U.S. exports might show a bias.

ever their age. Among the commodities that have much older dates than the high degree of differentiation might suggest:

533   Pigments, paints, varnishes
571   Explosives and pyrotechnics
679   Iron and steel castings, forgings, etc.
694   Nails, screws, nuts, bolts, etc.
717   Textile and leather machinery
842   Fur clothing and fur articles

Other goods are very young, but nevertheless highly standardized. Two separate cases seem to appear: goods which are genuinely new, but naturally standardized, and standardized goods whose newness, if not a quirk of the dating method, can only be explained by changing industrial or consumer fashions. In addition, there are some commodities, for example nickel and tin, which are not at all new but which have been *exported* only very recently by the United States. Among those commodities which have younger dates than the high degree of standardization would indicate are:

651   Textile yarn and thread
652   Cotton fabrics
672   Ingots, other primary forms
674   Universals, plates, sheets
683   Nickel
687   Tin
688   Uranium, thorium, etc.
712   Agricultural machinery
725   Domestic electrical equipment
732   Road motor vehicles
733   Bicycles, trailers, invalid carriages
893   Plastic articles

Without these eighteen items, the rank correlation between product age and standardization would improve, perhaps to about 0.5. Even this correspondence is not terribly large. It must be recognized that different goods start their lives with different intrinsic degrees of standardization. Over the product cycle any given good may become more standardized, but, because of differences at birth, there will never be an exact correspondence between product age and product standardization.

Indeed, as measured by coefficient (5), goods may never change their degree of differentiation very much. Production techniques could well become more familiar and standardized with time, but no correspondence need exist between product age and product standardization. In that event, the success of coefficient (5) would reflect the arguments put up by Drèze rather than a temporal sequence. Drèze contended that small and less developed nations would concentrate on internationally standardized goods because such nations cannot achieve long runs making differentiated items. Drèze might also have noted that differentiated goods require more skills in manufacture and for this reason tend to be the province of developed countries. True, Drèze emphasized international standardization while coefficient (5) measures product group standardization, but some similarity probably marks the two concepts.

Given the existence of these possible explanations, what luck does differentiation have as an explanatory characteristic? As with first trade dates, gross domestic product per capita is the national attribute assumed to determine differentiation in exports. Table 5 shows a Spearman correlation of .724 between this attribute and the trade characteristic. Canada and Australia, "new" rich countries with highly standardized exports, are the principal deviant nations. Elimination of Canada raises the Spearman coefficient to .788. The weighted rank coefficient for twenty-four nations is .763, and the simple correlation is .749.

These coefficients bear out the Vernon-Drèze hypothesis that advanced nations specialize in differentiated exports. Whether the hypothesis owes its success to a product cycle thesis, or to the intrinsic difficulties of making and marketing differentiated goods, is not a question that can be answered from static cross-section analysis.

SUMMARY

What can be said about an evaluation which finds virtue everywhere? Considering the unlikely, indeed almost improbable, statistics used in certain instances, the discovery of little truths in every nook is perhaps surprising. Much better to pour academic hot oil on two or three accounts than to broadcast olive branches!

Had the analysis been extended to more countries, and had a broader definition of manufactures been employed, less sympathetic findings might have emerged. But distinctions based on the experience of small exporting countries or on commodities with a large natural resource component would scarcely convince anyone. If a theory is to be condemned, it must be condemned after sympathetic examination.

In retrospect, it must be conceded that many different characteristics express themselves in export patterns. No one theory monopolizes the explanation of manufactures trade.

This seemingly prosaic finding is not altogether commonplace. The characteristics themselves, when matched against the 102 SITC commodities on a weighted rank correlation basis, show five strong intercorrelations: the expected coincidence between wages and human skills; the correspondence between human and physical capital; the overlap between the consumer-producer goods dichotomy and the light-heavy industry dichotomy; the match between standardized and skilled goods; and the correspondence between scale economy and skilled goods. To a certain extent, therefore, the "different" characteristics do nothing more than catch different glimpses of the sophistication that accompanies economic development.

But the seven commodity characteristics, when applied to national export patterns, yield much more similar country rankings than the underlying correspondence between characteristics themselves might lead us to expect. The Kendall coefficient of concordance between country rankings exceeds .700, a value which is easily significant at the 1 per cent level. When the export-embodied characteristics of twenty-four nations are compared on a simple correlation basis, the same picture emerges. Out of the twenty-one bilateral correlations between the export-embodied characteristics of the twenty-four-nation sample, all are significant but 4 (Table 11). The average value of the twenty-one bilateral correlations is .683, whereas the average value of the twenty-one weighted rank correlations between commodity characteristics per se (Table 8) is only .303. Export patterns exercise an intriguing kind of selectivity. Commodities are favored which contain several characteristics suitable to the nation's economic structure. The composite trading pattern thereby agrees with various theoretical predictions.

TABLE 11

Simple Correlations Between the Export-Embodied
Characteristics of Twenty-Four Nations

	Capital per Man	Skill Ratio	Wages per Man	Scale Econ- omies	Con- sumer Goods Ratio[a]	First Trade Date	Prod- uct Differ- entia- tion
Capital per man	1.000						
Skill ratio	.597	1.000					
Wages per man	.826	.911	1.000				
Scale economies	.308*	.744	.695	1.000			
Consumer goods ratio[a]	.782	.849	.938	.645	1.000		
First trade date	.261*	.636	.588	.777	.481*	1.000	
Product differentiation	.382*	.923	.783	.786	.766	.674	1.000

Note: In this exercise the correlations between national values for different export-embodied characteristics are compared with one another.

Source: Table 2.

[a]The signs of the consumer goods ratio correlations have been reversed. Also see note (f) to Table A-2.

*Not significantly different from zero at the 1 per cent confidence level.

Earlier it was said that the neofactor proportions account, combining human and physical capital, performed so well that the role for other theories was doubtful. It is now apparent that another cluster of explanations—shall we call it the neotechnology account?—emerges as an equally strong contender.

The neofactor proportions story emphasizes tangible factors of production—physical capital and labor of different qualities—operating in a basically competitive world economy. This stress permits easy assimilation to the grand body of neoclassical economic reasoning. Questions of income distribution, international migration, savings, capital formation, and so forth, are easily handled starting from national endow-

TABLE 12

*Simple Correlations Between the Import-Embodied
Characteristics of Twenty-Four Nations*

	Capital per Man	Skill Ratio	Wages per Man	Scale Economies	Consumer Goods Ratio[a]	First Trade Date	Product Differentiation
Capital per man	1.000						
Skill ratio	.317*	1.000					
Wages per man	.261*	.668	1.000				
Scale economies	.197*	.740	.577	1.000			
Consumer goods ratio[a]	.267*	.719	.749	.654	1.000		
First trade date	-.608	.026*	.483*	.162*	.184*	1.000	
Product differentiation	-.141*	.596	.761	.416*	.720	.604	1.000

Note: In this exercise, the correlations between national values for different import embodied characteristics are compared with one another.

Source: Table 3.

[a]The signs of the consumer goods ratio correlations have been reversed. See also note (f) to Table A-2.

*Not significantly different from zero at the 1 per cent confidence level.

ments of productive resources. And the dichotomy between consumer and producer goods can be accompanied as a minor garnish.

The neotechnology account, however, points to production "conditions" in a setting of monopolistic competition: [52] economic returns to scale, product age, and product differentiation. If this trilogy were somehow combined into a single characteristic, that characteristic might prove as powerful as Lary's single measure (value added per man) of human and physical capital in explaining trade flows.[53]

[52] For the distinction between perfect and monopolistic competition as an underlying presupposition of international trade theory, see H. G. Johnson [24].

[53] For results of correlations incorporating value added per man as the dependant variable, see the note by Lary in this volume.

But the neotechnology approach is not geared to answering the traditional questions of economic inquiry. It can as yet offer little to compare with Samuelson's magnificent (if misleading) factor-price-equalization theorem. The theoreticians may remedy this shortcoming. In the meantime, the technology approach has illuminated some new fields of inquiry. For example, it helps explain the composition of direct investment flows [76]. And it provides the foundation for understanding why trade refuses to wither and die when nations grow more similar.

GAINS FROM TRADE

Orthodoxy vs. Linder

According to the prevalent orthodoxy, international trade makes possible greater output by reallocating resources among substantially different activities. *Dissimilar* goods, so the argument runs, are the mainspring of exchange. Maximum benefit accrues when each nation concentrates on its own, relatively efficient, lines of production. The first six theories enumerated in Table 1 presuppose this basic orthodoxy.

S. B. Linder offers a different story, at least for commerce in manufactured goods [44, pp. 86–109]. In Linder's version, the qualities and kinds of manufactured goods consumed by a nation are peculiar to its own industrial structure and level of per capita income. Exports of manufactures are an outgrowth of a home production which caters to majority dictates, while imports accommodate the slightly different needs of the minority.[54] The factor proportions approach may adequately explain commerce in primary goods, but international trade in manufactures must be seen as an extension of the internal market.

Linder's core hypothesis yields various suggestive insights. Flavored with ingredients from the theory of monopolistic competition, it rationalizes the flourishing exchange between Renaults and Fiats, between Budweiser and Loewenbrau. It explains the creation and extinction of trade as a function of each partner's travelling speed through its income zone. An empirical corollary which Linder casually examined is the connection between bilateral trade intensity and per capita income; but,

[54] H. G. Grubel finds confirmation of Linder's commodity composition argument in the *growth* of European Common Market trade [15].

as Linnemann subsequently demonstrated, the intensity of bilateral trade can hardly be evaluated without explicit reference to distance. Here we examine another Linder corollary relating to the commodity composition of trade in manufactured goods.

The assertion tested is that the composition of nation i's manufactured exports will be more similar to the composition of nation j's imports as i and j more closely resemble each other in per capita income and economic structure. In the extreme case, the export and import menus for a given country should be highly similar. As Linder himself says [44, p. 91]: ". . . the range of potential exports [of a country] is identical to, or included in, the range of potential imports." And, somewhat later [44, p. 138]: "Potential exports and imports are—when they are manufactures—the same products. An *actual import* product today is a *potential export* product today and may be an *actual export* product tomorrow." The gains from this sort of exchange stem from the marginal satisfaction which differentiated consumption brings to the buyer, from the reduction of monopoly returns to labor and capital, and from the elimination of economic rents on technological know-how.

The assertions of the orthodox school as opposed to those of Linder regarding export-import similarity can be interpreted at two levels. They can mean that dissimilarity (similarity) should exist between actual *commodities* imported and exported by a given nation. Or they can mean that dissimilarity (similarity) should exist between commodity *characteristics* embodied in imports and exports. Both interpretations are examined in the following sections.

Before proceeding to the numerical exercises, it must be admitted that the Linder-orthodoxy distinction has been phrased too strongly, at least so far as the "orthodox" scale economy and product cycle theories are concerned. In a few offhand remarks, Linder allows these latter explanations a role in accounting for trade among manufactured goods [44, pp. 102, 103, 129]. The remarks afford Linder a potential escape hatch for explaining commodity specialization, so long as that specialization is based, not on "tangible" factor endowments (including human skills), but on "ephemeral" production conditions, like innovation and scale. Since Linder's text spends very little time developing this escape hatch, we are perhaps justified in giving it only editorial notice.

SMILAR COMMODITIES?

Country i's commodity composition of exports may be expressed by vector X_i, where each element, x_{in}, represents exports of commodity n as a percentage of that country's total manufactures exports. Country j's commodity composition of imports may be expressed by vector M_j, where each element, m_{jn}, represents imports of commodity n as a percentage of its total manufactures imports. The cosine of vectors X_i and M_j provides an index of trade similarity: [55]

$$(6) \qquad \text{Cos } X_i M_j = \frac{\sum\limits_{n} x_{in} \cdot m_{jn}}{\sqrt{\sum\limits_{n} x_{in}^2 \cdot \sum\limits_{n} m_{jn}^2}}$$

When Cos $X_i M_j$ equals one, the two vectors are identical: when the cosine equals zero, they are completely dissimilar.

FIGURE 2

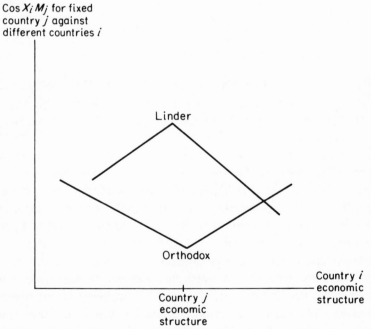

Cos $X_i M_j$ for fixed country j against different countries i

Linder

Orthodox

Country j economic structure

Country i economic structure

[55] This measure is presented in R. G. D. Allen [1, p. 381] and critically examined by H. Linnemann [45, pp. 140–143].

FIGURE 3

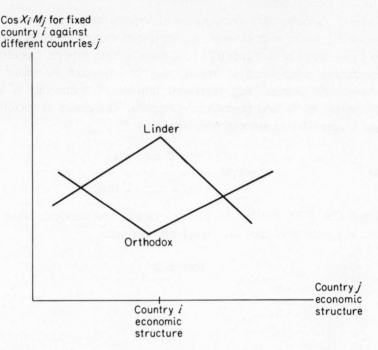

Cos $X_i M_j$ for fixed country i against different countries j

Linder

Orthodox

Country j economic structure

Country i economic structure

By extension of Linder's argument, the Cos $X_i M_j$ values, when graphed for a given country's *import* vector, should resemble the tent shape depicted in Figure 2; for the same country's *export* vector, the Cos $X_i M_j$ values should resemble the tent shape of Figure 3. This extension depends on the assumption that a country's actual *trade* with all countries represents the range of its *potential* trade with any given country. Thus, actual total imports of country i will be more similar to actual total exports of country j as i and j more closely resemble each other in economic structure; and the same statement applies to total exports of country i when compared with total imports of country j.

Conversely, orthodox theory suggests that imports of countries in a given economic zone will not match their exports, because trade, rather than merely extending the internal market, compensates for international economic differences. The orthodox position yields the expectation, depicted in Figures 2 and 3, of a "V" shaped distribution of Cos $X_i M_j$ values. Table A-3 sets forth the matrix of Cos $X_i M_j$ values derived from the 1965 three-digit trade statistics for manufactured goods. Whether the matrix in Table A-3 reflects a tent or a "V" can be suggested by application of the following regression equations, where A_i and A_j measure economic structure.

(7) $\text{Cos } X_i M_j = c_1 + a_1 A_j + b_1 A_i$, when $A_j \leq A_{ij}$;

and

(8) $\text{Cos } X_i M_j = c_2 + a_2 A_j + b_2 A_i$, when $A_j \geq A_i$.

If Linder's argument is correct, then c_1 should be less than c_2, a_1 should be positive, b_1 should be negative, a_2 should be negative, and b_2 should be positive. The converse relationships would support the orthodox position.

In estimating the parameters of (7) and (8), per capita GDP has been used as the sole measure of economic structure. Since GDP per capita offers a well correlated proxy for most other aspects of economic structure (Table 9), this restriction should not prove fatal.

The parametric results from (7) and (8) support neither Linder nor orthodoxy. The shape of export-import cosines represents neither a tent nor a "V." Instead, as Table 13 shows, the typical export vector grows *continuously* more similar to the import vector of an opposing nation, as the importing nation is more developed. This holds not only for manufactures exports from the United Kingdom and Sweden, but also for exports from Portugal and Hong Kong: export vectors mesh better with import vectors when the importing country is a richer nation. Likewise, the typical import vector grows continuously more similar to the opposing export vector, as the exporting nation is more developed. The United States and Germany offer a wider selection of exports than Mexico and India.

Broadly speaking, these findings represent nothing more than the diversification of exports and imports which accompanies greater affluence. Owing to concentration, especially export concentration, the opposing trade vectors of two poor countries, say Hong Kong and Portugal, will substantially differ, while thanks to diversification the import-export vectors of two rich nations, for example the United Kingdom and Sweden, will roughly coincide.

Thus, as Table 13 shows, a_1, b_1, a_2, and b_2 all are positive, and to

TABLE 13

Similarity of Import and Export Vectors

I. National Import vs. Export Vectors

	Constant	Parameter of A_j	Parameter of A_i	R^2
Present results[a]				
$\text{Cos}X_iM_j =$				
$c_1 + a_1A_j + b_1A_i,$	.30331	.00006	.00012	.235
when $A_j \leq A_i$	(±.20183)	(±.00002)	(±.00002)	
$\text{Cos}X_iM_j =$				
$c_2 + a_2A_j + b_2A_i,$	.17781	.00004	.00026	.503
when $A_j \geq A_i$	(±.17442)	(±.00002)	(±.00002)	
Linnemann results[b]				
$\log\text{Cos}X_iM_j =$				
$c_3 + a_3\log A_j + b_3\log A_i$	c	.18	.35	

II. National Export Vectors[a]

	Constant	Parameter of $|A_i - A_j|$	Parameter of $\sqrt{A_iA_j}$	R^2
Linnemann results[b]				
$\text{Cos}X_iX_j = c_4 +$	.33517	−.00011	.00015	.318
$a_4|A_i - A_j| + b_4\sqrt{A_iA_j}$	(±.18400)	(±.00002)	(±.00002)	

Note: Symbols are

X = Export vector for the three-digit SITC classification, expressed as per cent of total country exports.

M = Import vector for the three-digit SITC classification, expressed as per cent of total country imports.

A = Per capita gross domestic product or gross national product.

i, j = Country subscripts.

a, b, c = Parameters and constants to be estimated.

[a] The present results are based on the cosine values reported in Tables A-3 (national import vs. export) and A-4 (national export vs. export). These cosine values pertain only to trade in manufactured goods.

(continued)

[b]The Linnemann results are based on H. Linnemann [45], Case AC 1, p. 82 and Case AC 29, p. 150. The equation in Case AC 29 was rearranged to make log C_{ij} (C_{ij} = Cos $X_i M_j$) appear on the left side as the dependent variable. The Case AC 1 value for log X_{ij} was then substituted in the rearranged Case AC 29 equation. The parametric relationship between C_{ij} and per capita income of importing country j is consequently found as the difference between the Case AC 1 and Case AC 29 values of ϕ_3, divided by ϕ_{16}. In our notation:

$$a_3 = \frac{\phi_3 \text{ (AC 1)} - \phi_3 \text{ (AC 29)}}{\phi_{16} \text{ (AC 29)}}.$$

Similarly:

$$b_3 = \frac{\phi_1 \text{ (AC 1)} - \phi_1 \text{ (AC 29)}}{\phi_{16} \text{ (AC 29)}}.$$

Five features should be observed about the implied relationships. First, Cases AC 1 and AC 29 are not based on exactly the same trade flows, and for this reason slight distortions are introduced. Second, parameters ϕ_1 and ϕ_3 are attached, in Linnemann's equations, to gross national product. The assumption that these parameters also describe the impact of cross-sectional changes in per capita gross national product depends on the tautology:

$$\phi_1 \log \text{(GNP)} \equiv \phi_1 \log \text{(per capita GNP)}$$

$$+ \phi_1 \log \text{(population)}.$$

Third, interactions between the commodity composition vector and terms other than per capita income have been ignored. Fourth, for all the foregoing reasons, the implied values of a_3 and b_3 probably differ somewhat from those that would be obtained by direct estimation. Fifth, the Linnemann results apply to all trade, not just manufactures trade.

[c]Not derived.

a much greater extent than their standard errors. To be sure, the explanatory powers of (7) and (8), as measured by R^2, are limited. But the positive parameter signs are unmistakable. Furthermore, the standard errors of c_1 and c_2 are so large that these coefficients cannot be statistically distinguished from one another.

If c_1 definitely exceeded c_2, then in terms of Figure 4 the orthodox position would receive support provided the other parameters fell in quadrant II. If c_2 exceeded c_1, Linder would get a boost provided the other parameters fell in quadrant IV. As it happens, c_1 and c_2 are indistinguishable, while the other parameters all land in quadrant I.

FIGURE 4

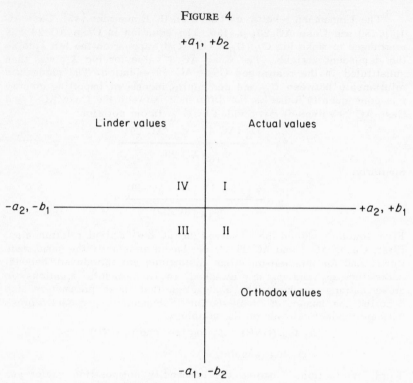

These results are obliquely confirmed by Linnemann's econometric work. Linnemann applied various "gravity" models on a cross-sectional basis to explain the size of 1959 bilateral trade flows (total trade, not just manufactures). Most of the models contain GNP and population of the trading partners, distance between them, and a dummy preference term (e.g., for Commonwealth trade) as explanatory variables. One model also includes the cosine between export and import commodity composition vectors as an independent variable. Assuming that commodity composition is a *dependent* rather than an independent variable, the results of this model—when contrasted with the results from a model without the cosine variable—imply certain parametric values for the impact of cross-sectional income changes on commodity composition. Table 13 performs and explains this exercise. The implied parameters indicate that import and export composition grow more similar with an increase in the per capita income of either partner.

For those who like theoretical admixtures, the parametric results of our own work, indirectly confirmed by Linnemann, may be rationalized by assigning orthodoxy and Linder each its own "sphere of influence." Judging solely from the cosine exercise, Linder—perhaps supplemented by product cycle and scale economy theory—works best in accounting for trade *within* the rich country zone. By the same token, orthodoxy— perhaps in the narrow tangible factor sense (including factors of nature) —does better at explaining the commodity composition of manufactures *within* the poor country zone. As for trade between zones, the cosine results agree with Linder if the zones are close together, and with orthodoxy when the zones are widely separated.

The "spheres-of-influence" reconciliation is at least compatible with a finding from the cross-sectional Gruber-Vernon work on the size of bilateral trade flows. Invoking a concept which dates from Tatemoto and Ichimura, Gruber and Vernon distinguish between "upstream" and "downstream" trade flows. Gruber and Vernon find that, as a country gets richer, its upstream exports increase about as rapidly as its down-stream exports.[56] As Linder might predict, trading relations do not particularly wither with those areas which the exporting country comes more to resemble.

Nevertheless the "spheres of influence" reconciliation critically depends on one assumption: that tangible orthodox considerations govern a

[56] W. H. Gruber and R. Vernon, "The Technology Factor in a World Trade Matrix," this volume, Table 10. The results quoted are derived by comparing the parameters for the group in which $H_i > H_j$ with the group $H_i < H_j$. H_j, used to distinguish between upstream and downstream trade, is the Harbison-Myers index of human resource development. Using the Gruber-Vernon notation, and heroically assuming that variables not mentioned in the formulation below are independent of per capita income, the elasticity of exports from i to j with respect to a change in the per capita income of i is given by:

$$\frac{\partial E_{ij}}{\partial PC_i} \cdot \frac{PC_i}{E_{ij}} = b_1 + b_3 \pm b_7 \left\{ \frac{PC_i}{|PC_i - PC_j|} \right\}$$

The range of per capita GNP covered in the Gruber-Vernon sample runs from about \$100 to about \$3000. For downstream exports, therefore, the average value of the term in braces applied to b_7, taking into account the range of possible trading partners j, is about 2; for upstream exports, it gets larger as the country gets richer. The sign of b_7 is positive for downstream sales, negative for upstream sales. Thus, for a country with per capita income of \$1,000, the elasticity of exports with respect to an increment in per capita income is about 1.2 for both upstream and downstream trade. This elasticity reflects the mean experience of eight high technology industries and sixteen other industries, giving each industry equal weight.

rather smaller segment of manufactures trade than the neotechnological considerations of Linder. For as a country gets richer, its export menu becomes rapidly more diversified. If Linder explains the trade between rich nations, then his arguments necessarily apply to a wider range and larger volume of goods.

Putting the matter in Linder's own phraseology, the range of potential imports expands somewhat with economic development, but the range of potential manufactured exports expands *very much more*.[57] Pakistan *already* imports a wide spectrum of manufactures, but its exports are virtually limited to textiles and leather goods. Judging from cross-section data, however, affluence diversifies the poor country export menu, rendering it more similar to world import menus. Affluence also diversifies the poor country import menu, but at a slower rate. Thus, in Table 13, parameters a_1, a_2, and a_3, representing the impact on cosine values of an increment in importing country income, are all significantly smaller than respectively b_1, b_2, and b_3, the parameters reflecting a change in exporting country income.

Obviously the proffered reconciliation demands an econometric investigation of bilateral trade composition. The reconciliation requires, among other things, that the cosines of bilateral trade become more similar as trading partners become richer. Trade vector analysis without this bilateral dimension can yield only speculation on the kinds of gain which characterize trade in manufactures.

SIMILAR CHARACTERISTICS?

What about the characteristics embodied in trade flows? Do export and import characteristics make up each other's deficiencies, or do they merely duplicate one another's qualities? Table 14 attempts to answer this question in a preliminary way by contrasting national export and import rank lists with respect to commodity characteristics. If trade compensates for national deficiencies, as each orthodox theory contends, then negative rank correlations should appear. Linder himself

---

[57] See M. Michaely [47, pp. 11–18]. Michaely's results cover all trade, not just manufactures. Similar results, however, should emerge from a comparative analysis of Cos X_iX_j and CosM_iM_j vectors limited to manufactured goods. See also the work of Gruber and Vernon, reported in this volume, which finds that an increase in the exporting nation's per capita income exercises a far more favorable impact on bilateral trading intensity than an increase in the importing country's income.

TABLE 14

Spearman Correlations Between Export Characteristics and Import Characteristics

Commodity Characteristic	Spearman Correlations Between Nations Ordered According to Characteristic Embodied in Exports and Characteristic Embodied in Imports
Capital per man	-.162*
Skill ratio	-.503*
Wages per man	-.183*
Scale economies	-.490*
Consumer goods ratio[a]	-.337*
First trade date	-.380*
Product differentiation	-.404*

Sources: Tables 2 and 3.

[a]See note (f) to Table A-2.

*Not significantly different from zero at the 1 per cent confidence level. With twenty-four observations, however, any coefficient greater than 0.342 in absolute value significantly differs from zero at the 10 per cent confidence level.

might agree that trade compensates for product cycle and scale economy characteristics, but he is reluctant to see either an exchange of physical capital for crude labor or an exchange of human skills [44, p. 86].

As a matter of fact, the Spearman correlations are all negative. Although none significantly differs from zero at the 1 per cent level, it is hardly coincidental that they all agree with the orthodox argument. Either through the selective workings of the marketplace, or through the deliberate imposition of trade barriers, exports and imports substantially compensate each other for skills, for scale economies, for product age, and for standardization, while the exchange of physical capital for crude labor power is limited.[58] The comparatively weak showing of Heck-

---

[58] Weighted rank correlations, not presented in Table 14, reinforce these conclusions. For big trading nations, there is virtually no exchange of crude capital and crude labor power, and the trade between producers' and consumers' goods is not at all robust.

TABLE A-1

Concordance between United Nations Standard International Trade Classification (SITC)[a] and United States Standard Industrial Classification (SIC)

512	**561**	**632**	**653**	**663**	**674**
2818	2871	2441	2221	3271	3312
2842	2872	2442	2231	3272	3316
2843	2879	2443	2262	3291	
		2445	2269	3292	**675**
513	**571**	2499	2296	3293	3312
2812	2892	2541		3295	3316
2813			**654**	3296	
2895	**581**	**633**	2241	3297	**676**
	2821	nil	2292	3299	3312
514					
2819	**599**	**641**	**655**	**664**	**677**
	2861	2621	2291	3211	3312
515	2891	2631	2295		3315
nil	2899		2298	**665**	
		642	3987	3221	**678**
521	**611**	2641		3229	3317
2814	3111	2642	**656**		
2815		2643	2299	**666**	**679**
	612	2644	2391	3262	3391
531	3121	2645	2392	3263	
2818	3131	2646	2393		**681**
		2647	2394	**667**	3339
532	**613**	2649	2395	nil	
nil	3992	2651	2396		**682**
		2652	2397	**671**	3331
533	**621**	2653	2399	3312	3341
2816	nil	2654		3313	3351
2851		2655	**657**	3321	3399
2893	**629**	2661	2271	3322	
	3011		2272		**683**
541	3069	**651**	2279	**672**	3339
2831		2281	3982	3312	3399
2833	**631**	2282		3323	
2834	2431	2283	**661**		**684**
	2432	2284	3241	**673**	3334
551	2433		3274	3312	3352
2087		**652**	3281		3399
		2211			3497
553		2261	**662**		
2844			3251		**685**
			3253		3332
554			**663**		
2841			3255		
			3259		

(continued)

TABLE A-1 (continued)

3356	**696**	**718**	3662	**733**	**841**
3399	3421	3531	3671	3751	2251
		3532	3672	3791	2252
686	**697**	3533	3673	3799	2253
3333	nil	3534	3674		2254
3356		3535	3679	**734**	2256
3399	**698**	3536		3721	2259
687	3411	3537	**725**	3722	2311
3339	3392	3551	3631	3723	2321
3356	3361	3554	3632	3729	2322
3399	3362	3555	3633		2323
	3369	3559	3634	**735**	2327
688	3492	2794	3635	3731	2328
3339	3493		3636	3732	2329
	3496	**719**	3639		2331
689	3499	3553		**812**	2335
3339	2591	3561	**726**	3231	2337
	3993	3562	3693	3261	2339
691	3964	3564		3264	2341
3441		3566	**729**	3269	2342
3442	**711**	3567	3622	3431	2351
3444	3511	3569	3623	3432	2352
3446	3519	3581	3624	3433	2361
3449		3582	3629	3494	2363
2542	**712**	3585	3611	3498	2369
	3522	3586	3641		2381
692		3589	3642	**821**	2384
3443	**714**	3599	3691	2511	2385
3491	3571		3692	2512	2386
	3572	**722**	3693	2514	2387
693	3576	3612	3694	2515	2389
3357	3579	3613	3699	2519	3151
3481		3621		2521	
	715			2522	**842**
694	3541	**723**	**731**	2531	2371
3452	3542	3643	3741	2599	
	3544	3644	3742		**851**
	3545			**831**	3021
695	3548	**724**	**732**	3161	3141
3423		3651	3713	3171	3142
3425	**717**	3652	3715	3172	
3429	3552	3661	3717		

(continued)

TABLE A-1 (concluded)

861	3861	892	893	3953	899
3811		2711	3079	3955	3199
3821	863	2721			3962
3822	nil	2731	894	896	3963
3831		2732	3941	nil	3981
3841	864	2751	3942		3983
3842	3871	2752	3943	897	3984
3843	3872	2753	3949	3911	3995
3851		2761		3912	
	891	2771	895	3913	
862	3931	2782	3951	3914	
2793		2789	3952	3961	

Note: There is no one-to-one correspondence between the two schemes. The same four-digit SIC industry frequently contributes to more than one three-digit SITC commodity, while some three-digit SITC groups find no counterpart four-digit industry. This concordance was used in estimating capital per man, wages per man, and scale economies for four-digit SITC groups. Other concordances were devised for converting the Japanese input-output data on consumer ratios, and the Census Bureau data on occupational skills, to the SITC basis. The input-output data was converted with the partial assistance of the United Nations concordance [62].

[a] SITC figures are bold face.

scher-Ohlin might be interpreted either as a modest triumph for Linder or as the inevitable outcome of restrictive tariffs and quotas. The major point, though, is that trade *does* involve some exchange of characteristics.

It would be interesting to quantify the characteristics exchanged on a bilateral basis, distinguishing between upstream and downstream trade. The speculation of the previous section, for what it is worth, suggests a shift from "tangible" factor proportions trade to "ephemeral" product cycle and scale economy commerce as the trading partners become richer and more similar.

Even a bilateral exercise, however, would leave open the question whether an exchange of "ephemeral" characteristics contributes much to welfare. Emile Despres, for example, argues that the important segment of commerce is Heckscher-Ohlin trade, and that other trade, large as it may be in volume, makes a much smaller welfare contribution per dollar of traffic.[59] Whether product cycle, scale economy, and other forms of interstitial commerce have redeeming qualities in spurring the diffusion of techniques, enhancing productivity, and curbing the power of local monopolies, is a question that might be debated for a very long time.

REFERENCES

1. Allen, R. G. D., *Mathematical Economics,* 2nd ed., London, 1959.
2. Arrow, K. J., Chenery, H. B., Minhas, B. S., and Solow, R. M., "Capital-Labor Substitution and Economic Efficiency," *Review of Economics and Statistics,* August 1961.
3. Balassa, B., "Tariff Protection in Industrial Countries: An Evaluation," *Journal of Political Economy,* December 1965.
4. Ball, D. S., "U.S. Effective Tariffs and Labor's Share," *Journal of Political Economy,* April 1967.
5. Bhagwati, J., "The Pure Theory of International Trade: A Survey," reprinted in *Surveys of Economic Development,* Vol. II, 1965. An addendum is forthcoming, J. Bhagwati, *Trade, Tariffs and Growth,* Cambridge, 1969.
6. Bharadwaj, R., and Bhagwati, J., "Human Capital and the Pattern of Foreign Trade: The Indian Case," *Indian Economic Journal,* October 1967.
7. Bharadwaj, R., *Structural Basis of India's Foreign Trade,* Bombay, 1962.
8. ————, "Factor Proportions and the Structure of Indo-U.S. Trade," *Indian Economic Journal,* October 1962.
9. Diebold, J., "Is the Gap Technological?" *Foreign Affairs,* January 1968.
10. Douglass, G. K., "Innovation and International Trade," Claremont, California, 1966, unpublished paper.
11. Drèze, J., "Quelques réflexions sereines sur l'adaptation de l'industrie belge au Marché Commun," *Comptes rendus des Travaux de la Société Royale d'Economie Politique de Belgique,* No. 275, December 1960.
12. ————, "Les exportations intra-C.E.E. en 1958 et la position belge," *Recherches Economiques de Louvain,* No. 8, 1961.
12a. Economic Commission for Latin America, "The Growth and Decline of Import Substitution in Brazil," *Economic Bulletin for Latin America,* March 1964.

[59] This view was offered by Professor Despres at a Stanford Seminar, October 1968. S. B. Linder takes a similar position [44, p. 140].

TABLE A-2

Characteristics of Traded Goods

SITC Two-Digit Division or Three-Digit Group[a]	Capital per Man[b]	Skill Ratio[c]	Wages per Man[d]	Scale Economies[e]	Consumer Goods Ratio[f]	First Trade Date[g]	Product Differentiation[h]
51 Chemical elements and compounds	**36,213**	**.1564**	**7,684**	**.041**	**.105(.293)**	**1946.4**	**.8934**
512 Organic chemicals	40,058		7,921	.086	.136	1947.2	.9175
513 Inorganic chemicals: elements, etc.	26,166		6,913	-.074	.035	1943.0	.7741
514 Other inorganic chemicals	26,371		7,318	-.058	.035	1943.2	1.1162
515 Radioactive materials	26,371*		7,318*	.000*	.035*	1953.4	2.4360
52 }521 Mineral tar and crude chemicals from coal, petroleum, natural gas	**24,188**	**.1564**	**7,287**	**.027**	**.301(.293)**	**1940.0**	**.8008**
	24,188		7,287	.027	.301	1940.0	.8008
53 Dyeing, tanning, coloring materials	**13,395**	**.1075**	**7,031**	**.060**	**.091(.291)**	**1938.8**	**.9122**
531 Synthetic organic dyestuffs, etc.	13,395*		7,921	.086	.048	1945.7	.9505
532 Dyeing and tanning extracts	13,385*		6,563*	.047*	.048*	1945.1	.4875
533 Pigments, paints, varnishes	13,395		6,563	.047	.138	1935.3	.9093
54 }541 Medicinal and pharmaceutical products	**13,646**	**.1926**	**6,806**	**.083**	**.804(.854)**	**1950.5**	**1.4745**
	13,646		6,806	.083	.804	1950.5	1.4745

Code	Description							
55	**Essential oils, perfume materials, toilet and cleansing goods**	19,506	.1564	6,273	.185	.804*(.854)	1940.5	.7488
551	Essential oils, perfume, flavor materials	42,967		6,217	.194	.804*	1948.6	.7454
553	Perfumery and cosmetics	10,000		5,342	.240	.804*	1930.1	.2990
554	Soaps, cleansing, polishing preparations	8,223		6,692	.158	.804*	1943.0	.7618
56 }	Manufactured fertilizers	17,103	.1564	4,980	.076	.141(.293)	1933.2	.4791
561 }		17,103		4,980	.076	.141	1933.2	.4791
57 }	Explosives and pyrotechnic products	7,703	.1564	6,190	-.079	.170(.293)	1942.6	1.2713
571 }		7,703		6,190	-.079	.170	1942.6	1.2713
58 }	Plastic materials, regenerated cellulose and artificial resins	24,788	.1564	7,126	.009	.257(.212)	1954.6	.9093
581 }		24,788		7,126	.009	.257	1954.6	.9093
59 }	Chemical materials and products, n.e.s.	19,489	.1564	6,094	.059	.505(.293)	1945.5	.7512
599 }		19,489		6,094	.059	.505	1945.5	.7512
61	**Leather, leather mfg., and dressed fur**	5,195	.0171	5,907	.104	.841(.691)	1934.9	.5898
611	Leather	4,586		5,201	-.058	.767	1935.3	.5896
612	Manufactures of leather	3,081		4,030	.060	.860	1931.9	.5896*
613	Fur skins	6,923		7,728	.400	.860*	1935.0	.5903

(continued)

TABLE A-2 (continued)

SITC Two-Digit Division or Three-Digit Group[a]	Capital per Man[b]	Skill Ratio[c]	Wages per Man[d]	Scale Economies[e]	Consumer Goods Ratio[f]	First Trade Date[g]	Product Differentiation[h]
62 Rubber manufacturers, n.e.s.	**9,361**	**.0604**	**6,356**	**.011**	**.316(.506)**	**1947.8**	**.7467**
621 Materials of rubber	9,361*		6,356*	.011*	.316*	1949.0	.8769
629 Articles of rubber	9,361		6,356	.011	.316	1947.5	.7106
63 Wood and cork manufacturers	**4,086**	**.0149**	**4,525**	**.013**	**.201(.223)**	**1946.1**	**.8468**
631 Veneers, plywood boards, etc.	4,087		4,933	.029	.058	1947.9	.6834
632 Wood manufactures, n.e.s.	4,086		4,340	.006	.482	1946.2	.9511
633 Cork manufactures	4,086*		4,340*	.006*	.482*	1934.3	.8320
64 Paper, paperboard, and manufactured paper products	**23,383**	**.0390**	**6,541**	**.088**	**.229(.285)**	**1948.8**	**.8487**
641 Paper and paperboard	26,456		6,740	.101	.215	1949.2	.8279
642 Articles made of paper pulp, paper or paperboard	7,558		5,516	.018	.272	1946.5	.9943
65 Textile yarn, fabrics, made-up goods	**6,437**	**.0208**	**4,083**	**-.001**	**.604(.603)**	**1948.1**	**.5367**
651 Textile yarn and thread	6,452		3,500	.066	.677	1950.9	.4592
652 Cotton fabrics, woven	6,077		3,832	-.050	.677*	1952.6	.4774
653 Other textile fabrics, woven	7,178		4,325	-.034	.677*	1946.9	.5954

Code	Description						
654	Tulle, lace, embroidery, etc.	5,018		3,972	-.004	.677*	1941.4	.6057
655	Special textile fabrics	7,097		5,218	.011	.440	1945.9	.6167
656	Made-up textile articles	2,903		3,940	-.014	.634	1943.6	.5873
657	Floor coverings, tapestries, etc.	12,925		4,566	.052	.449	1936.9	.5132
66	**Nonmetallic mineral manufactures, n.e.s.**	**14,561**	**.0500**	**5,163**	**.048**	**.142(.380)**	**1945.6**	**.7826**
661	Lime, cement, building materials	41,009		6,401	-.055	.022	1936.1	.6718
662	Clay construction materials	8,862		4,937	.023	.008	1945.3	.7651
663	Mineral manufactures, n.e.s.	8,851		5,660	.051	.043	1945.2	.7681
664	Glass	21,623		7,553	.039	.209	1946.4	.9109
665	Glassware	9,724		5,462	.112	.242*	1945.9	.6279
666	Pottery	2,206		4,498	.034	.242	1944.7	.6015
667	Pearls, precious, semiprecious stones	2,206*		4,498*	.034*	.242*	1947.7	.8435
67	**Iron and steel**	**22,547**	**.0502**	**7,188**	**.069**	**.027(.125)**	**1948.5**	**.6959**
671	Pig iron, sponge iron, ferro-alloys, etc.	20,541		7,116	.082	.004	1942.2	.6917
672	Ingots and other primary forms	22,722		7,307	.035	.027	1949.4	.5479
673	Bars, rods, angles, shapes	24,455		7,414	.058	.027	1941.5	.6916
674	Universals, plates, and sheets	24,581		7,410	.058	.027	1951.0	.5159
675	Hoop and strip	24,581		7,410	.124	.027	1949.3	.6101
676	Rails and track construction material	24,455		7,414	.058	.027	1945.2	.5494

(continued)

TABLE A-2 (continued)

SITC Two-Digit Division or Three-Digit Group[a]	Capital per Man[b]	Skill Ratio[c]	Wages per Man[d]	Scale Economies[e]	Consumer Goods Ratio[f]	First Trade Date[g]	Product Differentiation[h]
677 Wire, excluding wire rod	24,189		7,371	.019	.027	1941.6	.6908
678 Tubes, pipes, and fittings	20,000		6,688	.039	.027	1950.4	.8713
679 Castings and forgings, unworked	16,777		7,157	-.004	.027	1939.5	1.3266
68 Nonferrous metals	**20,915**	**.0735**	**6,634**	**-.079**	**.092(.152)**	**1942.3**	**.6360**
681 Silver, platinum	29,216		6,825	-.298	.042	1938.6	.3357
682 Copper	18,743		6,494	-.067	.101	1938.6	.5589
683 Nickel	29,300		6,476	-.104	.042	1951.1	.6729
684 Aluminum	20,607		6,911	-.032	.142	1947.0	.7498
685 Lead	21,261		6,509	-.022	.042	1945.7	.6040
686 Zinc	20,545		6,434	-.024	.042	1946.9	.7365
687 Tin	23,235		6,603	-.068	.042	1947.8	.3390
688 Uranium and thorium	29,216		6,825	-.298	.042	1958.1	.2650
689 Miscellaneous nonferrous metals	29,216		6,825	-.298	.042	1951.3	.9489
69 Manufactures of metals, n.e.s.	**6,974**	**.0966**	**5,935**	**.028**	**.288(.378)**	**1945.6**	**1.1631**
691 Finished structural parts and structures	4,917		5,786	.005	.017	1944.2	.8109
692 Metal containers for storage, transport	5,602		6,222	.041	.017	1948.6	1.3287

Code							
693	Wire products and fencing grilles	10,402		5,698	−.008	.334	1945.4	.8969
694	Nails, screws, nuts, bolts, rivets	8,160		6,441	−.023	.334	1931.3	2.0906
695	Tools for hand or machine	6,425		5,890	.071	.334	1949.2	1.2815
696	Cutlery	13,475		5,448	.174	.334	1941.9	.5900
697	Household equipment	8,823*		5,448*	.011*	.334	1941.3	.5870
698	Metal manufactures, n.e.s.	8,823		5,925	.011	.334	1946.5	1.0341
71	**Machinery, other than electric**	**7,595**	**.0913**	**6,485**	**.044**	**.116(.112)**	**1948.6**	**1.0199**
711	Power generating machinery	77,702		7,036	.084	.039	1949.8	.9855
712	Agricultural machinery	9,867		6,120	.062	.039*	1950.7	.5654
714	Office machines	7,894		6,889	.030	.039*	1946.1	.5958
715	Metalworking machinery	7,247		7,111	.031	.003	1948.6	1.3156
717	Textile and leather machinery	5,222		5,455	.003	.026	1939.0	1.1986
718	Machines for special industries	6,738		6,598	.030	.018	1948.3	1.2200
719	Machinery and appliances, n.e.s.	7,362		6,216	.036	.245	1950.8	1.2075
72	**Electrical machinery, appliances**	**5,627**	**.1523**	**6,068**	**.063**	**.061(.494)**	**1947.8**	**1.3671**
722	Electric power machinery, switchgear	6,586		6,231	.081	.033	1951.4	1.7492
723	Equipment for distributing electricity	4,865		5,364	.031	.033	1948.1	.8825
724	Telecommunications apparatus	3,868		6,294	.031	.033	1948.7	.9608
725	Domestic electrical equipment	5,894		5,922	.096	.527	1948.8	.5320
726	Electrical apparatus for medical purposes	6,613		7,064	.073	.071	1944.7	.5320*

(continued)

TABLE A-2 (continued)

SITC Two-Digit Division or Three-Digit Group[a]	Capital per Man[b]	Skill Ratio[c]	Wages per Man[d]	Scale Economies[e]	Consumer Goods Ratio[f]	First Trade Date[g]	Product Differentiation[h]
729 Other electrical machinery, apparatus	5,839		5,874	.064	.071	1945.6	1.5192
73 Transport equipment	**9,328**	**.1218**	**7,399**	**.137**	**.099(.338)**	**1951.1**	**.7886**
731 Railway vehicles	8,182		6,689	.011	.118	1948.6	.8476
732 Road motor vehicles	12,264		7,486	.058	.077	1951.1	.5504
733 Road vehicles, nonmotor	2,811		4,861	.110	.236	1948.5	.5108
734 Aircraft	4,460		7,469	.304	.086	1951.7	1.0225
735 Ships and boats	5,305		6,440	.006	.106	1949.5	1.3093
81 } Sanitary, plumbing, heating **812** } and lighting fixtures	**9,593** 9,593	**.0455**	**5,827** 5,827	**.065** .065	**.242(.256)** .242	**1946.0** 1946.0	**.9592** .9592
82 } Furniture **821** }	**3,470** 3,470	**.0197**	**4,408** 4,408	**.032** .032	**.326(.556)** .326	**1947.3** 1947.3	**.5360** .5360
83 } Travel goods, handbags, **831** } and similar articles	**1,217** 1,217	**.0138**	**3,720** 3,720	**.031** .031	**.860(.957)** .860	**1936.6** 1936.6	**.6300** .6300

Code	Description							
84	**Clothing**	**1,329**	**.0102**	**3,098**	**-.096**	**.878(.945)**	**1945.5**	**.5273**
841	Clothing except fur	1,316		3,051	-.097	.878	1945.7	.5137
842	Fur clothing	2,151		6,017	-.032	.834	1928.8	1.0717
85 851	}Footwear	**1,443** 1,443	**.0066**	**3,653** 3,653	**.052** .052	**.985(.957)** .985	**1927.7** 1927.7	**.6060** .6060
86	**Instruments, photographic goods, watches**	**6,619**	**.1622**	**6,300**	**.038**	**.689(.444)**	**1948.8**	**1.6355**
861	Scientific, medical, optical instruments	5,982		5,958	.034	.689	1948.7	1.2224
862	Photographic supplies	10,308		7,674	.060	.800*	1948.6	1.9434
863	Developed cinema film	10,308*		7,674*	.060*	.800*	1958.1	1.0325
864	Watches and clocks	5,354		5,306	-.013	.662	1943.8	1.1907
89	**Miscellaneous manufactures, n.e.s.**	**4,845**	**.0730**	**5,004**	**.060**	**.526**	**1947.9**	**1.3152**
891	Musical instruments, sound recorders	3,731		5,126	.089	.527	1950.9	1.5929
892	Printed matter	5,681		6,039	.034	.512	1947.1	1.3470
893	Plastic articles	6,314		5,037	.078	.527	1950.6	.5983
894	Perambulators, toys, sporting goods	3,988		4,076	.090	.527	1947.5	.7867
895	Office and stationery supplies	4,620		5,056	.066	.527	1944.4	.9424
896	Works of art, collectors' pieces	2,824*		4,798*	.032*	.527	1941.6	.9424*
897	Jewelry, goldsmiths' wares	2,824		4,798	.032	.527	1950.6	.9424*
899	Manufactured articles, n.e.s.	6,989		4,359	.055	.527	1944.2	.7360

(continued)

TABLE A-2 (concluded)

SITC Two-Digit Division or Three-Digit Group[a]	Capital per Man[b]	Skill Skill Ratio[c]	Wages per Man[d]	Scale Economies[e]	Consumer Goods Ratio[f]	First Trade Date[g]	Product Differentiation[h]
Selected Products Not Included In the Statistical Analysis							
013 Canned, prepared meat	7,840	.0179	5,955	.027	.996	1940.8	.4205
032 Canned, prepared fish	6,012	.0330	3,837	.081	.995	1943.9	.3576
046 Meal, flour, of wheat, maslin	11,588	.0180	6,183	.170	.976	1933.9	.2198
047 Meal, flour, of cereals, n.e.s.	13,256	.0180*	4,759	.244	.976	1938.9	.2620
048 Cereal preparations	7,529	.0180*	5,507	.135	.976	1934.5	.4364
053 Preserved fruit	7,937	.0330	3,993	.121	1.000	1941.3	.2617
055 Preserved vegetables	7,986	.0330	4,045	.119	1.000	1938.8	.4571
061 Sugar and honey	22,625	.0156	5,913	-.135	.715	1937.7	.4667
062 Sugar confectionery	5,498	.0156*	4,345	.144	1.000	1924.4	.6005
091 Margarine, shortening	19,852	.0452	6,558	-.039	1.000*	1943.6	.2640
111 Nonalcoholic beverages	7,428	.0277*	5,033	.089	.999	1939.3	.3705
112 Alcoholic beverages	18,869	.0277	7,101	.142	.996	1925.6	.4948
122 Tobacco manufactures	9,735	.0221	4,463	.153	1.000	1935.3	.1780
231.2 Synthetic rubber	35,683	.1564	7,733	na	.252	1954.6	.4298
242 Wood shaped, worked roughly	10,629	.0122	3,880	.081	.042	1948.3	.4511
251 Pulp, waste paper	36,821	.0620	7,099	na	.038	1942.2	.2267
266 Synthetic, regenerated fibers	24,867	.1124	6,193	.491	.462	1952.1	.3834
332 Petroleum products	21,374	.1468	6,185	-.014	.335	1939.2	.4583
421 Fixed vegetable oils, soft	18,512	.0532	5,331	.077	na	1951.2	.1889

Notes to Table A-2

[a]The descriptions here are somewhat abbreviated. Consult *Commodity Indexes for the Standard International Trade Classification, Revised* [63] for a complete description.

[b]Capital per man, measured in U.S. dollars of approximately 1963 vintage, refers to fixed plant and equipment immediately employed in making the commodity, as produced in the United States. The labor estimates represent total manufacturing employment. The capital estimates were synthesized from Leontief's 1947 estimates and the capital expenditure figures reported in various editions of *Census of Manufactures* [69]. Annual 2 1/2 per cent depreciation and 3 1/2 per cent inflation factors (both straight line) were applied to structures. Annual 5 per cent depreciation and 2 1/2 per cent inflation factors (again, straight line) were applied to equipment. The depreciation factor was first applied and the surviving plant and equipment was then inflated to 1963 values. It was assumed that the capital stock in 1947 was composed of 37 per cent structures and 63 per cent equipment; hence, given the stipulated depreciation and inflation factors, 38.3 per cent of the 1947 capital outfit was assumed to exist in 1963. Depreciation factors were based on data in Treasury Department, *Tables of Useful Lives of Depreciable Property* [75]. Inflation factors were based on indices appearing in *Statistical Abstract of the United States: 1965* [67]. The capital expenditures series were not always continuous from one year to the next, owing both to inadequate data received by the Census Bureau and to the reclassification of industries in 1958. Accordingly it was often necessary to interpolate figures and to reconstruct the series. Once labor and capital estimates were obtained, the data was reclassified according to the three-digit SITC. The two-digit estimates were obtained by weighting the three-digit estimates (excluding asterisked values) by the 1965 United States export pattern.

[c]Skill ratios refer to the percentage of the industry's labor force accounted for, in the United States, by professional, technical, and scientific personnel, The data was derived on a two-digit SITC basis, after appropriate reclassification. The basic statistics come from *U.S. Census of Population, 1960: Occupation by Industry* [70].

[d]Wages per man, measured in 1963 U.S. dollars, were derived from U.S. data by dividing the wage bill by total employees immediately occupied in making the commodity. The data was taken from the *Census of Manufactures: 1963* [69] and reclassified according to the three-digit SITC. The two-digit SITC estimates were obtained by weighting the three-digit estimates (excluding asterisked values) by the 1965 United States export pattern.

[e]Scale economies were equated with the exponent in the regression equation, $v = kn^{\alpha}$, where v is the 1963 ratio between value added in plants employing n persons and average value added for the four-

digit U.S. Census Bureau industry, and k is a constant. The data was taken from the *Census of Manufactures: 1963* (69). Four-digit industries were reclassified according to the three-digit SITC prior to running the regression analysis. The two-digit SITC estimates were obtained by weighting the three-digit estimates (excluding asterisked values) by the 1965 United States export pattern.

[f]After the statistical work was complete, I discovered that imports had been erroneously neglected in calculating the Japanese consumer goods ratios, and that some errors of classification had crept into the work. These shortcomings were partially remedied on an ad hoc basis for those three-digit SITC groups most affected, namely 512, 521, 531, 533, 541, 551, 553, 554, 561, 581, 599, 612, 613, 681, 683, 685-689, 715, 718, 719, 724, 725, 734, 812, 861, 862, 863, 892. The corrected values appear in Table A-2. However, no attempt was made to recompute the embodied characteristics appearing in Tables 2 and 3, or the subsequent statistical analyses, using the corrected values. These values would not materially alter the conclusions reached in the text. In principle, the consumer-goods ratio is measured as the percentage of commodity output and imports purchased, in Japan, by "final consumers" directly and on the "second round." "Final consumers" are defined as households plus government bodies, except when government bodies are clearly purchasing for investment purposes (as in the acquisition of transport equipment and machinery). Inventory changes and exports were netted out of total deliveries by each sector on the ground that they are divided between consumption goods and investment goods in the same ratio as other sales. The "second round" refers to the percentage of intermediate goods which find their way to final consumption after one pass through the input-output table. The consumer goods ratios were estimated from the 1960 Japanese input-output table, reclassified according to the three-digit SITC (see notes to Table A-1). The two-digit SITC estimates were obtained by weighting the three-digit estimates (excluding asterisked values) by the 1965 Japanese export pattern. Two-digit U.S. consumer-goods ratios, based on the 1958 input-output table, appear in parentheses. These were not used in the subsequent calculations. The figures in the last section of the table for "selected products not included in the statistical analysis" are approximate estimates, based on Japanese experience. The Japanese data came from *1960 Table of Industrial Relations* [23]. The United States data are based on "The Transactions Table of the 1958 United States Input-Output Table" [43].

[g]First trade dates are expressed in a decimal version of the Christian calendar. The dates were found by examining successive issues (beginning in 1917) of United States Census Bureau *Schedule B* (the detailed schedule of exportable goods) for the first appearance of specific commodities. The three-digit SITC estimates represent a simple average of all seven-digit commodities belonging to the three-digit group. The two-digit SITC estimates were obtained by weighting the three-digit estimates by the 1965 United States export pattern.

hProduct differentiation is measured as the coefficient of variation in unit values of 1965 United States exports destined to different countries. Differentiated goods are marked by higher coefficients of variation. Coefficients on a seven-digit SITC basis were derived from *United States Exports Commodity by Country* [72]. A simple average of the seven-digit coefficients is used for the three-digit SITC estimates. The two-digit SITC coefficients were obtained by weighting the three-digit estimates by the 1965 United States export pattern.

*Asterisked values represent arbitrary extrapolation from a "similar" commodity group.

13. Egendorf, A., "Plastic Materials and the Pure Theory of International Trade," A. B. thesis, Harvard University, 1966.

14. Felix, D., "Beyond Import Substitution: A Latin American Dilemma," in Papanek, G. F., ed., *Development Policy: Theory and Practice,* Cambridge, 1968.

15. Grubel, H. G., "Intra-Industry Specialization and the Pattern of Trade," *Canadian Journal of Economics and Political Science,* August 1967.

16. Gruber, W., Mehta, D., and Vernon, R., "The R&D Factor in International Trade and International Investment of United States Industries," *Journal of Political Economy,* February 1967.

17. Haldi, J., and Whitcomb, D., "Economies of Scale in Industrial Plants," *Journal of Political Economy,* August 1967.

18. Heckscher, E. F., "The Effect of Foreign Trade on the Distribution of Income," in *Readings in the Theory of International Trade,* Ellis, H. S., and Metzler, L. A., eds., Philadelphia, 1950.

18a. Hirsch, S., "Trade and Per Capita Income Differentials: An Empirical Test of Burenstam-Linder's Theory," Tel Aviv University, September 1969, draft manuscript.

19. ———, "The United States Electronics Industry in International Trade," *National Institute Economic Review,* November 1965.

20. Hirschman, A. O., "The Political Economy of Import-Substituting Industrialization in Latin America," *Quarterly Journal of Economics,* February 1968.

21. Hufbauer, G. C., *Synthetic Materials and the Theory of International Trade,* London, 1966, Appendix B.

22. International Labor Office, *Yearbook of Labor Statistics: 1965,* Geneva, 1966.

23. Japanese Ministry of International Trade and Industry, *1960 Table of Industrial Relations,* Tokyo, 1966.

24. Johnson, H. G., "International Trade Theory and Monopolistic Competition Theory," in Kuenne, R. E., ed., *Monopolistic Competition Theory: Studies in Impact,* New York, 1967.

TABLE A-3

Cosine Coefficients[a] between National Export and Import Vectors, Three-Digit SITC Basis

Importing Country	Exporting Country											
	Canada	U.S.	Austria	Belgium	Denmark	France	Germany	Italy	Nether-lands	Norway	Sweden	U.K.
Canada	.4308	.9280	.5160	.6746	.5627	.8807	.9564	.7938	.5637	.1905	.6379	.9611
United States	.7316	.6551	.6871	.8016	.3804	.7915	.6952	.7378	.6042	.4524	.6869	.7506
Austria	.3995	.8811	.5811	.6655	.6342	.8918	.9487	.8694	.6523	.2345	.6543	.9186
Belgium	.5044	.8264	.5431	.7924	.5028	.8456	.8829	.7934	.5972	.2936	.6338	.9316
Denmark	.5545	.8483	.7466	.7891	.6633	.9464	.8986	.8773	.7691	.4427	.7940	.8787
France	.4941	.8771	.7627	.7333	.7231	.8653	.8639	.8046	.7498	.3441	.7229	.8242
Germany	.5626	.7092	.8046	.7921	.5777	.8349	.7065	.8353	.7525	.3969	.6671	.7126
Italy	.4826	.8449	.7209	.6774	.6785	.8159	.8180	.7293	.7858	.3510	.6753	.7820
Netherlands	.4824	.8622	.7260	.7637	.6528	.9235	.9004	.9106	.7928	.2979	.6998	.8799
Norway	.2131	.4533	.4174	.4053	.6777	.5525	.5108	.5191	.5643	.6085	.7080	.4834
Sweden	.4229	.8797	.6512	.7604	.6533	.9410	.9454	.8994	.7093	.3083	.6907	.9177
United Kingdom	.5674	.6127	.6073	.6155	.5196	.5853	.5565	.5782	.6098	.4571	.5976	.6245
Australia	.5461	.9233	.5493	.6704	.5237	.8708	.8961	.7816	.6448	.2521	.6711	.9203
Japan	.3088	.6914	.4852	.4189	.5968	.5767	.5795	.5509	.6243	.3749	.4882	.5657
Israel	.2815	.5245	.4076	.6301	.4542	.5523	.5599	.4653	.4801	.2815	.5117	.6860
Portugal	.4145	.8188	.5727	.7793	.5422	.8673	.8938	.7617	.6262	.2233	.6137	.9184
Spain	.3450	.7757	.7420	.5450	.7409	.7166	.7539	.6578	.6675	.2917	.6304	.6729

	Australia	Japan	Israel	Portugal	Spain	Yugoslavia	Mexico	Hong Kong	India	Korea	Pakistan	Taiwan
Yugoslavia	.3663	.8015	.7374	.6828	.6874	.8543	.8464	.7485	.7083	.3360	.6627	.7836
Mexico	.4111	.9242	.5279	.5586	.6671	.8256	.9581	.7637	.5863	.2231	.6870	.8991
Hong Kong	.3388	.4956	.6029	.6472	.4472	.6330	.5285	.6091	.6495	.2425	.4593	.5963
India	.3646	.8171	.6825	.5836	.7371	.7460	.7935	.6656	.6289	.3169	.6783	.7421
Korea	.1960	.3010	.3139	.3754	.3024	.3920	.3223	.3701	.4534	.3867	.2469	.2698
Pakistan	.3403	.7603	.6479	.6026	.6757	.7666	.8034	.6766	.6752	.2995	.6481	.7403
Taiwan	.3212	.5847	.4765	.6196	.4719	.6960	.6288	.5623	.6129	.3782	.5416	.6591
Canada	.5549	.5495	.0521	.1915	.4586	.3421	.1851	.1185	.1189	.1860	.1193	.1600
United States	.5849	.6551	.2563	.3784	.4859	.4592	.2601	.3499	.2639	.4689	.1991	.3759
Austria	.5532	.5786	.0756	.2940	.5690	.4060	.3043	.1699	.2185	.2210	.2230	.2744
Belgium	.6243	.5531	.3724	.3688	.5196	.4158	.2532	.1750	.1957	.2320	.1623	.2307
Denmark	.5896	.7563	.1031	.3396	.5669	.5352	.3137	.2206	.2476	.3456	.2462	.3428
France	.6014	.6162	.1008	.2556	.5471	.4494	.3329	.1700	.1365	.2602	.1341	.2391
Germany	.6031	.6707	.1761	.4238	.5567	.5252	.4066	.3728	.3184	.4847	.2963	.4403
Italy	.6139	.6094	.0785	.2489	.5010	.4288	.3577	.1354	.1624	.2265	.1524	.2161
Netherlands	.5669	.6998	.1213	.3756	.5189	.4909	.2891	.3401	.2393	.3765	.2412	.3948
Norway	.3158	.7783	.0580	.1749	.5572	.7611	.1912	.1704	.0970	.2031	.1037	.1757
Sweden	.6105	.6929	.0903	.3032	.5602	.4972	.2898	.2654	.1974	.3401	.1935	.2956
United Kingdom	.5569	.4677	.5361	.4647	.4893	.4663	.3313	.2209	.2139	.3133	.1760	.3533
Australia	.5535	.5640	.0698	.2826	.5015	.3751	.1952	.1497	.2059	.2174	.2406	.2494
Japan	.4267	.3765	.1879	.2368	.4752	.3533	.3334	.0741	.1364	.1082	.0842	.1382
Israel	.4095	.5052	.7998	.4322	.3222	.3474	.1787	.0498	.1133	.1158	.0660	.1356

(continued)

TABLE A-3 (concluded)

Importing Country	Exporting Country											
	Australia	Japan	Israel	Portugal	Spain	Yugo-slavia	Mexico	Hong Kong	India	Korea	Pakistan	Taiwan
Portugal	.6070	.6052	.3073	.3046	.4376	.3222	.2983	.0917	.1099	.2056	.1281	.2102
Spain	.4564	.5122	.0619	.1866	.3955	.3354	.2876	.0630	.0474	.1665	.0667	.1863
Yugoslavia	.5191	.6588	.0640	.2330	.4686	.3763	.2846	.0746	.1575	.2461	.1485	.2081
Mexico	.5020	.4856	.0396	.1455	.4573	.3406	.2130	.0596	.0214	.0814	.0376	.1218
Hong Kong	.3661	.5846	.4853	.6857	.4029	.4215	.2646	.4423	.2919	.4437	.3985	.5622
India	.4796	.5487	.0776	.1523	.4317	.4439	.2513	.0337	.0252	.1362	.0471	.1401
Korea	.1905	.3601	.1193	.2472	.4061	.2222	.2065	.0424	.0977	.1166	.1324	.2427
Pakistan	.4598	.5991	.0496	.1840	.4480	.4340	.2798	.0715	.0286	.1524	.0654	.1626
Taiwan	.4771	.7113	.0673	.1682	.5072	.4595	.3065	.0491	.0643	.2093	.0887	.1897

[a]The cosine coefficient is defined as:

$$\text{Cos} X_i M_j = \frac{\sum\limits_{n} x_{in} \cdot m_{jn}}{\sqrt{\sum\limits_{n} x_{in}^2 \cdot \sum\limits_{n} m_{jn}^2}},$$

where x_{in} represents exports of commodity n as a percentage of country i's total manufactures exports, and m_{jn} represents imports of commodity n as a percentage of country j's total manufactures imports.

TABLE A-4

Cosine Coefficients[a] between National Export Vectors, Three-Digit SITC Basis

	Canada	U.S.	Austria	Belgium	Denmark	France	Germany	Italy	Nether- lands	Norway	Sweden	U.K.
Canada	1.0000											
United States	.4776	1.0000										
Austria	.5013	.5704	1.0000									
Belgium	.3932	.5892	.6157	1.0000								
Denmark	.2106	.6718	.6537	.3485	1.0000							
France	.4264	.8389	.7099	.8173	.5985	1.0000						
Germany	.3851	.9107	.5723	.6884	.6375	.9016	1.0000					
Italy	.3379	.7738	.6973	.6839	.6558	.8884	.8272	1.0000				
Netherlands	.3821	.6766	.6984	.5561	.6671	.7381	.6190	.7024	1.0000			
Norway	.6627	.2441	.4410	.2642	.4000	.3198	.2264	.2603	.3910	1.0000		
Sweden	.6790	.6739	.6785	.5044	.7063	.6621	.6921	.6079	.5969	.6435	1.0000	
United Kingdom	.4263	.9063	.5228	.7313	.5727	.8851	.9415	.8024	.6139	.2080	.6370	1.0000
Australia	.3960	.5271	.3909	.6166	.3011	.5917	.5629	.4681	.3969	.2255	.4215	.5846
Japan	.2515	.4942	.6356	.6611	.5724	.7434	.6025	.6929	.7426	.4463	.6276	.5913
Israel	.0402	.0632	.0829	.3329	.0584	.0992	.0593	.1083	.1335	.0562	.0402	.2559
Portugal	.1009	.1867	.3606	.3741	.2506	.3445	.1939	.4082	.4296	.1172	.1525	.3003
Spain	.2553	.4430	.4191	.4577	.4336	.5578	.4711	.5733	.5087	.3858	.4293	.4693
Yugoslavia	.2918	.3549	.4663	.3895	.5792	.4817	.3813	.5392	.4955	.5771	.5696	.3858
Mexico	.1480	.2064	.3021	.3014	.2377	.3257	.2208	.2732	.3136	.1083	.1786	.2429
Hong Kong	.0327	.0970	.3838	.2086	.2390	.2595	.1075	.4528	.2691	.0611	.0928	.1171
India	.0212	.0656	.2234	.2379	.0932	.2261	.0964	.3303	.3096	.0392	.0409	.1807
Korea	.1028	.1272	.4643	.3764	.2223	.3800	.1719	.4890	.3299	.0725	.1362	.1951
Pakistan	.0317	.0814	.2168	.2214	.0980	.2372	.0926	.2878	.3113	.0319	.0457	.1516
Taiwan	.1825	.1542	.3827	.3134	.2250	.3583	.1612	.4254	.4051	.1780	.1521	.1752

(continued)

TABLE A-4 (concluded)

	Australia	Japan	Israel	Portugal	Spain	Yugoslavia	Mexico	Hong Kong	India	Korea	Pakistan	Taiwan
Australia	1.0000											
Japan	.4143	1.0000										
Israel	.1248	.1205	1.0000									
Portugal	.1538	.3899	.4864	1.0000								
Spain	.3627	.5387	.1027	.3936	1.0000							
Yugoslavia	.3949	.6449	.0806	.3328	.6039	1.0000						
Mexico	.6211	.2374	.0805	.2191	.3917	.2946	1.0000					
Hong Kong	.0627	.3322	.1049	.4910	.2793	.4025	.0748	1.0000				
India	.0669	.3976	.1257	.4409	.2384	.1373	.0687	.1321	1.0000			
Korea	.1684	.4892	.1111	.4813	.2783	.3864	.1623	.7090	.3694	1.0000		
Pakistan	.0688	.3316	.0570	.4890	.2746	.1603	.1333	.2128	.7444	.3202	1.0000	
Taiwan	.1170	.3920	.1410	.5312	.3244	.3821	.2189	.5492	.2372	.7589	.3486	1.0000

[a]The cosine coefficient is defined as in note (a) to Table A-3, except that x_{jn} replaces m_{jn}, where x_{jn} represents exports of commodity n as a percentage of country j's total manufactures exports.

25. Keesing, D. B., "Labor Skills and International Trade: Evaluating Many Trade Flows with a Single Measuring Device," *Review of Economics and Statistics*, August 1965.

26. ———, "Labor Skills and Comparative Advantage," *American Economic Review*, May 1966.

27. ———, "The Impact of Research and Development on United States Trade," *Journal of Political Economy*, February 1967.

28. ———, "Labor Skills and the Structure of International Trade in Manufactures," in Kenen, P. B., and Lawrence, R., eds., *The Open Economy: Essays in International Trade and Finance*, New York, 1968.

29. ———, "Population and Industrial Development: Some Evidence from Trade Patterns," *American Economic Review*, June 1968.

30. Kendall, M. G., *Rank Correlation Methods*, 3rd ed., London, 1962.

31. Kenen, P. B., "Nature, Capital and Trade," *Journal of Political Economy*, October 1965.

32. ———, "Toward a More General Theory of Capital," Columbia University International Economics Workshop, December 1965, mimeographed.

33. Kenen, P. B., and Yudin, E., "Skills, Human Capital, and U.S. Foreign Trade," Columbia University International Economics Workshop, December 1965, mimeographed.

34. Kit, B., Yurow, J., and Millie, H., *Economic Impact of International Standardization on United States Industry and Trade*, Washington, June 1966.

35. Kravis, I. B., " 'Availability' and Other Influences on the Commodity Composition of Trade," *Journal of Political Economy*, April 1956.

36. ———, "Wages and Foreign Trade," *Review of Economics and Statistics*, February 1956.

37. Kuhn, T. S., *The Copernican Revolution: Planetary Astronomy in the Development of Western Thought*, Cambridge, 1957.

38. Kuznets, S., "Quantitative Aspects of the Economic Growth of Nations," Parts IX and X: "Level and Structure of Foreign Trade," *Economic Development and Cultural Change*, October 1964 and January 1967.

39. Lary, H. B., *Imports of Manufactures from the Less Developed Countries*, New York, NBER, 1968, pp. 36–37.

40. ———, "A Critique of Leontief's Findings on Factor Proportions in United States Foreign Trade," University of Wisconsin, Workshop in Economic Development, March 1968.

41. Leontief, W. W., "Domestic Production and Foreign Trade: The American Capital Position Re-examined," *Proceedings of the American Philosophical Society*, September 1953.

42. ———, "Factor Proportions and the Structure of American Trade," *Review of Economics and Statistics*, November 1956.

43. ———, "The Transactions Table of the 1958 United States Input-Output Table," *Survey of Current Business,* September 1965.

44. Linder, S. B., *An Essay on Trade and Transformation,* Stockholm, 1961.

45. Linnemann, H., *An Econometric Study of International Trade Flows,* Amsterdam, 1966.

46. Manne, A. S., ed., *Investments for Capacity Expansion: Size, Location, and Time-Phasing,* London, 1967.

47. Michaely, M., *Concentration in International Trade,* Amsterdam, 1962.

48. Mitchell, E. J., "Explaining the International Pattern of Labor Productivity and Wages: A Production Model with Two Labor Inputs," *Review of Economics and Statistics,* November 1968.

48a. Mookerjee, S., *Factor Endowments and International Trade,* Bombay, 1958.

49. Moroney, M. J., *Facts from Figures,* London, 1958.

50. Moroney, J. R., "The Strong-Factor-Intensity Hypothesis: A Multisectoral Test," *Journal of Political Economy,* June 1967.

51. Ohlin, B., *Interregional and International Trade,* rev. ed., Cambridge, 1967.

52. Posner, M. V., "International Trade and Technical Change," *Oxford Economic Papers,* October 1961.

53. Roskamp, K. W., "Factor Proportions and Foreign Trade: the Case of West Germany," *Weltwirtschaftliches Archiv,* 1963.

54. Roskamp, K. W., and McMeekin, G. C., "Factor Proportions, Human Capital and Foreign Trade: the Case of West Germany Reconsidered," *Quarterly Journal of Economics,* February 1968.

55. Smith-Gavine, S. A. N., "A Percentage Measure of Standardisation," *Productivity Measurement Review,* Paris, December 1963.

56. Stigler, G. J., "The Economics of Scale," *Journal of Law and Economics,* October 1958.

57. Stobaugh, R. B., Jr., "The Product Life Cycle, U.S. Exports, and International Investment," D.B.A. thesis, Harvard Business School, June 1968.

58. Stolper, W., and Roskamp, K. W., "Input-Output Table for East Germany with Applications to Foreign Trade," *Bulletin of the Oxford University Institute of Statistics,* November 1961.

59. Tatemoto, M., and Ichimura, S., "Factor Proportions and Foreign Trade: the Case of Japan," *Review of Economics and Statistics,* November 1959.

60. Travis, W. P., *The Theory of Trade and Protection,* Cambridge, 1964.

61. Tucker, J., *Four Tracts, Together with Two Sermons, on Political and Commercial Subjects,* Gloucester, 1774, pp. 9–48.

62. United Nations, *Classification of Commodities by Industrial Origin:*

Relationship of Standard International Trade Classification to the International Standard Industrial Classification, New York, 1966.

63. ――――, *Commodity Indexes for the Standard International Trade Classification, Revised*, New York, 1963.

64. ――――, Statistical Office, *Commodity Trade Statistics*, New York, various issues.

65. ――――, Statistical Office, *The Growth of World Industry: 1938–1961*, New York, 1963.

66. ――――, Statistical Office, *Yearbook of National Accounts Statistics: 1965*, New York, 1966.

67. United States, Bureau of the Census, *Census of Manufactures: 1958*, Summary Volume, Part 9, Washington, 1960.

68. ――――, *Schedule B—Statistical Classification of Domestic and Foreign Commodities Exported from the United States: January 1, 1958 Edition*, Washington, reprinted January 1, 1962.

69. ――――, *Census of Manufactures*, Washington, various editions, 1951 through 1963.

70. ――――, *U.S. Census of Population, 1960: Occupation by Industry*, Washington, 1963.

71. ――――, *Changes in Schedule B—Statistical Classification of Domestic and Foreign Commodities Exported from the United States: January 1, 1965 Edition*, Public Bulletin B-1, Washington, 1965.

72. ――――, *United States Exports Commodity by Country* (FT 420), Washington, December 1965.

73. ――――, *Statistical Abstract of the United States*, Washington, 1965, 1966.

74. ――――, *U.S. Commodity Exports and Imports as Related to Output 1962 and 1963*, Washington, 1966.

75. United States, Treasury Department, *Tables of Useful Lives of Depreciable Property* (Bulletin "F"), Washington, 1955.

76. Vernon, R., "International Investment and International Trade in the Product Cycle," *Quarterly Journal of Economics*, May 1966.

77. Vietorisz, T., and Manne, A. S., "Chemical Processes, Plant Location and Economies of Scale," in Manne, A. S., and Markowitz, H. M., eds., *Studies in Process Analysis*, New York, 1963.

78. Waehrer, H. Y., "Inter-Industry Skill Differences, Labor Earnings and United States Foreign Trade: 1960," Ph.D. dissertation, Columbia University, 1966.

79. Wahl, D. F., "Capital and Labor Requirements for Canada's Foreign Trade," *Canadian Journal of Economics and Political Science*, August 1961.

80. Walker and Company (in collaboration with UN Statistical Office), *Supplement to the World Trade Annual: 1964*, New York, 1966.

81. Wells, L. T., "International Trade and Business Policy," D.B.A. dissertation, Harvard Business School, 1966.

The Technology Factor

in a World Trade Matrix

WILLIAM H. GRUBER

NORTHEASTERN UNIVERSITY

RAYMOND VERNON

HARVARD UNIVERSITY

One of the external economies that an author can draw upon in a collection of papers such as these is the expository background which the other papers provide. Elsewhere in this collection, the reader will find a number of accounts of the past efforts of economists to find an efficient explanation of international trade—efficient in terms of its ability to describe, predict, and explain the level and composition of such trade. To relate our contribution appropriately to what has gone before, there is no need to make more than the briefest reference to those past efforts.

The mainstream of international trade analysis proceeds, of course,

NOTE: This paper was made possible by a grant from the Harvard University Program on Technology and Society under a long term grant from the International Business Machines Corporation. Support also was provided by Harvard University's Center for International Affairs. Computer facilities were provided by the M.I.T. Computation Center. Although the article is a joint product of the authors, Gruber was principally responsible for the trade matrix and the related variables and Vernon was principally responsible for the analytical structure. The authors are grateful to Vincent Foxworthy for his assistance in programming and to Herbert Cremer for his work on the data. Gordon Kaufman's occasional guidance on the statistical techniques used in this paper was of immense value to the authors.

from an analytical structure identified with Ricardo, Marshall, Heckscher, and Ohlin, stressing comparative advantage doctrine and factor proportions theory. It hardly needs to be said that analyses in this tradition generally take consumer preferences as given, the market as atomistic, knowledge as free and universal, the production function as invariant, and unit costs as invariant or increasing. The composition of trade is then explained primarily in terms of the differences in factor proportions and consumer preferences between countries.

A number of other lines of analysis have appeared in recent years, however, which have based their search for explanations of international trade on rather different factors. One strand of this aberrant tendency seeks to determine to what extent the leads and lags in technological innovation among countries determine the level and composition of their trade; [1] the departures from the mainstream that are involved in this approach usually include the assumption that technical knowledge or skill is not a costless or universally available good and the assumption that the possession of knowledge or skill creates a transitory advantage for the exporting country. A second theme, not wholly dissociated from the first, has emphasized the relation between the export performance of a nation and a market "horizon"—including both the knowledge and the perception of market risk—of the nation's businessmen; once again, the new emphasis consists mainly of introducing knowledge as a hitherto neglected variable. [2] Still another approach to international trade emphasizes the role of economies of scale, whether internal or external, whether in production or in marketing, as a powerful explanatory variable. [3] Finally, there have been explanations that appeal to systematic institutional factors, such as the parent-subsidiary relation of the buyer and seller or the bilateral trade arrangement of the buying and selling countries. Behind these explanations there usually lies the assumption that buyers and sellers are engaged in a trade-off between risk avoidance and cost, forsaking the freedom to select source or market solely on a price basis, in favor of the advantages of longer run assurances [16].

---

[1] Williams [21], Kravis [11], Keesing [7], Kindleberger [12], Vernon [18], Hirsch [3], Wells [19], Tsurumi [17], and Stobaugh [15].

[2] H. G. Johnson has pointed out the introduction of skill and knowledge can be readily accommodated within the structure of classical theory [6].

[3] See the sources cited in footnote 1, as well as: Linder [13], Linnemann [14], Hufbauer [5], and Keesing [9].

The purpose of this paper is to provide grist for the mill of theory. The analysis in the paper is based upon a matrix of world trade for manufactured goods relating to one year, 1964. The fact that the data are confined to manufactured goods and the fact that they relate to a single year substantially limit the contribution one can hope to make. Theories that rely on comparative cost concepts to explain international trade generally cannot be tested very rigorously unless all of the trade of the importing and exporting countries is included in the test. And theories that rely on leads and lags for their causation cannot be tested very well unless they are exposed to data over periods of time. Still, there is much that the analysis has to suggest about the relative strength of forces underlying international trade flows.

The central question of the analysis is this: To what extent are the international trade flows of an industry associated with the technological aspects of the industry, and how do these associations vary according to the countries of origin and destination of the trade flow? To explore the question adequately, however, numerous ancillary issues have to be investigated, including the relation between the trade of an industry and its nontechnological characteristics.

TECHNOLOGICAL INPUTS AND WORLD TRADE

Before introducing the world trade matrix that is the *pièce de résistance* of this paper, it will help to summarize some of the findings of earlier studies that have an immediate bearing.

One finding of central relevance to this analysis is that, as far as the United States is concerned, industries associated with a relatively high "research effort" also tend to export a relatively high proportion of their output. It does not matter very much how "research effort" is measured, whether by industry research and development expenditures as a percentage of industry sales, or by technical personnel as a percentage of total industry employment; the results are still very much the same. Various studies done by us and by others have confirmed this relationship [8, 2]. Table 1 extracts some data from one of our earlier studies to illustrate the main point.

In interpreting the results in Table 1, there are a number of difficulties

TABLE 1

Research Effort and World Trade Performance
by United States Industries, 1962

	5 Industries with Highest Research Effort	14 Other Industries	All 19 Industries
Research effort			
Total R&D expenditures as percentage of sales	6.3	0.5	2.0
Scientists and engineers in R&D as percentage of total employment	3.2	0.4	1.1
Export performance			
Exports as percentage of sales	7.2	1.8	3.2
Excess of exports over imports, as percentage of sales	5.2	-1.1	0.6

Source: W. H. Gruber, Dileep Mehta, and Raymond Vernon [2],
Table 1, p. 23.

to be faced. One of these, as we shall have occasion to point out several times in the course of this paper, is the fact that high R&D activity in U.S. industry is strongly correlated with various other industry characteristics; there is an especially close association, for example, with the comparatively intensive use of high-level manpower in general. Accordingly, one cannot readily determine whether the R&D effort of an industry or its pattern of manpower use in general is the prime factor influencing the export performance of the industry. Yet for some policy purposes, the distinction can be critical.

The statistical tie between strong export performance and skilled manpower use is not limited to U.S. industry alone. The same tie seems to exist in Canadian industry. An illuminating analysis of the performance of sixty-three branches of Canadian industry demonstrates a fairly strong association between (1) male professional and technical workers as a percentage of total employment and (2) exports as a percentage of domestic production [20]. More fragmentary evidence suggests that a similar association may exist for the industries of a number of other countries, but that the tendency weakens and may even be reversed as one moves from developed to less-developed economies.

It is not self-evident why R&D-intensive, skill-intensive industries should characteristically export a relatively high percentage of their output. All that the literature contains at this stage are fragmentary tests of some general hypotheses, linking such behavior to issues of monopoly, scale, and innovational lags [5, 18]. But one cannot yet exclude such mundane explanations as the possibility that the products of such industries are of high value in relation to weight and bulk, or that they are especially free from import impediments such as high tariffs and embargoes.

Having started these hares, it has to be acknowledged at once that the existing data are not good enough to pursue them very far, at least not in terms of the measures presented in Table 1. Figures on the relationship of exports to production, broken down by industrial groupings that can be matched with R&D variables, are available for only a few countries. In order to throw light on the problem from a different direction, therefore, we turn to the analysis of the world trade matrix that constitutes the core of this paper.

AREA EXPORT SHARES IN WORLD MARKETS

One can think of the export trade of any area as being a function of the economic characteristics of the industries that generate the exports. Symbolically, for exporting country i:

$$\sum_{j=1}^{n} E_{ijk} = f(a, b, c, \ldots)$$

where: E_{ijk} specifies the volume of exports from area i to area j in product category k; and

$a, b, c, \ldots$ specify various economic characteristics applicable to industries producing manufactured goods.

(The introduction of *j*, the importing area, at this point should not throw the reader off; it does not play an operational part in the discussion until much later and is introduced simply to permit the use of consistent notations throughout the paper.)

When a relationship of this sort is computed separately for each of the exporting areas in the world trade matrix, the basis has been laid for developing two kinds of information.

One type of information is the *similarities* from area to area in the export performance of industries with specified characteristics. Can one say, for instance, that industries in which technological activity or degree of concentration are very marked also generally have large exports, irrespective of the characteristics of the exporting area?

Another kind of information is the *differences* in the export behavior of given kinds of areas. Do capital-rich economies, for instance, systematically exhibit more prominence for capital-intensive industries in their export mix than economies that are relatively less well endowed with capital? More generally, does the export mix seem to be a function of the resource endowment of the exporting country?

So much for prelude. The data developed by us for mounting this phase of the analysis are described in Appendix A. They consist of the 1964 exports of specified manufactured goods, broken down into twenty-four categories, from each of ten exporting areas (United States, United Kingdom, West Germany, France, "Rest of EEC," "Rest of EFTA," Canada, Japan, Mexico, and Brazil) to each of twelve importing areas (the first eight enumerated above plus the white Commonwealth countries, Africa minus South Africa, Latin America, and Asia.)

The choice of areas and industry breakdowns embodied the usual procrustean compromises that research of this sort is bound to require. Given the limitations of resources and data, we adopted a much more highly aggregated classification system of areas and industry than is optimal for work of this sort. As the reader will shortly see, the limitations imposed by the classification of industries proved particularly restrictive. But despite these handicaps, the results provide many insights into the role of the technical factor in international trade.

Table 2 presents the 1964 export data separately for each of twenty-four industries from each of the ten exporting areas. The table also presents summary figures grouping eight "technology-intensive" indus-

TABLE 2

Exports from Ten Areas by Twenty-Four Industries Normalized by Total Exports of Area, 1964

(exports from each area as per cent of twenty-four-industry total from that area)

Industries (SIC number)	U.S.	U.K.	West Germany	France	Rest of EEC	Rest of EFTA	Canada	Japan	Mexico	Brazil	All 10 Areas
All twenty-four	100.0	100.0	100.0	100.0	100.0	100.0	100.0	100.0	100.0	100.0	100.0
Eight technology-intensive	41.7	31.2	31.0	27.8	29.2	22.4	18.1	23.6	11.8	3.3	29.8
Aircraft (372)	6.7	1.2	.3	1.8	.9	.2	2.2	.2	a	.3	2.1
Office machines (357)	2.4	1.1	1.4	1.1	1.4	1.0	1.1	.3	a	.1	1.4
Drugs (283)	1.6	1.6	1.3	1.6	1.1	2.1	.2	.5	2.6	.1	1.3
Chemicals (minus drugs) (other 28)	13.8	10.0	12.2	10.9	9.2	6.6	7.7	7.0	5.4	2.2	10.2
Electrical machinery (36)	7.9	8.8	9.1	5.9	8.6	6.0	2.8	11.9	.7	.2	7.8
Instruments (38)	3.1	2.4	3.8	1.9	1.7	4.9	.7	3.3	.4	a	2.8
Agricultural machinery (352)	3.8	3.5	1.4	.9	.6	.8	2.9	.2	.1	a	1.9
Petroleum and coal (29)	2.4	2.6	1.5	3.7	5.6	.8	.6	.4	2.7	.3	2.4
Sixteen other	58.3	68.8	69.0	72.2	70.8	77.6	81.9	76.4	88.2	96.7	70.2
Transport equipment (minus aircraft) (other 37)	6.3	16.6	18.4	10.8	8.2	6.5	3.3	12.3	.6	.5	10.3
Other machinery non-electrical (other 35)	20.6	17.4	20.8	9.0	8.2	12.8	5.1	6.9	1.0	.8	14.0
Nonferrous metals (other 33)	3.3	3.7	2.2	2.2	4.2	4.0	15.5	1.0	15.4	a	4.0
Rubber, and plastics n.e.c. (30)	1.3	1.5	1.4	2.0	1.4	.5	.4	2.1	.1	.6	1.3

(continued)

TABLE 2 (concluded)

Industries (SIC number)	U.S	U.K.	West Germany	France	Rest of EEC	Rest of EFTA	Canada	Japan	Mexico	Brazil	All 10 Areas
Ferrous metals (331 & 332)	3.8	5.6	8.3	11.7	10.5	5.6	3.6	15.0	2.8	1.9	7.5
Fabricated metals (34)	2.7	3.8	4.6	2.8	2.9	2.7	1.2	4.0	1.4	a	3.1
Stone, clay, glass (32)	1.3	2.0	2.3	2.1	2.8	1.6	.3	3.2	1.9	a	2.0
Paper (26)	3.3	1.3	1.0	1.6	1.5	11.2	26.1	1.1	.4	.2	4.4
Textiles (22)	2.2	6.2	3.6	7.8	9.2	4.7	.7	15.9	5.3	.7	5.7
Food (20)	9.0	6.0	2.0	13.1	12.3	15.9	13.2	5.6	56.4	85.8	10.4
Tobacco (21)	.6	.5	.1	.1	.4	.4	.1	a	a	a	.3
Furniture and fixtures (25)	.2	.3	.6	.4	.7	1.1	.1	.2	.2	a	.5
Leather products (31)	.4	1.1	1.0	2.3	2.2	.7	.3	1.9	.3	.1	1.2
Printing and publishing (27)	1.3	1.3	.7	1.2	.9	.7	.2	.3	1.2	a	.9
Apparel (23)	1.1	1.4	1.5	3.8	4.7	4.1	.3	4.9	.3	.1	2.6
Lumber and wood (24)	1.0	.1	.5	1.3	.7	4.9	11.6	2.1	.6	5.9	2.0

aLess than .05 per cent.

tries and sixteen other industries. As noted earlier, measures of the intensity of research activity and measures of the intensity of use of highly skilled manpower in general are so strongly associated that we cannot hope to avoid the problem of collinearity in any industry classification system.[4] Accordingly, the ambiguity in the phrase "technology-intensive" may have a certain virtue, reminding the reader of the unavoidable ambiguity in the meaning of the classification. In any event, the eight technology-intensive industries are all those which in 1964 employed scientists and engineers in excess of 6 per cent of their total workforce, as measured by U.S. data. To make comparisons somewhat easier for the eye, the export figures for each industry in each area are expressed as a percentage of the total exports of manufactured goods of that area. In the notation system used here, the figures for a given industry in Table 2 are:

$$\frac{\sum\limits_{j=1}^{12} E_{ijk}}{\sum\limits_{j=1}^{12} \sum\limits_{k=1}^{24} E_{ijk}}$$

The eight technology-intensive industries, it is evident, are major contributors to world trade totals in manufactures. As a benchmark to measure that importance, one has only to note that they account for almost 30 per cent of the exports of the ten exporting areas in Table 2, even though the contribution of those industries to world output probably is well below 20 per cent. Apart from the general level of the exports of these industries, however, one is also struck by the faithful way in which the relative importance of the eight technology-intensive industries declines as the eye moves across the table—that is, from the highly developed United States, to the middle range of development represented by Europe and Japan, and finally to the less-developed areas represented by Mexico and Brazil.

A more systematic way of observing the similarities and differences for the industry shares is provided by the figures in Table 3; in that

---

[4] The Pearsonian coefficient of correlation for the twenty-four industries in Table 2 between (1) scientists and engineers as per cent of total workforce and (2) scientists and engineers in R&D as per cent of total workforce was +.97. Both these measures also were very highly correlated with indirect labor as per cent of total workforce.

table, the logs of the export shares of each of the twenty-four industries for each exporting area are correlated with the logs of the shares of each other exporting area in the matrix.

The figures in Table 3 demonstrate widespread similarities in the forty-five pairs of export profiles. To be sure, the similarities tend to be stronger when the export profiles of advanced countries are paired than when the profiles of such countries are matched with those of less-developed areas; the profiles of the United Kingdom, West Germany, France, Japan, and "Rest of EEC" resemble one another more closely than any of them resemble Mexico or Brazil. In fact, Mexico and Brazil are somewhat less certain matches not only for the advanced countries but even for one another. Still, the data in Table 3 suggest similarity in export profiles more strongly than they suggest difference.

The significance of these similarities, however, must not be exaggerated. A part of the parallelism may be generated by such simple explanations as the existence of universal frictions that prevent the export of some kinds of products from any country. For instance, bulky products, low in value, may be less likely to enter international trade than high-value products, whatever the source. Or the correlations may be simply a reflection of the industry classification system used; large industries are likely to generate more exports than small industries if the industries are not homogeneous in product and cost structure.

In order to distinguish among these possibilities and others, some added analysis on different lines is helpful. By relating each area's exports in a given industry to the exports in that same industry from all ten areas, the variations in export mix among the ten areas are more clearly highlighted. Symbolically, the measure for analysis is:

$$\frac{\sum\limits_{j=1}^{12} E_{ijk}}{\sum\limits_{i=1}^{10} \sum\limits_{j=1}^{12} E_{ijk}}$$

Observe some of the characteristics of this measure. If the industry distribution of a given exporting area is exactly like the industry distribution of world exports, then for that area the measure is identical in value for all twenty-four industries. Stated differently, variations in the measure from industry to industry for any exporting area reflect the

TABLE 3

Exports from Ten Areas by Twenty-Four Industries Normalized by Total Exports of Area, Compared by Pairs of Areas, 1964

(each cell shows Pearsonian coefficient of correlation for logs of export shares of twenty-four industries between indicated areas)

Exporting area	U.S.	U.K.	West Germany	France	Rest of EEC	Rest of EFTA	Canada	Japan	Mexico	Brazil
U.S.	+1.00	+ .79	+ .67	+ .67	+ .61	+ .51	+ .69	+ .43	+ .32*	+ .47
U.K.		+1.00	+ .86	+ .78	+ .81	+ .52	+ .39	+ .61	+ .45	+ .28*
West Germany			+1.00	+ .83	+ .81	+ .68	+ .43	+ .83	+ .44	+ .30*
France				+1.00	+ .92	+ .64	+ .52	+ .88	+ .61	+ .61
Rest of EEC					+1.00	+ .67	+ .43	+ .80	+ .63	+ .50
Rest of EFTA						+1.00	+ .63	+ .73	+ .59	+ .43
Canada							+1.00	+ .43	+ .35	+ .45
Japan								+1.00	+ .56	+ .47
Mexico									+1.00	+ .30
Brazil										+1.00

*Indicates coefficient not significant at the 5 per cent level.

differences in the relative importance of the exports of these industries for the particular area, as compared with the relative importance of these industries in world export totals. The measure therefore captures for each area only the deviations of that area from world export patterns.

Bearing these properties of the measure in mind, Table 4 demonstrates that the areas which are prominent exporters of technology-intensive products, according to our crude twenty-four-industry classification, are also the most prominent exporters of other manufactured products. The exports of the United States, for instance, take first place in both the technology-intensive and the "other" group of industries; West Germany and "Rest of EEC" share second- and third-place honors in both groups, and so on. But Table 4 also affirms what had already begun to be suggested by the figures in earlier tables, namely that the technology-intensive industries occupy an especially prominent place in the export mix of the United States and a less-than-proportionate place in the export mix of most areas toward the lower end of the development spectrum.

There is a good deal more that can be ferreted out, however, regarding the similarities and differences in the industry profiles of the different areas. And as a first step in these added probes, one can repeat the performance of Table 3, cross-correlating the export profiles of all possible pairs of areas. This time, however, export profiles are measured by the data in Table 4, that is, by industry-normalized, not area-normalized, shares.

In Table 5, unlike Table 3, marked similarities in export patterns are no longer in evidence. Quite obviously, the similarities in Table 3 are based in good part on factors that are common to the industries for all the areas rather than to the areas themselves. But some new correlations emerge in Table 5—correlations that are much more telling for analytical purposes.

Although the relations are not very strong and are often not significant in a probability sense, the United States emerges as a distinctive area, its export profile being negatively related to each of the other areas except the United Kingdom and Canada. Canada also offers a maverick profile; it, too, exhibits a negative relation to most other areas. For the rest, there are interesting similarities: the United Kingdom with West Germany; and France, Japan, and "Rest of EEC" with one another.

TABLE 4

Exports from Ten Areas by Twenty-Four Industries Normalized by Total Exports of Industry, 1964

(industry exports from each area as per cent of total industry exports from all ten areas)

Industries (SIC number)	U.S.	U.K.	West Germany	France	Rest of EEC	Rest of EFTA	Canada	Japan	Mexico	Brazil	All 10 Areas
All twenty-four	20.7	11.6	16.2	8.5	16.5	11.3	6.5	7.0	.7	1.1	100.0
Eight technology-intensive	28.9	12.1	16.8	7.9	16.1	8.5	3.9	5.5	.3	.1	100.0
Aircraft (372)	67.5	6.9	2.5	7.5	7.3	.9	6.8	.3	a	.2	100.0
Office machines (357)	36.5	9.0	16.1	6.8	16.7	8.5	5.1	1.3	a	.1	100.0
Drugs (283)	24.8	13.6	15.8	10.0	13.4	17.8	.9	2.4	1.3	.1	100.0
Chemicals (minus drugs; (other 28)	28.0	11.4	19.3	9.0	14.8	7.3	4.8	4.8	.4	.2	100.0
Electrical machinery (36)	21.1	13.2	19.1	6.5	18.3	8.8	2.3	10.7	.1	a	100.0
Instruments (38)	22.7	9.9	21.9	5.6	9.9	19.8	1.7	8.4	.1	a	100.0
Agricultural machinery (352)	41.1	21.5	12.1	4.2	5.6	5.0	9.9	.6	a	a	100.0
Petroleum and coal (29)	19.9	12.2	9.9	12.8	38.0	3.7	1.5	1.1	.7	.1	100.0
Sixteen other industries	17.3	11.4	15.9	8.8	16.6	12.5	7.6	7.6	.8	1.5	100.0
Transport equipment (minus aircraft; other 37)	12.7	18.7	28.9	8.9	13.2	7.2	2.1	8.3	a	.1	100.0
Other machinery non-electrical (other 35)	30.5	14.4	23.9	5.4	9.6	10.3	2.3	3.4	a	.1	100.0

(continued)

TABLE 4 (concluded)

Industries (SIC number)	U.S.	U.K.	West Germany	France	Rest of EEC	Rest of EFTA	Canada	Japan	Mexico	Brazil	All 10 Areas
	17.2	10.8	8.8	4.8	17.5	11.3	25.2	1.8	2.6	a	100.0
Nonferrous metals (other 33), Rubber, and plastics n.e.c. (30)	20.1	13.5	17.3	12.8	17.9	4.8	2.0	11.1	a	.5	100.0
Ferrous metals (331 & 332)	10.6	8.8	18.0	13.3	23.2	8.5	3.1	14.0	.3	.3	100.0
Fabricated metals (34)	17.9	14.1	23.5	7.7	15.4	9.9	2.4	8.8	.3	.1	100.0
Stone, clay, glass (32)	14.1	12.0	18.7	9.3	23.7	9.2	1.1	11.2	.6	a	100.0
Paper (26)	15.6	3.4	3.8	3.0	5.7	28.6	38.0	1.8	.1	a	100.0
Textiles (22)	8.1	12.8	10.2	11.7	26.7	9.4	.8	19.5	.6	.1	100.0
Food (20)	18.0	6.7	3.2	10.7	19.5	17.3	8.2	3.8	3.6	9.0	100.0
Tobacco (21)	40.2	17.2	4.6	2.4	18.9	15.3	1.2	a	a	.1	100.0
Furniture and fixtures (25)	9.7	8.3	20.6	7.9	22.8	26.1	1.6	2.5	.3	a	100.0
Leather products (31)	6.8	11.1	13.6	16.8	31.1	7.3	1.8	11.3	.2	.1	100.0
Printing and publishing (27)	29.6	16.6	13.2	11.8	16.1	8.5	1.3	2.1	.9	a	100.0
Apparel (23)	8.8	6.5	9.3	12.5	30.3	18.3	.8	13.4	.1	a	100.0
Lumber and wood (24)	9.9	.8	4.3	5.3	5.8	26.8	36.7	7.0	.2	3.2	100.0

aLess than .05 per cent.

TABLE 5

Exports from Ten Areas by Twenty-four Industries Normalized by Total Exports of Industry, Compared by Pairs of Areas, 1964

(each cell shows Pearsonian coefficient of correlation for
logs of export shares of twenty-four industries between indicated areas)

Exporting area	U.S.	U.K.	West Germany	France	Rest of EEC	Rest of EFTA	Canada	Japan	Mexico	Brazil
U.S.	+1.00	+ .31*	- .18*	- .43	- .45	- .47	+ .13*	- .71	- .41	- .05*
U.K.		+1.00	+ .54	+ .15*	+ .35	- .38	- .60	- .13*	- .03*	- .42
West Germany			+1.00	+ .31*	+ .27*	+ .04*	- .51	+ .50	- .05*	- .42
France				+1.00	+ .64	- .29*	- .50	+ .60	+ .33*	+ .26*
Rest of EEC					+1.00	- .03*	- .65	+ .28*	+ .35	- .04*
Rest of EFTA						+1.00	+ .09*	+ .21*	+ .29*	- .09*
Canada							+1.00	- .19*	- .08*	+ .15*
Japan								+1.00	+ .27*	+ .12*
Mexico									+1.00	+ .04*
Brazil										+1.00

*Indicates coefficient not significant at the 5 per cent level.

Brazil and Mexico bear little similarity to the advanced countries, and no similarity to one another.

With these broad impressions as an introduction, we are ready for the next question: Area by area, are the industry-normalized export measures related in some systematic way to the economic characteristics of the industries that generate the exports?

The selection of appropriate industry characteristics is, of course, critical to the exercise. The characteristics used in this analysis were intended to reflect, with fine impartiality, both the kinds of factors that are relevant to a comparative-cost approach and those that might be surrogates for monopoly effects and scale effects. They were:

L, *a raw-labor intensity measure*—employees per dollar of value added, as reported for U.S. industry

T, *a technology-intensity measure*—scientists and engineers as percentage of total employment, as reported for U.S. industry

K, *a capital-intensity measure*—fixed assets as percentage of sales, as reported for U.S. industry

S, *an intermediate-good specializing measure*—output delivered to other business as percentage of total output, as reported for U.S. industry

C, *an industry-concentration measure*—a measure based on the relative importance of the largest firms, as reported for U.S. industry

M, *a crude materials input measure*—inputs of crude materials as percentage of total output, as reported for U.S. industry.

The first three measures are intended to correspond respectively to three factors: labor in a raw or unimproved state; human skills embodied in labor (sometimes referred to as human capital); and fixed capital.

Although the measures are defined and discussed in more detail in Appendix A, one should be aware at once that they suffer from numerous inadequacies and inelegancies. First of all, although some of the measures purport to reflect the intensity of different inputs in the product of the industry to which they are related, these measures are actually based on the characteristics of the industry responsible for only the final fabricating stage of the product; they are not the sum of the direct and indirect inputs to the product, such as might be derived from an inversion of the national input-output matrix. Second, the measures purporting to gauge inputs are inconsistent in the sense that some of them are related to sales (S and M), while others are related to value added or to a conceptual equivalent (T and L). The analysis is relying—perhaps too heavily—upon the fact that measures of this sort usually display considerable insensitivity to greater refinement, especially at the gross levels of industry aggregation that we have been obliged to use here. The refinement of the industry-characteristic measures is quite clearly an area in which more work needs to be done.

Another point to be emphasized is that the "industry characteristics" used in these tests and others are characteristics based on U.S. industry data. Just how damaging that fact may be for the analysis is not clear; the debate over the existence and strength of factor inversions as an element in international trade is still going on and the results are not all in. Our use of U.S. characteristics commits us to the assumption that the relative factor position of given industries is similar in different countries. If this should prove to be the case, then the use of U.S. data is not overwhelmingly disconcerting [5, App. B, pp. 115–120; 12; 4]. But some pitfalls are opened up by this limitation, a fact that requires special care in the interpretation of the results.

On the other hand, the independent variables used in this analysis enjoy certain elements of strength that are not immediately apparent. The selection of these variables was the result of a tedious weeding-out process—a process that involved as many as a dozen different industry measures at various stages in the analysis. As a result of this process, the interrelations among various industry characteristics were well explored, adding somewhat to our sense of confidence both in the selection of variables and the interpretation of the results.

To what extent does intercorrelation exist between the measures that are to serve as the descriptive variables for our twenty-four industries? In responding to this question, one has to recognize that some of the measures—those relating to factor intensity—cannot fail to be inter-correlated, simply because of what they purport to represent. Factor-intensity measures purport to reflect the relative use of different inputs; if some are used relatively heavily, others must have been used relatively lightly. If, for instance, the product of a given industry is represented as highly capital-intensive, then the combined use of other factors in that product should be of lower than average intensity. If not, some major input is being wholly missed by the measures, or else there is something wrong with the measures used.

The results of the tests for intercorrelation between the industry variables are presented in Table 6. On the whole, the relationships in the table show a gratifying tendency toward rationality. There is a modest correlation between the technology-intensity measure, T, and the capital-intensity measure, K. But none of the factor-intensity measures—L, T, or K—shows a very strong positive correlation with any other. On the other hand, there are some strong negative correlations: both the technology-intensity measure and the capital-intensity measure are negatively correlated with the raw-labor measure.

There are other signs of rationality and consistency in the various measures descriptive of the twenty-four industries. The index purporting to measure technology intensity proves to be positively correlated with the measure representing industry concentration—a relationship frequently observed in other studies. And where a high use of raw labor exists, the industries involved tend to exhibit a low degree of concentration. The measure for industries specializing in intermediate goods output is positively correlated with the index of capital intensity, conjuring up an image of steel mills and aluminum smelters; and the measure for crude material use shows a similar tie to capital intensity, fortifying the image. Finally, consistent with earlier studies, the capital-intensity measure shows no significant relation with the measure of industry concentration; evidently capital-intensive processes afford no sure road to oligopoly power, at least when measured by the structure of U.S. industry [2].

Although the various industry measures offer a certain satisfying internal consistency, the reader will already have noted that they suggest special difficulties in the clarification of a major issue. If high technology inputs go hand in hand with high concentration, this fact is bound to imperil any statistical effort to discern what part of the export advantage of any given country in such industries may be due to the abundance and low cost of the technology inputs and what part to the exploitation of monopoly advantage. If technology intensity goes hand in hand with industry concentration, which is cause and which effect? And which is the necessary and sufficient condition to successful exports?

TABLE 6

Relations Between Descriptive Measures of Twenty-Four Industries

(each cell shows Pearsonian coefficient of correlation between indicated measures for twenty-four industries)

Industry Measure[a]	L Raw Labor Intensity	T Technology Intensity	K Capital Intensity	C Industry Concentration	S Intermediate Goods Specialization	M Crude Material Intensity
L Raw labor intensity	+1.00	− .65	+ .46	− .60	+ .05*	− .19*
T Technology intensity		+1.00	+ .41	+ .66	− .01*	− .09*
K Capital intensity			+1.00	+ .24*	+ .67	+ .43*
C Industry concentration				+1.00	− .08*	+ .13*
S Intermediate goods specialization					+1.00	+ .11*
M Crude material intensity						+1.00

Source: Based on U.S. industry data.

*Indicates coefficient not significant at 5 per cent level.

[a]Correlations are based upon logarithms of the underlying measures.

Even with that particular analytical objective in peril, however, there is still much to be learned by comparing the export measures on which Tables 4 and 5 are based with the characteristics of the industries to which they are related. Table 7 presents some of the results of such an analysis. In computing the net regressions and other data shown in Table 7, the dependent variable subjected to analysis was, of course, the same as that used in Tables 4 and 5, converted to log form. At the same time, all the independent variables were also expressed in log form. The purposes of this conversion are the usual ones. Because of the statistical skew that is found in most of the series, the conversion generates a distribution that is more in accord with the normal-distribution assumption of the statistical significance tests applied here. At the same time, the conversion permits the analyst to compare the apparent influence on exports of the various industry characteristics in each of the different exporting areas, expressing that influence in a common unit—the unit of the elasticity concept.

One hardly needs to be reminded that as a model purporting to explain the comparative performance of various exporting areas in different products the structure in Table 7 is incomplete. Some of the lacunae are self-evident. For instance, each exporting area confronts a different array of markets, remote or proximate, protected or otherwise. Moreover, each exporting area has a different propensity for serving its foreign markets by way of direct investment in overseas subsidiaries. Failure to deal with these variables affects any product category differently for the various exporting areas. The indications provided by a model such as that in Table 7 are predictably incomplete.

As it turns out, the statistical relationships shown in Table 7 prove to have appreciable "explanatory" power for only three of the exporting areas—the United States, Japan and Mexico—as indicated by the value of the coefficient of multiple correlation. For all the other areas, systematic deviations from the world export profile are feeble.

The fact that there is not much to be inferred from the table regarding the export patterns of the areas just below the United States in development, from the United Kingdom to "Rest of EFTA," is reassuring in one sense. This result means that the industry export profiles of these areas exhibit few tendencies that distinguish them from the world pattern as a whole, at least as gauged by the industry measures used

TABLE 7

Net Regressions Derived from Relating Industry-Normalized Exports
of Twenty-Four Industries to Selected Industry Characteristics, 1964
(Figures in parentheses under net regressions are *t* values;
those under correlation coefficients, *F* values)

$$\log \frac{\sum\limits_{j=1}^{12} E_{ijk}}{\sum\limits_{i=1}^{10} \sum\limits_{j=1}^{12} E_{ijk}} = a + b_1 \log L + b_2 \log T + b_3 \log K + b_4 \log C + b_5 \log S + b_6 \log M$$

Net regressions for:

Exporting area	L Raw labor	T Technology	K Capital	C Industry concentration	S Intermediate goods	M Crude material	R Multiple correlation
U.S.	− .804 (2.75)	+ .169 (1.73)	− .641 (2.59)	+ .296 (1.07)	+ .456 (1.76)	− .017 (.89)	.85 (7.27)
U.K.	− .611 (1.17)	+ .009 (.05)	− .360 (.81)	+ .522 (1.06)	− .077 (.17)	− .013 (.38)	.58 (1.40)
West Germany	+.029 (.05)	+ .119 (.58)	+ .206 (.40)	− .342 (.59)	− .056 (.10)	− .032 (.80)	.36 (.43)
France	+ .100 (.23)	+ .062 (.43)	+ .028 (.07)	− .507 (1.23)	+ .021 (.05)	+ .004 (.15)	.36 (.42)
Rest of EEC	− .030 (.06)	− .210 (1.31)	+ .278 (.68)	+.250 (.55)	− .342 (.81)	− .004 (.14)	.37 (.44)
Rest of EFTA	− .329 (.57)	− .196 (1.02)	+ .228 (.47)	− .701 (1.29)	− .354 (.70)	+ .024 (.63)	.58 (1.46)
Canada	+1.065 (1.07)	− .058 (.17)	+ .706 (.84)	+ .398 (.42)	− .002 (.01)	− .010 (.15)	.41 (.56)
Japan	+1.983 (2.09)	+ .414 (1.30)	+ .254 (.32)	−1.554 (1.73)	+ .717 (.85)	+ .072 (1.16)	.73 (3.18)
Mexico	−2.06 (1.74)	− .420 (1.05)	+ .997 (.99)	−2.54 (2.53)	− .153 (.15)	+ .062 (.79)	.74 (3.33)
Brazil	− .505 (.28)	+ .233 (.39)	− .945 (.62)	− .643 (.38)	+.910 (.57)	+ .210 (1.77)	.44 (.68)

here. That is what one should expect of some major group of exporters; in this case, the fact that the exporters occupy the conceptual middle ground in the analysis adds a little to the credibility of the interpretation with regard to the United States and Japan.

For the United States, according to the figures, relatively high shares of world exports are associated with a trilogy of factors: with high technology-intensity, with low raw-labor intensity, and with low capital-intensity. Since these intensities are not independent, there is a certain artificiality involved in commenting on them one at a time; one should, perhaps, confine his observations to industries incorporating the whole syndrome. Still, it is worth noting that the labor result is consistent with expectations. The capital result would probably have been resisted before the Leontief paradox was exposed; but perhaps, by now, it is part of conventional wisdom. The strength of the technology factor is consistent with other studies and with Leontief's solution of his paradox; on the other hand, it is also consistent with the possibility that "technology" is a surrogate for "oligopoly," given the existence of collinearity between the variables.

In the case of Japan, the industry characteristics conducive to high export shares in world markets prove to be raw-labor intensity and capital intensity—once again, a pair of intercorrelated characteristics. The results with respect to the raw-labor measure are as expected. Those with regard to capital are no doubt influenced by her strong position in "ferrous metals"—iron and steel—and by her weak position in many of the industries with low capital intensity. The explanation for Japan's strength in the capital-intensive industries may well be the converse of the explanation for U.S. weakness: either a classical explanation of the type proposed by Leontief, or a national capability for paying labor at less than its marginal productivity.

The Mexican figures defy easy explanation. Without more investigation, it is not very fruitful to speculate over their meaning.

To sum up: The analysis to this point tends to confirm much of what had generally been suspected. It supports once again the right of the technology factor (or, since the two are not statistically separable, the human skill factor) to be regarded as one type of factor endowment that may contribute to an explanation of international trade flows. It suggests, if further corroboration were needed, that the factual observations underlying both the U.S. and the Japanese versions of the Leontief paradox were not mere statistical aberrations. But it does not resolve the tension between the classical and eclectic "explanations" of these phenomena; and it offers the seeds for some new disputes over the critical factors determining the patterns of trade.

TRADE BETWEEN AREAS

The search for an explanation of the trade performance of the technology-intensive industries is pursued here in still another direction. Up to this point, the export figures used for analysis were for given industries from given areas, totaled for all destinations. In attempting to understand the forces behind the trade in technology-intensive industries, however, the characteristics of the importing areas may impart as much information as those of the exporting areas. In short, the world trade matrix for any given industry can be viewed as a network of bilateral trade flows whose structure is determined by various economic characteristics of the exporting and importing areas concerned.

The approach in this section is to analyze the bilateral trade networks of each of our twenty-four industries in terms of selected variables that are based on the exporting and importing areas. The object is not only to identify the variables that help to explain the trade flows but also to detect systematic variations in the value and direction of those variables from one kind of industry to the next.

For any k:

$$\log E_{ijk} = f(PC_i, PC_j, GNP_i, GNP_j, D_{ij}, P_{ij}, |\ \Delta PC_{ij}\ |, \text{ and } |\ \Delta H_{ij}\ |)$$

where:

PC_i = log of per capita income of exporting area

PC_j = log of per capita income of importing area

GNP_i = log of gross national product of exporting area

GNP_j = log of gross national product of importing area

D_{ij} = a function of the distance between i and j

P_{ij} = a dummy variable representing the presence (1) or absence (0) of a preferential trade arrangement between i and i

$|\Delta PC_{ij}|$ = log of the absolute difference between PC_i and PC_j

$|\Delta H_{ij}|$ = log of the absolute difference between "index of human resource development" in the exporting area (H_i) and such an index in the importing area (H_j); the index, which is based on educational attainment patterns, is known as the Harbison-Myers index.

A more detailed description of these measures appears in Appendix A.

The first six independent variables are fairly familiar in this sort of analysis; they are measures which have been employed by others, with varying success, to "explain" international trade flows.[5] These variables bear a close affinity to standard gravity models, where distance and mass are the key "explanatory" variables.

The other two variables, $|\Delta PC_{ij}|$ and $|\Delta H_{ij}|$, are more novel. These variables are introduced in order to test a family of hypotheses which hold that countries whose national environments differ considerably will have a different pattern of trade relations than those whose national environments are very much alike; and, further, that these differences will vary systematically by the nature of the product. The difference between the per capita incomes of any two areas, $|\Delta PC_{ij}|$, may be taken as a crude index of the difference in consumption patterns. The difference in human resource development, $|\Delta H_{ij}|$, to the extent that its descriptive power differs from $|\Delta PC_{ij}|$, is thought of as stressing the side of production. In short, the human resource level is thought of as the measure of an input, generated by investments in education and knowledge, whereas per capita income is related to the structure of the economy's demands.

Despite the ambitious coverage of the independent variables, some of the limitations previously encountered in Table 7 remain painfully evident. The role of import barriers, including the effective tariff rates, import licensing regimes, and other such impediments, is not explicitly accounted for. Nor is the influence of the existence of direct investments abroad by the industries of the various exporting countries. Our limited resources did not permit us to try to fill these gaps, and the reader will

[5] Linnemann [14] uses a very similar form of equation. However, he confines his analysis principally to aggregate trade flows and only ventures tentatively into the question of the differences in trade flows among different types of commodities.

have to be on his guard to detect where these omissions may have led us astray.

Before exploring the aggregate explanatory power of the variables that were included, there is the usual indispensable threshold question: To what extent are the independent variables intercorrelated? Table 8 sets out a matrix of correlation values for all possible pairs of the independent variables.

One can see at once that the variables are intercorrelated in a web of relations, complicating somewhat the interpretation of everything that is to follow. Not surprisingly, the logs of per capita income are positively associated with the logs of the gross national product to which they relate; any other result would be somewhat suspect. Distance, D_{ij}, is related to per capita income differences, $|\Delta PC_{ij}|$; where small distances exist between countries, the per capita income differences are also small, while larger distances are associated with larger per capita income differences. But this relation may have no causal significance and may simply be a reminder of the fact that seven of the eight rich exporting areas and seven of the nine rich importing areas in our trade matrix are relatively close together, in Europe and North America, while the poor areas of our trade matrix are far away from most of their trading partners.

The two measures of area differences, $|\Delta PC_{ij}|$ and $|\Delta H_{ij}|$, also exhibit some relationship to one another. But it is apparent that they are far from being carbon copies. While there is, of course, an intimate relation between the per capita income and the human resource development index of any area, the correlation of the absolute differences in these measures for pairs of areas is weak. This reflects the aberrant behavior of several areas including Canada, Japan, and "Rest of EFTA." Canada is on the low side as measured by the human resource development index in view of its per capita income, while Japan and "Rest of EFTA" project the opposite picture.

Regressing the logs of the trade flows on the eight variables presented in Table 8, industry by industry, a set of twenty-four industry equations are derived. The net regressions in these twenty-four equations for 1964 data are shown in Table 9, below, together with the value for the multiple correlation coefficients.

One of the striking aspects of Table 9 is the remarkable consistency

TABLE 8

*Relations Between Descriptive Measures
Relating to Exporting and Importing Areas, 1964*
(each cell shows Pearsonian coefficient of
correlation between indicated measures)

Measure	PC_i	PC_j	GNP_i	GNP_j	D_{ij}	P_{ij}	$\lvert\Delta PC_{ij}\rvert$	$\lvert\Delta H_{ij}\rvert$
PC_i log per cap income, export area	+1.00	a	+.79	a	− .17	+ .08*	+ .10*	+ .06*
PC_j log per cap income, import area		+1.00	a	+ .50	− .35	+ .09*	− .11*	− .06*
GNP_i log GNP export area			a	− .07*	− .02*	+ .02*	+ .17	+ .21
GNP_j log GNP import area				+1.00	− .22	− .06*	+ .10*	+ .22
D_{ij} function of distance between areas					+1.00	− .43	+ .54	+ .18
P_{ij} trade preference dummy variable						+1.00	− .32	− .35
$\lvert\Delta PC_{ij}\rvert$ log difference between PC_i and PC_j							+1.00	+ .46
$\lvert\Delta H_{ij}\rvert$ log difference between human resource development indexes								+1.00

*Indicates coefficient not significant at 5 per cent level. Although $n = 114$ for most correlations in the table, $n = 10$ for the PC_i, GNP_i correlation and $n = 12$ for the PC_j, GNP_j correlation.

[a] not calculated.

TABLE 5

Net Regressions and Multiple Correlations Reflecting Relations Between
Bilateral Trade Flows and Characteristics of Trading Areas, 1964

$$logE_{ijk} = a + b_1 logPC_i + b_2 logPC_j + b_3 logGNP_i + b_4 logGNP_j + b_5 logD_{ij} + b_6 P_{ij} + b_7 log|\Delta PC_{ij}| + b_8 log|\Delta H_{ij}|$$

Industries (SIC number)	Net Regressions for:								Multiple R Correlation
	PC_i	PC_j	GNP_i	GNP_j	D_{ij}	P_{ij}	$|\Delta PC_{ij}|$	$|\Delta H_{ij}|$	
Eight technology-intensive									
Aircraft (372)	−.111*	−.154*	+1.194	−.006*	−.364*	+.412	+.318*	−.055*	.69
Office machines (357)	+.506*	−.019*	+.652	+.350	−.430	+.206*	−.103*	+.106*	.79
Drugs (283)	−.005*	−.590	+.796	−.161*	−.794	+.226*	+.265*	−.088*	.70
Chemicals (minus drugs) (other 28)	+.929	−.513	+1.079	+.686	−.735	+.332	+.013*	−.124*	.92
Electrical machinery (36)	+.396*	−.408	+1.156	+.294*	−.712	+.366	+.119*	−.012*	.83
Instruments (38)	+.024*	−.123*	+1.197	+.370	−.394	+.232*	−.064*	+.015*	.76
Agricultural machinery (352)	+.119*	−.162*	+.854	−.203*	−.986	+.349	+.132*	+.281	.74
Petroleum and coal (29)	−.629	−.363	+1.330	−.168*	−1.463	+.255*	+.241*	+.165*	.76
Sixteen other									
Transport equipment (minus aircraft) (other 37)	+.684	−.455	+.854	+.134*	−.855	+.524	+.182*	+.111*	.75
Other machinery non-electrical (other 35)	+1.098	−.457	+1.056	+.298	−.724	+.392	−.015*	+.055*	.90
Nonferrous metals (other 33)	+1.293	−.121	−.043*	+.582	−.927	+.503	+.253*	+.156*	.85
Rubber, and plastics n.e.c. (30)	−.482*	−.385	+1.126	+.233*	−.716	+.430	−.100*	+.297	.74
Ferrous metals (331 & 332)	+.172*	−.467	+.971	+.468	−1.000	+.618	+.034*	+.126*	.77
Fabricated metals (34)	+.250*	−.372	+.819	+.251*	−.761	+.416	+.151*	+.133*	.78
Stone, clay, glass (32)	+.567	−.185*	+1.224	+.274*	−.896	+.344	+.154*	+.033*	.76
Paper (26)	+1.296	−.355	−.051*	+.152*	−1.057	+.470	+.324	+.263	.79
Textiles (22)	−.294*	−.406	+1.382	+.419	−.802	+.475	−.018*	−.058*	.73
Food (20)	−.467*	−.382	+.861	+.602	−1.238	+.427	+.500	+.167*	.76
Tobacco (21)	−.754	−.107*	+.922	+.076*	−.089*	+.180*	+.308	−.143*	.46
Furniture and fixtures (25)	−.372*	−.399	+.922*	+.108*	−1.311	+.334	+.395	+.207	.72
Leather products (31)	−.406*	−.108*	+.864	+.331*	−.725	+.505	+.139*	+.023*	.67
Printing and publishing (27)	+.189*	−.085*	+.736	−.070*	−1.050	+.139*	+.287	+.077*	.70
Apparel (23)	+.500*	−.161*	+1.152	+.216*	−.825	+.462	+.125*	+.068*	.69
Lumber and wood (24)	+.406*	+.001*	+.124*	+.240*	−.886	+.488	+.324*	+.096*	.65

*Indicates not significant. For net regressions, based on t-test at 5 per cent level; for multiple correlations, based on F-test at 5 per cent level.

in the trade behavior of the different products, almost irrespective of product type. The only seeming difference between the behavior of the eight technology-intensive industries and the sixteen other industries—and that difference feeble at best—is the explanatory power of PC_i, the per capita income of the exporting country. In this variable, consistent with conventional wisdom, one detects the prevalence of a positive relation to trade levels in the technology-intensive industries and of a negative relation in the industries at the other end of the technology spectrum. But the relations are weak and wavering.

The fact that there are so few consistent differences between the two groups of industries is a finding that generates very mixed reactions. As will shortly be evident, the seeming consistency may be due in part to the relative grossness of our industry classifications, a grossness that may have the effect of grouping a broad band of industrial activities within each of the twenty-four industry groups in Table 9. We shall return to that issue later in the discussion. For the present, the consistencies themselves are worth noting.

As indicated by many earlier studies, the distance factor, D_{ij}, has strong explanatory power for most product classes, large distances being associated with low trade. There is a temptation to equate the distance factor with some simple economic equivalent, such as transport cost. But the pervasive strength of that factor, including its appearance in such industrial categories as "drugs" and "agricultural machinery," suggests that more may be involved in this measure than mere transport cost. Perhaps what one sees here is a measure that captures not only the effect of transport cost but also the effect of other frictions associated with distance, such as limitations on businessmen's knowledge about sources and markets.

According to Table 9, the preference factor, P_{ij}, like the distance factor, significantly affects the trade flows in most of the twenty-four industry groups, conducive to higher trade levels. Here, one cannot be sure whether the tariff treatment is the moving force, or whether the market familiarity and market knowledge that go with the existence of a preferential trade relation are the causal factors of the higher levels of trade.

Table 9 also shows that irrespective of industry the size of the gross national product of the exporting country, GNP_i, is strongly correlated with the level of trade flows; but the size of the gross national product of the importing country is much more feebly and uncertainly related. Hypotheses that stress the internal and external scale economies of large countries as a source of export strength in manufactured products seem supported by this finding.

The per capita income figures for importing countries throw added light on the sources of trading strength. On the whole, the higher the per capita income of the importing country, PC_j, the lower its imports of the products covered by this matrix; this is a relation, of course, that is purportedly net of the GNP effects. One has to be cautious about interpreting the meaning of the partial relationships between per capita levels and trade flows in view of the positive correlation of the per capita figures with the GNP data. If the relationship is not a mere quirk of the data, it reflects either a perverse consumption pattern for manu-factured goods in high-income countries or the ability of such countries to engage in import substitution more effectively than others. On sheer plausibility grounds, the second possibility is more appealing than the first. If import substitution in manufactured goods is more extensive in high-income countries, is this a phenomenon other than that of mere scale? Does it perhaps reflect a greater capacity for high-income coun-tries to assemble the ingredients of technology, capital, and entrepre-neurship, whenever the existence of a domestic market is evident?

The likelihood that scale alone may not be the critical variable in explaining the results is indicated by the consistent direction in the regression values generated by $\mid \Delta PC_{ij} \mid$ and $\mid \Delta H_{ij} \mid$. In both these cases, as Table 9 indicates, large differences between importing and exporting countries are associated with high trade levels. The tendency is not very strong, but it is stubbornly persistent; nineteen of the twenty-four industry groups exhibit positive net regressions both for $\mid \Delta PC_{ij} \mid$ and for $\mid \Delta H_{ij} \mid$. If gaps in per capita income and human-resource development between importer and exporter have any effect on the level of world trade, that effect is to augment such trade, not to reduce it.

How seriously is one to take the results of an analysis of this sort?

At a minimum, with an analysis so complex and a set of independent variables so intimately interrelated, one wants to be sure of the sensitivity of the results to different structures of the model. Two features of the model are especially bothersome: the pervasive role of per capita income in the specification of the independent variables; and the unweighted character of the observations, which gives each bilateral flow as much weight as any other in the statistical generalizations.

Troubled by these aspects of the model, we sought to test the persistence of the principal results by altering the model in numerous ways. In one series of variants, one or more independent variables were dropped. In another series, geographical areas that appeared at the upper or lower end of the range—the United States in one variant, Mexico and Brazil in another—were dropped from the analysis. Through all of these, the major findings continued to appear: Distance and preference played their usual roles. Countries with a large GNP were stronger exporters of manufactured goods than countries with small, but a large GNP was no sure indicator of large imports. And finally $| \Delta PC_{ij} |$ and $| \Delta H_{ij} |$ persisted in exhibiting a mildly positive relation with trade levels for practically every type of product.

Among the variants in the model that were tried was one that separated out the bilateral trade flows affected by preference from those in which no preference existed. There were 17 preference-related bilateral flows out of the 114 flows of the 12 x 10 matrix, resulting principally from the existence of the EEC, EFTA, and the British Commonwealth preferences. Having in mind the complexity of the forces at work in these preference situations, the question was whether the tendencies manifested in the 114-pair matrix would continue to appear in the 17-pair and 97-pair matrices.

The answer is yes and no; no, in general for the 17 pairs of preference relations, and yes with undiminished strength in the 97 no-preference pairs. In the 17-pair preference group, only one or two of the explanatory variables show much strength. GNP_i, measuring the size of the exporting area, continued to be an important explanatory factor. But the distance variable, D_{ij}, lost its explanatory power as did the human resource development index. Preferential areas, it appears, have their own *modus vivendi*. In the 97-pair no-preference group, however, all of the explanatory variables took on added strength and pervasiveness among the industry groups.

Still another decomposition of the 114 bilateral flows was suggested by the strong hints of significance of $| \Delta H_{ij} |$ as an explanatory variable.

That variable, it will be recalled, seemed to bear a slight positive relation to trade flows, even for technology-intensive products. The possibility that differences in human resource development levels might encourage exports from the more highly developed to the less developed areas seems plausible enough. One might also entertain the possibility that, at least for certain kinds of products, human resource differences encourage trade to flow from the less developed to the more highly developed areas. But it seems improbable a priori that the trade stimulus would be similar in intensity and direction for all types of products.

In order to sort out the influence of the human resource measure with somewhat greater clarity, export flows were separated into two groups: those that represented an "upward" flow, from areas with low human resource indexes to areas with higher indexes; and those that moved in the opposite direction. There were 61 flows of the first sort, and 53 of the second, making up the usual 114-flow total.

From other compilations of the underlying data—compilations derived as by-products of the first main part of this study—a good deal was already known or easily inferred regarding the differences in the industrial mix of exports. High-income areas, as Table 2 had demonstrated, had a heavier representation of technology-intensive goods in their total export mix than lower-income areas. Beyond that, if one subjected the measures in Table 4 to systematic analysis, one could demonstrate that the high-income areas showed a positive tie between the prominence of a given industry in their export profile and the technology intensity of the industry, whereas that tie was absent or even negative for the low-income areas.

On the basis of various exploratory compilations done in connection with the first section, it also had been learned that any exporting area when selling down the income ladder to lower-income areas displayed a larger stress on technology-intensive goods in its export mix than when selling to areas of similar or higher income. In the case of the middle range of developed countries from the United Kingdom to Japan, for instance, it is known that the eight technology-intensive industries accounted for 19.8 per cent of their total exports to the United States, but for 27.8 per cent of their total exports to each other, and 30.7 per cent of their total exports to the less developed areas. Could one add to an understanding of the forces affecting upstream and downstream trade by reference to the variables in Table 9? The data in Table 10 provide some glimmerings of an answer.

The first impression to be drawn from Table 10 is the marked similarity in the results between the 61 "downstream" trade flows and the 53 "upstream" flows.

Observe the contribution of GNP_i, the gross national product of the exporter, in the two groups of cases. In both instances, a large GNP is strongly related to a high level of exports; for most industries, whether or not they are technology-intensive, the size of the exporting economy is important in determining the level of exports.

Note, too, the persistence in the tendency for per capita income in the importing country, PC_j, to be associated negatively with trade flows, both for upstream and for downstream trade flows. There is a suggestion in the table that this tendency is stronger in the eight technology-intensive industries than in the sixteen others; if that is so, the hypothesis that the negative correlation may reflect a greater capability of high-income countries for import substitution gains a bit more credence.

Finally, Table 10 tells us that the size of the income gap and the size of the human resource gap between exporter and importer continue mildly but persistently to be related to the level of bilateral trade flows. These tendencies seem somewhat weaker in the downstream trade of the technology-intensive industries than in the upstream trade in those industries; but there are no other clear differences in relative impact.

In terms of classical theory, there is no great surprise in the fact that exporting countries should find an especial affinity with markets most different from themselves in per capita income and human resource characteristics. What is difficult to accept is that this tendency should exist even for upstream exports in technology-intensive products. In this case, no doubt, we are the victims of the grossness in the system of industry classification on which the analysis is based. One strongly suspects that if the data could be broken down adequately, the products being exported upstream under the "technology-intensive" label would be a fairly standardized, relatively uncomplicated type of product, demanding little in the way of skill or technology from the exporting country.

TABLE 10

Net Regressions and Multiple Correlations Derived from Analysis of
Sixty-One Trade Flows $(H_i>H_j)$ and Fifty-Three Trade Flows $(H_j>H_i)$, 1964

$$\log E_{ijk} = a + b_1\log PC_i + b_2\log PC_j + b_3 GNP_i + b_4\log GNP_j + b_5\log D_{ij} + b_6 P_{ij} + b_7\log|\Delta PC_{ij}| + b_8\log|\Delta H_{ij}|$$

Net Regressions for:	Sixty-One Case Group, $H_i>H_j$			Fifty-Three Case Group, $H_j>H_i$		
	Mean Value	Number with Same Sign as Mean	Number Statistically Significant[a]	Mean Value	Number with Same Sign as Mean	Number Statistically Significant[a]
Eight Technology-Intensive Industries						
$\log PC_i$	+.030	5	1	+.199	6	2
$\log PC_j$	−.431	8	4	−.507	7	2
$\log GNP_i$	+1.113	8	8	+1.466	7	7
$\log GNP_j$	+.364	7	4	−.173	5	1
$\log D_{ij}$	−.918	8	7	−.724	8	6
P_{ij}	+.442	8	4	+.110	6	0
$\log|\Delta PC_{ij}|$	+.167	6	1	+.240	8	1
$\log|\Delta H_{ij}|$	+.043	4	0	+.322	7	5
Multiple correlation, R	.79	—	8	.78	—	8
Sixteen Other Industries						
$\log PC_i$	−.472	12	4	+.024	6	4
$\log PC_j$	−.281	14	6	−.055	8	1
$\log GNP_i$	+.751	16	11	+1.259	13	10
$\log GNP_j$	+.123	10	1	+.172	11	3
$\log D_{ij}$	−1.106	15	15	−.705	16	11
P_{ij}	+.512	16	13	+.348	14	4
$\log|\Delta PC_{ij}|$	+.379	15	7	+.142	13	0
$\log|\Delta H_{ij}|$	+.168	13	3	+.241	14	5
Multiple correlation, R	.75	—	16	.78	—	16

[a] For net regressions, based on t-test at 5 per cent level; cases with sign different from mean are not included.
For multiple correlation coefficients, based on F-test at 5 per cent level.

On looking back at the various provocative indications afforded by the models, two generalizations stand out. One is the explanatory power of some of the forces that are implicit in the gravity model; large exporters (but not necessarily large importers) generate large trade flows, but the frictions associated with distance dampen down such flows. The other conclusion relates to the explanatory power of the quality of labor. To plagiarize and modify Ricardo, the data may be displaying the dominance of an exchange of brain-created goods for brawn-created goods. As suggested by the analysis presented earlier, differences in capital and resource availability may be of less importance. Perhaps nations inadequately endowed with capital and natural resources can substitute for these to some extent or import them if necessary, without much loss of competitive position [cf. 1]; but it may be more difficult to substitute for a lack of highly skilled manpower and more uneconomic to substitute for a lack of unskilled labor.

STATIC AND DYNAMIC FACTORS

In interpreting the findings in this paper, one has constantly to recall that the findings have nothing to say about the temporal sequence of events—that they represent simply and unabashedly a cross-sectional analysis of world trade relationships. Sometimes the researcher has no choice but to try to infer what may happen over time by exploiting the indications provided from cross-sectional data. In international trade, however, that kind of exercise seems especially hazardous.

One major difficulty with moving from static to dynamic concepts in international trade has to do, as usual, with the temporal interdependence of critical variables.

The patterns of trade in an early time period may have a great deal to do with the strength of the independent variables in the period that follows. Because trade has expanded in the past, the frictional effects of distance upon future trade may decline and the lubricating effects of preferences may increase.

Moreover, although trade may be thought of as a substitute for the movement of the factors in any given time period, it may also be a stimulant for the movement of those factors in the periods that follow; investment may follow the market, and human resources may follow the investment. Trade in one period, therefore, may be the instrument for the displacement of trade in the periods that follow.

Although one has to proceed with caution in applying static observations to dynamic concepts, it is possible to reconcile the temporal sequences suggested by dynamic product-cycle or market-cycle theories with the static cross-sectional snapshot presented here.

As various dynamic models suggest, it may well be that when manufactured products first enter international trade, they tend to find their initial export markets in areas very like that of the exporter, rather than in areas that differ markedly from the exporter in human resource development terms. Our results suggest, however, that this is no more than a transitional stage; eventually, imports are cut back by domestic production and the exporter moves on to other more remote markets. What endures in international trade seems to be the commodity flows that are based on gross differences in factor endowments, differences not readily bridged by the regroupment of local factors in new combinations or the import of foreign factors to supplement those that are in local short supply.

One can speculate that the factors relating to human resource development are especially hard to replace or supplement where they are inadequate. The capabilities that go with a high level of human resource development, whether applied through cost and price or through monopoly power, may be difficult to match; and the capabilities that accrue from an adequate supply of raw labor may also be among the more enduring advantages of a trading nation. If that is so, then, the static cross-sectional pattern of world trade may well be dominated by these relatively intractable factors.

APPENDIX A

This appendix deals with the sources and methods of compilation of the trade data, the industry data, and the area data used in the study.

Trade data

Trade data were taken from OECD, *Statistical Bulletins,* Series D, Numbers 1 to 6 for January to December 1964; and the United Nations,

Statistical Papers, *Commodity Trade Statistics,* January to December 1964. The following conversion of SITC to SIC categories was used:

Industry	SIC	SITC
Food and kindred products	20	Total food shipments (0) minus nonmanufactured food (041, 043, 044, 045, 051) plus beverages (111, 112)
Tobacco products	21	122
Textile mill products	22	651 minus 651.6, synthetic fibers, 652, 653, 654, 655, 657
Apparel and related products	23	841, 842, 656
Lumber and wood products	24	631, 632, 633, 243
Furniture and fixtures	25	82
Paper and allied products	26	641, 642, 251
Printing and publishing	27	892
Chemicals and allied products	28	5, 231, 651.6
Drugs	283	541
Chemicals minus drugs	28 minus 283	5, 231, 65.6, minus 541
Petroleum and coal products	29	332
Rubber and plastic products n.e.c.	30	621, 629, 893
Leather and leather products	31	611, 612, 831, 85
Stone, clay, and glass	32	661, 662, 663, 664, 665, 666
Ferrous metals	331, 332	671, 672, 673, 674, 675, 676, 677, 678, 679
Nonferrous metals	33 minus (331 + 332)	681, 682, 683, 684, 685, 686, 687, 688, 689
Fabricated metal products	34	691, 692, 693, 694, 695, 696, 697, 698
Machinery, except electrical	35	711, 712, 714, 715, 717, 718, 719
Office machines	357	714
Agricultural machinery and implements	352	712
Other machines except electrical	35 minus (357 + 352)	711, 715, 717, 718, 719
Electrical machinery	36	722, 723, 724, 725, 726, 729, 891.1, 891.2
Transport equipment	37	731, 732, 733, 734, 735
Aircraft	372	734
Other transport	37 minus 372	731, 732, 733, 735
Instruments and related products	38	86, 891 minus (891.1 + 891.2)

Country groupings provided by the OECD were used in those cases where it was possible. A number of difficulties were encountered in the raw data, e.g., different figures in the English and French texts. In a few cases, subtraction of figures for West Germany and France from the EEC total left a negative value for the rest of EEC. Similar difficulty occasionally appeared in the subtraction of U.K. data from EFTA totals. Such cases, however, were infrequent and involved small volumes of trade. When this occurred, a value of 0 was assumed. Some U.S. exports in industries 36 and 372 were unspecified as to destination; it was assumed that these were exports of defense products and that they were distributed to Asia, 60 per cent, Latin America, 30 per cent, and Africa, 10 per cent. In some cases, data were available on an exporter basis and in other cases on an importer basis. Where observations were separately available both for the exporter and for the importer, the differences were not always consistent in an obvious sense. Some of the unexplained variance in the statistical analysis must be attributed to the poor quality of the data.

"Africa" includes all of Africa except South Africa. "Latin America" includes Spanish-speaking and Portuguese-speaking areas of South and Central America, and of the Caribbean and Mexico; it does not include non-Spanish-speaking or non-Portuguese-speaking Caribbean, Central and South American territories. "Asia" includes all of Asia and the Near East, except the U.S.S.R. and mainland China.

Industry data

The number of scientists and engineers, by industry, is from: Bureau of Labor Statistics Bulletin No. 1418, *Employment of Scientific and Technical Personnel in Industry,* Washington, 1964, Table A-14.

Total employment by industry is from U.S. Bureau of Labor Statistics Bulletin No. 1312–4, *Employment and Earnings Statistics for the United States, 1909–1966,* Washington, 1964.

Value added by industry is from U.S. Bureau of the Census, *Census of Manufactures: 1963,* Washington, 1968.

The capital/output ratio was calculated from data in FTC-SEC *Quarterly Financial Reports.* Capital was defined as net property, plant and equipment; output as sales. The data for two industries was not available from the FTC-SEC reports. Office machines were calculated from the annual reports of Control Data and SCM; agricultural equipment from the annual reports of International Harvester and John Deere & Co.

The industry concentration measure was calculated from *Census of Manufactures: 1963*. Each industry value was based upon the share of total industry shipments held by the largest eight firms. Four-digit SIC data were weighted by shipments and summed to create the variables at the two-digit and three-digit level used in the study.

Intermediate output, crude materials input, and the output by industry used in the intermediate goods specialization and crude materials input measures were calculated from: "The Transactions Table of the 1958 Input-Output Study and Revised Direct and Total Requirements Data," *Survey of Current Business,* September 1965, pp. 33ff. Definitions of crude materials input and intermediate goods output were taken as given, with one exception: Although the output of SIC 241 appears in the original source as an intermediate output, it was reclassified as a crude material input for the paper industry.

Country data

GNP and population figures were taken from Table 3 of *Gross National Product; Growth Rates and Trend Data,* Washington, AID, 1967, pp. 8–14. For this purpose, "Latin America" is: Costa Rica, El Salvador, Guatemala, Honduras, Nicaragua, Argentina, Bolivia, Brazil, Chile, Colombia, Dominican Republic, Ecuador, Mexico, Panama, Paraguay, Peru, Uruguay, Venezuela, Jamaica, Trinidad and Tobago. "Africa" includes: Ethiopia, Ghana, Kenya, Morocco, Nigeria, Rhodesia, Sudan, Tanganyika, Tunisia, Uganda, Zambia; note the omission of a few important countries including Egypt and Algeria. "Asia" includes: Cyprus, Greece, Iraq, Israel, Jordan, Turkey, Ceylon, India, Pakistan, Burma, China (Taiwan), Korea, Malaysia, Philippines, Thailand; note that Indonesia is omitted.

The human resource development index is defined by its authors as the "arithmetic total of (1) enrollment at second level of education as a percentage of the age group fifteen to nineteen, adjusted for years of schooling, and (2) enrollment at the third level of education as a percentage of the age group, multiplied by a weight of 5." See F.

Harbison and C. A. Myers, *Education, Manpower and Economic Growth,* New York, 1964, pp. 31–48, for a more detailed definition of the index and some correlations between the index and other measures of economic development.

EFTA, EEC, LAFTA, the British Commonwealth preference, and the French Union preference determined the preference classification. Distance in miles was used to create a distance-from-exporter-to-importer index. Where possible, the midpoints of regions were used as terminal points. Distances were measured in one-thousand-mile units. Land distances were weighted by a factor of 2. Values less than 1 were assigned a value of 1, and those over 10 a value of 10.

REFERENCES

1. Cooper, R. W., *The Economics of Interdependence,* New York, 1968, Chap. 3.

2. Gruber, W. H., Mehta, D., and Vernon, R., "The R&D Factor in International Trade and International Investment of United States Industries," *Journal of Political Economy,* February 1967, pp. 20–37.

3. Hirsch, S., *Location of Industry and International Competitiveness,* Oxford, 1967.

4. Horowitz, M. A., Zymelman, M., and Herrnstadt, I. L., *Manpower Requirements for Planning, An International Comparison Approach* (2 vols.), Boston, 1966.

5. Hufbauer, G. C., *Synthetic Materials and the Theory of International Trade,* Cambridge, 1966.

6. Johnson, H. G., "Comparative Cost and Commercial Policy Theory for a Developing World Economy," Wicksell Lectures of 1968, mimeographed.

7. Keesing, D. B., "Labor Skills and Comparative Advantage," *American Economic Review: Papers and Proceedings,* May 1966, pp. 249–58.

8. ———, "The Impact of Research and Development on United States Trade," *Journal of Political Economy,* February 1967, pp. 38–45.

9. ———, "Population and Industrial Development," *American Economic Review,* June 1968, p. 448.

10. Kindleberger, C. P., *Foreign Trade and the National Interest,* New Haven, 1962.

11. Kravis, I. B., " 'Availability' and Other Influences on the Commodity Composition of Trade," *Journal of Political Economy,* April 1956, pp. 143–55.

12. Lary, H. B., *Imports of Manufactures from Less Developed Countries,* New York, NBER, 1968, Chaps. 2 and 3.

13. Linder, S. B., *An Essay on Trade and Transformation,* New York, 1961.

14. Linnemann, H., *An Economic Study of International Trade Flows,* Amsterdam, 1966.

15. Stobaugh, R. B., Jr., "The Product Life Cycle, U.S. Exports, and International Investment," Ph.D. dissertation, Harvard Business School, 1968.

16. Tilton, J. E., "The Choice of Trading Partners: An Analysis of International Trade in Aluminum, Bauxite, Copper, Lead, Manganese, Tin and Zinc," *Yale Economic Essays,* Fall 1966.

17. Tsurumi, Y., "Technology Transfer and Foreign Trade: The Case of Japan 1950–1966," Ph.D. dissertation, Harvard Business School, 1968.

18. Vernon, R., "International Investment and International Trade in the Product Cycle," *Quarterly Journal of Economics,* May 1966, pp. 190–207.

19. Wells, L. T., Jr., "Product Innovation and Directions of International Trade," Ph.D. dissertation, Harvard Business School, 1966.

20. Wilkinson, B. W., *Canada's International Trade: An Analysis of Recent Trends and Patterns,* Montreal, 1967.

21. Williams, J. H., "The Theory of International Trade Reconsidered," *Economic Journal,* June 1929, pp. 195–209.

COMMENTS

JAGDISH N. BHAGWATI
Massachusetts Institute of Technology

I should like to make a few comments on Mr. Hufbauer's excellent paper.

(1) The attempt at running comprehensive tests, using a common set of data, for a variety of competing "theories" of trade patterns is welcome. However, I find Hufbauer's use of U.S. coefficients for *other* countries quite difficult to accept. While it is true that we have to work with the "best" data that are available, it is not true that we do not have the kinds of coefficients required by Hufbauer for his many countries. For example, we do have data (even if not fully comparable with U.S.) on skills in different activities for countries such as India. It would be worthwhile for Mr. Hufbauer to work through his exercises by actually using the coefficients of at least one other country and examining how far the use of U.S. coefficients everywhere biases his results. Ultimately, we can develop confidence in his results only if the coefficients used are those actually obtained from these other countries.

(2) Further checking of his other statistical indices would also be useful. For example, his estimate of the scale factor in different industries (for the United States) is admittedly open to extremely serious, and in my judgment overriding, objections. But here also, I suspect that Hufbauer could try to improve his results by comparing his statistical results, at the least, with the results derived with superior techniques by economists such as Stigler (who uses the "survival" technique), Haldi, and Manne.

(3) It should also be noted that Hufbauer uses only "direct" coefficients in his tests.

(4) The work on "human capital" in international trade has been carried out by Bharadwaj and Bhagwati for India's pattern of trade and by Roskamp and McMeekin for West Germany, in addition to Peter Kenen and Elinor Yudin for the United States. Merle (Yahr) Weiss' introduction of "human capital" in the estimation of C. E. S. production functions, yielding elasticities of substitution close to unity and hence reversing the conclusions of Minhas, is also relevant.

(5) Finally, while Hufbauer is to be congratulated for bringing Leontief's exercise up to date, I would like to record my student B. R. Hazari's comment that a full test of the Heckscher-Ohlin theorem in a multicommodity system requires that *each* exportable commodity from the United States should have a higher capital/labor ratio than each importable commodity. Working with aggregate capital/labor ratios for exports and imports as groups would not be an adequate test. Thus, even if the latter test were passed, the stricter test may not hold at a significant level; but if the former test were failed (as in the paradox), clearly the latter will also have failed.

DONALD B. KEESING
Stanford University

The studies by Hufbauer and, by Gruber and Vernon, for all the dissimilarities in their methods and approaches, complement each other very effectively. Together they mention and attempt to test, explicitly or implicitly, virtually the whole bewildering array of explanations that are now competing in trying to account for international trade in manufactures. The main results of each paper help, it seems to me, to confirm the same general picture of the causes of trade; yet the differences in interpretation and emphasis leave us free to describe this picture in many alternative ways. Indeed, it is striking that the authors often manage to give the same strands of contemporary thinking decidedly different conceptual and empirical twists.

I think the most striking joint implication of the two papers is that, at least at an operation level, we can no longer go back to any single, simple explanation of trade. Our new findings have been pushed to the point where we are now irreversibly aware of several basic, real-life causes operating in combination.

The strong roles in trade of natural resources, distance and preferences, which the Gruber-Vernon study helps to confirm, would seem almost trivially obvious in terms of microeconomics, except for the role of distance in products for which transport costs are minor. To explain this, as others have suggested, may require an information or communication approach to the subject.

The most obvious challenges for theory, and ultimately for policy, are the other apparent causes of trade. These are not only all highly interrelated, but, perhaps even more significant, they are all intimately related to the growth and development process. I am tentatively inclined to think of these would-be explanations in three clusters: the first group has to do with human resources, skills, and education; a second group relates to scale economies, external economies, total national income, and the dimensions (including the demand characteristics) of national markets; and the third group, elusive to formulate in parallel with the others, relates to R&D, innovation, new products, standardization, and levels of technological development. I suspect that the information and communication side of trade, if we were to investigate it further, would also prove to be related in none-too-simple ways with development, skills, scale, and technology.

I am not optimistic about our ability (1) to sort out these causes of trade or (2) to unify them into an operationally meaningful theory, on the basis of empirical and theoretical work focused on trade itself. Indeed, I expect that within a few years we will have largely exhausted what can be done to map the causes of trade which are based on trade patterns together with commodity characteristics. The main outlines are already becoming clear from the two papers we are considering and their empirical predecessors.

Rather, I would like to suggest that the challenge must ultimately be resolved through the unifying effect of advances in growth and development theory, which will probably take a long time to be realized. So that the really central challenge for empiricists is to build up a detailed knowledge of the technical interrelationships underlying growth and development. Trade theory is foredoomed to become an extension of growth and development theory; but the latter is still struggling toward its first successful synthesis. Until we possess adequate models of the growth and development process, trade theory will remain a temporary patchwork spread over a void and the sense of crisis and general dissatisfaction that now pervades the field will continue.

Turning to the individual papers, Professor Hufbauer has done a remarkably ingenious job of devising new quantitative proxies for economies of scale, first trade date, and standardization. There are obvious shortcomings in each of his novel measures; but these measures can probably be combined with others, derived from other countries and approaches, to quantify these concepts better in the future.

Hufbauer's biggest problems arise out of the underlying associations among the various commodity characteristics which he tries to measure, and the overlaps in the theories and the proxies he uses for them. Three-digit rank correlations between his characteristics, which he used originally on an unweighted basis, fail to show the real degree of multicollinearity among the explanations themselves. The bulk of world trade in manufactures consists of machinery, electrical machinery, certain types of transport equipment, and complex chemicals—a few trade categories in all—in which the industries at one and the same time are very skill-intensive, involve substantial scale economies, produce a large proportion of new, unstandardized products, and conduct much R&D. The pattern of trade in these products, both absolutely and compared to other manufactures, reflects quite consistently the trading countries' levels of development and their economic size.

I write these comments before seeing Hufbauer's revisions; but I trust that he will have explored further both the underlying associations I have just mentioned and the very high correlations in the relative standings of countries when his various commodity characteristics are applied to the same trade flows. These patterns of association, to judge by my own experiments with his data, turn out to be rather different according to whether rank or linear correlations are used. On a linear basis, for example, capital per man performs substantially worse than the other explanations; wages per man cease to be the "best" performer; and the ratio of consumer to intermediate goods does quite a fair job, despite the weakness of the underlying "theory." In either sort of correlation, at any rate, there are some intriguing mysteries. For example, when applying his measure of scale economies to exports, why should the results correlate very closely with GDP per capita? Why, for that matter, do his results for scale economies correlate so well with his results for standardization?

It must also be seriously questioned whether some of his proxies, borrowed from other people's studies, correspond to the theories to which he relates them. It is certainly conspicuous that Hufbauer regards professional and technical workers in an industry as a measure of a skill theory of trade, while Gruber and Vernon consider the same proxy to be a measure of their "R&D factor." [1] Again, the high, unweighted Spearman rank correlation of .920 (not shown in the Hufbauer article), between Hufbauer's export results with U.S. wages per man and a country's GDP per capita, does not necessarily confirm a skill theory of trade; for, in practice, U.S. wages per man in an industry reflect not only the skills and education of the labor force, but also the industry's success in terms of R&D and new products, economies of scale, and even trade itself. After all, U.S. labor is not averse to raising wages when profits permit.

I for one cannot get excited about Hufbauer's new evidence on capital and the Leontief paradox. It seems to me that the physical capital version of the Heckscher-Ohlin-Samuelson theory is almost irrelevant to observed trade patterns, probably because both financial capital and capital goods are far more mobile internationally than other key inputs such as skills, technical knowledge, organizational know-how, and externalities from the surrounding economy. Hufbauer's capital measure is easily the worst of his seven "explanations" of trade, at least on a linear-quantitative basis. That he got a positive result at all is at least partly because he used capital per man, which is positively associated with skills, R&D, and the like, rather than capital relative to output, for which this association is blurred because of the productivity effects of the other factors.

One last point on this paper: although Hufbauer has done an ingenious job of trying to test Linder's hypothesis with countries' aggregate trade data, the job really calls for data on bilateral trade flows, along the lines of Gruber and Vernon's matrix. It seems to me

[1] Editor's note: The final version of the Gruber-Vernon paper adopts the Hufbauer concept.

that their Tables 8, 9, and 10 shed a good deal of light on the under-lying question. As I read this evidence, Linder's explanation will scarcely survive as a single or separate theory of trade; but his hypothesis has helped to call attention to distance, scale, and market size effects that are extremely important in practice.

Gruber and Vernon's paper really reports two different empirical studies, the first climaxing with Table 7 and the second with Tables 9 and 10. The paper is ingenious and well written, and the findings are very suggestive, especially those of the second empirical study. The empirical tests and findings are not linked to theory with the same explicitness and rigor as in Hufbauer's study; but an even wider range of theories are implicitly tested, and the results present intriguing further challenges for theory, while complementing Hufbauer's in many ways.

I have a number of qualms about their first empirical study as it was originally presented. I am not clear, much less convinced, of the theoretical basis for selecting advertising intensity, intermediate good specialization, and industry concentration as characteristics to be tested in Tables 6 and 7. I would rather see these characteristics dropped and a proxy for scale economies included instead.[2]

I am even more bothered by methodological aspects of the regressions shown in Table 7, where the dependent variable is the country's share of the ten areas' total exports. Since each country's share is negatively related to the other countries' shares, the regression results for one country are not independent of those for the next one; and the result is that for any characteristic one or two countries tend to be on each opposing side, while most wind up with inconclusive results in the middle. Moreover, since export characteristics turn out to be a function of levels of industrial development, it is hardly surprising that for several areas that fall into the weighted middle of the Gruber-Vernon sample in terms of income, namely the United Kingdom, the rest of EFTA, and Canada, no independent variable significantly explained their trade-share patterns. Surely there are ways around this problem. At the very least, regressions such as these should be attempted on other measures of trade shares, such as a country's share of an industry's exports when U.S. exports are excluded and more poor countries are

2 Editor's note: The final version of the Gruber-Vernon paper is partially responsive to this criticism.

included; or, perhaps even better, a country's exports of the product relative to the exports of countries with higher and lower per capita incomes.

Their second study yields extremely interesting results. My only serious reservations relate to the implicit nature of much of their theoretical framework and to the presence in Tables 9 and 10 of so many separate independent variables related to income. This is especially serious in that income is a good proxy for not only demand but many supply conditions associated with development. I consider it a forceful testimonial to the strength of the many trade effects linked with development that so many significant coefficients appeared for these variables, despite all the underlying multicollinearity.

Let me add that, against the background of the existing literature, I find quite exciting Hufbauer's effects with scale economies and the Gruber-Vernon effects with total national income, as well as their results using differences in the Harbison-Myers index.

This large-scale testing of theories has many of us wondering which important explanations of trade might have been overlooked up to now. Let me therefore call attention here to the case of Israel, as discussed by Seev Hirsch in a later paper in this volume. In that country—in which rather impressive human resources have been thrown together recently and are now being combined into new organizations—export success in complex, skill-intensive products seems to be taking much longer than in simple, standardized products. This helps to suggest that we might build a useful line of theory around organization-building and the theme that the capabilities of a productive organization can be much more than the sum of the factors it employs. In such an explanation one would want to combine somehow Arrow's learning by doing, Leibenstein's X-efficiency, and Gabriel's corporate skills. Organization-building and learning effects would seem to me to be most important in technologically complex, R&D-intensive, fast-changing, skill-intensive industries. Unfortunately, however, it may prove impossible to define such an approach so as to be operational and measurable.

Together the Hufbauer and Gruber-Vernon papers should stand as a landmark in our empirical research; but there is still room for considerable further research along similar lines. In view of the identification problems implied by their results, the point will soon be reached where we will need to test such relationships by applying advanced econometric methods to explicit alternative systems of equations.

I have already suggested, however, that, by their nature, studies of the relationships among trade patterns and commodity characteristics cannot give us anything like a unifying explanation of trade patterns. Success in achieving such an explanation will only come, I expect, through empirical and theoretical advances in our understanding of the basic technical interrelationships underlying development. Given the difficulty of this task, it will probably be a long time and a lot of work before we can put the Humpty Dumpty of trade theory together again.

C. P. KINDLEBERGER
Massachusetts Institute of Technology

The papers before us are in the new but distinguished tradition of using the capacity of the computer for massive manipulation of numbers to verify the theory of international trade, and in particular to see which of a variety of competing theories dominates the explanation of trade in manufactures. The authors think the time is past for the identification of possible theories or taxonomy. As Hufbauer says of the new theories: "They often perform very well when applied to a single group of commodities or a limited range of countries." But some theories must be better than others, and some one theory must be best. So our authors pile up the numbers for selected countries and areas, arranged overall in one case and in matrix form in the other, and we are off.

There is no faulting the ambition or the technical virtuosity of our authors. I admire the first and envy the second, even though I am not always clear what some of the manipulations imply in detail. It is useful to test our theories empirically, even though it seems impossible at this stage of our knowledge and data to establish any one theory as dominant, or even to disprove much.

My scepticism about proving a great deal about the theory of trade from manufacturing data goes back a long way to the "proofs" of comparative advantage put forward by MacDougall, Balassa, and Stern, and based on the Ricardian labor theory of value. In these cases, a discarded theory was proved by empirical demonstration, using bilateral trade and trade of two similar countries with third countries. The proofs seemed to satisfy few observers, neglecting as they did the contribution of capital to comparative advantage and omitting such industries as chemicals. The Leontief paradox moved the discussion back to the Heckscher-Ohlin-Samuelson model with variable factor proportions.

The Leontief paradoxical results showing that United States exports were labor-intensive and imports capital-intensive, produced an explosion in the theory of trade, despite little agreement on the explanation of the untoward results. Agreement is lacking between the Hufbauer and the Gruber-Vernon papers on this point, since Hufbauer's results confirm the Leontief findings only for the United States and restore the Heckscher-Ohlin-Samuelson findings with respect to capital and wages for other countries (How reconcile with Ichimura and Tatemoto for Japan, and with Roskamp for Germany?), while Gruber and Vernon seem to find capital out of line throughout their world trade matrix.

Hufbauer classifies seven explanations of trade, six orthodox and converging, and one, that of Linder, heretical. The orthodox explanations are grouped into a neofactor proportions account, combining human and physical capital, and a neotechnological account relying mainly on economies of scale, product innovation, and product differentiation; Linder's is a preference-similarity theory. It is not clear, however, that the neofactor and the neotechnological theories converge analytically. Neofactor proportions theories assume that there is a standard world technology and that factor endowments determine the direction of trade. Neotechnological theories assume that technology is continuously changing unevenly, and that these changes alter the trade pattern. Innovations lead to exports; the spread of technology to the world establishes a pattern based on factor proportions, which may or may not differ from that induced by the initial gap. To the extent that the pattern based on factors differs from that based on innovation, the neofactor and neotechnological explanations differ rather than harmonize.

The papers, it should be noted, discuss only one sort of technological theory, when there are in fact two. Innovation can take place in product or in process. The authors here identify technical change with new products rather than with producing old products in new and lower-cost ways. The widespread disdain among empiricists today for factor reversals is based on the same view. There is strong evidence to support the position, as Lary has shown in his work, but it cannot be ruled out by assumption. We know that factor reversals exist in some fields, as in rice which is produced in labor-intensive ways in the Far East, but the United States, using capital-intensive methods of sowing and fertilizing from aircraft and harvesting by outboard motorboat, is today its leading world exporter. And it is well to remember the work of Tyzynski who corrected the results of the German Enquête Ausschuss of the 1920's which emphasized new goods with high income elasticity as a source of trade growth, by pointing to the Japanese case which the earlier data had overlooked. In addition to the commodity and country effects taken to be high for "new products," based on goods, incomes, and income elasticities, there is the competitive effect which may be based on process innovation in old goods.

It may be noted that within the field of product innovation the product-cycle theory emphasizing supply and the Linder theory focusing on demand may each either explain trade or trade's drying up. Assume that technology spreads abroad. Direct investment may substitute for trade as a means of holding the market against local competition and may stop there. Trade is cut off, rather than reversed. In this instance it is hard to see how aggregated trade data can prove or disprove such a theory. In Linder's theory, rising incomes in a country may induce consumers to shift to products which are too expensive for the export market, i.e., American-type large cars which suit the home market but are too big and too voracious as consumers of taxed gasoline for the foreign market. Exports of large cars decline. Imports of small cars, however, reflect the demand for a different product, the second or third car in a family, which has a different income and price elasticity from the first car. The Linder theory can thus be used in slightly different circumstances to explain flourishing trade between countries on the same level of living, or a decline in such trade when incomes pass through certain zones. Rank-order correlations which fail to account for the distances between incomes will miss this possibility.

Let me now raise some technical problems. Both papers rely on cross-sectional analysis. Gruber and Vernon apologize for using the matrix of

a given year to verify a dynamic model of trade. Hufbauer is uncon-
cerned with the problem. If, however, different commodities find themselves at different stages of the product cycle, it is not clear what the
average position portrays. One should normalize by the stage of the
product cycle, and this cross-section data do not do. To measure the
average height of a family with children of various ages produces no
interesting result.

Both papers use United States coefficients widely and apologize for
the practice. Hufbauer uses national attributes in his Table 4, but all
except one of the product characteristics in his Table A-2 are of United
States origin. This raises fundamental questions when it comes to
measuring foreign industries. With no factor reversals and identical
production functions, factor-input ratios may be compared only on the
assumption of identical factor prices. None of these conditions is
guaranteed. There is something of a presumption of no reversals on the
basis of Lary's work, as I have said, but identity of production functions is excluded by the product-cycle hypothesis, and identical factor
returns can be eliminated by casual empiricism. Gruber and Vernon
particularly have trouble, it seems to me, when they assume that the
same industries are research-intensive all over the world, and the same
industries advertising-intensive. In fact, they express surprise that Japan
does so well in advertising-intensive industries and seek to explain it by
implicit theorizing to the effect that Japan compensates for lack of
advertising by cutting costs—a hint of innovation in process rather than
product which is otherwise missing from both papers.[1]

I also find unsatisfactory the implicit theorizing which adduces a
new explanatory variable, the propensity to apply marginal pricing, to
explain why the United States exports little and Japan a great deal in
capital-intensive industry. This variable may differ from country to
country, along with other sociologically and economically determined
propensities which affect foreign trade, such as readiness to apply
tariffs in periods of falling prices (Germany, France and Italy did so
in wheat in the 1880's, but Denmark, Britain and the Netherlands did
not); or business propensity to push exports in periods of slack domestic

---

[1] Editor's note: The references to advertising intensity, which appeared in the
conference version of the Gruber-Vernon paper, were eliminated in the final
version.

business, which is remarked to be high in Germany and low in the United States. But such explanations must not be introduced casually to explain away statistical results which depart from a priori expectations. If they are to be used they must be addressed explicitly and the basis for national differences demonstrated.[2]

In Hufbauer's paper, dating and standardization present particular problems. One can sympathize with the problem of trying to find intellectually satisfactory measures for these concepts on a world basis, but why limit the United States data, if one is restricted to a single country, to exports? The addition of imports would have helped, especially for the standardization coefficients. Hufbauer notices that cotton textiles a priori seem satisfactory in standardization but curious in first date. To limit unit values to 1965 exports eliminates cotton gray goods from the standardization index, the most important single item in world cotton-textile trade. It may even be that the United States did not export gray goods in the period since 1917, although, of course, it has imported them. First-date averages by countries in Table 2 seem very odd indeed, with no country having an average composition of 1965 exports earlier than 1944 and the latest country average coming only to 1948. It seems hard to say anything interesting about the product-cycle or technological gap theories of trade with data which average out most of the timing differences between countries and produce sixteen out of twenty-four averages in two years, 1946 and 1947.

Gruber and Vernon try to allow for distance, while Hufbauer apologizes for leaving the problem alone. But the Gruber-Vernon solution is not completely satisfactory for it fails to distinguish those goods (weight-losing or bulk-gaining) in which distance inhibits trade and those foot-loose industries in which it does not. The distance factor is important both for petroleum and coal and for furniture and fixtures. But what can one make of identical net regressions in Table 9 for drugs, on the one hand, and stone, clay and glass, on the other $(-.005)$ and $(-.567)$? If more than physical distance is meant (i.e., such factors as established trade channels, market horizons customarily scanned, and the like), it is not certain that distance is an ideal proxy, especially when, in some goods, it has strong economic effects of a physical nature.

[2] Editor's note: These points also were stricken from the Gruber-Vernon paper in response to criticism such as this.

Tariff barriers are ignored in both papers, although Gruber and Vernon include a variable for preferences, apparently on the assumption that tariffs are otherwise uniform. This is a dubious omission, especially if one believes, with Hufbauer and Travis, that tariffs may be sufficiently distortionary to account for the Leontief paradox.

On scale economies, Hufbauer did not consider the work of Jacques Drèze in two interesting, important, but difficult-to-obtain papers.[3] Drèze observes that Belgium concentrates its production and exports on standardized products, not only by broad classes such as semifinished iron and steel, flat glass, and photographic film, but within categories which vary in standardization. Thus Belgium produces white china, but not colored or decorated (i.e., the standardized quality rather than the qualities subject to taste) and, within automobile components, such products as standardized batteries, tires, windows, upholstery fabrics, wiring harnesses and radiators, rather than engines, bodies, and their components, which vary among producers, models, and countries. This extends Hufbauer's analysis, though he does not allow for production of standardized products for export by small countries beyond mentioning it. But Hufbauer is puzzled by the phenomenon which Drèze fails to take into account, the specialization by Denmark, the Netherlands, and Sweden in scale-economy goods to a greater extent than their manufacturing output would justify. Switzerland could be added to this list, if its trade had been covered. These countries are style-setters which achieve their scale economies through exports. The attempt to identify scale economies with certain goods, and associate these goods with certain size countries in exports, must be modified on two counts: first, the possibility that small countries can achieve exports in scale-economy goods where the standardization is set by large countries; and second, the possibility that the differentiated products of small countries, such as Dutch electrical equipment, Swedish machinery and telephones, Danish furniture, and Swiss pharmaceuticals (but not Belgian products), get accepted as the international standard.

But it is time to conclude. The Hufbauer and Gruber-Vernon papers,

[3] See "Les exportations intra-C.E.E. en 1958 et la position belge," *Recherches Economiques de Louvain,* 1961, and "Quelques réflexions sereines sur l'adaptation de l'industrie belge au Marché Commun," *Comptes Rendus des Travaux de la Société Royale d'Économie Politique de Belgique,* No. 275, December 1960.

for all the nitpicks of details I have produced, are surely in the right direction—that of empirical verification of the theory of trade overall and on the average, even though contrary examples and exceptions abound in the small.

Hufbauer and Gruber and Vernon differ in the evaluation of their overall findings. Gruber and Vernon find the persistent strength in explaining trade of differences in human-resource development "a major fresh conclusion." [4] Hufbauer characterizes his conclusion that physical-capital and human-skill theories produce enviable results with little *ad hoc* manipulation or theoretical amplification "distressingly simple and orthodox." One may wonder on the basis of the pioneering work of Kenen and Keesing how fresh is the discovery of human resources as a basis for trade. And a textbook writer who has just finished a new edition may be pardoned if he does not find the simple and orthodox view "distressing."

IRVING B. KRAVIS
University of Pennsylvania

The Hufbauer and Gruber-Vernon papers are similar in that each represents an imaginative effort to extend our understanding of the factors that determine the commodity composition of international trade in manufactures. They are alike also in the success each enjoyed in the choice of explanatory variables, including one or two that might at first blush appear rather unlikely.

Several of the explanatory variables in each paper represent factor proportions of one sort or another such as capital-labor ratios in the Hufbauer paper, the capital-output ratios in the Gruber-Vernon paper, and the relative importance of highly qualified workers in both papers. Other explanatory variables represent the economies of scale, such as Hufbauer's elasticity of value added with respect to the number of employees per establishment. Still others reflect monopolistic elements

---

[4] Editor's note: The final version of the paper is more modest in tone and does not contain this reference.

arising either from technological gaps, such as Hufbauer's measure of the lateness of the appearance of each category of exports in trade, or resulting from industrial concentration such as Gruber-Vernon's use of the concentration ratio. With one exception in the Hufbauer paper, the values of each of the explanatory variables assigned to each export category are derived from U.S. data; thus, it is assumed that there are no factor reversals.

Another important assumption which the two papers have in common is that factor scarcities can be judged purely in physical terms without reference to demand factors. In this respect they follow the practice developed by Leontief in his famous paper suggesting the factor paradox for U.S. trade, and their findings tend to confirm the fact that U.S. exports are not particularly intensive in physical capital. The expansion of the concept of capital to include human capital, suggested by Peter Kenen and others, and the capitalized value of the knowledge produced by R&D expenditure, recently suggested by Harry Johnson, will probably operate so as to increase the relative quantity of capital in the U.S. economy and the relative quantity embodied in U.S. exports.

There is, however, a potentially important factor on the demand side which has been overlooked and which would in a sense tend to place a greater burden of explanation on these suggestions for broadening the concept of the capital supply. It is the capital intensity of U.S. consumption patterns relative to that of foreign consumption patterns. Housing and durable goods, the consumption categories in which the excess of U.S. over foreign per capita consumption tends to be largest, absorb large amounts of capital. In 1958, the last date for which Goldsmith, Lipsey, and Mendelson prepared a national balance sheet,[1] nonfarm households actually held tangible assets which in value were almost 30 per cent greater than those held by nonfinancial corporations, the entities which presumably generated our manufactured exports. The value of residential structures owned by nonfarm households was almost twice the value of nonresidential structures held by nonfinancial corporations, and consumers' durables were almost 15 per cent higher than producers' durables held by nonfinancial corporations. This large household demand for capital must be taken into account in any assessment of

[1] R. W. Goldsmith, R. E. Lipsey and M. Mendelson, *Studies in the National Balance Sheet of the United States,* II, Princeton for NBER, 1963, pp. 68–69.

relative factor scarcities in the U.S. economy compared to that of other countries.

There are of course differences as well as similarities in the approach followed by the two papers. The authors of the two papers have, for example, organized their data differently. The advantage of the Hufbauer approach is that he uses a more detailed breakdown of exports of manufactures, involving more than a hundred three-digit SITC groups. Gruber and Vernon, on the other hand, set a much more demanding test for themselves. In the first part of their paper, they seek to explain the relative size of each country's exports of manufactures in terms of their explanatory variables; that is, they correlate each country's export shares for each of the twenty-four industries with certain characteristics of each industry. (In the second part of their paper they correlate, for each of the twenty-four industries, the size of the bilateral trade flows of the exporting and importing partners with certain national characteristics, or with differences in these characteristics.) Hufbauer works only with successive correlations of the ranks of countries when they are arrayed according to two different variables, one measuring the relative amount of a given characteristic embodied in each country's total exports of manufactures and the other measuring the amount of the corresponding national attribute found for each country.

A major disadvantage which both studies encounter, in common with other empirical investigations of trade flows, is that the classifications used for industrial production and international trade really are not relevant to the purposes at hand. Now it may be thought that this objection is not valid in view of the high degree of success of both papers in explaining international trade flows by variables which are calibrated in terms of the existing categories. However, there is no reason to believe that the classifications are equally appropriate or equally inappropriate for each of the several explanatory variables. It is possible, for example, that the categories may contain groups of products that are more homogeneous with respect, say, to the skill ratio than with respect to the economies of scale. Indeed, there is some reason to believe that the classifications are particularly deficient for purposes of measuring economies of scale. Scale economies are a function not only of the size of plant, which can be measured in terms of the existing classifications and which Hufbauer does measure, but also of the product mix within plants, which is more difficult to measure and which is omitted from

Hufbauer's net. In the case of the United States, at least, the scale economies that are important in exports are often more a function of the size of the market than of the size of plants or establishments. In the study of international price competitiveness that Robert Lipsey and I have been conducting at the National Bureau,[2] we have encountered a number of cases in which the size of the U.S. market enables U.S. producers to reach large volume production for relatively specialized product variants for which markets are thin in any one of the smaller, competing economies. In the antifriction bearing industry, for example, the U.S. imports commonly used bearings which can be produced in large volume both here and abroad, but the United States has nevertheless enjoyed a net export position in bearings owing to exports of specialized kinds capable of meeting precision needs, resisting heat or rust, or bearing great weight.

Scale economies that may or may not be unique to the U.S. economy also arise where there is a high degree of product specialization by each of a large number of small firms. Brown and Rosenberg have reported this situation as characterizing the machine tool industry;[3] each plant type typically produced one or at most only several types out of the four hundred kinds of tools produced in the industry.

It may also be questioned whether either study has found a satisfactory measure of product differentiation. Hufbauer attempts, with great ingenuity, to measure product differentiation in terms of the coefficient of variation for U.S. export unit values to different destinations for each of his three-digit categories of goods. However, even if we put aside the well-known erratic character of unit value data, export unit values to various destinations may vary widely for a number of reasons not just because of product differentiation. In the first place, a wide variety of standardized products may be found even in some of the seven-digit classifications which Hufbauer uses to build up his three-digit measures, and the product mix sent to different destinations may be different. Even a cursory check of U.S. 1965 export data [4] brings up some suggestive illustrations: unit values of exports to different destinations for

[2] *Price Competitiveness in World Trade*, Chap. 2, forthcoming.

[3] M. Brown and N. Rosenberg, "Prologue to a Study of Patent and Other Factors in the Machine Tool Industry," *The Patent, Trademark and Copyright Journal of Research and Education*, Spring 1960, p. 45.

[4] U.S. Department of Commerce, *U.S. Exports, Commodity by Country*, FT 410, December 1965.

"screws, rivets, washers, and similar articles of iron or steel" (Schedule B commodity number 6942130) ranged from 22.6 cents per pound (to Korea) to $4.26 per pound (Greece), while for "industrial sewing machines except shoe sewing machines, new" (7173030) the range went from $214 (to Salvadore) to $988 (to Vietnam) per unit; the coefficients of variation were 0.74 for screws, etc. and 0.52 for industrial sewing machines. It is rather doubtful that these differences in range and variation of the unit values to different destinations reflect the relative impact upon these two categories of the product cycle. Secondly the seven-digit classification sometimes includes used machinery along with new, as in the printing machinery categories (7182210 to 7182960 inc.), and in other instances it provides separate categories for used equipment, as in industrial sewing machinery (7173040). Thus, the coefficient of variation is sometimes affected by the extent to which used machinery is exported to some destinations and new machinery to others, and it cannot be assumed that the relative importance of second-hand products is the same from one category to another. Finally, price discrimination as between different destinations, which is not unknown even in U.S. export trade, would also affect unit values.

The a priori doubts about the adequacy of the standardization coefficient are reinforced by an examination of the way in which the coefficient ranks the three-digit groups. While the author is correct in saying "reasonable coefficients seem to emerge, at least in some instances," there are many that appear to be unreasonable. According to this measure, for example, office machinery (SITC 714) and agricultural machinery (712) are more standardized than zinc (686) and paper and paperboard (641). A perusal of Hufbauer's Table A-2 will show that such outcomes are not uncommon.

It is possible, however, that the significant correlation between the ranks of the various countries with respect to their export-weighted coefficients of variation for export unit values and their ranks with respect to manufacturing sophistication (as measured by GDP per capita) has another and important meaning. It may reflect the greater variety of goods available in high income countries rather than measuring the extent to which sophisticated countries are able to offer differentiated products.

Putting this implication aside for the moment, it is worth pointing out that an important new line of investigation is suggested explicitly by the Gruber-Vernon paper and implicitly by Hufbauer's paper, although not very much explored in either. In the empirical and theoretical work dealing with the commodity composition of trade over the past twenty or twenty-five years, the main effort has been devoted to the search for explanations of the contrasting trade patterns of different countries. Gruber and Vernon remind us that something can be learned by studying the similarities of trading patterns; perhaps we have given inadequate attention to the difference between tradeable goods and home goods. Economists of a former generation used to describe the characteristics of traded goods in three terms: homogeneous, high in value in relation to bulk, and in universal demand. Perhaps technological progress, particularly the reduction of the cost of transport, has altered the restrictive impact of all three of these characteristics upon the kinds of goods that are traded. Perhaps with the spread of industrial production and with higher real income levels, differentiated goods are as prone or more prone to be traded than homogeneous products.

Although the point about homogeneous versus differentiated goods is speculative, the similarity of export patterns of the main manufacturing countries is clearly shown by the Gruber-Vernon correlations. This similarity of export patterns is not dependent on the use of twenty-four relatively large industrial categories but persists, I have found, when the exports of manufactures of the major industrial countries are correlated at the three-digit level (about 100 categories); the Spearman coefficients in the matrix of correlations involving the United States, the United Kingdom, Germany, and Japan range from .54 to .82.[5]

What is the significance of these similarities? One possibility is that all advanced manufacturing countries tend to produce highly similar baskets of goods and to export them to nonmanufacturing countries. It is true that there are striking similarities in the structure of production among the important manufacturing countries; for example, the Spearman coefficient for the rank correlation between nineteen two-digit industries is 0.72 for Japan and the United States and 0.83 for Germany and the United States.[6]

[5] Using OECD data on 1964 exports.
[6] Based on data in United Nations, *The Growth of World Industry, 1953–65,* New York, 1967.

Such an explanation cannot, however, be more than part of the story, since, as is well known, intratrade among the industrial countries is quite important. Indeed, in 1964, half of U.S. and U.K. manufactures exports and three-quarters of Germany's went to OECD countries.[7]

Conceivably, for purposes of this intratrade, each major industrial country might specialize in a different group of industries, but this seems unlikely in view of the similarities in the industrial composition of their exports. Also, a direct check of a single case, U.S. and German intratrade, indicates a significant degree of similarity in the industrial pattern of each country's exports to the other; the Spearman coefficient was .53 for eighty-six three-digit categories for which OECD data for 1964 exports were available. This coefficient, which is significant at the 1 per cent confidence level, leaves room for some industry specialization, but it also indicates a considerable amount of what looks like cross exporting.

It is possible that a better explanation of this trade might come from a comparison of the economic characteristics of home goods and tradeable goods. Neither of these papers tells us, for example, whether the goods that are generally exported in relatively large volume by the major manufacturing countries are particularly capital-intensive, or unusually subject to the economies of scale as compared to goods that are exported in smaller volume. Neither do they indicate whether there are differences between the economic characteristics of the manufactures the industrial countries export to one another and those they send to other destinations. Until we have the answers to questions like these, we shall not fully understand the forces that determine the commodity composition of trade.

Meanwhile, it is possible to outline a hypothesis to explain this intratrade that can be viewed in one sense as an extension of the availability argument I offered some years ago;[8] that is, trade consists to a significant degree of products, or still more importantly, of product variants that are not available in the recipient country. Before drawing on the Gruber-Vernon and Hufbauer papers to suggest why this occurs, I may call attention to two bits of evidence (both reported in the forthcoming

[7] See also H. Grubel, "Intra-Industry Specialization and the Pattern of Grade," *The Canadian Journal of Economics and Political Science,* August 1967.

[8] " 'Availability' and Other Influences on the Commodity Composition of Trade," *Journal of Political Economy,* April 1956.

study by Lipsey and me) that indicate that the availability factor does operate for manufactures and particularly for machinery, as businessmen perceive the situation. The first suggests that U.S. exports of metal products and machinery depend to a considerable extent upon differences in design and other aspects of product differentiation. The second is a survey by the IFO Institute of Munich in which German firms that purchased foreign factory equipment reported that 63 per cent of their purchases were due to the fact that the desired equipment was not available at home; another 12 per cent was purchased because of the superiority of foreign equipment; and only 7 per cent for price advantages.

Some of the reasons underlying the availability of different products or product variants in various supplying countries are found in the technological gap or in the kind of product differentiation along national lines (Belgian lace, French wine, British china, etc.) which I mentioned earlier. In addition, the combination of an increase in the variety of products—for producers' goods as well as for consumer goods—and the economies of long production runs may result in specialization by product variant rather than by industry or type of product.

Although economies of long production runs explain why countries are led to concentrate on a limited range of products, even when they are capable of producing the full range, the determination of the particular variants each country will specialize in depends on systematic as well as random factors. In general, the larger the market the wider the range of products for which the country will be able to obtain the economies of long runs,[9] and the more likely it is to be able to export a variety of materials and equipment catering to specialized needs which have a demand extensive enough to warrant production beyond the handicraft, custom, or special-order stage and yet infrequent enough to prevent the attainment of scale economies in smaller markets.

A country with a small home market would specialize in the less esoteric and more widely demanded products in which it could achieve

---

[9] A recent study of the Canadian economy shows the cost disadvantages that ensue from the attempt to produce a wide range of product variants in a small market. See D. J. Daly, B. A. Keys, and F. J. Spence, *Scale and Specialization in Canadian Manufacturing*, Staff Study No. 21, Economic Council of Canada, March 1968.

long production runs; this has been pointed out by Drèze who has advanced a "standardization" hypothesis to explain Belgium's export pattern in which semimanufactures are important.[10]

As between countries with the same size market, the one with greater physical and human capital might provide the leadership in developing new variants, losing its comparative advantage in each new variant as it became more widely used in the other country. As between countries equal in market size and in physical and human capital, the pattern of specialization in the production of different variants in long runs might depend on systematic elements such as differences in tastes and natural resource endowments or on chance factors.

An important systematic element is the tendency for domestic production in each country to consist of product variants that cater to the tastes and needs of the home market. Drèze and (I think) Linder, among others, have seen this trade-creating aspect of product differentiation chiefly in connection with consumers goods. Lipsey and I have been struck in the course of our National Bureau study with a number of examples of a similar phenomenon in connection with producers' goods. Equipment is usually designed in each country to meet local conditions such as the usual scale of output and the prevailing relative factor prices. In each country, however, there is apt to be a small demand for equipment which is different from that which serves most local needs. This small demand can be better satisfied by equipment designed for conditions that happen to prevail in another country. European equipment for such industries as printing, baking, and pharmaceuticals, for example, is designed for smaller volume, lower speed, and greater versatility than American equipment for the same industries. In each area most domestic needs are met by domestic production, but Americans do import some low-volume versatile machines from Europe and export some high-volume specialized machines to Europe.

Obviously, this basis for specialization is closely related to the diseconomies of small-scale production or of special orders. However, one

[10] Jacques Drèze, "Quelques réflexions sereines sur l'adaptation de l'industrie Belge au Marché Commun," *Comptes rendus des Travaux de la Société Royale d'Économie Politique de Belgique*, No. 275, December 1960.

may suppose that the ability of a country to participate in this trade, particularly in sectors of rapidly changing technique, is related to its possession of the attributes which are required for the production and development of special designs of equipment—viz., physical and human capital, particularly R&D skills.

An explanation along these lines is consistent with the similarity of export profiles found by Gruber and Vernon, the associations between commodity characteristics and national attributes stressed by Hufbauer, and the importance of intratrade pointed out above.

This is not to claim that specialization by product variant can explain all intraindustrial country trade flows in manufactures. The truth probably is that manufactures move across international boundaries owing to a variety of causes. Some—and probably a significant fraction—can be explained in terms of the classical factor proportions theory. The emergence of textile exports from developing countries, despite hostile commercial policies by the developed countries, may be a reflection of such tendencies. Other flows are due to favorable financing, to past flows (parts for machinery, extensions of past installations of systems such as railroad, electrical, and telephone), and to speed of delivery. Lipsey and I are inclined to the view that the importance of delivery speed in accounting for U.S. exports has not been given sufficient weight. To take an extreme example, the United States was able to export ships after the Suez Crisis in 1957 despite prices that were perhaps double those abroad. This suggests, as do some of our authors' results, that the factors that are important in explaining one country's trade may differ from those that loom large in explaining another country's, and that there is some evidence that the main forces at work in influencing U.S. trade patterns in particular tend to differ from those operating in other countries.

Doubtless other explanations and hypotheses about the meaning of the results that have placed before us by Gruber and Vernon and Hufbauer will be forthcoming. Their work has broken new ground in the effort to understand the factors that determine the commodity composition of trade. They have, to amend slightly the words of one of the papers, provided valuable grist for the mill of theory.

MORDECHAI E. KREININ
Michigan State University

Although the papers presented at the conference fall within the realm of the "pure theory" of international trade, it appears that various speakers address themselves to three different questions, to wit: (1) an assessment of the gains from international trade (Arrow); (2) an explanation of the commodity composition of trade (Hufbauer, and Gruber and Vernon); and (3) the development of a guide for trade policy for individual nations, particularly within a development context (Bruno). These are certainly not mutually exclusive, and an "ideal" theory should contain answers to all three. But within an empirical context, one would be doing well to test for one or two of them at a time. The following remarks are addressed to the Hufbauer and Gruber-Vernon papers on the supposition that their main objective is to explain the commodity composition of international trade.

In the received theory of exchange both supply and demand play a role in the process of price determination. Translated into the (barter) theory of international trade—based on the doctrine of comparative advantage—we find supply factors determining the boundaries to mutually beneficial trade and demand considerations determining the commodity terms of trade within these boundaries. But the Heckscher-Ohlin model, as tested by Leontief and in the vast literature that ensued, assumes away international differences in demand. Likewise, most of the theories tested in these two papers are exclusively of the supply variety.

In actual fact, supply models can be expected to explain rather well the portion of world trade that consists of homogeneous commodities. When it comes to industrial products, which constitute the bulk of trade among the developed countries, the patterns of demand and the degree to which they are influenced by product differentiation can be expected to play an important role. None of the models tested here can shed light on the mutual exchange of Fiats, Renaults, and Volkswagens among the three major EEC countries. On a priori grounds, supply factors would dominate trade relationships only when they result in a price differential large enough to swamp the demand effects in monopolistically competitive markets. Consequently, it would make sense to test the supply models only for these commodities which differ substantially in the product characteristic being tested. This brings me to the next operational suggestion.

The papers under discussion are of immense value in analyzing the various characteristics of commodity groups entering international trade. It would have been preferable to carry out such an analysis for each of the five-digit SITC categories; but evidently this is precluded on practical grounds. Now, by running multiple regressions and adding independent variables, one can certainly increase the portion of the variance being explained. But as this process progresses, the theory loses operational simplicity and therefore practical significance. The logical simplicity of a theory (like that of the Heckscher-Ohlin model) has a value which should be preserved even while the theory is made more sophisticated. Moreover, even by employing dozens of variables, we may not reach satisfactory explanations of all trade by all countries.

I would therefore like to suggest an alternative method of using the data gathered in the papers. As a first stage we wish to test the explanatory power of each commodity characteristic by relating it to the respective structure of the economy. (Incidentally, this link is missing in the first half of the Gruber-Vernon paper because the country-endowments counterpart of each industry characteristic is not given.) Assume, for example, that we start by testing the factor proportions model. I propose that we rank all commodity groups by capital per man and then eliminate from the test, say, a fifth of the industries which fall right in the middle. Better cut-off points can perhaps be decided upon after an examination of the data; but any decision would of necessity be arbitrary. We test the theory with the industries at the two ends—those falling in two groups that contrast sharply with each other in terms of capital per worker—thus generating a powerful "supply effect." Homogeneous products can perhaps be included even if they fall in the middle group.

One can proceed in the same fashion with the other characteristics to be tested; namely, by excluding the respective "middle group" and testing the theory for those industries which differ considerably from each other. A theory that cannot explain trade in its own "end group" products can be discarded.

Subsequently, in order to compare the relative effectiveness of the theories, an iterative process can be employed. For each commodity characteristic one can start from the two ends and work toward the middle by adding industries, until the explanation loses power. The characteristic that explains a larger share of world trade is presumably the superior one. From there we can proceed with a theoretical and empirical approach based on reasonable combinations of the characteristics which came out well in the tests.

In sum, what is suggested here is that instead of attempting an explanation of all trade using a multiplicity of variables, it might be better to try to explain a portion of total trade by a simple theory. But instead of deleting a country, as Hufbauer has done, it is proposed here to exclude commodities. It is reasonable to expect that much of the unexplained portion would be due to differences in demand patterns under monopolistically competitive conditions, and unexplainable by supply models.

Having completed this stage of the analysis, one can embark on two alternative courses. The first course would involve merging the explanatory factors that came out well into a composite variable on grounds that make theoretical sense. Hufbauer's suggestion of neofactor proportions and neotechnology variables come to mind in this connection. And, if necessary, the relative explanatory power of the competing composite variables can be assessed by the same iterative procedure outlined above. The second alternative is to incorporate in the theory different explanations for trade in different types of commodities. Such a result might emerge if the various factors were equally powerful in explaining trade in different, but distinct, types of goods.

HAL B. LARY

National Bureau of Economic Research

In the concluding summary of that part of his paper concerned with the "nature of trade," Hufbauer refers to the explanatory power of a measure I have employed elsewhere [1] to explain trade flows—i.e., value added per employee as an index of the combined inputs of physical and human capital into different manufacturing industries. It may therefore be useful to add this composite variable to Hufbauer's list of product characteristics embodied in exports and imports and to relate the results to whichever of his national attributes seems most appropriate.[2] Gross domestic product per capita commends itself for this purpose, given the broad content of value added by manufacture.

Table 1 gives the average value added per employee obtained by applying U.S. coefficients for different industries to the product composition of each of the twenty-four countries' exports and imports of manufactures. When the export series (of primary interest for reasons given by Hufbauer) is matched with GDP per capita, the following correlations are obtained (comparable to those given in Table 5 of Hufbauer's paper):

Rank correlations, unweighted
24 countries .765
23 countries (Mexico excluded) .871
Rank correlation, weighted .928

These results compare favorably with those given by Hufbauer's skill analysis, being distinctly higher than the correlations with skill ratios embodied in trade and slightly lower than the correlations with wage rates. Conceptually, the value-added criterion seems more appealing. As Harry Johnson says in his paper in this volume, "it picks up not only the neofactor proportion elements of material and human capital, but also to some extent the neotechnology elements of scale economies, and of product age and differentiation, insofar as these last are reflected in selling prices." This may be true of still other inputs of "intellectual capital" into the production process.

[1] *Imports of Manufactures from Less Developed Countries,* New York, NBER, 1968. As explained there (pages 21–22), "Differences from industry to industry in value added per employee are here assumed to measure differences in the aggregate flows of services from the factors of production employed in the manufacturing process (and exclude therefore indirect factor inputs such as materials used). It is further assumed that these services may be ascribed either to human capital or to physical capital, and that, in interindustry comparisons, the wage-and-salary part of value added is a good proxy for the first and the remainder of value added a good proxy for the second."

[2] I am grateful to Professor Hufbauer for his interest in this exercise and for putting his basic trade data at my disposal and grateful also to his assistant, Melissa Patterson, for doing the computations.

TABLE 1

*Value Added by Manufacture per Employee, Embodied in 1965 Exports
and Imports and GDP Per Capita, Twenty-Four Countries*
(in dollars; rank order given in parentheses)

| | Value Added Per Employee | | GDP Per Capita |
	Exports	Imports	
Canada	14,671 (2)	13,820 (12)	2,110 (2)
United States	14,340 (4)	13,079 (21)	3,000 (1)
Austria	12,319 (15)	13,747 (13)	1,030 (13.5)
Belgium	13,235 (10)	13,529 (15)	1,460 (10)
Denmark	12,346 (14)	13,492 (16)	1,680 (8)
France	14,071 (6)	14,239 (7)	1,580 (9)
Germany	14,276 (5)	13,265 (19)	1,770 (6)
Italy	12,572 (13)	14,709 (3)	1,030 (13.5)
Netherlands	13,469 (9)	13,332 (18)	1,430 (11)
Norway	13,721 (7)	12,465 (22)	1,880 (4)
Sweden	13,196 (11)	13,429 (17)	2,100 (3)
United Kingdom	13,715 (8)	13,209 (20)	1,710 (7)
Australia	14,397 (3)	13,893 (11)	1,810 (5)
Japan	11,880 (16)	15,212 (2)	720 (15)
Israel	8,841 (21)	12,227 (24)	1,090 (12)
Portugal	9,813 (19)	14,102 (9)	420 (18)
Spain	13,116 (12)	14,403 (5)	550 (16)
Yugoslavia	11,564 (18)	14,211 (8)	250 (19)
Mexico	15,909 (1)	15,500 (1)	430 (17)
Hong Kong	7,845 (24)	12,418 (23)	200 (20)
India	8,634 (22)	13,637 (14)	80 (23.5)
Korea	9,084 (20)	14,508 (14)	140 (21)
Pakistan	8,157 (23)	13,918 (10)	80 (23.5)
Taiwan	11,795 (17)	14,397 (6)	130 (22)

Source: Value-added averages are obtained by applying coefficients
derived from U.S. 1963 Census of Manufactures (converted to SITC in
accordance with Hufbauer's Table A1) to the percentage distribution of
each country's exports or imports among the 102 three-digit SITC
categories used in Hufbauer's analysis. The GDP series is taken
directly from his Table 4.

As would be expected, the import series in Table 1 is negatively related to GDP per capita, though much less strongly than exports.[3] Most countries with high average value added in exports show the opposite for imports, and vice versa. It is particularly noteworthy that, on this more comprehensive definition of capital inputs, the export average is distinctly higher than the import average for the United States. This result—not surprising in the light of previous findings by Kravis, Keesing and others relevant to the skill content of exports and imports— suggests that a basic flaw in the Leontief paradox was reliance on an inadequate physical concept of capital.

Mexico and Israel stand out as the most deviant countries, the first with a much higher, the second a much lower, average value added in exports than their GDP per capita would lead one to expect. Hufbauer has already commented on the reasons for Israel's behavior. That of Mexico is strongly influenced by the fact that nonferrous metals and certain pharmaceuticals and chemicals—all strongly resource-oriented— make up more than half of its exports of manufactures according to Hufbauer's grouping. In a ranking excluding all nonferrous metals and chemicals, Mexico falls to fifteenth place in exports on the value-added criterion.[4] As Hufbauer indicates, there is reason to look critically at his coverage of "manufactures." The same question arises with regard to the Gruber-Vernon selection, which contains even more essentially resource-oriented items.

The computations given here on value added per employee may be criticized, as the Hufbauer and Gruber-Vernon computations have been, because of the use of American coefficients. Strong similarities across countries in the pattern of value added per employee according to industry make me doubt that this is, in fact, a major weakness in the analysis.[5] But, clearly, there is room for further empirical work using and comparing other countries' coefficients.

[3] The simple correlation is −.407 compared with .668 for exports.

[4] The unweighted rank correlations obtained on this basis (.856 for all twenty-four countries and .9185 with one country, Israel, omitted) are higher than those reported above for all products in Hufbauer's selection, but the weighted correlation (.914) is slightly lower. More study, however, needs to be given to the criteria of selection and, in particular, to the identification and exclusion of industries whose location is determined mainly by natural resources rather than by labor, capital, technology, or other factors.

[5] See Chapter 3, "International Comparisons of Factor Intensities," in *Imports of Manufactures from Less Developed Countries*.

Case Studies

Transfers of

United States Aerospace

Technology to Japan

G. R. HALL & R. E. JOHNSON

THE RAND CORPORATION

Economists have usually regarded the situs and dispersion of technology as exogenous factors, the concern primarily of historians [15]. Although differential endowments of technology are of fundamental importance for the central body of economic theory and doctrine, there has been little attention given to the question of how these differences are established or modified. This situation is changing, however. Many recent theoretical models and empirical studies incorporate the transfer or diffusion of technology,[1] but so far only a few case studies have explicitly treated the expected benefits that create a demand for someone else's technology, and the process and costs of meeting this demand [3].

This paper deals with the last topic, the process and the attendant costs of transferring technology among companies in highly developed economies. It is a case study of four interfirm transfers to Japan in the 1950's and 1960's [6, 20]. Interfirm transfers are one of many types of international technology transplantation that are occurring with increasing frequency, but the histories of these four transfers illustrate some

NOTE: The views expressed in this paper are those of the authors. They should not be interpreted as reflecting the views of The RAND Corporation or the official opinion or policy of any of its governmental or private research sponsors.

[1] Examples include: Behrman [4]; Gruber, Mehta, and Vernon [5]; Hirsch [7]; Keesing [13]; Mansfield [14]; Nelson [17]; Nelson, Peck, and Kalachek [16]; Spencer [20]; Vernon [22]; U.S. Department of Commerce [21].

general considerations relevant to all types of international movements of technology.

During the 1950's and 1960's there were numerous international aerospace manufacturing programs, many of them involving the production of complete aircraft, as can be seen in Table 1. From 1950 to 1967, more than 10,000 sophisticated aircraft, with a market value of over $5 billion, were produced by firms under license from the original designers.

During this period, Japan was particularly active in acquiring aerospace technology, most of it from the United States. Their skill in doing so confirmed the reputation the Japanese have had for over a hundred years as skilled importers of technology; but economists have too often merely expressed their admiration for Japanese astuteness and left the matter there. Sociological and cultural factors are important, of course, but the relevant issue is how the Japanese actually formulate plans and proceed to acquire technology. The aircraft manufacturing programs to be analyzed here show that the process involves difficult decisions about what and how much technology to acquire and the process by which it is acquired. Correct decisions importantly affect the success and costs of international transplantation of technology.

SOME CONCEPTUAL CONSIDERATIONS

We often speak of technology being transferred or knowledge migrating, but are seldom precise about the process involved.[2] Precision is important because technology as an abstraction cannot move—things and people are transferred.

Technology can be transferred in two basic forms. One form embraces physical items such as drawings, tooling, machinery, process information, specifications, and patents. The other form is personal contact. Put simply, knowledge is always embodied in something or somebody, the form being important for determining the transfer process and its costs. The process is simpler if knowledge is embodied in purely physical

---

[2] Technology is knowledge or information that permits some task to be accomplished, some service rendered, or some product produced. Conceptually, technology can be distinguished from science, which organizes and explains data and observations by means of theoretical relationships. Technology translates scientific relationships into "practical" use.

TABLE 1

International Production of Aircraft Under License, 1950–67

Location of Licensor	Location of Licensee	Bombers		Fighters		Other Military		Helicopters		Civilian Transports		Total	
		No.	$ Million	No.	$ Million	No.	$ Million	No.	$ Million	No.	$ Million	No.	$ Million
U.S.	Europe	–	–	1,393	2,046	100	3	2,183	294	–	–	3,676	2,343
U.S.	Other	–	–	2,532	1,002	568	241	570	94	–	–	3,670	1,337
Europe	U.S.	403	484	–	–	–	–	–	–	278	148	681	632
Europe	Europe	–	–	899	365	669	109	–	–	–	–	1,568	474
Europe	Other	48	372	669	109	–	–	100	20	44	66	861	567
	Total	451	856	5,493	3,522	1,337	353	2,853	408	322	214	10,456	5,353

Source: R. E. Johnson and J. W. McKie, *Competition in the Reprocurement Process*, The RAND Corporation, RM-5657-PR, May 1968, p. 24. For data on the underlying programs, see Appendix C of the same study.

items. If it is embodied in people's expertise, a personnel transfer may be necessary—often in the form of a technical assistance program. Within a single organization, the process may be more informal: people simply meet to talk or work together.

In any case, the ease and cost of transfer hinge on the industrial skill the recipient already possesses. A firm skilled in the manufacture of some general line of products—voltage regulators, let us say—will probably have little trouble in mastering the technology for a new regulator; in turn, the transferring firm will probably find it easy and inexpensive to impart the required information. The opposite will hold if the transfer entails a substantial advance in the technical level of the new producer. This fact has led us to distinguish among types of information that may be transferred. We refer to these as general, system-specific, and firm-specific technologies.

General technology refers to information common to an industry, profession, or trade. At one extreme this category includes such basic skills as arithmetic, and at the other such specialized skills as blueprint reading, tool design, and computer programming. The same general knowledge is possessed by all firms in an industry and hence is the ticket of admission to the industry.

System-specific technology refers to the information possessed by a firm or individuals within a firm that differentiates each firm from its rivals, and gives a firm its competitive edge. Some of this specific information will have been acquired through engaging in certain tasks or projects. It comprises ingenious procedures connected with a particular system, solutions to unique problems or requirements, and experiences unlike those encountered with other systems. System-specific technology is when a firm, in manufacturing an item, acquires information that is peculiar to that item. Were any other firm to manufacture that item, it too would probably obtain the same technology.

Firm-specific knowledge differs from system-specific knowledge in that it cannot be attributed to any specific item the firm produces. Firm-specific knowledge results from the firm's overall activities. Some organizations possess technical knowledge that goes beyond the general information possessed by the industry as a whole; another firm manufacturing the same products would not necessarily acquire this same technology. For example, a firm may have special capabilities in thin-wall casting or metallurgical techniques not possessed by other firms, and not necessarily attributable to any specific item the firm has produced.

To illustrate the differences among the three types of technology, some of the information required for the manufacture of, say, the F-5 aircraft is common to all firms with an aircraft manufacturing capability; this we call general technology. The particular firm that manufactures the F-5 has acquired some specific information about this system not possessed by other firms; this is system-specific information. Certain other technology is possessed by this producer that other firms do not share, but which is not attributable to the F-5 (or other specific system); this is the producer's firm-specific knowledge.

The kind of information necessary for performing a certain task, and the form in which it is embodied, importantly influence the diffusion of technology and its costs. Diffusion and its costs in turn importantly influence the scope or integration of a firm and the barriers to entry encountered by potential new suppliers.[3]

A firm's willingness to diffuse its technology depends on the form in which the knowledge is embodied and the extent to which well-functioning markets for technical information exist. Assume that a firm's specific technology is protected by property rights, e.g., by a patent, and that perfect markets exist for property rights, for factors of production, and for the products or services for which the technology is used. Then the firm should be indifferent as to whether it sells the technology to other producers or uses it to produce goods and services. The value of the technology to the possessor should be the same in both cases. If markets are lacking or highly imperfect at the product level, however, the firm may be forced to sell the property rights in order to realize a return from them. Imperfect factor markets may mean, on the one hand, that the firm will be unable to obtain the resources needed to utilize the technology "in-house" at prices as low as its competitors', so it may find the sale of technology relatively more profitable. On the other hand, effective competition in the labor market may mean that the technology is diffused so rapidly that in the absence of recognized

[3] The literature on technology and market structures has been more concerned with the generation of technology than with diffusion of technology. The literature is surveyed and extended in Nelson, Peck, and Kalachek [16, pp. 66–88].

intellectual property rights, the firm has no intellectual capital to sell. If markets for property rights are lacking or imperfect, it may pay the firm to use the technology within its own organization. If the technology is not invested with property rights, the firm cannot sell it, and the best option is to try to keep the information secret and use it within the firm. In short, the decision to sell technology or utilize it within the firm depends primarily on the intellectual property system and the perfection of markets for ideas, factors, and product.[4]

The ease with which a new firm can enter an industry depends on the considerations just discussed, as well as on the type of technology required to be an effective competitor. Established firms may be wholly unable to deter a new firm from obtaining the general technology it needs to enter an industry. If this information is publicly available, as in textbooks, other open literature, and skills of people in the general labor market, any new firm may be able to master the basic arts with minimum expense. However, even if general technology is not openly available to a newcomer, existing firms may not try to withhold it from a would-be new competitor. A well-established firm with many rivals may look with equanimity on having another competitor in the industry. It may be willing to render technical assistance at something like the direct costs involved in transferring the information. A firm with few competitors, however, may look darkly on the arrival of another one on the scene and be much less willing to sell technology. As with specific technology, existing firms are likely to have some control over access and this may be a competitive barrier that firms try to protect.

These considerations go far to explain why international, interfirm transfers of technology appear to be more common than intranational, interfirm transfers. Market position, tariffs, transportation costs, and marketing costs are undoubtedly more significant internationally. Also, "political" considerations are often overriding in determining which firms will be allowed in a market. Consequently, the international market for technology is undoubtedly better developed than national markets. Internationally, firms often buy and sell technology in situations

---

[4] This discussion abstracts from uncertainty, although in international markets characterized by imperfect information, uncertainty is a vital determinant of the extent, nature, and cost of technology transfers. For a discussion of this see Y. Aharoni [1].

where domestically they would invest or do without rather than deal with a competitor.

These same considerations also contribute to the importance of the multinational corporation as an agent of transfer. Internationally, firms trading in a market may find it advantageous to establish local facilities whereas they would not do so domestically in a similar local market within a nation in which other production facilities existed [22, 1]. The multinational corporation is particularly well suited to technology transfer in such circumstances. If it is already exporting to the market in question, it has information about demands, competitive conditions, the political climate, and so forth. Also, because technology transfer is an intrafirm matter, the response to a decision to establish the technology locally may often be quicker and less expensive than establishing an interfirm market relationship through a multiple-firm program.

Thus, international corporate transfers of technology may involve a market transaction in which technology is bought and sold, or a single firm may be integrated in such a manner that the market transaction is replaced by intrafirm activities. Both arrangements have been substantial during the 1950's and 1960's. Although this study is limited to interfirm transfers, it is important to note that transfers within multinational corporations are of equal or greater importance.

Regardless of their attitude toward general technology, virtually all firms regard their specific technology as a valuable asset. Their attitude toward supplying information to other firms, however, may depend on whether it is firm-specific or system-specific technology that is to be transferred. If a firm views its firm-specific technology as giving it a competitive edge over its rivals, the firm may be loath to divulge it. There is less concern over system-specific technology; in fact, there is a substantial trade (particularly international) in designs, process information, and the like. Two factors seem to be at work here. System-specific technology is more likely to be protected by patents or other property rights, or by generally accepted proprietary claims, so the original possessor has more protection in using the information and trade is easier. Probably more important, the firm is likely to regard the technology as relevant only to one particular product. If another firm sets out to produce a competitive product, it will rediscover the technology. That being so, the original producer is likely to regard transfer of the technology as merely saving the new producer time and expense, rather than revealing some secret that could have been maintained. Ordinarily, then, system-specific knowledge is transferred more willingly than are other types of technology.

The important point is that one firm's willingness to transfer technology to another will partly depend on whether the technology is embodied in a form that can be sold, and upon the financial inducements. Willingness will also depend on whether the firm views the prospective recipient as a potential competitor. These factors in turn depend to a considerable degree upon the kind of knowledge required—that is, on whether it is general, firm-specific, or system-specific.

The process of transfer and its costs also depend upon the nature of the technology to be transferred and the form of its embodiment. General technology will probably be more costly to transplant than will firm-specific knowledge, and firm-specific more costly than system-specific, because the latter is often embodied in patents, designs, drawings, tooling, and other physical forms. Even when system-specific information is embodied solely in personnel, the transfer is still less difficult than in other kinds of technology, since the task is merely one of teaching lessons learned in other ways.

Firm-specific technology may be embodied both in physical form and in "know-how" resulting from interpersonal working relationships within an organization that are in some way difficult to separate from the firm as an entity. Firm-specific technology, therefore, can be costly to transfer.

The transplantation of general technology may be the most difficult and costly of all, since it requires intensive yet broad education in practices and procedures peculiar to an industry. Although these practices may be embodied in manuals and standard operating procedures, it may still necessitate costly experience to master them. Transfer of general technology blends into the process of general education for development.

All three types of technology were transferred in the co-production of aircraft by U.S. and Japanese companies. Although the Japanese did not methodically use these categories in deciding what technology to acquire, the categorization helps in understanding their decisions.

EARLY CO-PRODUCTION PROGRAMS

Japan's impressive World War II aviation industry came to a halt in 1945. The Western Allies prohibited Japanese aircraft production and research and development activities until April 9, 1952. When the ban was lifted, the Japanese had virtually no aircraft capability. Wartime bombings, earthquakes, and other disasters had destroyed much of the plant and equipment, experienced personnel were retired or working in other fields, and postwar advances in aerospace technology left Japan's skills and equipment largely obsolete.

The rebirth of the industry can be roughly divided into three periods. The first period began with the lifting of the ban in 1952 and lasted until about 1954, when the F-86F and T-33A programs began. During this period, the industry concentrated on repair and overhaul work for the Japanese Air Self-Defense Force (JASDF) and the U.S. Air Force [20]. At the same time, R&D and prototype production took place for several trainers and liaison planes for the Japanese Defense Agency (JDA).

In the second period, from about 1954 to 1964, the industry added a substantial manufacturing effort to its overhaul and maintenance activities. Most of the planes produced were designed by U.S. firms, but Fuji Heavy Industries, Ltd., designed and produced two small jet trainers, and Ishikawajima-Harima Heavy Industries Co., Ltd. (IHI) developed and produced the J-3 jet engine. Several R&D programs were begun that have been important in the third period beginning in 1965. This period has also included the production of Japanese-designed commercial aircraft and several new design efforts.

Japan's aircraft industry in the mid-1960's was small, having about 20,000 employees and above $200 million in annual sales. Over 100 firms claimed membership in the industry, but 5 firms accounted for most of the output. These firms, components of major industrial groups of *zaibatsu*, all had license agreements with U.S. aerospace firms, the ties being shown in Figure 1. The middle column of Figure 1 lists U.S. aircraft and engine systems manufactured in Japan from 1954 to 1966.

Between 1952 and 1964, the Japanese industry turned out 1,422 planes with total sales prices amounting to $781.7 million ($787.7 million adjusted for price changes). Of this production, JDA took 1,117,

FIGURE 1

Co-production of U.S. Planes, Helicopters, and Engines in Japan, 1954–66

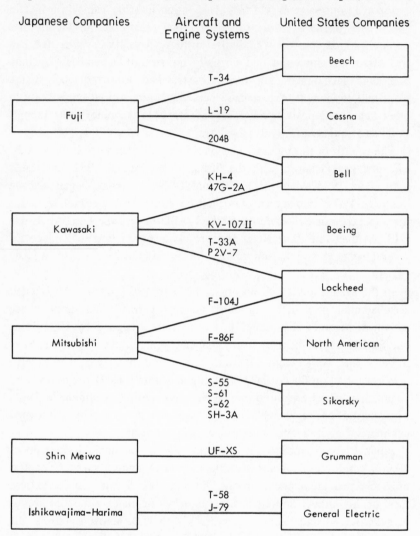

Japanese Companies — Aircraft and Engine Systems — United States Companies

Japanese Companies	Aircraft and Engine Systems	United States Companies
Fuji	T-34, L-19, 204B	Beech, Cessna
Kawasaki	KH-4, 47G-2A, KV-107 II, T-33A, P2V-7	Bell, Boeing
Mitsubishi	F-104J, F-86F, S-55, S-61, S-62, SH-3A	Lockheed, North American, Sikorsky
Shin Meiwa	UF-XS	Grumman
Ishikawajima-Harima	T-58, J-79	General Electric

the U.S. Government 27, and domestic civilian customers 206, while 72 went for export and reparations. Manufacturing accounted for about three-fourths of the revenues earned, and repair and related activity for the rest.

Japanese aircraft manufacturing activity really began in earnest in 1957. Between 1957 and 1967, the industry turned out between 100 and 230 aircraft each year. Most were produced under U.S. license, but in later years the Japanese were increasingly involved in design projects. A short-range Japanese turboprop-airliner, the YS-11, was sold in several countries, including the United States. Plans were under discussion for production of a domestically developed interceptor and possibly a military transport.

The point is that in a very short period—largely as a result of skillful importation of technology—the Japanese acquired a small but capable and profitable aerospace industry. A key element in this accomplishment was the Japanese Government's sponsorship of military aircraft co-production programs. Co-production refers to interfirm transfers of manufacturing technology in which the developer of an item provides data, technology, and other assistance to enable another firm to manufacture the item. The first three such programs were the manufacture by Mitsubishi Heavy Industries (MHI) of the North American Aviation F-86F fighter, and the Kawasaki Aircraft Company (KAC) manufacture of the Lockheed Aircraft Corporation's (LAC) T-33A trainer and P2V-7 antisubmarine aircraft. These programs established the industry and facilitated the later manufacture of the more sophisticated Lockheed F-104J interceptor.

This study focuses on the costs of transferring the F-104J technology from the United States to Japan, a program representative of many corporate transfers of technology between countries with developed industrial capabilities. To set the stage for this discussion, however, a brief summary of the earlier programs is in order.

The transplantation of general information about U.S. aerospace practices, firm-specific information about Lockheed and North American, and even some system-specific information about the T-33A and F-86F, had begun even before co-production was instituted. Japanese firms, including those later involved in the production progress, had contracts with the USAF for aircraft work; Mitsubishi, for example, had a contract for an inspection-and-repair-as-necessary program for F-86 aircraft. This involved some importation of technology; for example, North American Aviation set up a small technical assistance program to support MHI. Mitsubishi officials state that both the direct experience with the

F-86 system and the general familiarity the firm gained with NAA procedures and systems were helpful when the F-86F co-production program began.

Co-production increased the rate, amount, and kinds of technical information provided the Japanese by several orders of magnitude. Both North American and Lockheed provided their co-production partners with extensive packages of data about corporate policies and practices, and there were many more contacts between American and Japanese personnel. For the F-86F program, for example, a group of MHI officials spent several months during 1956 at North American's facilities learning about NAA's operations. The data packages furnished contained detailed information about managerial, drafting, and other corporate procedures. (Much of this information was embodied in manuals and statements of standard procedures.)

It is easily seen that abundant general and firm-specific information was made available; it is difficult to determine exactly how much the Japanese used and how valuable they found it. But discussions with the U.S. and Japanese officials connected with the programs indicate that the Japanese airframe manufacturers adopted a considerable body of U.S. general aerospace technology and Lockheed and North American firm-specific technology. It is clear that adoption was neither slavish nor automatic. The Japanese innovated and adapted many of the basic procedures they adopted [6, pp. 80–89].

On the vendor and subcontractor level, the transplantation of general and firm-specific technology sometimes resembled that between prime contractors, and sometimes did not. The experience of some firms paralleled that of MHI and KAC; others apparently possessed all the general and firm-specific information they were interested in, and consequently desired access only to system-specific technology. For example, it appears that for generators and other electrical systems little technology except system-specific flowed to Japan.

The transfer of system-specific information about the T-33A, F-86F, and P2V-7 is easier to analyze. In general, the Japanese received all product designs and specifications and all process specifications. In particular, they had the benefit in every case either of the tooling or of the tool design information used by the developer in his production activities. They also received a great deal of planning information.

And since important data exist in the notes and black books of foremen and other production line personnel, these too were collected and made a part of the data package.

The blueprints, design drawings, and similar data transferred had to be adapted because of differences between manufacturing practices in the two countries. First, they had to be "upgraded," that is, made more detailed, because U.S. toolmakers and machinists are expected to surmise more than are their European and Japanese counterparts.[5] Second, the data and drawings in the early programs had to be translated into Japanese and into the metric system. During the peak year (1956) of the F-86 program, for example, there was a design group at MHI of about sixty people. They devoted about 70 per cent of their effort to translating drawings and specifications into the Japanese language and converting them into the metric system. From this experience MHI was subsequently able to use the Lockheed drawings for the F-104J program without translation.

Access to technical information was not a problem. When discussing data transfers, U.S. aerospace officials were emphatic in saying that their co-production partners could have access to any document. One U.S. executive flatly stated, "We were paid to put them in business, and we gave them everything we had." Nor does the story change when talking to Japanese executives. When asked if they would have liked fuller information from their U.S. co-production partners, the Japanese invariably replied that they had no problem getting blueprints and other documents.

But what about the kind of information not found in documents? This "know-how" is usually assumed to be a part of the experience of men and organizations rather than written records. One pertinent measure

---

[5] This requirement illustrates the general problem of adapting technology to international differences in labor skills, training, and practices. The U.S. machinist is expected to take more independent responsibility than is his counterpart in other countries. The revision of U.S. drawings to make them compatible with Japanese shop practices required a considerable fraction of the U.S. technical assistance efforts. Another example of necessary adaptation of U.S. practices to Japanese procedures occurred in quality control. To give their decisions the ring of authority, and to save face among workers whom they implicitly "criticized," Japanese inspectors had to be given a higher rank in the corporate organization than their U.S. counterparts enjoyed. See Hall and Johnson [6, p. 82]. The point is obvious but vital. Sophisticated technology can seldom be transplanted without adaptation to local practices and skill levels. The costs of such adaptation are often significant.

of the extent to which the relevant aerospace manufacturing technology was embodied in people is the technical assistance that was furnished licensees.

For the T-33A program, LAC sent 59 advisors to Japan. Because few of them stayed the full three years, the total number of man-years spent by LAC was considerably less than 177. The team included 5 administrators, 1 manager, 1 "leg man," 1 training specialist, 1 personnel man, 8 to 10 tooling specialists (who were in Japan for only one year), 10 to 15 manufacturing planners, 2 material procurement specialists, and production specialists or others with production experience. Lockheed hired some members of the group specifically for the program. The tooling supervisor, however, was a long-time LAC employee, and Lockheed considered it important for the transfer of technology and learning to find tooling specialists familiar with Lockheed procedures.

The P2V-7 program also used a team of about 60 technical men and about the same number of man-years as the T-33 program. The contract called for 1,462 man-months of overseas technical assistance; it also provided 775 man-months of technical assistance in the United States, and an allowance of up to 78 man-months for short-term and emergency specialists.

The NAA technical assistance program was much smaller than the LAC programs. No more than 29 employees were in Japan at a time. Fewer man-months of effort were expended on F-86F technical assistance; less than 400 man-months were expended on the entire program. Of the 32 people who worked on the F-86F, all had had similar responsibilities on other F-86 programs.

The technical assistance teams were coupled to the Japanese licensees in different ways by LAC and NAA. Lockheed used what it calls the "counterpart system." Each man who went to Japan was assigned a "counterpart" Kawasaki employee at the supervisor level, and an interpreter. This system meant that a group of three worked together, and each KAC employee was able to go up the chain of command until he reached a supervisor with an American counterpart, from whom he was able to obtain assistance or advice. LAC argues that the best way to succeed in a co-production program is to participate directly in the problems of the partner. Indeed, LAC emphasizes that a large, integrated team is the key to co-production success.

North American did not integrate its team with the MHI organization nor get directly involved in MHI's activities; instead the team made itself available for advice upon request. NAA believes that its system created less friction with MHI, a firm proud of its capabilities and achievements. The NAA system also required a smaller technical assistance team.

Both methods succeeded, but LAC believes that its procedures led to better airplanes and better success in meeting schedules. NAA and MHI both hold that schedules and quality were not serious problems for the F-86F program and that some of the T-33A assistance provided by LAC was redundant.

These differences in judgment may be due to the fact that the NAA and LAC technical assistance efforts transferred different kinds of technology. The NAA team was composed of NAA employees of long standing, most of whom had had extensive experience with the manufacture of the F-86F. LAC, by contrast, hired some people with aerospace experience but who had not necessarily worked for Lockheed or worked with the T-33 before they went to Japan. This evidence indicates that NAA viewed the technical assistance requirements as the transfer of the technology specific to the F-86F, but that LAC was concerned with transfers of other types of technology as well, a fact which may explain the difference in the sizes of the teams. The implication is that system-specific technology is more susceptible to transfer in written form. General and firm-specific technology, it appears, require a process of education and occupational training with more personal interaction.

The relative importance attached to general and firm-specific technology as opposed to system-specific technology may be related to differences between MHI and KAC. When co-production began in Japan, MHI was technically a more sophisticated firm than KAC. Thus the difference in the sizes of the LAC and NAA teams may also be partly explained by the difference in the technological base of the two licensees: the larger the base, the less the general and firm-specific technology required. It is extremely difficult to analyze this hypothesis, however, because of personal considerations that confuse the data.

KAC appears to have been more willing than MHI to enter into close working relationships with U.S. firms. The F-104J program, on which Lockheed worked with MHI, should provide some basis for comparison, since Lockheed is the only American company to have worked with both MHI and KAC. Unfortunately, that information is ambiguous. MHI felt that LAC preferred Kawasaki as the prime contractor. Suspicions and doubts between the two may have led to the more formal relationship for the F-104J program than had existed between LAC and KAC on the T-33A and P2V-7 program. The F-104J program, then, cannot readily be compared with these earlier co-production efforts.

Although the amount of general and firm-specific technology transferred depends on the technology base of the licensee, it also depends on the sophistication of the system to be developed. Much of the technical assistance in the T-33A program was devoted to the transfer of general and firm-specific knowledge. The relatively arge technical assistance effort required for the P2V-7, however, according to LAC sources, was due to KAC's need for the system-specific technology required for producing a more complex aircraft.

The time pattern of transfer

All programs had the same general schedule. One or more planes of each model were manufactured and test-flown in the United States, then shipped to Japan. These were followed by other U.S.-manufactured aircraft shipped in progressively less assembled form. These "knock-down" aircraft were assembled by the licensee, who thereby gained experience in assembly operations. At some point in the program, when the licensee's own assembly tools were completely operable, knockdowns were replaced by shipments of component parts. As production tooling was completed, Japanese-manufactured parts entered assembly. Another major milestone was Japanese assumption of full manufacturing responsibility, with U.S. material support primarily limited to "hardcore" items. Although the U.S. licensor supplied some parts throughout the entire manufacturing stage, these decreased in number and importance as time went on.

The contribution of this phase-in procedure to the success of the co-production programs can hardly be overemphasized. It permitted the Japanese firm to meet relatively tight production schedules while learning from the licensor.

Tooling

The provision of tooling may be the most important part of the transfer process, insofar as the transfer of learning is concerned. It can be argued that a considerable degree of production efficiency is embodied in the design of the jigs and fixtures used by production personnel, because tooling design determines the basic physical relationships between men and machines. In all co-production programs, either tool design information or the actual tooling was transferred. Although there is no way for us to judge the relative importance of these two transfers, provision of one or the other is the primary factor in the transfer of the developer's manufacturing experience to a new company.

There was considerable diversity among the programs. For the F-86F program NAA provided Mitsubishi with a complete set of tooling from its plant in Columbus, Ohio, which was being phased out of F-86 production. MHI had to refurbish some of the equipment, but in general there was far less toolmaking than starting from scratch would have required. It is impossible to quantify this statement, since MHI was building up its labor force and many people designated for production were assigned to tool building to keep them busy.

In contrast to the MHI F-86F program, KAC received only the master tools required to control interchangeability for the T-33A.[6] KAC received copies and plans necessary to reproduce all of the approximately two thousand other tools required.

Methods used for both the previous programs were used for the P2V-7 program. KAC made some tools; it also bought twenty-seven international master tooling gauges from LAC to control mating. KAC was also given two large shipments of production tooling owned by the U.S. government and no longer needed by LAC. Naturally, this reduced KAC's toolmaking expense considerably.

The special tooling required for each program was extensive, involving thousands of items. Some items were manufactured in the United States,

---

[6] Master tools or gauges are used to locate specific points on the airframe for maintaining or checking accuracy.

but most were produced in Japan from designs, models, samples, and so forth, provided by the U.S. licensor.[7]

Parts and manufacturing support

The provision of parts and material support required two activities, interrelated and yet separate parts of the licensors' contractual obligations: (1) the provision of knockdown aircraft, component parts, hardcore parts, and raw materials from the United States, and (2) technical assistance in developing Japanese sources of supply.

The provision of knockdown assemblies and component parts has already been discussed as part of the interaction between phase-in and scheduling activities of production. Supply arrangements for items not produced by the U.S. co-production partner varied in each of the three programs. Lockheed dealt directly with its subcontractors for KAC. MHI procured items for the F-86F program directly from the NAA subcontractors, but NAA purchased a number of items for MHI that had been furnished by the U.S. government for the production of the F-86F.

Hardcore items—the components, parts, and materials imported from the United States—were defined by the P2V-7 contract as those items "beyond the capability of the Japanese industry to produce or . . . economically unfeasible for production in Japan." Both U.S. and Japanese sources emphasized the effort made to minimize hardcore items. The Japanese government was prepared to pay a premium to initiate domestic production. The U.S. firms assisted the implementation of this policy by accepting most of the items selected by the Japanese for the hardcore list. Many items that were furnished as hardcore in the early programs were produced domestically in later ones, since each program increased the Japanese aircraft industry's capability.

The provision of tools, assemblies, parts, and materials by the United States served a number of ends. It assured international interchangeability of certain items. It decreased Japanese production costs by

---

[7] Much of the technology—and many of the improvements in technology as a result of "learning" phenomena—are embodied in tool design and changes to tooling for sophisticated products. Therefore, the role of tooling in technical assistance programs and material support deserves close attention. For more discussion of the tooling and tool designs furnished the Japanese, see Hall and Johnson [6, pp. 94–96, 107–08].

furnishing tooling the firms would otherwise have had to build and by permitting importation of parts that would have been expensive to produce in Japan. As a result, Japan had to invest only a little less than $17 million in facilities. Supply by the United States also permitted tight delivery schedules for planes to JDA. Most important, manufacturing support permitted the transfer of technology at reasonable cost.[8]

A general observation

Some quantitative features of the three early programs are summarized in Table 2. It is harder to summarize the results of the programs. Japan obtained 552 planes for its military forces which it could have purchased from NAA and LAC assembly lines, but we do not know the relative costs of importation and domestic production at that time. There were some identifiable direct spillovers as, for example, the landing gear on the commercial airliner, the YS-11, which is an adaptation of the P2V-7 landing gear. Yet, in general, these benefits are small compared with the basic outcome of the early programs: the acquisition of sufficient general and firm-specific technology to qualify Japan as a producer of advanced commercial and military aircraft.

THE F-104J PROGRAM

The three programs previously described above exemplify technology transfer from an industry with an established capability to an industry trying to establish a new capability.[9] Mitsubishi's production of the F-104J illustrates another type of transfer—between two countries with established industries.

Description of the program

On November 7, 1959, Mitsubishi Heavy Industries was notified that it would be the prime contractor for Japanese production of the

[8] The relationship between extent of domestic production and cost has been instructively developed by Baranson in [3] and in an International Bank for Reconstruction and Development report [12].

[9] Although Japan did not have an established aircraft industry, it did have a substantial and well-developed industrial base. Thus, the early aircraft programs differ from technology transfers to less-developed countries in which more general technology must be transferred to make a co-production program successful.

TABLE 2

Japanese Co-production of U.S. Military Aircraft, 1955–63

Program Feature	Type of Aircraft		
	T-33A	P2V-7	F-86F
Total number of aircraft involved:	210	42	300
Knockdowns from U.S.	20	6	10
Component parts from U.S.	10	8	60
Fabricated in Japan	180	28	230
Items supplied from U.S.:			
Data	limited rights and all data	limited rights and all data	limited rights and all data
Technical assistance	59 men	about 60 men	32 men
Tooling	13 key masters from U.S.; about 21,000 built in Japan from U.S. designs	27 key masters some production tools from U.S.; rest built in Japan from U.S. designs	complete set from U.S.
Manufacturing support	selected parts, engines, armament	selected parts, engines, armament, some electronics	selected parts, engines, armament
Companies involved:			
U.S.	Lockheed	Lockheed	No. Amer.
Japanese	Kawasaki	Kawasaki	Mitsubishi
Period of production	1955–59	1958–63	1955–61

Lockheed F-104 Starfighter, with Kawasaki Aircraft Company as a major airframe subcontractor.[10] In the intervening period between notification and contract effective date, a two-nation agreement was negotiated, the U.S. financial contribution was determined, a license was signed between MHI and Lockheed, and several purchase agreements and contracts were made between the companies concerned. The contract between Mitsubishi and the Japanese Defense Agency, signed March 31, 1961, initiated the C-1 program for the production of 180 F-104Js and 20 trainer planes, called the F-104DJ. This program ended March 1965; it was followed early in 1966 by the C-2 program for 30 additional aircraft.

The total C-1 program cost about $269 million, of which the U.S. government contributed $75 million. It involved the Japanese manufacture of most of the airframe and J-79 engine components, plus assembly of some of the electronic items. Three F-104J planes were manufactured, assembled, and test-flown in the United States; 17 knockdowns and sets of component parts were manufactured in the United States and assembled in Japan; 160 F-104J planes were manufactured and assembled in Japan; and 20 F-104DJ planes were manufactured in the United States and should be assembled in Japan. The 30-plane C-2 program increased the proportion of engine components manufactured in Japan and added additional Japanese responsibilities for assembly and manufacture of electronics.

Data and technical assistance

The involvement of U.S. firms can be usefully divided into data, technical assistance, and material support. In the data category the most important information transferred to Japan was probably tool designs. Most tooling was built in Japan from Lockheed designs. The Japanese imported the master tools from the United States in some cases; in others, they imported plaster copies from which they made their own master tools. They also purchased tooling for tricky designs or parts hard to produce from blueprints alone.

The LAC-MHI license agreement specified a technical assistance

[10] About 70 per cent of the airframe by weight was manufactured by Mitsubishi and about 30 per cent of Kawasaki. In dollars, the percentages were 80 and 20, Horikoshi [10].

program of approximately 1,400 man-months in Japan, paid for by the U.S. government. The major subcontractor, Kawasaki, also received LAC technical assistance. The third technical assistance effort of any size was between General Electric Company and Ishikawajima-Harima Heavy Industries Company, Ltd. (IHI) for the production of the J-79 engine. General Electric provided thirteen engineers, or about 131 man-months, at a total cost of $285,000. Other licensors of parts and components also provided some technical assistance to licensees.

Much of the technical assistance involved design changes that distinguished the F-104J from the basic F-104. Because the Japanese wanted a heavier airframe and better electronics, more manufacturing technology was required than in the earlier programs.

Unlike its experience with Kawasaki, which actively sought technical assistance, Lockheed found the Mitsubishi organization much more formal. Assistance was requested, but there was not as close a relationship between the two firms as there had been between LAC and KAC. Indeed, Mitsubishi officials expressed skepticism about the need for such a large Lockheed technical assistance team. Since the technical assistance was paid out of the U.S. contribution, however, MHI was not inclined to protest the size of the effort.

Material support—airframes

The hardcore list for the F-104J reflects Japan's interest in increasing the capability of her aircraft industry. Subject to total budgetary restrictions, everything was built in Japan that could be [10, p. 3].

The budget constraint meant that relative U.S. and Japanese production costs influenced the decision as to what technology to acquire. This fact in turn made the size of the program and rate of production important determinants of the hardcore list. As an illustration of this point, the consortium producing the European F-104G, although it had a larger budget, bought fewer hardcore items and curtailed importation of many items from the United States earlier in their program than did the Japanese because the European program was larger and the rate of production higher than in Japan [11, p. 1194].

Japan already possessed most of the required technology and facilities. In the opinion of J. Horikoshi, an MHI official during the F-104J program, the important technological capabilities acquired by the Japanese were limited to chemical milling techniques,[11] the spray-mat process to control icing,[12] and the improved capability to form and handle high-heat-treatment (4340) steel [10, p. 7].

The general qualifications of the Japanese firms are indicated by the composition of the hardcore lists. The initial hardcore list contained 226 items. By mid-1965 this number had fallen to 181. Further, 22 items originally procured as finished parts were being shipped to Japan as rough castings and forgings at this time. The 181 items on the final hardcore list were determined by the three criteria that LAC and MHI used at their conferences: (1) Capital equipment expense; (2) Project tooling expense; (3) Technical capability. As shown in Table 3, no item was classified hardcore solely from lack of technical capability; and in fact, for only 10 of the 181 items was this lack among the determining factors.

The price breakdown of Table 3, though crude, is revealing. The total cost of hardcore per aircraft was approximately $38,000. The items

TABLE 3

Items (Hardcore) Acquired From Outside Japan for F-104J Program
(classified by price and reason for acquisition)

Reason for Acquisition	No. of Line Items	Unit Price in dollars			
		0–100	101–500	501–1000	Over 1000
High capital equipment expense (1)	25	19	3	2	1
High project tooling expense (2)	70	42	20	7	1
Technical capability limitations (3)	0	0	0	0	0
Combination of 1 and 2	76	27	47	2	0
Combination of 1 and 3	0	0	0	0	0
Combination of 2 and 3	3	0	0	3	0
Combination of 1, 2, and 3	7	0	2	4	1
Total	181	88	72	18	3

Source: Lockheed Aircraft Corporation.

[11] Produced under a Turco Products, Inc., license.
[12] Produced under an English Electric Company (NAPIER) license.

Lockheed supplied to Mitsubishi were primarily inexpensive; about half the total hardcore amount is accounted for by items costing from $100 to $500.

A hardcore list can be extensive for either of two mutually exclusive reasons: an item may be so sophisticated and complex that its manufacture would be difficult and expensive to transfer to another firm; or an item may be so simple and widespread in application as to be uneconomical to produce except in large quantities. In the first case, the high costs of transfer could place the item on the hardcore list. In the second case, transfer, although probably inexpensive, might be unattractive because of the economies of scale. The F-104J hardcore list reflects economies of scale more than high costs of transfer. The relatively few expensive items on the F-104J hardcore list include the air intake duct inner skins, radomes, wing skins, fuselage main frames, fuselage keelsons, empennage beams, and fuselage longerons. Inexpensive items included because of the economies of scale were mostly small pieces of hardware such as blind rivets and hi-lock bolts.

In contrast to the airframe part of the program, most of the expensive electronics items were imported. As will be discussed later, these items seem to have fallen into the category of high transfer costs rather than the second, or economies-of-scale, case.

The extent of technology transfer

The material support from the United States raises the question of how much of the F-104J was really Japanese-produced, or conversely, how much was merely Japanese assembly of U.S. manufactured items. To answer this question, data were obtained from leading Japanese participants in the program to separate vendor and subcontractor purchases from value added. The sample included five suppliers of airframe items, the engine manufacturer, and three electronics companies.

One conclusion stands out clearly. The airframe, engine, and electronics firms differed widely in their degree of domestic production.

To understand the role of these three groups, and to provide a comparison for cost figures to be presented later, Table 4 shows the average costs for sixty F-104Gs purchased in the United States in 1964 from Lockheed Aircraft Corporation. The G version is similar to the J version so it provides a good basis for cost comparisons. Note

TABLE 4

Flyaway Cost of U.S.-Produced F-104G Aircraft, Fiscal Year 1964

Item	Thousands of Dollars	Per Cent
Airframe	789	65.8
Engine	184	15.3
Electronics[a]	227	18.9
Total	1200	100.0

Source: Based on information provided by the F-104 System Program Office, USAF on a fiscal year 1964 Military Assistance Program procurement of approximately sixty aircraft.

[a]Includes estimated prices on miscellaneous items of government-furnished equipment.

that the airframe accounts for approximately two-thirds of the cost of the system, and the engine and electronics for about one-sixth each.

Table 5 presents data on the airframe part of the Japanese program. MHI, the prime contractor, produced about 80 per cent of the total value of the airframe. As the major subcontractor, KAC was responsible for the complete empennage, the forward and aft fuselage sections, and some other items.

Table 5 divides the MHI and KAC parts of the C-1 program among outside domestic purchases, imports, and the value-added by the firm.[13] About 31 per cent of MHI's purchases and about 33 per cent of KAC's were imported. Compared with the total cost of manufacture, imports were about 17 per cent for MHI and about 18 per cent for KAC. Hardcore items accounted for about 30 per cent of MHI's imports. Raw material imports were relatively insignificant. Most of the purchased items came from Japanese firms.

The value-added percentages, 45 per cent for Mitsubishi and 46 per

[13] The twenty trainers and twenty knockdowns in which MHI and KAC were only middlemen for LAC are not shown. The discussion is limited to the 160-aircraft portion of the program and its related spare parts production. The MHI figure for the KAC subcontract differs in Table 5 from the total of the KAC column because it includes the cost of KAC's assembly activity for the 20 aircraft assembly-only portion of the program.

TABLE 5

*Production Experience of MHI and KAC in
160-Aircraft Portion of C-1 Program*

Item	MHI		KAC[a]	
	$ Millions	Per Cent	$ Millions	Per Cent
Total imports[b]	19.95	17.1	3.52	18.0
Raw material	1.89		0.71	
Parts	12.00		2.81	
Hardcore[c]	6.06			
Total domestic purchases	44.64	38.3	7.15	36.4
Raw material	1.32		1.06	
Parts	20.48		6.09	
KAC subcontract	22.84			
Value added by firm	51.94	44.6	8.95	45.6
Total	116.53	100.0	19.62	100.0

[a]Excludes spare parts and the assembly work on the first 20 F-104J aircraft.

[b]Airframe experience only (excludes MHI import of $23.45 million of electronics).

[c]Purchased separately from LAC out of U.S. dollar contribution.

cent for Kawasaki, provide a check on the extent of the technology transfer. Had the value-added percentages been low, we would have suspected that the Japanese firms were merely importing U.S.-produced items and no significant transfer of technology was involved; but the MHI and KAC figures are about the same as the value-added percentages for U.S. airframe producers, implying that MHI and KAC were manufacturing rather than transshipping the F-104.

Since Mitsubishi purchased about $22 million worth of items from Japanese firms other than KAC, we must go below the prime-contractor level and examine the source of inputs for the Japanese vendors in order to obtain a picture of the relative Japanese and U.S. contributions

TABLE 6

Production Experience of the Three Largest MHI Vendors,
160-Aircraft Portion of the C-1 Program
(in per cent)

Item	Shinko Electric Co., Ltd.		Shimadzu Seisakusho Ltd.		Sumitomo Precision Products Co., Ltd.	
Imports	9.5		61.3		32.3	
Raw materials		0		0		11.8
Parts		9.5		61.3		20.5
Domestic purchases	14.4		11.9		46.3	
Raw materials		5.3		3.4		4.1
Parts		9.1		8.5		42.2
Value-added by firm	76.1		26.8		21.4	
Total	100.0		100.0		100.0	
Products	generators, voltage regulators		air conditioners, starters		landing gear	
Purchased by MHI	9.3		14.7		13.1	
U.S. licensor	Bendix Corp.		Garrett Corp.		Cleveland Pneumatic	

to the F-104J. Table 6 shows the production experience of the three MHI suppliers. These firms, Shinko, Shimadzu, and Sumitomo were not only quantitatively important suppliers, accounting for a third of Mitsubishi's purchases, but illustrate three different domestic supply conditions.[14]

Shimadzu's experience is an example of a supplier that made extensive use of imports. Over 80 per cent of its sales to MHI were accounted for by one product—the air conditioning system. Because this compact

[14] For further information on Japanese subcontractors and suppliers, see Hall and Johnson [6, pp. 122–34].

and sophisticated system was unlike anything the firm had previously manufactured, most of the parts were imported from the U.S. licensor, the Garrett Corporation. Because of this one product, approximately 61 per cent of Shimadzu sales to MHI were foreign product imports. There appears to have been a severe barrier to the transfer of technology, perhaps resulting from the extreme difference in the technological base of the licensor and licensee, because this heavy reliance on imports is not characteristic of Shimadzu. Under another Garrett license, Shimadzu manufactured an electric actuator. Imports for this simpler item, of which Shimadzu was an experienced manufacturer, accounted for only 17 per cent of total sales.

Sumitomo Precision presents an intermediate case of reliance on imports. It manufactured landing gear components under a license with Cleveland Pneumatic, with imports accounting for about one-third of the total sales to MHI. At the time of the C-1 program, the Japanese industry lacked a capability for forging hard steel (especially forgings that required large-capacity double-action presses).[15] Many of the imported items required hard-steel forgings with only modest amounts of machining. The relatively heavy reliance on domestic purchases reflects primarily the involvement of Daikin Kogyo Company, Ltd., one other firm producing landing gear components.

The experience of Shinko Electric illustrates the third position on imports. Note the very low reliance on imports, even though the products are somewhat complex (voltage regulators, generators, etc.), manufactured to Bendix Corporation designs. Shinko officials state they had almost no difficulty in manufacturing the items they supplied. The reason for importing parts from the United States was primarily comparative manufacturing costs; the imports were not necessarily the most sophisticated parts, and there had been practically no technical interaction between licensor and licensee.

In short, most of the F-104J airframe was manufactured in Japan, and U.S. imports of finished items accounted for a small part of the airframe value. There was a very gradual and, on the whole, modest decline in the reliance on imports during the C-1 program; and for the C-2

[15] Japan was also limited in five-axis milling, precipitation hardening, phosphate finishing, and nitriding.

program (for thirty follow-on craft), very little import substitution was programmed for MHI, KAC, and the three leading MHI vendors.

Differences among the MHI vendors in their reliance upon imports were substantial and reflect the differences in the requirements for a successful transplantation of technology. When only system-specific information is required, transfer is easy and inexpensive even if the item is complex and the technology sophisticated. Transfer appears more difficult for items substantially different from a firm's current product, with licensees likely to rely heavily on imports of finished items from their licensors.

Material support—engines

In sharp contrast to the modest decline in imports for the airframe portion of the F-104J, the role of imports in engine co-production changed dramatically. The first twenty-nine "Japanese" engines (procured by the Japan Defense Agency from the prime contractor) were actually supplied from the United States as partly assembled knockdowns. By the end of the C-1 program, imports accounted for less than one-third of the total invoice price. IHI was the prime contractor for the J-79/GE-11A engine, with both KAC and MHI as subcontractors. Table 7 indicates the average cost experience for the C-1 program, and the IHI estimates for the follow-on C-2 program. Note the difference between the C-1 and the C-2 programs in the reliance on imports. Over half the price of an engine can be attributed to U.S. imports in the C-1 program, while in the C-2 program imports were programmed to be less than one-quarter of the price of the completed engine.

The list of C-2 program imports from General Electric Co. contained only a handful of components having unit costs of $500 or more—a small fraction of the number of such components imported for the C-1 program. A few major components were supplied by U.S. vendors, but the bulk of the imports were "nuts and bolts," in the words of one IHI official.

Compare the IHI figures with those in Table 5 for MHI and KAC. IHI had a programmed value-added of about 44.2 per cent for the C-2 phase, or about the same as that of MHI and KAC for the C-1 program. But note that in the C-1 program IHI "in-house" work accounted for

TABLE 7

IHI Production Experience of J-79 Engines: 160-Aircraft Portion of the C-1 Program and C-2 Program Estimates

Items as per cent	Program			
	C-1		C-2	
Imports	51.3		24.5	
Total domestic purchases	13.2		31.3	
MHI subcontract		6.1		9.4
KAC subcontract		1.7		2.5
Other		5.4		19.4
Value added by IHI	35.5		44.2	
Total	100.0		100.0	
Program size in $ millions[a]	44.39		7.14	

[a]Contract information supplied by JDA

only about 35.5 per cent of the total engine price. Domestic purchases differ even more. For the C-1 program only 13.2 per cent of the engine price was spent on IHI purchases from Japanese firms; comparable figures for MHI and KAC were 38.3 and 36.4 per cent. IHI's domestic purchases were programmed for about 31.3 per cent for the C-2 program. In other words, IHI's sources of supply for the C-2 program were about the same as MHI's and KAC's were for the C-1 program. This means that Japan's engine self-sufficiency lagged behind its airframe self-sufficiency by about five years.

Material support—electronics

Most F-104J electronics were not co-produced in the same sense that the airframe and engine were co-produced. The twenty F-104DJ aircraft and the first twenty F-104J aircraft were completely equipped with electronics from U.S. suppliers. For the remaining 160 F-104J aircraft in the C-1 program, 160 sets of major items of electronics were imported.

To learn more about the Japanese role in providing spare electronics

TABLE 8

Selected JDA Expenditures on Electronics: C-1 Program

Item	Quantity	Supplier	Imports		Value Added in Japan		Total Imports and Value Added	
			$ Mil.	Per Cent	$ Mil.	Per Cent	$ Mil.	Per Cent
NASARR	27	Mitsubishi Electric	3.2		0.9		4.1	
Stable platform	24	Mitsubishi Precision	0.9		0.4		1.3	
Air data computer	24	Shimadzu Seisakusho	0.6		0.2		0.8	
Total			4.7	75.8	1.5	24.2	6.2	100.0

units, data were assembled on the North American Search and Range Radar (NASARR) fire control system procured from Mitsubishi Electric, the stable platform procured from Mitsubishi Precision, and the air data computer procured from Shimadzu. These three items accounted for about three-fourths of the total cost of the electronics items. (See Table 8.) Imports accounted for over 75 per cent of the total sales price. Discussions with the Japanese corporate officials confirmed that the Japanese firms had only assembled and tested imported parts.

The relative costs of imports and domestically assembled components for the electronics part of the F-104J program were high. The average unit cost of the completed items imported is about 20 per cent lower than the cost of the parts for the components assembled in Japan. Table 9 compares the average prices paid by the Japanese government for the components assembled in Japan with the unit costs of complete components imported from the United States. Subtracting the value-added in Japan from the unit cost gives the cost of the imported parts used in assembly. The costs of these parts are uniformly higher than the costs of the completely assembled components imported.

The implication of these data is that the Japanese electronics assembly part of the program was subsidized by the Japanese government to enable Japanese manufacturers to gain familiarity with the more sophisticated electronic products.

TABLE 9

Average Unit Costs of Selected Items of Electronics
(thousands of dollars)

Item	U.S. Unit Cost	Quantity	U.S.-Supplied Imported Parts Used in Assembly	Spare Units Assembled in Japan		
				Value-Added in Japan	Total Unit Cost, Japan	Quantity
NASARR	95.5	160	119.4	33.1	152.5	27
Stable platform	31.5	160	36.8	16.5	53.3	24
Air data computer	23.2	160	26.5	8.1	34.6	24

Summary of material support data

Some key features of the F-104J program are shown in Table 10. A major share of the fabrication of the F-104J took place in Japan, but the transplantation of U.S. technology varied considerably among different parts of the program. Most of the airframe was produced in Japan after the first twenty aircraft were assembled. By 1966 most of the engine was produced in Japan, but it took the entire C-1 program for the necessary technology to be transferred completely. Very little of the electronics technology was transferred.[16]

Through previous overhaul and airframe co-production programs, Japanese airframe manufacturers had acquired substantial command over most of the general airframe manufacturing technology. Since very little general technology was required, the transplantation was rapidly accomplished. The airframe situation also appears characteristic of various component suppliers such as Shinko Electric, the generator producer.

The electronics situation contrasts sharply with the airframe experi-

TABLE 10

Japanese Co-Production of the F-104J, 1961—67 —Lockheed-Mitsubishi

Total number of aircraft involved:	207
Knockdowns from U.S.	7
Component parts from U.S.	10
Fabricated in Japan	190
Items supplied from U.S.:	
Data	limited rights and all data
Technical assistance	about 60 men
Tooling	11 key masters and over 5,000 plaster splashes and Mylar reproductions. Tooling built in Japan from U.S. designs.
Manufacturing support	selected parts, some engines, armament, most electronics.

[16] In dollar terms, the airframe accounted for about 60 per cent of the cost of the aircraft, and the other two categories for about 20 per cent each.

ence. Japan's reputation in the field of commercial electronics might lead one to expect that the F-104J electronics gear would be manufactured in Japan without difficulty. In fact, however, little electronics manufacture took place on the C-1 program. Most major electronics items were imported from the United States.

The explanation given by Japanese executives is that there are substantial differences between sophisticated military electronics and the commercial field in which Japanese firms are experienced—in physical characteristics and in specifications. This indicates that production of items such as the NASARR or the stable platform would have required the transfer of general technology associated with the military electronics field rather than merely the specific technology associated with the particular systems.

Through assembly and spare parts manufacturing, the Japanese generally have been acquiring the general technology of military electronics. Future aircraft programs should show a pattern in electronics more like that in the airframe portion of the F-104J program.

The J-79 engine experience tends to support this prediction. Unlike electronics, the Japanese had had some experience in jet engine production at the outset of the C-1 program; by the end of the C-1 program the engine was produced almost entirely in Japan. The transfer process for engine technology took much longer than did the airframe, probably because the Japanese had had extensive prior experience in airframe production, which gave them a relatively large stock of general manufacturing technology.

The F-104J experience illustrates that the transfer of technology need not be an all-or-nothing matter. The ability to import parts, supplies, materials, and technical assistance permits a gradual and partial transfer of the technology required for an item. This process is well exemplified by the engine and electronics portions of the program.

The F-104J experience suggests that the ease of transferring manufacturing technology for an aircraft importantly depends upon the amount of general knowledge that must be included in the transfer. If the backgrounds of the firms are so different that the transfer of general technology is necessary, a firm is likely to limit its initial activities to assembly and repair—activities that appear to facilitate the gradual transfer of general technology.

THE ECONOMICS OF TRANSFER

Two classes of costs are incurred when technology is transferred from one firm to another. First, there are direct costs, or the financial outlays required to move the necessary technology. Second, there are indirect costs in the form of increased production costs incurred because manufacturing responsibility is divided rather than concentrated at a single point. The direct and indirect costs of the F-104J technology transfer will first be considered; then the total cost of producing the F-104J will be compared with that of another F-104 model produced in the United States.[17]

Direct costs

The major direct costs were license fees, royalties, and technical assistance payments.[18] Considering royalties and license fees first, each Japanese producer of a U.S. proprietary item had to make some financial arrangement for manufacturing and data rights. MHI paid Lockheed $1.5 million plus a royalty of about $31,500 for each of the 160 F-104Js manufactured in Japan during the C-1 program. These payments followed the pattern set in the earlier programs.

There were many additional license agreements at the vendor level, usually amounting to about 5 per cent of the invoice price of the licensee's product, with a modest initial payment or none at all. That portion of the invoice price represented by parts and materials purchased by the licensee from the licensor was ordinarily excluded from royalty payments.

---

[17] Only occasional reference will be made to earlier programs, since they took place before Japan had a fully developed aircraft industry.

[18] The license between Lockheed and Mitsubishi covered ten years. It provided for manufacturing rights, development activities, technical data, technical assistance, and all warranties. Only items designed by Lockheed were included in the license. LAC provided all data required for manufacture, including revisions during the license term. The assembly of the plane and all LAC-designed items were warranted, but not items of other firms' design. Mitsubishi had exclusive rights to sell the F-104J, but only to the Japanese government. MHI agreed to pay LAC $5.8 million to develop the J version of the airframe: a fixed fee of $1.5 million for the manufacturing rights and data, plus a royalty on each plane made in Japan, this to be $32,000 for the first plane, dropping to $25,000 on the 201st plane. On spare parts not purchased from LAC, MHI agreed to pay a 5 per cent royalty.

Estimated total royalties on the airframe portion of the program are shown in Table 11. Total royalties have been estimated at 5 per cent of the total work performed by Japanese vendors, or $765,000.' This figure was obtained from Table 5, which shows that MHI's purchases in Japan were $21.8 million, excluding the KAC subcontract. Approximately 30 per cent of this amount in turn went to purchases from U.S. vendors. For the remaining 70 per cent ($15.3 million), we assume an average royalty payment of 5 per cent. The unit cost figures shown in

TABLE 11

Payment for Rights and Technical Assistance in the F-104J Program
(thousands of dollars)

Item	Cost
Airframe technology	Per Airframe
Technical assistance	20.8^a
Total manufacturing rights	42.8
Initial payment to Lockheed	7.5^b
Royalty to Lockheed	31.5^c
Vendors' royalty to Lockheed	3.8^d
Total	63.6
Engine technology	Per Engine
Technical assistance	1.1^e
Total manufacturing rights	10.8
Initial payment to GE	10.0^f
Royalty payment to GE vendors	0.8^g
Total	11.9

[a] Technical assistance of $4.16 million/200 airframes.
[b] Payment of $1.5 million/200 airframes.
[c] Average for the first 160 airplanes.
[d] Estimated as 0.05 x 15.3 million/200 airframes.
[e] Technical assistance of $0.28 million/250 engines.
[f] Payment of $2.5 million/250 engines.
[g] Estimated as 0.05 x 4.1 million/250 engines.

Table 11 were obtained by allocating costs (except for the Lockheed royalty) to approximately two hundred airframes.[19]

For the J-79 engine, $2.5 million was paid by IHI to GE for three hundred engines on a royalty-free basis. IHI also made royalty payments to certain GE vendors. These were computed from the data in Table 7, assuming there were no royalty charges for IHI domestic purchases that were ultimately supplied by U.S. vendors. For the remainder ($4.1 million) a 5 per cent average royalty was again assumed. These charges were allocated to 250 engines, the approximate C-1 and C-2 production.

Payments for technical assistance have been allocated in the same fashion as payments for rights. Japanese vendors received minimal technical assistance from licensors. Those technical assistance programs of significant size were with MHI, KAC, and IHI.

We are now in a position to examine the direct costs of transfer in relation to total production costs.[20] For this purpose the F-104G costs shown in Table 4 will be used. According to Table 11, direct costs of airframe technology transfer amounted to $63,600 per plane or about 8.1 per cent of the total F-104G airframe cost. Direct costs for engine technology transfer were $11,900 per engine, or about 6.5 per cent of the comparable U.S.-produced engine cost. Together, these represent about 7.8 per cent of the total cost of the airframe and engine. Technical assistance amounted to more than a quarter of the total direct costs of transfer.[21]

[19] The 200-airframe figure was obtained by adding the 160-unit C-1 program to the 30-unit C-2 program and assuming that the production of a substantial number of spares in the C-1 program was equal to ten complete airframes. The 20 F-104DJ's and the 20 F-104J's supplied in the form of knockdowns were excluded. Because there was little or no Japanese production for these parts of the C-1 program, it is inappropriate to allocate royalties, license fees, etc., to these planes.

[20] No figures are presented for the electronics part of the program, since it is not clear how much or what type of technology was transferred.

[21] The payments for technical assistance differ from the payments for licenses and rights. The former are payments for a new service—the activities required to diffuse knowledge. Licenses and royalties, on the other hand, are economic rents; they are not payments for the production of any new goods or service. Thus, the "real" economic cost of transfer of technology is less than the nominal financial costs. Present institutional arrangements, however, give firms property or quasiproperty rights in the ideas, data, and designs embodied in a finished system. Transfer requires payments to the owner of these rights in order to induce them to forego their rights not to disclose their knowledge.

Indirect costs

Production costs are influenced by the rate of learning and the economies of scale. These factors are in turn determined by the rate of production, the volume of production, and the delivery schedule. This relationship can be formally stated as

$$C = f(x, V, T, m),$$

where C denotes the cost, x the rate of output, V the scheduled volume of output, T the time output begins, and m the length of the output period. T and m fix the production period measured from the time the program begins. Note that there are only three degrees of freedom; specification of any three variables fixes the fourth.[22]

The rate of production is the central variable in the economic literature on costs, while the volume of production is the central variable in the literature on learning or progress curves. Our present concern is not with the total costs of production attributable to each variable; it is how these costs vary with the number of producers in a program, and what costs can be avoided when production responsibility is concentrated in a single firm. To this end we will discuss each variable.

The relationship between costs and the rate of production is traditionally divided into two parts: the relationship between output and investment in plant and equipment (economies of scale), and the relationship between output and variable factors of production (economies of plant utilization). Let us consider investment first. Both Lockheed and Mitsubishi had the factory space and basic equipment required for F-104 production. Few new facilities had to be added in Japan specifically for the program. About $10.1 million worth of capital investment in Japanese aircraft capability was designated for the F-104J; private investment accounted for about $8.4 million of this total. Most of this investment was for the J-79 engine. IHI invested $5.3 million and the Japanese Government an additional $1.1 million in J-79 engine facilities.

Tooling costs are more easily attributed to a specific program than are plant and facility investment expenditures. The extra tooling costs in a co-production program greatly depend on how much tooling is transferred from the original producer. Usually, this means that the

---

[22] This information and much of the discussion to follow is based on the work of Alchian and Hirshleifer [2, 9, 8].

tooling expense attributable to co-production depends on the extent to which production in the new and old locations overlaps.

Precise tooling costs for the F-104J program are unavailable, but a reasonable estimate can be derived from MHI's man-hour figures. MHI invested about 1.5 million man-hours in the original tooling. (Total MHI man-hours for all portions of the C-1 program were about 7.0 million.) The MHI tooling experience appears reasonable when compared with Lockheed's original tooling for the F-104A, about 1.4 million man-hours.

Costing the Japanese tooling expenditure is difficult, but if we use the Japanese aviation industry rule of thumb, which estimates labor costs at $3 per hour, we arrive at a tooling cost of about $4.5 million, plus some allowance for overhead and indirect expenses. Added to this figure should be the tooling costs of the other firms in the program, but little relevant information on that is available. MHI did most of the airframe tooling, and it appears that the only other major tooling expenditure was for the engine, for which no data are available.

The cost for MHI's tooling is somewhat overstated because some personnel destined for work on other parts of the program were put to work building tools. This extra expense, however, is properly regarded as a setup cost that could have been avoided if Lockheed had produced the F-104Js.

In sum, as a rough and probably high estimate, we can attribute to the investment costs of the airframe portion of the C-1 program, $3.7 million for plant and facilities and $4.5 million for direct tooling labor. Dividing this total by two hundred planes yields a unit-fixed-cost of $41,000. It was noted earlier that Lockheed sold the F-104G airframe for about $789,000 per copy, and it appears likely that the Japanese could also have bought airframes from LAC for this price. We may therefore conclude that the avoidable fixed cost amounted to a little more than 5 per cent of the airframe cost.

It does not appear that the relationship between the rate of production and tooling costs should importantly affect the costs attributed to dividing production rather than concentrating it within a single firm. The tooling for the original producer would have been designed with some particular rate of production and total output in mind. Transfer of the program to another manufacturer would not affect the total quantity to be bought nor should it affect the rate of production unless the transfer required so much time that the total volume for the program could not be produced with the originally scheduled rate of production. In that case, either the length of the production period would have to be extended or the rate of production would have to be increased. Increasing the rate of production would therefore be a cost attributable to the separation.[23] The important consideration is the impact of separation on scheduling.

The usual view is that the shorter the period between the start of a program and the delivery of the first item, the greater the cost. In a domestic program with a specified volume of production and a specified rate of production, higher costs can be expected if an early target date is established for the first delivery. In international co-production programs, however, the date of first delivery will partly govern the amount and type of imports. The earlier the date of delivery, the more knockdown and component parts will be acquired from the original supplier. The cost impact will depend on the relative costs of foreign and domestic production.

The schedule may affect costs in still another way. The longer the time between the start of a program and the date of first delivery, the less hurried the process of transferring the technology can be. The direct costs and effectiveness of transfer may be related to the speed of transfer. Certainly the phase-in process, previously emphasized as a key to successful transfer of learning, is likely to be hindered by a tight schedule.

The important point is that technology transfer is not a single event, but a series of events occurring over a period of time. Considerable flexibility is possible in adjusting the transfer of programs and technology to meet delivery schedule requirements. Such adjustment, of course, requires substantial and careful planning, but skillful planning can minimize the impact of transfer on the rate of production.

---

[23] The relationship between co-production and the costs associated with the rate of production depend on how the co-production program is organized. Recall the equation $C = f(x, V, T, m)$, and assume V is fixed. If T and m (the schedule) can be adjusted for the time required to transfer the program, or if no extra time is required to effect the transfer, x is not affected by co-production. If, however, transfer takes time and T and m are fixed, x will have to increase. If we make the usual assumptions about the relationship between C and x, there will be some additional indirect costs.

Turning to the indirect cost implications of the volume of production, it should be kept in mind that we are concerned with the cost associated with dividing a single program between two firms. The underlying determinants of total cost are not at issue. Consequently, our interest in the influence of production volume centers on the impact of co-production on progress or learning curves. In the consideration of progress curves, as Hirshleifer has pointed out, costs are influenced by two aspects of volume: the actual output and the scheduled total output [9, pp. 239–40]. Increasing familiarity with production processes should increase labor-force productivity and thereby progressively lower unit costs [8, pp. 146–47]. For this effect, it is the actual output that is important. An increase in the scheduled volume of output will lead to different managerial decisions about investment in facilities and tooling and to different production procedures that should also lead to progressively lower unit costs [9, p. 240]. For this latter effect the scheduled output, rather than the actual output, is significant. Here, since actual and scheduled outputs were the same, we cannot distinguish between the two situations. More generally, however, in analyzing the costs of transferring technology, it is important to specify whether actual or scheduled production is the measure.

Two interfirm comparisons of the volume-cost relationship are of interest. Assume that the first firm has a total cumulative production equal to N units. Also assume that the second firm is going to take on a co-production program of n units. One comparison is between the cost of the original producer's first n units and the second firm's costs for n units. This comparison indicates (assuming all adjustments for other cost effects such as economies of scale have been made and that the firms are equally efficient) the extent to which the first firm's learning was transferred to the second firm.[24]

The second comparison is between the cost of n units produced by the new manufacturer and the cost of units N to $N + n$, had they been manufactured by the original producer. This comparison indicates the cost impact of splitting the production run between two firms. The comparisons will be considered in order.

For the first comparison, if the two firms have identical progress

---

[24] L. E. Preston and E. C. Keachie discuss the relationship between learning and economies of scale [18].

curves, no learning has transferred. If the licensee's unit cost is lower for the first unit than that experienced by the first producer, or if his curve shows a steeper "slope," [25] then some learning has been transferred. If the new firm's initial unit cost equals the licensing firm's unit cost at the time of transfer, and if the slope of the progress curves for both firms from that point on is the same, all learning has been transferred.

Figure 2 illustrates these relationships. Following the usual practice in progress curve measurement, the figure shows direct labor hours per aircraft as a function of total number of units produced. The line *A-A* represents the licensor's progress curve. Assume that a co-production program is established at point *X* after ten units have been produced by the licensor. If all of the licensor's learning has been transferred, the licensee's man-hour requirements for his first unit will correspond to those needed by the licensor for the eleventh unit. This 10-unit advan-

FIGURE 2

Learning Transfer Effects; Illustrative Progress Curves

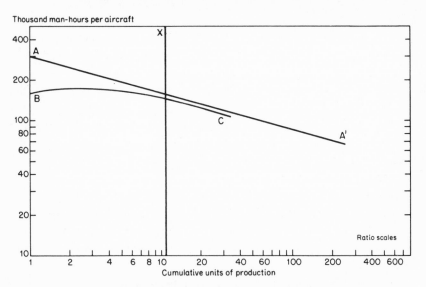

Thousand man-hours per aircraft

Cumulative units of production

[25] "Slope" has a meaning in progress-curve analysis different from its mathematical meaning. Here it refers to the ratio $[c_t/(c_t/2)]100$ where c_t is the production cost of the tth unit of output.

tage would remain with the licensee throughout his production. This situation is shown by the progress curve *B-C*, which approaches the licensor's curve asymptotically. Of course, if none of the licensor's learning is transferred and interfirm differences are ignored, then the licensee's progress curve will be identical to that of the licensor.

In most programs, some but not all of the licensor's learning will be transferred. Thus, the licensee's initial position will lie somewhere between *A* and *B*. Moreover, the slopes of the two curves may or may not converge in the manner shown, depending on differences in efficiency and factor prices which have been ignored for the sake of illustration. The important point, however, is that the transfer of learning results in the new producer requiring fewer man-hours for his initial production than were required by the original producer.

Let us examine the F-104J in this manner. Early in the program, LAC officials made estimates of the direct manufacturing man-hours required by MHI and KAC. LAC officials stationed in the Japanese plants observed that these early estimates conformed reasonably well to the actual man-hour expenditures of the two firms. Although these early estimates have some speculative aspects, they provide a basis for quantitative estimates of the amount of learning actually transferred.

In order to compare the Japanese and U.S. experience, some data had to be adjusted in the following manner: we know that a number of airframe items were manufactured in the United States, and some were purchased from Japanese vendors; both these factors must be accounted for. We estimate the price of that part of the airframe produced at Lockheed, which excludes equipment-purchase items, to be about $520,000, or roughly two-thirds of the total airframe costs shown in Table 4. Imports of hardcore airframe shown in Table 5 accounted for approximately $38,000 per airframe. LAC officials estimate total imports of airframe items to be approximately $50,000 per airframe. This, plus an estimated $40,000 for airframe purchases from Japanese vendors, shows us that approximately 17 per cent of the total airframe effort was performed outside the MHI and KAC facilities. As shown in Table 12, we can now estimate the total direct man-hours as 21 per cent more than the amounts actually spent by MHI and KAC.

The Japanese data are now in a form that can be compared with Lockheed experience. Choosing the LAC base is difficult, however. Our

TABLE 12

Direct Man-Hours, Manufacturing: 160 F-104J Airframes
(in millions)

MHI	3.98[a]
KAC	1.71[a]
Other	1.19[b]
Total	6.88

[a]Estimated by officials of LAC.

[b]Estimated at 21 per cent of the total MHI and KAC man-hours. Total outside work was approximately $90,000 per unit. Exclusive of equipment purchase items, LAC airframes cost about $520,000, and 90/(520-90) = 21 per cent.

choice is the first 160 F-104As and F-104Cs. However, the F-104J airframe was at least 20 per cent heavier and in other ways differed from U.S. versions. Indeed, on a cost-per-pound basis, as progress curves are sometimes expressed, the Japanese experience would be much more impressive than on the cost-per-plane basis used here. The Lockheed production of F-104Gs or F-104J knockdowns might also be introduced, but it would be difficult to adjust the data for learning accumulated from previous models or for the assembly operations not performed. Consequently, we have preferred to use the F-104A and F-104C for the comparison even though doing so may understate the U.S. cost relative to the Japanese cost. This means that any statistical biases are in the direction of understating the interfirm transfer of learning.

LAC and MHI progress curves are shown in Table 13. For the first 10 F-104s produced by each firm, MHI used substantially fewer man-hours than did LAC. The LAC man-hour rate per plane was slightly less than the MHI rate per plane by the time each had completed 160 aircraft. Direct man-hours used for the first 160 airframes by the Japanese were only about 90 per cent of the total LAC man-hours for the first 160 F-104s built in the United States.

The relationship between the two learning curves is shown in Figure 3. The rate of learning in Japan (85 per cent slope) is well below the U.S.

TABLE 13

Comparison of U.S. and Japanese Direct Man-Hours, Manufacturing
(in thousands)

Numbers of Aircraft	First U.S. Program F-104A, F104C	First Japanese Program F-104J
1-10 (average)	101.0	76.4[a]
150-160 (average)	30.5	33.1[a]
1-160 (total)	7590.0	6880.0

[a]Based on Lockheed estimates of MHI direct man-hours, inflated by the ratio of total Japanese man-hours to MHI man-hours shown in Table 12 (6.88/3.98 = 1.73).

FIGURE 3

Comparative F-104 Progress Curves

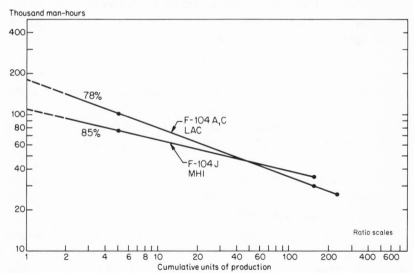

rate (78 per cent slope). However, the lower cost in Japan for the first units meant that the total Japanese man-hour expenditure was lower than Lockheed's expenditure for the first 160 planes it produced. Average man-hours per plane for the first 160 produced by each firm were 43,000 for MHI and 47,400 for LAC.

We are now in a position to answer the first of our two questions: How much learning was transferred from LAC to MHI? If we assume that the firms were equally efficient and that the rate of production and delivery schedule did not affect man-hour improvement, some summary estimates can be made.

One measure would be to assume that in the absence of a transfer of learning, MHI would have had the same man-hours for the first unit as LAC had for its first unit. Actually, MHI's figure was about 25 per cent lower, or about the number of man-hours LAC used to produce the fourth plane.

On the other hand, one might take the entire 160-plane program as the basis. Since the rate of improvement for MHI was less than for LAC, this gives a lower figure, about 10 per cent. The higher estimate of the amount of learning transferred seems the more reasonable one, considering the fact that the Japanese labor system results in high factory manning levels.

Employment by a large Japanese firm implies a lifetime commitment. Therefore, one often observes more labor hours per unit of Japanese output than are technically required, or than are typically observed in the United States. Probably more important, there are large differences in wage rates between the United States and Japan. Differences by a factor of three are not uncommon in the "blue collar" aerospace skills. Capital equipment is, if anything, more expensive in Japan, so it is not surprising that the Japanese tend to use larger work forces to reduce idle equipment time. In general, because of different factor prices, we would expect the Japanese to use more labor-intensive processes than do U.S. firms. These considerations imply that more man-hours per plane would be expended in Japan than in the United States, regardless of the amount of learning transferred.

In short, it appears reasonable to conclude that a substantial amount of learning was transferred—enough so that the man-hours used on the first MHI F-104 were 25 per cent less than those required for the first

LAC F-104. For the program as a whole, the learning transferred saved MHI about 10 per cent of the man-hours required by LAC for its first 160 aircraft.

Addressing the second comparison, i.e., between the man-hours used by MHI and those that would have been required had the 160 F-104Js come off the LAC assembly line, the problem is to compare the total MHI man-hours for 160 aircraft (6.9 million) with the total LAC would have required to produce an additional 160 aircraft. Based on very limited data about the F-104G, the total output by LAC of all F-104 models at the time of transfer, and LAC's rate of learning discussed earlier (78 per cent), we estimate that total LAC man-hours for an additional 160 aircraft would have been 3.7 million, or about 23,000 man-hours per plane. On this basis it appears the MHI man-hours were nearly twice what LAC would have required.[26]

Even if Japanese production did require perhaps twice as many man-hours, total labor costs appear to have been lower. Although international comparisons with Japanese labor rates are tricky, knowledgeable Japanese officials believe that a good order of estimate might be about one-third the U.S. rates. On the basis of the total cost data for the F-104J program, this estimate appears slightly high, or else our estimate of the man-hour requirements is slightly high, or most likely, both are high. Nonetheless, the total cost figures to be discussed shortly indicate that as orders of magnitude, these estimates are credible.

Technology transfer incurs not only direct costs, such as royalties and technical assistance payments, but also the indirect costs associated with the loss of economies of scale and with learning and scheduling. The direct costs can be estimated with some precision. For the F-104J program, for example, the direct costs amounted to about 7.8 per cent of the price of the complete airframe and engine. Technical assistance accounted for about a quarter of the direct costs.

Indirect costs are harder to estimate. Splitting production between

[26] Actually, 87 per cent greater, were such computational accuracy warranted: $[(6.9 - 3.7)/3.7] = 87$ per cent. The estimate of Lockheed man-hours is understated for two reasons. First, it assumes a constant progress-curve slope; the curve might have flattened out. More important, with each new model of the F-104 at Lockheed, the progress curve shifted upward. Undoubtedly, if the F-104J had been produced in the United States the man-hours for the first J version plane would have been higher than the end-point of Lockheed's F-104 progress curve shown for the earlier period.

two sources can affect production rates, lot sizes, and schedules. Each of these impacts affects production costs.

The production rate or economies-of-scale effects and the schedule effects importantly govern the extent of the "hardcore" lists—the components, parts, and materials imported. Extensive economies of scale or tight delivery schedules imply larger amounts of imports.

Transplantation of technology will almost always entail some loss of learning due to lower total quantities of production at any single location. This impact, however, can be lessened by the transfer of learning from the original producer to the technology recipient. In the F-104J program, it appears that between 10 per cent and 25 per cent of Lockheed's progress-curve advantage was transferred to Mitsubishi.

Total cost of production

Let us now examine the total cost of F-104Js to the Japanese government and compare it with the price Japan might have paid for finished airplanes in the United States.

It is well known that the Japanese co-production programs required more man-hours than would have been required in the United States. It is also well known that certain parts and materials produced in Japan cost more than the U.S. counterparts. Furthermore, some investment and set-up costs were incurred that could have been avoided by purchasing from a "hot" production line. As a result, it has been commonly assumed that the Japanese planes cost anywhere from 20 to 100 per cent more than they would have in the United States. The actual cost data for the F-104J program confute these common notions, however.

In fact, no premium was paid. The Japanese obtained the planes at a lower cost than they would have paid in the United States.

The high materials costs for the F-104J program appear to have been more than offset by the lower labor costs in Japan. Although it is impossible to estimate precisely the impact of the differences in factor prices, the figures in Table 13 indicate that the factor-cost saving must have been large.

Table 14 shows that in Japan for 160 aircraft the cost for an airframe was $620,000 as against a U.S. cost of $789,000 for an F-104G bought in smaller lot sizes. For the engine, the Japanese cost was higher— $232,000 compared with $184,000. Adding these two totals gives an

TABLE 14

Comparison of U.S. and Japanese Average Unit Production
Costs for F-104 Aircraft
(thousands of dollars)

Item	Japanese Production (F-104J Aircraft)	U.S. Production (F-104G Aircraft)
F-104 airframe[a]	620[b]	789
J-79 engine	232[c]	184
Total	852	937

[a]Includes all items of installed equipment other than electronics.
[b]Includes payments to Lockheed for technical assistance, tools, data, and cataloging shown in Table 11, allocated to 200 airframes.
[c]Includes payments to General Electric for technical assistance shown in Table 11, allocated to 250 engines.

F-104J unit cost of $852,000—about seven-eighths the U.S. price of a comparable plane.

The Japanese costs include technical assistance ($20,800 for airframe, $1,100 per engine); rights ($42,800 per airframe, $10,800 per engine); tooling and start-up costs (direct costs were about $41,000 per airframe); and all other manufacturing costs. The unit-cost estimates are therefore slightly exaggerated, because none of these costs are allocated to the C-2 program or spare parts production. The only identifiable cost not included is the fixed investment for the program; it was omitted because LAC had some government-furnished plant and equipment, and its facilities were used on programs other than the F-104. Therefore, it was not clear what the corresponding figure for the United States should be. Even leaving the F-104J costs unadjusted, however, and allocating all fixed investment earmarked for the F-104J program, the basic conclusion remains the same. Allocating the investment would increase the airframe cost by $23,000 and the engine cost by $32,000. This total increase of $55,000 would give a total figure for the F-104J of $907,000. This is still approximately 10 per cent below the price Lockheed charged for the F-104G.

Electronics are not included in the calculation for two reasons. First, they were not co-produced in Japan during the C-1 program, certainly not in the sense that airframes and engines were co-produced. Second, the J and G versions of the F-104 differ substantially in electronics, even though the planes are essentially identical in terms of airframes and engines. Since the C-1 electronics were imported, they do not affect the cost comparison.

Differences in factor prices tend to cloud the issue. Nonetheless, quite apart from any beneficial effects to the Japanese aviation industry, it is clear that the decision to co-produce the airframe was economically advantageous for Japan.

CONCLUSIONS

This paper has considered the costs of international transfers of sophisticated technology. The reasons for desiring such a transplantation are outside the scope of this analysis, but a few comments are in order. Most interfirm transfers, at least among firms in countries with developed economies, occur because a firm perceives some profit advantage from establishing a local production capability [7]. Some transfers, of which the cases considered here are examples, occur for reasons other than simple, short-run economic gain. The exportation of United States aerospace technology to Japan in the 1950's and 1960's resulted from Japan's military decisions and its political climate. There are military advantages to local production of weapons, but even more important in Japan's case was the political controversy over importation of weapons. Because the aircraft manufactured in Japan were regarded as Japanese weapons, local support was generated for Japan's military strategy and force-level decisions.

It turned out, at least in the F-104J case, that the transfers were also economically advantageous. The costs of the Japanese-produced F-104Js were at least 10 per cent less than the probable cost had Japan bought the aircraft off the Lockheed production line. The benefits perceived when the decisions were made, however, were political rather than economic.

Regardless of whether economic, political, social, or some mixture of factors lead a firm or government to consider substituting an importation of technology for an importation of products, the costs of transfer are a factor in the decision and its outcome. These costs depend upon the amount of technology transferred and the process of acquisition.

At the start, costs depend on whether the transfer is limited to system-specific and firm-specific knowledge, or whether a substantial amount of general technology is required to establish the manufacturing capability. If the firm or country already possesses the general technology required to manufacture the product in question, transfer is likely to be relatively inexpensive. Transfers involving substantial amounts of general technology can be extremely expensive.

Even if the transplantation is limited to system-specific technology, transfer is not an all-or-nothing matter. The ability to import components, parts, and materials provides considerable flexibility in the extent of transfer. In the F-104J case, for example, the technology for the airframe was substantially transferred early in the C-1 program. However, the transfer of technology for the jet engine required practically all the C-1 program to complete, and little or no manufacturing technology for the electronics gear was transferred. Japanese involvement in electronics consisted of assembly of components and parts.

Transfer entails not only a movement of ideas in the form of blueprints, drawings, and other data, but a movement of material and men. Put differently, a transfer of manufacturing technology for a sophisticated product usually involves a transfer of rights and data, a technical assistance program, and material support. The success and costs of a transfer are importantly influenced by the amount of each class of support.

In the rights and data area, tooling designs and related information are particularly important. Much of the original producer's technology and learning advantages are embedded in his tools and the changes he makes to these tools. Transfer of tooling data, therefore, not only is essential to a technology transplantation, but it also influences the cost level that the new producer can achieve relative to the original producer.

Technical assistance is usually required since much technology, know-how, or learning is embodied in people rather than physical items. The amount and nature of technical assistance varied considerably in the Japanese aerospace co-production programs. The differences were partly related to the kind or amount of technology transferred. System-specific knowledge seemed to require much less personal contact than did firm-specific or general technology. In part, the differences appear to have reflected differences in corporate attitudes towards technical assistance. Since technical assistance accounts for a relatively small part of the costs of transfer, however, generous provision of it would seem an appropriate transfer tactic.

Material support may involve furnishing constructed tooling and other equipment, or it may be limited to hardcore imports of components, parts, and material. As we have seen, the hardcore list will contain items with opposite characteristics: low-cost, simple, standardized items on the one hand, and expensive, complex, and specialized items on the other. Decisions about the composition of the hardcore list can obviously lead to importing too much or too little technology, judged either by the costs of transferring the technology or by the total costs of the resultant products.

Costs of transfer are both direct and indirect. Direct costs include royalties, technical assistance payments, and similar expenses. Indirect costs occur because the establishment of a new production source affects production rates, total quantities of production at a single location, and schedules. Put differently, there are indirect cost impacts due to loss of scale or learning economies when production is divided into two locations. For the F-104J the direct costs amounted to about 7.8 per cent of the sales price of the aircraft. Indirect costs are harder to estimate, but it is clear that much of their impact was lessened by a substantial transfer of learning from Lockheed to Mitsubishi. Analysis of the progress curves of the two firms indicates that between 10 per cent and 25 per cent of Lockheed's accumulated learning was acquired by Mitsubishi as part of the technology transfer.

The expense required to transplant knowledge is a major determinant of international flows of technology. This case study of interfirm transfers of the manufacturing technology for a sophisticated product among firms in countries with developed economies is, of course, only one of many types of technology transfer. Intrafirm transfers by multinational corporations, transfers from highly developed to less-developed countries, and transfers of less sophisticated technologies, all have special cost characteristics different from those for the United States-Japanese aerospace transfers in the 1950's and 1960's. Nonetheless, technology transfer will require a process basically similar to that described here.

There will have to be transfers of rights, data, technical assistance, and material support. These will be direct costs involved in payments for these transfers, as well as indirect costs due to losses of advantages from economies of scale and learning impacts. More knowledge about the process for international transfers of technology and the cost relationships involved should enhance our understanding of international trade and investment and promote more effective public and private policies toward trade and investment.

REFERENCES

1. Aharoni, Y., *The Foreign Investment Decision Process,* Cambridge, 1966.

2. Alchian, A., "Costs and Outputs," in Abramowitz, M., *et al., The Allocation of Economic Resources: Essays in Honor of B. F. Haley,* Stanford, 1959, pp. 23–40.

3. Baranson, J., *Manufacturing Problems in India,* Syracuse, 1968.

4. Behrman, J. N., "Promoting Free World Economic Development Through Direct Investment," *American Economic Review,* May 1960, pp. 271–81.

5. Gruber, W., Mehta, D., and Vernon, R., "The R&D Factor in International Trade and International Investment of United States Industries," *Journal of Political Economy,* February 1967, pp. 20–37.

6. Hall, G. R., and Johnson, R. E., *Aircraft Co-Production and Procurement Strategy,* The RAND Corporation, R-450, 1967.

7. Hirsch, S., *Location of Industry and International Competitiveness,* Oxford, 1967.

8. Hirsch, W. Z., "Manufacturing Progress Function," *Review of Economics and Statistics,* May 1952, pp. 143–55.

9. Hirshleifer, J., "The Firm's Cost Function: A Successful Reconstruction?" *The Journal of Business of the University of Chicago,* July 1962, pp. 235–55.

10. Horikoshi, J., "F-104J Production Program as Viewed from the Japanese Standpoint," AIAA Paper 65-804, presented at the American Institute of Aeronautics and Astronautics Meeting, Los Angeles, November 1965.

11. *Interavia,* "Four Countries Build the Super Starfighter," August 1963, p. 1194.

12. International Bank for Reconstruction and Development, *Automotive Industries in Developing Countries,* Washington, D.C., 1968.

13. Keesing, D. B., "The Impact of Research and Development on United States Trade," *Journal of Political Economy,* February 1967, pp. 38–48.

14. Mansfield, E., *Industrial Research and Technological Innovations: An Econometric Analysis,* New York, 1968.

15. Murphy, J. J., "The Transfer of Technology: Retrospect and Prospect," in Spencer, D. L., and Woroniak, A., eds., *The Transfer of Technology to Developing Countries,* Washington, D.C., 1966, pp. 8–36.

16. Nelson, R. R., Peck, M. J., and Kalachek, E. D., *Technology, Economic Growth and Public Policy,* Washington, D.C., 1967.

17. Nelson, R. R., *International Productivity Differences in Manufacturing Industry: Problems with Existing Theory and Some Suggestions for a Theoretical Restructuring,* The RAND Corporation, P-3720, November 1967.

18. Preston, L. E., and Keachie, E. C., "Cost Functions and Progress Functions," *American Economic Review,* March 1964, pp. 100–06.

19. Spencer, D. L., "An External Military Presence, Technological Transfer, and Structural Change," *Kyklos,* 1965, pp. 451–74.

20. ———, *Military Transfer of Technology,* Washington, D.C., 1967.

21. U.S. Department of Commerce, *Technology and World Trade,* Washington, D.C., 1967, pp. 119–43.

22. Vernon, R., "International Investment and International Trade in the Product Cycle," *Quarterly Journal of Economics,* May 1966, pp. 190–207.

COMMENTS

JACK BARANSON
International Bank for
Reconstruction and Development

The Hall-Johnson paper contributes to our general understanding of the elements of comparative advantage in a spectrum of industrial activity. It analyzes the market structure and commercial considerations influencing the cost and feasibility of technological transfer. The paper also deals with the research and skill component in an array of industrial activity. The empirical evidence contained in the Hall-Johnson piece reinforces the view that Japan's ability to adapt and absorb foreign technology has been a basic ingredient of its competitive advantage in many areas of world trade. In our efforts to reformulate trade theory, this type of knowledge helps us to understand the technological component of traded goods and, more important perhaps, the ingredients of technological advantage.

Several characteristics of the Hall-Johnson paper warrant special mention. To begin with, not only does the paper deal with the required production time, resources, and capabilities, but it has also broken down the industrial product into components and parts. This is a significant step beyond the usual analysis based upon standard industrial classification product groups. Attention is drawn to the differences in technical sophistication and optimal scale requirements within product families and subassembly groups which affect comparative costs and manufacturing capability. In my own studies of diesel engine manufacture and automotive production,[1] I have found it is essential to analyze relative costs and technical requirements at the component and parts level.

[1] *Manufacturing Problems in India,* Syracuse, 1967; and *Automotive Industries in Developing Countries,* World Bank Staff Occasional Paper No. 8, Baltimore, 1969.

Second, important distinctions are drawn in the paper among the various kinds of received technology—general, system-specific, and firm-specific. Implicit in this categorization are certain technical and commercial characteristics that affect both marketability as viewed by private corporations and the related cost and feasibility of transfer. The importance of these aspects are highlighted by Raymond Vernon, who has drawn attention to corporate earnings at various phases in the product cycle, and A. T. Knoppers, who analyzes profit motivation in transferring "marketable technology." [2] This, in part, is what is meant by "market force analysis of international flows of technology"—a market that has been structured by Japan's industrialization policies. The need for general versus system-specific or firm-specific knowledge depends upon the stage of sector development within each firm. Resource costs and phase-in time are also a function of the stage of industrial development. Japanese firms were apparently much further advanced in general airframe manufacturing technology than in aircraft electronics. In the electronics field, there was extensive need for general and system-specific knowledge as a prelude to the more costly and intricate firm-specific knowledge needed for actual production.

Firm-specific knowledge is an outgrowth of comparative development and experience. A longstanding policy of the Japanese government has been to give special subsidy or financial support to technologically weak sectors of the Japanese economy, and to expand or reinforce technical capabilities at the plant level. For example, the Japanese Development Bank finances projects to modernize plant equipment or develop new product designs with a view toward "enhancing the Japanese economy's competitive position in world trade."

A third point made in the Hall-Johnson paper relates to the components and parts that Japanese aircraft manufacturers continued to import rather than procure from local sources. These hardcore items included (1) sophisticated components or subassemblies that were

[2] Raymond Vernon, "International Investment and International Trade in the Product Cycle," *The Quarterly Journal of Economics,* May 1966, pp. 190–207; Antonie T. Knoppers, "Development and Transfer of Marketable Technology in the International Corporation: A New Situation in Applied Science and World Economy" (paper presented to the Committee on Science and Astronautics, U.S. House of Representatives for the Ninth Meeting of the Panel on Science and Technology, February 1968), Washington, D.C., 1968, pp. 63–72.

difficult or expensive to transfer to domestic firms (such as special pumps and valves and electronic guidance devices), and (2) simple items (such as bolts and rivets that would be costly to reproduce domestically in limited quantities). From such evidence, two important insights emerge. First, industrial goods entering world trade depend in part upon the stage of development of the supply structure in overseas markets. Thus, protective tariffs nurture less efficient industries which displace industrial goods in world trade. Second, the development of local supplier capability is a function of domestic capabilities to adapt and absorb foreign technology. David Granick points out that Soviet metal-working plants in the 1930's had neither the technical skills nor the framework of industrial integration necessary to absorb the more advanced technologies then available from abroad.[3] In short, Japanese comparative advantage is something much more than cheaper labor. It is a composite of technological know-how, scale economies, and production strategies— the combination alluded to in Harry Johnson's illuminating "State of the Theory."

Much can be drawn from a study of this type about the nature of dynamic comparative advantage, the limitations of industrialization based upon import substitution, and the development of the technological ingredients for specialization in world trade. Defining the comparative advantage range as a contribution to long-term economic growth has been a topic of increasing concern in the field of development.[4] The technical and commercial considerations revealed in the Hall-Johnson paper need to be viewed in the broader context of trade and development policies which influence production costs and innovational environments. Harry Johnson has drawn attention to the stultifying effects of economic nationalism which often inhibit the development of indigenous technological capabilities.[5]

The Hall-Johnson paper draws attention to several other aspects affecting development strategies. Implicit in the Japanese experience are investments in research capabilities and technical skills to convert

---

[3] David Granick, *Soviet Metal-Fabricating and Economic Development: Practice versus Policy,* Madison, Wisconsin, 1967.

[4] Wilfred Malenbaum, *et al.,* "Comparative Costs and Economic Development," *American Economic Review, Papers and Proceedings,* May 1964, pp. 390–434.

[5] Harry G. Johnson, *Economic Nationalism in Old and New States,* Chicago, 1966.

and absorb imported technology. I found in my study of diesel engine manufacture in India that the manufacturing capabilities that took less than two years to transfer to Japan will take at least fifteen years in India.[6] This is because there is a severe shortage in India of the critical engineering and technical skills that are much more abundant in Japan. High engineer density in Japan acts as a major contributing factor to the country's success in competing in world markets. Equally important is the technical assistance rendered to small supplier plants by the larger industrial firms in Japan. Foreign licensing regulations in Japan have also contributed to their success in world trade.[7]

Another revealing point made in this case study of technological transfer is the role played by multinational firms in imparting industrial design and manufacturing techniques. Much depends upon their willingness to share know-how, which is related to global marketing and manufacturing strategies. But even more important than the imparting of technical knowledge and manufacturing capabilities is the ability and willingness to implant indigenous engineering and design capability for continued technological transformation.[8]

JAGDISH N. BHAGWATI
Massachusetts Institute of Technology

Apropos the comment of Jack Baranson regarding the adaptability of technology to local conditions, I would like to relate the example of how a certain radio manufactured in India with the assembly-line method turned out to contain several bugs in it because labor found it extremely difficult to adapt itself to the "moving line." A technology which was therefore appropriate to the transferring country was not optimal when

[6] See Baranson, *Manufacturing Problems in India*, pp. 68–69.

[7] Terutomo Ozawa, *Imitation, Innovation, and Trade: A Study of Foreign Licensing Operations in Japan*, University Microfilms, 1967.

[8] Jack Baranson, "Transfer of Technical Knowledge by International Corporations to Developing Economies," *American Economic Review, Papers and Proceedings*, May 1966, pp. 259–67; see also Baranson, *Automotive Industries in Developing Countries*, pp. 79–80.

applied to the recipient country with different qualities in its labor force (although, given time, the labor force could almost certainly be trained up to the required level of discipline).

This example, in turn, raises the question as to why it was that such a technological transfer, presumably inefficient from an economic point of view, did not "lose out" in the competitive struggle. Or to put it in an alternative way, should economists really worry about such inefficient transfers if the market will make sure that they are eliminated by efficient transfers through the working of the market mechanism? In the Indian case, any such inefficient transfers showed surprising capacity to survive because the recipient country's policies frustrated the working of the market mechanism rather directly. Import controls prevented competition from abroad (through importation of competitively produced radios) whereas domestic restrictions on entry of new firms, via industrial licensing, prevented the emergence of more efficient rivals with superior technological processes. Thus, the existence of inefficient governmental policies elsewhere made it possible for firms to get away with importing inferior technologies. This conclusion, of course, begs the question as to why inferior technology should have been imported at all if better technology were available. In assessing this question, the facts that the market for sale of technology is imperfect and that information about alternatives not readily available are relevant.

Thus, in the end, the relevant questions seem to me to boil down to, *not* whether technology does get transferred at all, but whether the market for such transfers is perfect and, if it is not (in some defined sense), what is the pattern of optimal intervention that is called for. If the authors of the interesting paper on the transfer of aero-technology to Japan had focused on this question, we should have had answers of considerably greater interest to economists.

Technological Factors in the

Composition and Direction of

Israel's Industrial Exports

SEEV HIRSCH

TEL-AVIV UNIVERSITY

I. INTRODUCTION

In his celebrated paper "International Trade—The Long View," J. R. Hicks summed up his disappointment with the failure of economic theory to explain the composition and flow of international trade. Hicks felt that the classical theory could indeed explain the flow of minerals, raw materials, and agricultural produce from countries where they are naturally or easily available to those where they are not:

"All that, however, is very obvious—it needs no subtle economic reasoning to explain these comparative advantages. The crucial test for the factor-scarcity theory (and indeed, as we have seen, for any international trade theory) is to explain the advantages of the industrialized countries. And on that side, the factor-scarcity theory is not too successful." [5]

Hicks of course was not the only economist who felt that the law of comparative advantage in its classical, Ricardian sense or, in its more recent interpretation, in terms of the Heckscher-Ohlin "factor proportions" theorem failed to give a satisfactory explanation of the composition and flow of international trade. In view of the persistent dollar shortage in the decade that followed the war and following Leontief's claim that U.S. export industries are less capital-intensive than the country's import-competing industries, growing interest has been evidenced in the relationship between technology and trade (see Leontief [9], MacDougall [10], Hoffmeyer [7], and Posner [12]).

Some of the more interesting findings in this field concern the relationship between innovation and international competitiveness. In his study of the world plastics industry, C. Freeman showed that countries tend to enjoy a strong competitive position in world markets in plastic products developed by indigenous firms (Freeman [2]). Subsequent research conducted by Freeman into the electronics equipment industry yielded similar results [3]. These findings were confirmed by G. C. Hufbauer in his study of synthetic fibers [9] and by Gruber, Mehta, and Vernon, who studied the relationship between investments in research and development in a number of industries and the competitive position of the countries where this kind of investment took place [4]. All these researches tended to confirm the assertion that countries which pioneer new products tend to enjoy a quasi- or even absolute monopoly over these products in world markets, for a while. They enjoy this position even in those cases where they have no obvious comparative advantage in the inputs contained in the products.

This paper discusses the findings of yet another empirical study, conducted over the period 1965 to 1967, which sought to identify and explain some of the technological and other factors affecting the composition and direction of Israel's exports.

The approach used in this research and the methods adopted were determined by the basic premise that export performance as evidenced in statistics cannot be explained in terms of costs, market conditions, or even technological factors alone. Part of the explanation must be sought by reference to the exporting firm, the organization which transforms comparative advantage from an abstract concept into reality. Many firms could export some or all of their output, yet only some choose to become exporters whereas others stick to the domestic markets. Certain firms export the bulk of their output, whereas the exports of others, even in the same industry, may be negligible. Only in very few industries is export performance uniform; polished diamond manufacturers in Israel export, as a rule, the bulk of their output, and manufacturers of citrus products export, as a rule, a high proportion of their output. By contrast, few firms in the Israeli shoe industry engage in export. In most other industries, export performance varies between firms and between products, variations being almost infinite with respect to share of output exported, concentration of products, shares of different countries in exports, etc.

Numerous factors are undoubtedly responsible for these variations: among them, size, technology, factor costs and factor intensity, product policy, and government policies. Some of these factors, such as product policies, are within the control of the firms, whereas others, such as wage rates, are outside it. Certain factors, the exchange rate, for example, are established by governments, whereas others, such as availability of raw materials or the size of a potential export market, must be considered as given, as far as both the firm and the whole economy are concerned. Interaction among all these variables eventually produces export performance.

We reasoned that because individual firms have considerable latitude in their response to environmental factors, and because those factors influence but do not uniquely determine the firm's performance in the domestic and foreign markets, our research would be focussed on the individual firms. We sought to explain some aspects of the economy's export performance by studying their policies and behavior. Our basic postulate was that a significant proportion of variations in export performance of individual firms can be explained by reference to the characteristics of their products, which, in turn, are affected to an important degree by the skill intensity of the labor force employed in their manufacture. The model which our research was intended to test is spelled out, in some detail, below.

Products manufactured by skill-intensive firms (i.e., firms employing a high proportion of scientists, engineers, and highly skilled employees) have certain characteristics which distinguish them from products manufactured by firms with low skill intensity.

Firms employ a high proportion of skilled workers, engineers, and scientists when their products are comparatively new. At this stage, production runs are short, specifications are loose, and the production process must be frequently adjusted to take care of changes in specifications, design, or methods. To cope with these frequent changes and adjustments, the labor force must have high skill intensity. Existing, or mature products, by contrast, have different characteristics; the technology has been stabilized, specifications change rarely, designs are frozen, and production runs are long. Consequently, comparatively fewer scientists, engineers, and skilled employees are employed by the firms manufacturing these products.

The different characteristics of the high and low skill-intensive firms affect the manner in which they are able to export their products. Demand for skill-intensive products tends to be inelastic because substitution among competing products made by relatively few manufacturers is rather imperfect, and price competition is not very keen. Quality, reliability, and service are important determinants of the competitive position of the individual manufacturer. None of these ingredients can be taken for granted by the buyer, who must be in close and direct contact with the manufacturer to inform him of his specific needs.

The situation in respect to low skill-intensive products is different. Demand is characterized by high price elasticity, since close substitutes are readily available. Specifications, performance characteristics, and quality standards are well established, and users of the products are fully aware of what they can expect to get for the well publicized prices they pay.

To sell new, skill-intensive products, the manufacturer must inform potential buyers of the availability of his product, while ascertaining that it suits their requirements. He must often provide pre-sale and post-sale services to ensure that the product does indeed conform to the needs and specifications of the buyer. To perform these tasks, connection with the market must be intensive and communications between manufacturer and buyer must flow freely and frequently.

Manufacturers desiring to export high skill-intensive products must maintain their own marketing organization, if they are to compete successfully. They are usually at a disadvantage vis-a-vis domestic competitors because of distance, high costs of communications, and high marketing overheads. These expenses must be duplicated in every market regardless of its size. To compete successfully in export markets, low skill-intensive manufacturers have a far less onerous task—they must merely meet the price of their competitors, be they domestic or foreign. Since specifications, performance characteristics, and quality of their products are familiar to potential buyers, they do not have to invest heavily in marketing organizations and communications. Services, if necessary, can be performed by agents, and costs of marketing may be shared with other firms.[1]

---

[1] The characteristics of high and low skill-intensive products are discussed by the writer in greater detail in [6].

If the above outline of the problems facing manufacturers and exporters of high versus low skill-intensive products represents a reasonable approximation of reality, then certain differences in the organization, policies, and behavior of the firm manufacturing these two kinds of products ought to be observed:

High skill-intensive firms will tend to regard prices and costs as a comparatively unimportant determinant of their competitive posture. Their export performance will tend to be strongly affected by their marketing effort and by maintenance of close connections with the markets. Successful exporters will have their own marketing departments, and the most successful ones might even have some sort of proprietary association with the organizations marketing their products abroad.

Low skill-intensive firms are, by contrast, expected to be much more affected by price and cost considerations. Export performance need not be correlated with the existence of a marketing department or with maintenance of proprietary connections in foreign markets. Similarly, communications and direct connections with the market need not be as intensive as in the case of the high skill-intensive firms.

Positive correlation between size and export performance is to be expected because of the high costs and more complex tasks performed by exporters; yet size is likely to figure less importantly in the case of low skill-intensive firms, which need invest comparatively less in export marketing and whose comparative disadvantage vis-a-vis domestic competitors is less marked.

Finally, we expect certain relationships between the geographic distribution of exports and the skill intensity of the products. Since price is assumed to be the main determinant of the competitiveness of low skill-intensive products, these products may be expected to be exported mainly to markets where price competition prevails. The markets of Western Europe and North America are undoubtedly more competitive in this sense than the markets of Eastern Europe or of the developing countries of Africa, Asia, or South America, where competition is often restricted. Moreover, low skill-intensive products are, because of their technological characteristics, among the first candidates for domestic production in countries where industrialization is in its early stages. Such countries tend to grant administrative and tariff protection to their domestic industries should they be challenged by foreign competition. Consequently, a comparatively small proportion of low skill-intensive products will tend to be exported to the markets of the developing countries.

The exports of high skill-intensive products are expected to be distributed quite differently. Only a small proportion of high skill-intensive products exports are likely to be exported to the developed countries where manufacturers have a marketing cost advantage over foreign competitors. Many of the high skill-intensive products are not manufactured in the developing countries because of the scarcity of skilled workers, engineers, and scientists, and because of the small domestic markets. Israeli manufacturers of high skill-intensive products compete in the markets of the developing countries with other foreign manufacturers, who do not necessarily have a marketing cost advantage over the Israelis. Consequently, Israeli manufacturers of high skill-intensive products are expected to sell a high proportion of their exports in the developing countries.

These postulates are reformulated in Parts II, III, and IV, where they are tested against empirical data. Part II discusses the findings pertaining to the manufacturing process and pricing policies adopted by the firms which we interviewed and relates them to their skill intensity. Part III deals with the relationships between skill intensity, organization of the export marketing function and export performance. Part IV reviews the geographic distribution of the respondents' exports and relates it to their skill and capital intensities.

In Appendix A we discuss the methods used in selecting the firms which constitute our sample. The composition of the sample is discussed in Appendix B. Skill intensity, production concentration, and export performance are defined in Appendixes C, D, and E respectively.

II. PRODUCT CHARACTERISTICS IN RELATION TO SKILL INTENSITY .

A number of postulates concerning the relationship between the skill intensity of the respondents and the nature of the products manufactured by them are formulated and tested in this part. The characteristics examined include production concentration, production to customer orders and to customer specifications, methods of price determination, and capital intensity.

Concentration of production

Firms with high skill intensity which manufacture new products whose specifications frequently change, and whose production runs are short, as suggested in our model, might be expected to produce more products than the low skill-intensive firms whose production runs are long and whose products' specifications vary infrequently. One way of testing this proposition is to examine the degree of production concentration—how does the proportion of the most important products (in terms of value) vary with skill intensity?

A partial answer to this question is given in Table II.1 where data on production concentration are broken down by skill-intensity groups. The table shows that production concentration tends to decrease with skill intensity in accordance with our expectations. A more complete analysis requires that both size and industry be held constant since production concentration of a plant employing thirty workers is not quite comparable to that exhibited by a plant with five hundred

TABLE II.1

Distribution of Firms by Skill Intensity and Production Concentration

	Skill Intensity[b]							
	Number of Firms				Per Cent			
	Low	Medium	High	Total	Low	Medium	High	Total
Low	12	22	20	54	26	38	39	35
Medium	13	25	20	58	28	44	39	38
High	21	10	11	42	46	18	22	27
Total	46	57	51	154	100	100	100	100

Note: Inaccuracies due to rounding.

[a] For derivation of index see Appendix D.

[b] For definition of skill intensity and its measurement see Appendix C.

employees. Similarly, production concentration indexes of chemical plants employing continuous process methods should not be interpreted in exactly the same way as indexes calculated for metal fabricating plants where manufacturing is done in units or batches. Owing to the limited size of the sample, however, neither size nor industry was held constant. Correlation between skill intensity and production concentration might have been even more marked had this procedure been followed.

Production to order and to customers' specifications

We suggested in Part I that specifications for new products are worked out in cooperation with the market to a greater extent than those of mature products, whose specifications are stable and well known. If this is indeed the case then high skill-intensive firms should manufacture a higher proportion of their output to customers' order or to their specifications, than low skill-intensive ones.

Of the two measures, the proportion of production to customers' specifications is probably a better indication of the need for communications between customer and manufacturer, since communications between the two are implied by the definition of the term. On the other hand, production to customers' orders rather than to stock may be undertaken by the firm even when sales do not require intensive communications with customers, as when orders for a particular product are infrequent, or when unit costs are high. Our model suggests nevertheless the existence of a positive correlation between skill intensity and production to customers' orders because this method of production is likely to require, on the whole, more intensive communications with the customers than when the firm adopts the policy of producing to stock.

The evidence is presented in Tables II.2 and II.3 which show the relationship between skill intensity and the proportion of output manufactured to customers' orders and to customers' specifications respectively. The distribution of the respondents tends to conform to our expectations: skill intensity varies inversely with both variables. The figures also show that variations of the second measure are more strongly associated with skill intensity than those of the first.

TABLE II.2

*Distribution of Firms by Proportion of Firm Output Manufactured
to Order and by Skill Intensity*

Proportion of Firms' Total Output Manufactured to Order	Skill Intensity							
	Number of Firms				Per Cent			
	Low	Medium	High	Total	Low	Medium	High	Total
Per Cent								
0 - 35	30	18	20	68	54	27	34	38
36 - 80	11	24	22	57	20	36	37	31
81 - 100	15	25	17	57	26	37	29	31
Total	56	67	59	182	100	100	100	100
Average	33	58	58	50				

Note: Inaccuracies due to rounding.

TABLE II.3

*Distribution of Firms by Production to Customers' Specifications
and by Skill Intensity*

Proportion of Firms' Total Output Manufactured to Customers' Specifications	Skill Intensity							
	Number of Firms				Per Cent			
	Low	Medium	High	Total	Low	Medium	High	Total
Per Cent								
0	34	24	16	74	61	35	27	40
1 - 60	15	25	25	65	27	37	42	36
61 - 100	7	19	18	44	12	28	31	24
Total	56	68	59	183	100	100	100	100
Average	11	25	36	25				

Note: Inaccuracies due to rounding.

Methods of price determination

It was asserted in Part I that the demand for high skill-intensive products is less price sensitive than the demand for low skill-intensive products. This assertion was based on the assumption that manufacturers of high skill-intensive products enjoy a certain degree of monopoly since they have few or no competitors, at least in the short run. Low skill-intensive products, on the other hand, are marketed under competitive conditions, and their sellers must adjust their prices to those prevailing on the market.

To test this proposition, respondents were asked to indicate what proportion of their sales is priced on the basis of one of the following considerations: market price, institutional arrangements, average costs, and marginal costs. It was assumed that those who establish their prices on the basis of prevailing market prices have no control over prices since they are selling in a competitive market. Prices can be established on the basis of institutional arrangements when manufacturers cooperate in price fixing. Such cooperation is common in Israel where the Government encourages firms to cooperate in establishing agreed export prices and, in certain cases, even domestic prices. Where prices can be effectively established by cooperating manufacturers, competition is, by definition, reduced. Similar conclusions must be reached regarding the other pricing methods; if a firm can base its prices on costs, then it may be said to possess a certain degree of monopoly.

Tables II.4 and II.5 show the distribution of the respondents by skill intensity and by the dominant method they use to establish prices in foreign and domestic markets respectively. The tables show that most respondents consider their prices to be determined by the markets. Some difference, however, clearly exists between them. The dominant share of the market as the major determinant of price varies inversely with skill intensity. The higher the skill intensity, the lower the number of firms which regard their prices as being determined mainly by the market. This is especially noticeable in the domestic market, where competition is more subject to modification than in export markets. Here, less than half of the high skill-intensive firms report their prices to be determined by the market and nearly one-quarter price their products by means of institutional arrangements. The distribution of

TABLE II.4

Distribution of Firms by Dominant Method of Export Price Establishment and by Skill Intensity

	Skill Intensity							
Methods of Price	Number of Firms				Per Cent			
Establishment	Low	Medium	High	Total	Low	Medium	High	Total
Market determined	33	34	33	100	80	83	78	81
Institutional								
arrangement	4	1	0	5	10	2	–	4
Average costs	2	4	4	10	5	10	10	8
Marginal costs	2	2	5	9	5	5	12	7
Total	41	41	42	124	100	100	100	100

Note: Inaccuracies due to rounding.

TABLE II.5

Distribution of Firms by Dominant Method of Domestic Price Establishment and by Skill Intensity

	Skill Intensity							
Method of Price	Number of Firms				Per Cent			
Establishment	Low	Medium	High	Total	Low	Medium	High	Total
Market determined	38	49	26	113	72	72	48	64
Institutional								
arrangement	4	3	12	19	7	4	22	11
Average cost	9	15	16	40	16	22	30	23
Marginal cost	2	1	–	3	5	1	–	2
Total	53	68	54	175	100	100	100	100

Note: Inaccuracies due to rounding.

this group varies considerably from that of the medium and low skill-intensity groups.

Finally, we ought to consider the possibility of bias. It is of course possible that respondents tended to overstate the importance of the market as the dominant price determinant, but as long as this bias was equally distributed among the three skill-intensity groups, then the conclusion that prices of high skill-intensive firms are less determined by the market than prices of the low skill-intensive firms must stand.

Capital intensity

Elsewhere we have argued that new products tend to be products characterized by high skill intensity and to be less capital intensive than mature products. As products become more mature, increasing substitution of capital for labor becomes both technically and economically feasible because the manufacturing process becomes more stable, and longer runs of relatively uniform specifications are made easier [6].

This argument refers, however, to the *trend* of capital intensity over the life cycle of a product; it does not apply to the *level* of capital used in conjunction with other inputs at any particular point in time in the manufacture of different products. Hence we have no particular expectations regarding the relationship between skill and capital intensities in a cross-section analysis of the kind undertaken here.

Analysis of the data suggests, however, that skill and capital intensity are associated with each other. Table II.6, which shows the distribution of capital intensity by skill-intensity groups, points to the existence of a positive correlation between the two variables.

The association found between skill and capital intensity in Israeli industrial firms suggests an interesting hypothesis: that capital and unskilled (but not skilled) labor are substitute inputs and skilled labor and capital are, by contrast, complementary inputs.

Capital intensity as depicted in Table II.6 is measured by the assets per employee ratio, and the denominator of this ratio—the number of employees—is, it will be recalled, also the denominator used here to measure skill intensity. If capital were a substitute for unskilled (but not for skilled) labor, as suggested by this hypothesis, skill and capital intensity would increase when capital is substituted for labor and decrease when labor is substituted for capital. This conclusion, moreover, does not depend on the method of measurement. If capital intensity were

TABLE II.6

Distribution of Firms by Capital Intensity and by Skill Intensity

Assets Per Employee (£ Israeli)	Skill Intensity							
	Number of Firms				Per Cent			
	Low	Medium	High	Total	Low	Medium	High	Total
Less than 16,000 -	15	21	11	47	43	40	22	34
16,000 - 32,500	13	18	15	46	37	35	30	34
32,501 - 320,000	7	13	24	44	20	25	48	32
Total	35	52	50	137	100	100	100	100

differently measured, by the ratio of depreciation plus interest costs plus profits to value added, for example, and if the hypothesis advanced here does indeed conform to reality our conclusion would remain unaltered. In that case, an increase in the quantity of capital raises the value of the numerator of the capital-intensity measure and reduces the value of the denominator of the skill-intensity measure, thus giving rise to a positive correlation between skill and capital intensities.

To summarize, we have found that skill intensity is associated with certain product characteristics as suggested by our model. Skill intensity varies inversely with production concentration and directly with the propensity to produce to customers' orders and to customers' specifications. In comparison with low skill-intensive firms, high skill-intensive firms appear to have more control over the pricing of their products, especially in the domestic market where price competition can be modified and controlled with relative ease. Finally, while not expecting any particular relationship between skill and capital intensities, the data show that the two variables are positively correlated. The existence of this correlation suggests that capital and skilled labor may be complementary inputs whereas capital and unskilled labor may be substitutes.

Next we examine certain characteristics of the firms.

III. CHARACTERISTICS OF THE FIRM IN RELATION TO SKILL INTENSITY AND EXPORT PERFORMANCE

The distinction between product characteristics discussed in Part II and firm characteristics considered in this part is based on the assumption that the former are determined mainly on the basis of technological and economic considerations over which the firm has little influence. Once a product has been chosen, production techniques, pricing methods, capital intensity, etc., are more or less dictated to the firm by the prevailing supply and demand conditions. Management, on the other hand, appears to have more discretion in establishing the size of the firm and its domestic and foreign marketing policies. By analyzing firm characteristics separately from product characteristics, we focus attention on those aspects of performance in general, and export performance in particular, which are determined to an important degree by management's "subjective" preferences.

Size of the firm

We have postulated in Part I that export performance varies with size: the larger plants tend to have a better export performance than the small ones because firms cannot export unless they invest in market research in foreign servicing and in the maintenance of stocks. These costs are partly fixed and can be recouped only if sales volume is sufficiently large.

It was further postulated that the marketing cost advantage enjoyed by domestic suppliers over foreign competitors increases with the skill intensity of the product because of the crucial role of communication in the marketing of high skill-intensive products. Obviously, the cost of communication, and especially of face-to-face communication, increases with distance, thus raising the relative marketing costs of the exporters. To be able to export, the manufacturer of high skill-intensive products must have a substantial cost advantage in manufacturing, and a large enough sales volume to enable him to reduce unit costs to a competitive level.

Relationship between size and export performance is shown in Table III.1, where respondents are divided into three size groups on the basis

TABLE III.1

Distribution of Firms by Number of Employees and by Export Performance[a]

Number of Employees

Export Performance	Number of Firms				Per Cent			
	0–59	60–159	160+	Total	0–59	60–159	160+	Total
Zero exports	30	20	1	51	52	32	2	30
Low	15	9	13	37	26	14	26	22
Medium	8	18	18	44	14	29	35	26
High	5	16	19	40	8	25	37	23
Total	58	63	51	172	100	100	100	100

Note: Inaccuracies due to rounding.

[a] For definition of export performance see Appendix E.

of the number of their employees. The table shows that size does indeed vary with export performance as expected. Medium and large firms appear to be superior to small firms as export performers.[2]

We examine next the proposition that export performance is more strongly correlated with size in the case of high skill-intensive firms. The evidence is presented in Table III.2 where the data given in Table III.1 are regrouped in skill-intensity groups. Analysis of the data does not confirm our expectations. Although there appears to be a reasonably strong correlation between export performance and size in the low and even the medium skill-intensity groups, the high skill-intensive group exhibits no such correlation.

The relationship between size, skill intensity and export performance was analyzed by an alternative method which is shown in Table III.3. The table shows the firms ranked by the volume of their output and exports from the largest firm down, and grouped in deciles against the volume of their output and export expressed in cumulative percentages.

[2] These findings agree with those reported in a survey conducted under the auspices of P.E.P. in Britain in 1963 where a strong positive correlation was found between size and export performance [11].

TABLE III.2

Distribution of Firms by Export Performance, by Number of Employees, and by Skill Intensity

	Plants With			Per Cent of Plants With		
Export Performance	0–59 Empl.	60–159 Empl.	160+ Empl.	0–59 Empl.	60–150 Empl.	160+ Empl.
Low Skill Intensity						
Zero export	7	5	1	50	25	6
Low	3	1	3	21	5	19
Medium	1	7	4	7	35	25
High	3	7	8	22	35	50
Total	14	20	16	100	100	100
Medium Skill Intensity						
Zero export	16	11	0	70	48	0
Low	5	4	2	22	17	14
Medium	1	5	7	4	22	50
High	1	3	5	4	13	36
Total	23	23	14	100	100	100
High Skill Intensity						
Zero export	7	4	0	33	21	0
Low	7	4	8	33	21	42
Medium	6	5	6	29	26	32
High	1	6	5	5	32	26
Total	21	19	19	100	100	100

Note: Inaccuracies due to rounding. Average number of employees per firm for the three categories of skill intensity: *low*, 168; *medium*, 185; *high*, 285.

The method enables us to gauge the degree of inequality in the distribution of output and exports between the firms. Two conclusions are suggested by the figures: (1) that exports of all skill-intensity groups are less equally distributed than domestic sales; and (2) that the

TABLE III.3

Distribution of Firms by Output Volume, by Export Volume, and by Skill Intensity

(in cumulative percentages)

Deciles[a]	Low Skill Intensive		Medium Skill Intensive		High Skill Intensive		All Firms	
	Output	Exports	Output	Exports	Output	Exports	Output	Exports
First	42.5	46.7	48.8	42.7	50.3	68.7	49.0	56.2
Second	62.3	67.9	66.1	69.4	66.5	82.7	68.2	75.3
Third	73.9	82.0	75.7	86.4	77.0	91.5	77.7	87.0
Fourth	82.9	89.2	82.4	93.2	83.1	95.4	84.4	92.9
Fifth	88.4	93.5	87.8	97.6	87.7	97.7	88.9	96.3
Sixth	92.8	96.7	91.5	99.1	91.3	99.1	92.6	98.4
Seventh	96.3	98.4	94.8	99.6	94.1	99.8	94.5	99.4
Eighth	98.4	99.2	97.3	99.9	96.6	99.9	97.6	99.8
Ninth	99.7	99.8	99.1	100.0	98.4	100.0	99.0	100.0
Tenth	100.0	100.0	100.0	100.0	100.0	100.0	100.0	100.0

[a]Firms are ranked by output and exports, from the largest firm downward.

inequality increases with skill intensity. Although both conclusions are consistent with our hypothesis, we must point out that export performance in Table III.3 refers to absolute volume and not, as elsewhere in this paper, to growth rates multiplied by export shares.[3] The apparent contradiction between the conclusions suggested by Tables III.2 and III.3 is probably due to the concentration of exports in a very few firms. The five large, high skill-intensive firms with high export performance shown in Table III.2 are probably the same firms which appear in the first decile in Table III.3.

Existence of a marketing department

The marketing function need not be performed by a special department; it may be performed by groups or individuals attached to other departments or even to no particular department. This is probably truer of small than of large firms, though other considerations (such as the type of the product and the practice of the industry) undoubtedly influence the decision to establish a marketing department.

Here we wish to test the proposition that export performance is affected by the existence of a marketing department, and that the connection is especially evident in high skill-intensive firms. This proposition is based on the assumption that high skill-intensive firms which give formal recognition to the marketing function and establish a department to perform it have a better export performance than those which do not. No such assumptions are made regarding the low skill-intensive firms.

Table III.4 gives the data on the existence of marketing departments in the three skill-intensity groups and their export performance. The table shows that a higher proportion of the high skill-intensive firms have marketing departments than the low skill-intensive firms. It also shows that few high skill-intensive firms with no marketing departments have a high export performance. Although the table indicates that high skill-intensive firms which have a high or even medium export performance tend to have a marketing department, it does not imply that the establishment of such a department is necessarily correlated with high export performance; 29 per cent of the high skill-intensive firms

[3] For details see Appendix E.

TABLE III.4

Distribution of Firms by Export Performance, by Existence of Marketing Departments, and by Skill Intensity

Export Performance	Number			Per Cent		
	Firms With Market Dept.	Firms Without Market Dept.	All Firms	Firms With Market Dept.	Firms Without Market Dept.	All Firms
Low Skill Intensity						
Zero export	7	6	13	24	29	26
Low	2	5	7	7	24	14
Medium	9	3	12	31	14	24
High	11	7	18	38	33	36
Total	29	21	50	100	100	100
Medium Skill Intensity						
Zero export	12	15	27	40	50	45
Low	6	5	11	20	17	18
Medium	5	8	13	17	27	22
High	7	2	9	23	6	15
Total	30	30	60	100	100	100
High Skill Intensity						
Zero export	3	8	11	8	38	19
Low	11	8	19	29	38	32
Medium	14	3	17	37	14	29
High	10	2	12	26	10	20
Total	38	21	59	100	100	100
Grand Total	97	72	169	57	43	100

Note: Inaccuracies due to rounding.

with marketing departments were low export performers. Low skill-intensive firms appear, as expected, to be less dependent on a marketing department for a high export performance.

It may be argued at this point that we should not expect export performance to depend on the existence of a marketing department at all; that, if there is a relationship between the organization of the marketing function and export performance, it should be sought in the existence of an *export* department. This reasoning, however, does not appear to apply to Israeli firms, most of which seem to be too small to be able to have an independent export department. The few firms which have export departments are distributed equally between the three skill groups. Although the distribution of export performance of firms having marketing departments definitely varies with that of firms which have no marketing departments, the number of the firms in the first group is too small to draw definite conclusions. The pattern that emerged is nevertheless worth noting since it differed somewhat from that exhibited in Table III.4. A high proportion of low skill-intensive firms with no marketing departments have a high export performance, and a low proportion of high skill-intensive firms with no marketing department have a high export performance. Possession of a marketing department is generally associated with medium or high export performance in all three skill-intensity groups.

In summary, it may be stated that high skill-intensive firms which have a high export performance tend to have marketing departments, though many which have a marketing department are not high export performers. The association is even less clear in the case of the low skill-intensive firms where a considerable proportion of the high export performers do not have a marketing department.

Proprietary association abroad

Another form of association we were looking for was between proprietary associations abroad and export performance. One inevitable conclusion suggested by our previous analysis is that firms which have parent companies, subsidiaries, sales offices, or other proprietary connections abroad will tend to have a superior export performance because of the marketing connections which this form of association provides. We would also expect that the relationship between proprietary association abroad and export performance is more decisive for the high skill-intensive firms, which require particularly close communications with the markets, than for the low skill-intensive firms, which do not.

The data are given in Table III.5. Let us first examine the marginal

TABLE III.5

*Distribution of Firms by Export Performance, by
Foreign Proprietary Connections Abroad and by Skill Intensity*

Export Performance	Number			Per Cent		
	Firms With Foreign Prop. Con.	Firms Without Foreign Prop. Con.	All Firms	Firms With Foreign Prop. Con.	Firms Without Foreign Prop. Con.	All Firms
			Low Skill Intensity			
Low	0	7	7	0	21	19
Medium	2	10	12	67	29	32
High	1	17	18	33	50	49
Total	3	34	37	100	100	100
			Medium Skill Intensity			
Low	3	8	11	30	35	33
Medium	2	11	13	20	48	39
High	5	4	9	50	17	28
Total	10	23	33	100	100	100
			High Skill Intensity			
Low	3	16	19	17	53	40
Medium	7	10	17	39	33	35
High	8	4	12	44	14	25
Total	18	30	48	100	100	100
Grand Total	31	87	118	26	74	100

Note: Inaccuracies due to rounding.

distributions which appear to be quite interesting. Of thirty-one firms having proprietary associations abroad, well over one-half were high skill intensive, about one-third were medium skill intensive, and less than one-tenth low skill intensive. Turning next to the analysis of the relationship between proprietary association abroad and export performance, we note that nearly all high export performers among the low skill-intensive group had no proprietary associations abroad, whereas three-quarters of the high export performers among the high skill-intensive group did have proprietary associations abroad.

These figures suggest that the expectations regarding the association between proprietary associations of the three skill-intensity groups and export performance are largely confirmed.

The degree of confidence in the conclusions which emerge from the above analysis should, however, not be exaggerated. True, a definite association was found between export performance of the high skill-intensive firms and proprietary associations abroad; it was not shown, however, whether exports are sold in the markets where the responding firms have their associates. It may well be that a firm having a parent company in the United States exports the bulk of its output to Iran. As long as the connection between geographic distribution of exports and location of foreign associates is not known, no cause-and-effect relationship can be claimed with confidence between the foreign associations of high skill-intensive firms and their export performance.

It is perhaps proper to claim even at this stage that high skill-intensive firms with foreign associations appear to be conscious of international marketing opportunities and to realize them to a larger extent than high skill-intensive firms which have no such associations. The existence of foreign proprietary associations appears, by contrast, to be definitely unrelated to the export performance of the low skill-intensive firms.

Time spent abroad on export business

Finally, we analyze the relationship between the length of time spent abroad by senior executives of firms belonging to the three skill-intensity groups and the export performance of the firms. As in the previous case, we postulate that, *ceteris paribus,* high skill-intensive firms' executives must spend more time abroad if they are to have a satisfactory export performance. The nature of the products and of the marketing function demands intensive and, occasionally, personal communication with customers. Personal communication with the buyers is required to a lesser extent by manufacturers of low skill-intensive products.

To test this postulate we asked respondents to state the number of months spent abroad by the general manager ("president" in American terminology), marketing manager, and other executives, on matters pertaining to exports. The responses were divided into three groups: zero months, less than two months, and more than two months. Table III.6 gives the data on the distribution of the time spent by senior executives abroad, by skill intensity, and by export performance groups. The figures refer to total time spent by all executives abroad.

The table shows striking differences between the skill groups. Few of the high export performers among the low skill-intensive firms spent

TABLE III.6

Distribution of Firms by Export Performance, by Length of Time Spent Abroad, and by Skill Intensity

	Number of Firms				Per Cent of Firms			
Export Perform-ance	0 Months Abroad	0–2 Months Abroad	2+ Months Abroad	All Firms	0 Months Abroad	0–2 Months Abroad	2+ Months Abroad	All Firms
	Low Skill Intensity							
Low	3	4	0	7	50	19	0	19
Medium	0	7	4	11	0	33	44	31
High	3	10	5	18	50	48	46	50
Total	6	21	9	36	100	100	100	100
	Medium Skill Intensity							
Low	2	6	3	11	50	38	25	34
Medium	2	6	4	12	50	37	33	38
High	0	4	5	9	0	25	42	28
Total	4	16	12	32	100	100	100	100
	High Skill Intensity							
Low	4	10	5	19	66	67	19	41
Medium	2	3	11	16	34	20	42	34
High	0	2	10	12	0	13	38	25
Total	6	15	26	47	100	100	100	100
Grand Total	16	52	47	115	14	45	41	100

Note: Inaccuracies due to rounding.

two or more executive months abroad in export matters. By comparison, there appears to be a positive correlation between export performance and executive time spent abroad in the medium and especially in the high skill-intensive groups.

As in the previous section, which discussed the relationship between proprietary associations abroad and export performance, not too much faith should be put in the apparent relationships. Although these appear to confirm our expectations, it ought to be remembered that the table does not describe the relationship between executive months spent in particular markets and export performance in these markets; it only shows relationship between total executive time spent abroad and export performance in all markets. Therefore, the most that can be said about the relationship between the three variables at this stage is that high skill-intensive firms which demonstrate their awareness of foreign marketing opportunities by having their senior executives spend time abroad have a higher export performance than firms which do not adopt this policy. There appears to be a weaker association between executive time spent abroad and export performance in the case of low and medium skill-intensive firms.

Summary

Part III has discussed certain characteristics of firms and their relationships to skill intensity and to export performance. In accordance with our expectations size appears to be associated with export performance; a higher proportion of large firms than of small ones have a high export performance. Contrary to expectations, however, we found no particular association between export performance and size in the high skill-intensity group. A different test of the hypothesis revealed that a small proportion of the firms accounted for a high proportion of total exports in each of the skill-intensity groups. In agreement with our hypothesis, the inequality was most pronounced in the high skill-intensity group.

Several aspects of the firms' marketing policies were analyzed in the remainder of Part III. Firms possessing marketing departments appear to have higher export performances than firms which do not. The associations between the existence of a marketing department and export performance appeared to be more marked in the case of the high than in the case of the low skill-intensive firms.

Similar associations were found between export performance and the existence of proprietary associations abroad, as well as the length of time spent by senior executives abroad. In both cases, associations with export performance were more marked in the case of the high skill-intensive firms.

These findings tend to confirm the hypothesis that in order to export, high skill-intensive firms must maintain close communication with the markets. Such communication appears to be less essential in the case of the low skill-intensive firms, because they can obtain the necessary market information and maintain the required contacts with their customers through less direct methods.

IV. GEOGRAPHIC DISTRIBUTION OF EXPORTS

Certain propositions pertaining to the geographic distribution of Israel's exports have been suggested in Part I, viz.: that low skill-intensive industries sell a high proportion of their exports to developed and a small proportion to developing countries, whereas high skill-intensive industries sell a high proportion to developing and a low proportion to developed countries.

Another question to consider is the relationship between capital intensity and geographic distribution of exports. We noted earlier that there appears to be a definite association between skill and capital intensity, that high skill-intensive firms tend to have a high ratio of assets to employment. We shall therefore examine the extent to which capital intensity is associated with the destination of exports and discuss the implications of such an association.

Skill intensity and geographic distribution of exports

The respondents' exports, grouped by skill intensity and by markets in the years 1964 and 1967, are shown in Tables IV.1 and IV.2. Changes in the distribution of exports during the four-year period are shown in Table IV.3.

Table IV.1 shows that exports in 1964 tended to be distributed according to our expectations. The developed countries, which bought two-thirds of total exports, imported the bulk of the exports of the low skill-intensive firms, whereas their share of the exports of the medium

Case Studies

TABLE IV.1

Export Distribution by Skill Intensity and by Country Group, 1964

Country Group	Skill Intensity of Industry			
	Low	Medium	High	Total
Distribution by Importing Countries ($ thousands)				
Developing countries	998	3,465	7,693	12,156
Eastern Europe	126	653	7,309	8,088
Developed countries	24,142	6,023	11,274	41,437
Total	25,266	10,141	26,274	61,681
Distribution by Importing Countries (per cent)				
Developing countries	4	34	29	20
Eastern Europe	1	6	28	13
Developed countries	95	59	43	67
Total	100	100	100	100
Distribution by Skill-Intensity Group of Exporting Industries (per cent)				
Developing countries	8	29	63	100
Eastern Europe	2	8	90	100
Developed countries	58	15	27	100
Total	41	16	43	100

Note: Inaccuracies due to rounding.

and high skill-intensive firms was considerably smaller. An analysis of the shares of the different country groups of the respondents' exports shows that the developing countries and Eastern Europe imported mainly from high, and to a lesser degree, medium skill-intensive firms. The developed countries, on the other hand, bought well over half of their imports from low skill-intensive firms.

The figures in Table IV.2 are indicative of an interesting develop-

TABLE IV.2

Export Distribution by Skill Intensity and by Country Group, 1967

Country Group	Skill Intensity of Industry			
	Low	Medium	High	Total
	Distribution by Importing Countries ($ thousands)			
Developing countries	1,191	3,191	11,488	15,870
Eastern Europe	245	1,805	8,375	10,425
Developed countries	27,103	7,585	28,598	63,286
Total	28,539	12,581	48,461	89,581
	Distribution by Importing Countries (per cent)			
Developing countries	4	25	24	18
Eastern Europe	1	14	17	12
Developed countries	95	60	59	71
Total	100	100	100	100
	Distribution by Skill-Intensity Group of Exporting Industries (per cent)			
Developing countries	8	20	72	100
Eastern Europe	2	12	80	100
Developed countries	43	12	45	100
Total	32	14	54	100

Note: Inaccuracies due to rounding.

ment that appears to have taken place between 1964 and 1967. The developing countries and Eastern Europe continued to import mainly those products manufactured by high skill-intensive firms. But the developed countries, while continuing to buy practically all the exports of the low skill-intensive firms, increased their share of the exports of the high skill-intensive firms by a very substantial margin.

The change in the distribution of exports is analyzed in Table IV.3.

Case Studies

TABLE IV.3

Changes in Export Distribution by Skill Intensity and by
Country Group between 1964 and 1967

Country Group	Skill Intensity of Industry			
	Low	Medium	High	Total
	Distribution by Importing Countries ($ thousands)			
Developing countries	193	(274)	3,795	3,714
Eastern Europe	119	1,152	1,066	2,337
Developed countries	2,961	1,562	17,326	21,849
Total	3,273	2,440	22,187	27,900
	Distribution by Importing Countries (per cent)			
Developing countries	6	(11)	17	13
Eastern Europe	4	47	5	8
Developed countries	90	64	78	79
Total	100	100	100	100
	Distribution by Skill-Intensity Group of Exporting Industries (per cent)			
Developing countries	5	(7)	102	100
Eastern Europe	5	49	46	100
Developed countries	14	7	79	100
Total	12	9	79	100

Notes: Negative figures denoted by ( ). Inaccuracies due to rounding.

Nearly 80 per cent of the increase in exports between 1964 and 1967 was sold to the developed countries, which took practically all the additional exports of the low skill-intensive firms and a very substantial proportion of the additional exports of the high skill-intensive firms. The table also shows that high skill-intensive firms accounted for nearly 80 per cent of the additional exports between 1964 and 1967. The trend exhibited by these figures is highly significant, since they pertain to an increase of nearly one-half in the value of exports in the three year interval.

If the trend exhibited in the 1964–67 period continues, the pattern of Israel's exports might look roughly as follows by the middle of the 1970's: (1) The share of the high skill-intensive industries in the country's exports will rise at the expense of the low skill-intensive industries. (2) A larger proportion of exports will be directed toward the developed countries. (3) Exports to the developing countries will continue to consist mainly of high skill-intensive products. (4) The developed countries will increase their share of exports of both high and low skill-intensive industries. The increase in the share of the developed countries in exports of the high skill-intensive industries will be more marked, since their share in exports of the low skill-intensive industries is already very high.

This forecast of the future distribution of Israeli exports is based not only on the trends exhibited by total exports, but also on the export performance of the individual firms. Export performance, it will be recalled, measures both growth rate and proportion of output exported, and it varies considerably between the three country groups, as Table IV.4 clearly indicates. The table shows that the firms which concentrate their exports on the developed countries "outperform" those firms

TABLE IV.4

Export Performance by Major Country Group

	Export Performance			
Destination of Exports	Low	Medium	High	Total
	Number of Firms			
Developing countries	21	14	5	40
Eastern Europe	0	5	1	6
Developed countries	12	20	31	63
Total	33	39	37	109

Note: Exporting firms are distributed vertically according to the country group taking the largest share of their exports.

which export mainly to developing countries and to Eastern Europe in the sense that they either export a higher proportion of their output, or experience a higher rate of export growth, or both.

Capital intensity and geographic distribution of exports

It was reported in Part II of this paper that a positive correlation appears to exist between skill and capital intensity—high skill-intensive firms tend to have a higher ratio of assets to employment than low skill-intensive firms. Here we examine the question whether, and to what extent, this association tends to carry over into the distribution of exports to the three country groups.

The relevant data are given in Tables IV.5, IV.6 and IV.7, which show the geographic distribution of exports by capital intensity groups in 1964 and 1967 and the changes in distribution between the two periods.

There is a remarkable similarity between the figures in Tables IV.5 and IV.6 and those in Tables IV.1 and IV.2 showing the geographic distribution of exports by skill intensity. Looking at the margins, we note, first, that high capital-intensive exports are considerably larger than low capital-intensive exports in both 1964 and 1967, though low capital-intensive exports increased by a higher proportion between the two periods. Turning to the distribution among country groups, we note that low capital-intensive firms, like low skill-intensive firms, tend to sell the bulk of their exports to the developed countries and very little to the developing countries. The share of the latter group is much higher in the case of exports by high capital-intensive and high skill-intensive firms, though still less than that taken by the developed countries.

An analysis of changes in the two distributions shows, first that, although high skill-intensive products accounted for the bulk of the increase in exports between 1964 and 1967, this is not true to the same extent of high capital-intensive products, which accounted for less than 50 per cent of the increase. Also, while developing countries hardly increased their imports of low skill-intensive products, they increased their imports of low capital-intensive products by a considerable margin.

Two additional differences in the distribution are noteworthy. Exports

TABLE IV.5

Export Distribution by Capital Intensity and by Country Group, 1964

Destination of Exports	Capital Intensity			
	Low	Medium	High	Total
	Distribution by Importing Countries ($ thousands)			
Developing countries	642	1,700	7,101	9,443
Eastern Europe	42	287	8,823	9,152
Developed countries	9,894	18,172	15,530	43,596
Total	10,578	20,159	31,454	62,191
	Distribution by Importing Countries (per cent)			
Developing countries	6	9	23	15
Eastern Europe	—	1	28	15
Developed countries	94	90	49	70
Total	100	100	100	100
	Distribution by Capital-Intensity Group of Exporting Industries (per cent)			
Developing countries	7	18	75	100
Eastern Europe	1	3	96	100
Developed countries	23	41	36	100
Total	17	32	51	100

Note: Inaccuracies due to rounding.

of the medium skill-intensive firms tend to be distributed similarly to those of the high skill-intensive firms (with the notable exception of sales to Eastern Europe), while medium capital-intensive firms tend to resemble more closely the low capital-intensive firms in the distribution of their exports. The other dissimilarity also concerns the medium intensity group. While exports of the medium skill-intensive firms accounted for 16 per cent and for 14 per cent of total exports in 1964

TABLE IV.6

Export Distribution by Capital Intensity and by Country Group, 1967

Destination of Exports	Capital Intensity			
	Low	Medium	High	Total
	Distribution by Importing Countries ($ thousands)			
Developing countries	2,962	2,730	8,789	14,481
Eastern Europe	182	400	9,249	9,831
Developed countries	16,765	21,833	26,723	65,321
Total	19,909	24,963	44,461	89,633
	Distribution by Importing Countries (per cent)			
Developing countries	15	11	20	16
Eastern Europe	1	2	20	11
Developed countries	84	87	60	73
Total	100	100	100	100
	Distribution by Capital Intensity Group of Exporting Industries (per cent)			
Developing countries	20	19	61	100
Eastern Europe	2	4	94	100
Developed countries	26	33	41	100
Total	22	28	50	100

Note: Inaccuracies due to rounding.

and 1967, respectively, the share of the medium capital-intensive group in total exports was considerably higher, ranging from 28 per cent in 1967 to 32 per cent in 1964.

These findings, paradoxically enough, tend to agree with expectations derived from bilateral applications of the factor proportions theorem, which suggest that Israel, where capital is likely to be more expensive than in the developed countries and less expensive than in the develop-

TABLE IV.7

Change in Export Distribution by Capital Intensity and Country Group between 1964 and 1967

Destination of Exports	Capital Intensity			
	Low	Medium	High	Total

Distribution by Importing Countries
($ thousands)

Developing countries	2,320	1,030	1,668	5,038
Eastern Europe	140	113	426	679
Developed countries	6,871	3,661	11,193	21,725
Total	9,421	4,804	13,307	27,442

Distribution by Importing Countries
(per cent)

Developing countries	25	22	13	18
Eastern Europe	2	2	3	3
Developed countries	73	76	84	79
Total	100	100	100	100

Distribution by Capital Intensity Group of
Exporting Industries
(per cent)

Developing countries	46	21	33	100
Eastern Europe	20	17	63	100
Developed countries	32	17	51	100
Total	34	18	48	100

Note: Inaccuracies due to rounding.

ing countries, would tend to export low capital-intensive products to the former and high capital-intensive products to the latter. Before adopting this conclusion, however, we should recall that capital intensity, as measured here, reflects only direct capital and labor inputs at the manufacturing stage and does not include indirect inputs via materials purchased by the manufacturing firm. Capital intensity measured by direct inputs will be similar to that measured by total (direct plus indirect) inputs only when value added by manufacture is a high proportion of the value of output or when capital-labor ratios in manufacturing are not markedly different from those embodied in purchased materials.

Lacking the relevant data, we have no way of telling whether either of these alternatives does in fact occur. We must therefore conclude that we cannot regard our findings as being consistent with the factor proportions theorem, though they certainly do not conflict with it. Bearing in mind that several empirical research findings such as Leontief's and Bruno's were in direct conflict with this theorem, we should regard the findings reported here as worthy of note [9, 1].[4]

Our findings concerning the relationship between the skill intensity of different export products and their geographic distribution could also be interpreted in terms of Hufbauer's model [8]. Hufbauer distinguished between two kinds of products which enter international trade—"comparative advantage" and "technological gap" products. The former, consisting of those products which contain a high proportion of abundant inputs as suggested by the factor proportions theorem, will tend to be exported to countries with different factor endowments. Manufacturers of "technological gap" products have a competitive edge by virtue of the fact that they are first on the market. They can export their products to all countries even if they contain a high proportion of scarce inputs, because there is inevitably an "imitation lag" during which these products cannot be manufactured on a competitive basis by others.

How, then, do our findings fit into Hufbauer's model? Israel exports mainly high skill-intensive products to the developing countries. These products contain "technological gap" as well as "comparative advantage" elements; the former are reflected in their high skill content, and the latter in their high capital content. Israel's exports of low skill-intensive products to the developed countries may be regarded as belonging to the pure "comparative advantage" category. The high skill-intensive products which are exported in growing proportions to the developed countries also have elements of "technological gap" and of "comparative

---

[4] On the other hand we should take note that these findings agree with those of Tatemoto and Ichimura who showed that Japan exports labor-intensive products to the West and capital-intensive products to Asia [13].

advantage." The "technological gap" element is reflected in the high proportion of scientists, engineers and skilled employees in the labor force and the "comparative advantage" element in the relatively low cost of these production factors in Israel. This factor may, incidentally, compensate for the relatively high capital intensity of the high skill-intensive products.

Summary and conclusions

The expectation that Israel tends to export high skill-intensive products to developing countries and low skill-intensive products to developed countries is confirmed. An analysis of changes in the distribution of exports showed, at the same time, that a large proportion of the increase in exports between 1964 and 1967 consisted of high skill-intensive products sold mainly to the developed countries. If this trend continues, then the developed countries will absorb a growing share of the products exported by the high skill-intensive industries.

The analysis also showed that the capital intensity, like the skill intensity, of exports sold to Eastern Europe and the developing countries is higher than that of the exports sold to the developed countries.

Those findings pertaining to the geographic distribution of Israel's exports and to their skill intensity are undoubtedly welcome to the country's economic planners. Trade with most East European countries and with some of the developing countries is conducted within the framework of bilateral trade and payments agreements. The ability of Israel's industry to divert a growing proportion of its international transactions to markets where competition is less restricted and trade less subject to political direction signifies an improvement in its international competitiveness.

The conclusion regarding the trend in the distribution of exports by skill-intensity groups is perhaps even more significant. If Israel's exports in the future were to be dominated by products with a low-skill content, the country would have to compete increasingly with developing countries possessing abundant supplies of low-skill labor. Assuming that productivity per unit of labor in these industries does not vary widely between Israel and the developing countries, then average income cannot diverge too widely, either, in the long run. The average income level in Israel would therefore tend to be pulled toward that of its competitors. If, on the other hand, the country's major competitors are in the developed countries, and if we again assume that productivity variations are not too enormous, average income in Israel will tend to rise to the level enjoyed by those countries.

APPENDIX A, DISTINCTION BETWEEN FIRMS AND PLANTS

Distinction between firms and plants may be of crucial importance to a study which seeks to identify the role of the individual business unit in determining export performance. The need for such a distinction raises certain problems because of the difficulty involved in devising indexes and other measures which reflect equally well the operations and performance of single- and multiplant firms. Due to the composition of our sample, which contained fewer than ten plants owned by multiplant firms, the following procedure was adopted: (1) The unit for which data were gathered and on which analysis was performed, was the individual plant, except in those cases (two in the total) where data were available only for the entire firm; (2) services provided by multiplant firms to their individual units were recorded separately for each plant.

This procedure affects the analysis of product or firm characteristics in the sense that it ascribes to the plant certain characteristics possessed by the entire firm. For example, where a multiplant firm maintained a single marketing department, each plant was regarded as having its own marketing department. Although this procedure may overstate the marketing effort of the multiplant firm, it does not affect other centrally provided services such as R&D where the data provided by the respondents usually facilitated the allocation of costs, personnel, or other inputs between the individual plants.

In the text, the terms "plant" and "firm" are used interchangeably.

APPENDIX B, THE SAMPLE

The sample consists of 190 firms, operating in eleven industries, with which interviews were completed. The industries were chosen because they were major export industries in 1967 or were considered to be potentially significant exporters. The list of firms to be interviewed was provided by the Israel Government Central Bureau of Statistics on the basis of the following considerations:

1. The sample was to consist of 300 firms.

2. The probability of a firm's inclusion in the sample was proportional to the number of its employees.

3. Firms employing less than thirty people were excluded.

4. At least twenty firms per industry were to be included in the sample. In those industries which had fewer than twenty firms employing thirty people or more, all firms were included.

5. Classification by industry was based on the Central Bureau of Statistics classification system.

6. The list of industrial plants maintained by the Social Security Institution constituted the universe or the frame from which the sample was drawn.

Of the 306 firms included in the sample 190 were eventually interviewed. Of the 110 firms not interviewed, about one-third declined an interview. Most of the remainder were unsuitable because they were found to employ fewer than thirty people, because they had gone bankrupt or had merged with other firms, because of misclassification, or because they declined to give sufficient information to make their inclusion worthwhile.

Appendix Table 1 gives data on the industries studied in the survey and lists the number of firms employing over thirty people in each industry, the number of firms included in the sample, and the number of firms with completed interviews. About 35 per cent of the 544 firms in the eleven industries were interviewed. The share of these firms in the industries' exports in 1966 was roughly the same—37 per cent. However, if firms in the diamond industry are excluded from the calculations, the percentage of firms interviewed rises to 38 and that of exports to 68. Of the 190 respondents, 52 were nonexporters; the remaining firms exported varying proportions of their output.

Finally, a word of caution: since many of the findings are reported in the form of frequency distributions, totals or subtotals may be found to vary from table to table. These apparent inconsistencies are due to the fact that respondents did not usually answer all the questions posed to them. The reader is cautioned to bear this in mind when interpreting the findings.

APPENDIX TABLE 1

Distribution of Firms Employing over Thirty People in Eleven Industries in 1966

ISIC Industry Category (SITC equivalent in parentheses)	Number of Firms			Per Cent of Total	
	Total	in Sample	Interviewed	in Sample	Interviewed
Textiles 23 (65)	168	56	33	33	20
Leather and clothing 24, 29 (61, 84, 85)	103	38	20	37	19
Canned fruits and vegetables 203 (053)	31	31	16	100	52
Diamonds 394 (667.20)	86	25	16	29	19
Plastic products 399 (893)	27	27	16	100	59
Plywood and plumbing fixtures 251, 350 (695, 696, 631.21)	18	18	11	100	61
Nonmetallic mining 19 (27)	6	6	4	100	67
Chemicals 31-32 (51-59)	30	30	20	100	67
Electrical equipment 370 (72)	31	31	25	100	81
Electronics 370, 391, 392, (861, 724, 726, 729)	17	17	14	100	83
Machinery 36 (71)	27	27	15	100	56
Total	544	306	190	56	35

Source: For number of firms in each industry, Israel Government, Central Bureau of Statistics.

APPENDIX C, SKILL INTENSITY

The measure here employed is the share of engineers, scientists, and other employees having academic degrees and of highly skilled workers in the labor force. Holders of academic degrees were distinguished from other employees on the basis of a simple and objective criterion, whereas the classification of highly skilled employees was left to the respondents who were asked to include in this group employees in the three top grades of their skills or crafts. In certain crafts, such as welding, machine operating, wood working, etc., the classification is relatively simple, since it is based on formal examinations. In many other occupations, the classification is less formal and the respondents were asked to use their best judgment to classify their employees.

The skill-intensity index (SI) was constructed as follows:

$$SI = \frac{2.\,A + HS}{TE}$$

where A = employees holding academic degrees,

HS = highly skilled employees belonging to the three top grades of skill classification, or classified as such by management, and

TE = Total number of employees

Employees holding academic degrees were given a higher weight on the assumption that they contributed more to the special characteristics and the value of the products than did other skilled employees.

In the preceding analysis, firms are frequently grouped into three subgroups on the basis of the skill-intensity index. The distribution and the grouping are described in Appendix Table 2.

APPENDIX TABLE 2

Distribution of Respondents by their Skill Intensity Index

Skill Intensity Group	Range	Average	Number of Firms
Low	$0 < SI \leq 0.1$	0.06	56
Medium	$0.1 < SI \leq 0.3$	0.18	68
High	$0.3 < SI \leq 1.05$	0.48	60
Entire distribution	$0 < SI \leq 1.05$	0.26	184

APPENDIX D, CONCENTRATION OF PRODUCTION

The production concentration index (PC) is constructed as follows:

$$PC = \sum_{i=1}^{3} x_i^2$$

where x_i = share of product i in total output.

PC can range from zero to 1. It will assume the value 1 if only one product is manufactured and will decline in value as the number of products increases.

Respondents were divided into three production concentration groups on the basis of the following grouping of calculated index values:

Group	Index Value
Low	$0 < PC \leq 0.4$
Medium	$0.4 < PC \leq 0.8$
High	$0.8 < PC \leq 1.0$

APPENDIX E, EXPORT PERFORMANCE

The export performance of the firms interviewed is gauged from two points of view:
1. the proportion of output exported
2. the rate of growth of exports.

The proportion of output exported is obviously an important indicator of export performance. Firms whose export ratio is high are deemed to exhibit a better export performance than firms exporting a low proportion of their output. Growth rate, too, is indicative of export performance; firms whose exports increase at a high rate should be considered better performers than firms whose exports show little or no increase.

The export performance index (EP) is constructed as follows:

$$EP = \sqrt[n-1]{\frac{E_t}{E_1}} \cdot \frac{\sum_{t=1}^{n} t \, S_t}{\sum_{t=1}^{n} t} \qquad t = 1 \ldots 4$$

where E_t = Exports in year.

E_1 = exports in 1963.

E_2 = exports in 1964, etc.

S_t = Share of sales exported in year t. S_t is weighted, the weights varying from 1 (for share of exports in 1963) to 4 (for share of exports in 1966).

The share of sales multiplied by the weights and summed over the periods 1 to 4 is divided by the sum of the weights to obtain the weighted share of sales exported. The weight for a given year t is 0 if during that year no exports took place.

In theory the index could vary between 0 and infinity. In practice it varied between 0 (the value assigned to the export performance of firms which had no exports) and 5.70. The average value was 0.50.

In the analyses, respondents are frequently divided into four groups on the basis of their export performance index. The groups are analyzed in Appendix Table 3, which gives the breakdown of the respondents by export performance groups and indicates the extent to which their inclusion in a particular group was determined by both average annual export growth rate and weighted export share. An analysis of the feasible combinations of these two components of the export performance index suggests that the tradeoff permitted them is limited within a range, which makes intuitive sense. Thus, firms whose export share exceeds 0.25 can be included in Group I—low export performers—only if their exports declined between 1963 and 1966. In fact, not a single firm whose export share exceeded 0.25 was included in Group I. Turning to Group III—high export performers—we note that firms with negative export growth can be included only if their export share exceeds 0.5. The two firms included in Group III which met this criterion actually exported nearly 100 per cent of their output. Analyzing further the distribution within the various export performance groups, we note that most respondents in Group I are characterized by low or negative export growth rate and by low export shares. By contrast, most respondents in Group III have a high export share and a positive export growth rate.

The distribution of respondents belonging to the middle export per-

APPENDIX TABLE 3

Distribution of Respondents by their Export Performance Index and its Components

Group	Average Annual Growth Rate $G = \sqrt[t-1]{\dfrac{E_t}{E_1}}$	Weighted Share of Exports in Sales $S = \dfrac{\sum\limits_{t=1}^{n} t\, S_t}{\sum\limits_{t=1}^{n} t}$			
		$S \le .25$	$.25 < S \le 0.5$	$S > 0.5$	Total
52 Nonexporters					
EP = 0	G = 0	52	—	—	52
37 Low exporters					
0 < EP ≤ 0.1	G < 1	22	—	—	22
	1 < G < 1.3	5	n.f.	n.f.	5
	1.3 < G ≤ 2	6	n.f.	n.f.	6
	2 < G	4	n.f.	n.f.	4
44 Medium exporters					
0.1 < EP ≤ 0.5	G < 1	8	5	—	13
	1 < G < 1.3	7	9	n.f.	16
	1.3 < G ≤ 2	8	3	n.f.	11
	2 < G	4	n.f.	n.f.	4
40 High exporters					
0.5 < EP	G < 1	n.f.	n.f.	2	2
	1 < G < 1.3	n.f.	1	15	16
	1.3 < G ≤ 2	n.f.	5	10	15
	2 < G	2	3	2	7

Note: n.f. = not feasible. (Because of the criteria by which firms have been classified there are no entries in the indicated cells.)

APPENDIX TABLE 4

List and Rank of Respondents by Industry, Skill Intensity, and Export Performance

Industry	Average Skill Intensity Index	Rank	Average Export Performance Index	Rank
Nonmetallic mining	0.57	1	0.96	4
Chemicals	0.52	2	2.89	1
Electronics	0.36	3	2.20	3
Electrical equipment	0.31	4	0.65	6
Machinery	0.28	5	2.31	2
Plywood and Plumbing fixtures	0.27	6	0.45	8
Leather and clothing	0.18	7	0.22	10
Plastic products	0.15	8	0.06	11
Textiles	0.14	9	0.33	9
Canned fruits	0.12	10	0.46	7
Diamonds	0.04	11	0.85	5

formance group shows, as might be expected, a wider dispersion among the feasible combinations. Appendix Table 4 gives the breakdown of the respondents by industry, ranking each industry by average skill intensity and export performance.

REFERENCES

1. Bruno, M., *Interdependence, Resource Use and Structural Change in Israel,* Jerusalem, 1962.
2. Freeman, C., "The Plastics Industry: A Comparative Study of Research and Innovation," *National Institute Economic Review,* November 1963, pp. 22–62.
3. Freeman, C., "Research and Development in Electronic Capital Goods," *National Institute Economic Review,* November 1965, pp. 40–91.

4. Gruber, W., Mehta, D., and Vernon, R., "The R&D Factor in International Trade and International Investment of United States Industries," *Journal of Political Economy*, February 1967, pp. 20–37.

5. Hicks, J. R., "International Trade—The Long View," Central Bank of Egypt Lectures, Cairo, 1963, p. 6.

6. Hirsch, S., *Location of Industry and International Competitiveness*, London, 1967.

7. Hoffmeyer, E., *Dollar Shortage*, Amsterdam, 1958.

8. Hufbauer, G. C., *Synthetic Materials and the Theory of International Trade*, London, 1963.

9. Leontief, W. W., "Factor Proportions and the Structure of American Trade," *Review of Economics and Statistics*, November 1956, pp. 386–407.

10. MacDougall, D., *The World Dollar Problem*, London, 1957.

11. P.E.P., "Firms and Their Exports," *Planning*, London, November 1964.

12. Posner, M. V., "International Trade and Technical Change," *Oxford Economic Papers*, October 1961, pp. 323–41.

13. Tatemoto, M., and Ichimura, S., "Factor Proportions and Foreign Trade—The Case of Japan," *Review of Economics and Statistics*, November 1959, pp. 442–46.

COMMENT

ANNE O. KRUEGER
University of Minnesota

Professor Hirsch's paper contains a wealth of suggestive hypotheses and empirical evidence about firm behavior, product differences, and the nature of export markets. His essential thesis is that there are systematic relationships between types of products, the skill intensity of their production, and export market characteristics. The thesis is technological in that Hirsch believes that products requiring large skill inputs are generally comparatively new products with short production runs, loose specifications, much production to individual customer order, and considerable service and communications requirements by buyers. By contrast, established products are believed to have widely accepted specifications, standard technologies, and long production runs. This basic hypothesis generates a number of interesting corollaries with regard to the nature of price competition, size of firm, and the like. Hirsch then subjects these hypotheses to tests based on Israeli data for a sample of 190 firms.

Hirsch's paper contains too many provocative hypotheses and ideas to comment on them all in the time provided. These comments will focus upon only two aspects of his paper: (1) the relationship between technology, human capital, and the factor proportions model of international trade, and (2) the extent to which Hirsch's empirical research in fact tests the hypotheses with which he started.

Technology, human capital, the Heckscher-Ohlin model

Since Leontief [6] showed that American trade patterns could not be explained by the capital intensity of export- and import-competing production, the factor proportions explanation of trade has been suspect. It is evident that a simple two-factor model of trade cannot be used to predict or explain trade patterns. The basic question is, what is wrong? Is the Heckscher-Ohlin model based upon one or more assumptions in flagrant violation of reality, or has the model been misinterpreted empirically?

Some attempts have been made to develop alternative models of trade and determination of comparative advantage. However, most research efforts have been focussed upon the incorporation of either "technology" or "human capital" as an additional explanatory variable in trade theory. Kenen [5], Roskamp and McMeekin [7], and Keesing [4] have found that the incorporation of human capital into models of comparative advantage determination reversed the apparent paradox pointed out by Leontief. Keesing [3], Hirsch [2], Vernon [8], and Gruber, Mehta, and Vernon [1] have investigated the role of research and development (R&D) as an explanatory variable and believe that its explanatory power is high.

With both human capital and R&D showing considerable explanatory power, the significant question is the relationship between them and the relative importance of each in determining comparative advantage and trade patterns. From the viewpoint of trade theory, the essential question is the relationship between technology and production functions. The factor proportions model is based upon the assumption that the same technologies are available for production in all countries. If technologies differ, it is quite possible that labor-abundant countries might export capital-intensive goods because of superior technologies, and vice versa. If, on the other hand, technologies are the same between countries but some products require a relatively large input of skilled labor (including design to individual specification, servicing requirements, and the like), the prospect for standard trade theory is far brighter. Then, the factor-proportions explanation of trade, in its empirical application, needs to be amended to cover more factors of production. It would not be that the theory did not fit the world; it would be that the simple two-factor interpretation of the theory was in error.

The outline of a dynamic model of comparative advantage for incorporating human capital explicitly into trade theory has begun to emerge. There are four basic hypotheses: (1) Skill classes are imperfect substitutes, so that as countries accumulate more highly skilled individuals, wage differentials (in the absence of factor price equalization) tend to fall. (2) As suggested by Kenen [5], when countries increase their capital stock, it is allocated between investment in humans and investment in machines in such a way as to equate the rates of return on various investments. (3) With an increasing total capital stock per head, the rate of return on all types of investment declines, thereby changing (a) the skill-human capital proportions and (b) the relative distribution of skills among various classes. Little is known empirically about the directions of change. (4) For a given capital-rental and wage-differential structure, it will always pay firms to use more capital services with more skilled workers than with less skilled workers.

If these hypotheses are accepted, the rudiments of a theory can be pieced together. Rich countries will have to employ more skill and more capital per man in exports than will poor countries, and, conversely, poor countries will tend to export resource-intensive products, requiring less skill to produce. High per-capita-income countries will be those with a relatively large endowment of skills and physical capital. Technology can be regarded as an intermediate good produced with a high skill input. It would be used most intensively in the production of skill- and capital-intensive products. The ratios of physical capital to skill will vary with total capital endowment, but, without further assumptions or information, the direction of change cannot be specified. It might be the case that at intermediate income levels countries would have a higher ratio of physical to human capital than at high incomes, and that therefore they would find their comparative advantage in goods requiring relatively large amounts of physical capital, or vice versa.

Hirsch's results and Israel's comparative advantage

My chief concern with Hirsch's paper is that it is impossible to choose between the technological explanation and the skill explanation. Hirsch's findings are compatible with either the extended Heckscher-Ohlin model outlined above, or with a technological hypothesis.

Casual empiricism would suggest that Israel has a peculiar skill mix; many immigrants have come with very high skill levels, others have been virtually without skills. If this is true, Israel might well have a two-tail comparative advantage, concentrating her resources (1) in high skill activities to absorb her relative abundance of highly skilled workers and (2) in low skill activities to absorb the unskilled workers.

All this, of course, has to be taken in the context of other countries' comparative advantages (with a more normal skill distribution) as postulated above.

Such a hypothesis is consistent with Hirsch's findings. Hirsch does not use an independent measure of technology. Rather, he identifies technological firms as those having a high skill index and seeks to ascertain whether a high skill index [1] is correlated with the attributes of technological products he postulates. Hirsch's size measure fails his hypothesis, quite possibly because his unit is number of workers, rather than the amount of human capital or another more economically relevant unit. Hirsch was surprised to find the skill-intensive industries were also the capital-intensive industries. This is contrary to his technological hypotheses (although not essential to them) and consistent with the capital-accumulation view outlined above. The extended comparative advantage model would predict that Israel's skill-intensive industries would also be the capital-intensive industries, as Israel's relatively scarce capital stock would be allocated more toward the high skill workers than the low skill workers.

Hirsch finds that Israel's low skill and high skill industries, which he *identifies* with nontechnological and technological industries, have had a better "export performance" than the intermediate skill industries.[2] He

---

[1] Hirsch's skill index is open to criticism on several counts. He gives persons holding academic degrees a weight of two, other "skilled workers" a weight of one. Implicitly, he considers an academic degree holder a perfect substitute for two skilled workers and allows no substitution between these two groups and other employed persons. A comparable physical capital index might be the number of machines of twenty horsepower or less plus twice the number of machines of more than twenty horsepower divided by the total number of machines.

[2] Hirsch's export performance index is open to some criticism. Consider two firms with the following experience over a three-year period:

	Output		Exports	
Year	Firm 1	Firm 2	Firm 1	Firm 2
1	100	1000	50	100
2	90	1200	45	200
3	80	1500	40	300

I calculate the export performance of the first firm to be the cube root of .8 times one-half, or something in excess of .45. For the second firm, the export performance index is the cube root of three times .17, or less than .3. The first firm, with declining exports, outperforms the second firm, with tripled export sales and a rising share of exports in output.

explains this in terms of the existence of some resource-based industries. It would appear quite possible that the finding is a consequence of the two-tailed nature of Israel's comparative advantage, rather than the resource-base theory. Further support for this view comes from Hirsch's finding that Israel exports high skill products to the developing countries and low skill products to the developed countries. The double nature of Israel's comparative advantage appears, at least a priori, a more satisfactory explanation of this phenomenon than the technological content of the industries involved.

In summary, Hirsch has raised many interesting hypotheses about the nature of technology and its implications. From the viewpoint of international trade theory, however, he has not devised a test which can distinguish between the technological thesis and the human capital-physical capital explanation of orthodox trade theory.

REFERENCES

1. Gruber, W., Mehta, D., and Vernon, R., "The R&D Factor in International Trade and International Investment of United States Industries," *Journal of Political Economy,* February 1967.

2. Hirsch, S., *Location of Industry and International Competitiveness,* London, 1967.

3. Keesing, D. B., "The Impact of Research and Development on United States Trade," *Journal of Political Economy,* February 1967.

4. ————, "Labor Skills and International Trade: Evaluating Many Trade Flows with a Single Measuring Device," *Review of Economics and Statistics,* August 1965.

5. Kenen, P. B., "Nature, Capital and Trade," *Journal of Political Economy,* October 1965.

6. Leontief, W. W., "Factor Proportions and the Structure of American Trade," *Review of Economics and Statistics,* November 1956.

7. Roskamp, K. W., and McMeekin, G. C., "Factor Proportions, Human Capital and Foreign Trade: The Case of West Germany Reconsidered," *Quarterly Journal of Economics,* February 1968.

8. Vernon, R., "International Investment and International Trade in the Product Cycle," *Quarterly Journal of Economics,* May 1966.

Technical Change & Agricultural Trade:

Three Examples—Sugarcane,

Bananas, and Rice

R. E. EVENSON, J. P. HOUCK, JR., V. W. RUTTAN

UNIVERSITY OF MINNESOTA

The invention, diffusion, and adoption of new technology has long been a crucial, yet imperfectly understood, feature of agricultural development. Throughout man's history, agricultural productivity increases have come about (1) by the diffusion of traditional crops, animals, tools, and methods into new areas of settlement and (2) by the introduction of new crops, animals, tools, and methods into traditional agricultural systems [38]. During the last century, these processes have been accelerated by systematic efforts to identify, collect, and diffuse superior crop varieties, livestock breeds, and production practices throughout the major agricultural regions of the world. These systematic efforts have been supplemented by programs of adaptive research and extension designed to stimulate even more rapid diffusion of the best technologies from advanced regions and farms to less advanced regions and farms [6].

Technological advance is particularly important to producers and consumers of farm products moving in international commerce. Foreign exchange earnings from exports of primary agricultural products under-

NOTE: This essay is Minnesota Agricultural Experiment Station, *Scientific Journal Paper No. 6718*. The authors are Assistant Professor, Associate Professor and Professor, respectively, in the Department of Agricultural Economics, University of Minnesota.

pin the development programs of many poorer nations. Farm income and employment in many developing nations are major components of over-all national economic activity and depend heavily on foreign sales. On the other hand, consumers in both producing and importing nations have an important stake in international technological advance. When gains from innovation are passed along, consumers may benefit by lower prices and wider selections of food and fiber products.

The purpose of this paper is to examine three cases which provide some insight into the character of international transmission of technical change and its economic impacts and implications. These cases focus on three separate commodities—sugarcane, bananas, and rice. Each case presents different facets of the international movement of technological innovation.

Section I on sugarcane emphasizes the role of experiment station research in the development of new, higher yielding varieties and the subsequent diffusion of these varieties throughout the sugar-growing world. An attempt is made to assess the economic impact of the development of a new successful variety on the innovating nation and upon later adopters. Section II on the bananas trade illustrates how the development and adoption of disease-resistant banana varieties in Central America led to further innovations in marketing and processing techniques. The joint impact of these innovations is discussed in terms of changes in output, prices, and patterns of comparative advantage among producing nations. Section III on the rice trade illustrates how technical change in rice production in Japan was transferred to other producing nations, mainly Korea and Taiwan. The resulting increase in rice exports from these countries to Japan had substantial impacts on Japanese rice production and prices in the period before World War II. An attempt is made to measure these effects and to assess their economic implications.

Common threads run through each of these cases. A basic component of the technical changes examined in each of the three commodities is the development and diffusion of improved plant materials flowing from both public and private research efforts. In addition, each of these cases illustrates that, in one way or another, the pace of technical advance is linked to changes in economic incentives as viewed by individual producers and policy-making institutions. For each of these commodities, the complex web of international economic relationships has diffused the impact of a given technological advance far beyond those producers and nations actually developing the innovation or putting it into practice.

I. SUGARCANE [1]

This section explores the technical changes in sugarcane production that have resulted from the development and introduction of new sugarcane varieties. Four stages of progress in varietal development are identified and the relative contributions to varietal progress by the major sugarcane experiment stations of the world are evaluated. Intercountry and intracountry transmission of varieties is assessed and related to the stages of progress in varietal development. The implications for world sugar trade of the particular pattern of generation and transmission of technical change exhibited in this industry are explored.

Production and yield data are presented for eighteen major sugarcane producing countries in Table I.1. In this table, as throughout this paper, quantitative measures of "sugar" refer to material with 96 per cent sugar content. The relative position of a number of countries has changed considerably over time. The increased importance of production in Brazil and Mexico and the decline in production in Indonesia (Java) are especially striking. The yield data are incomplete, but the substantial increases taking place in India, South Africa, the continental United States (Louisiana and Florida), Hawaii, Taiwan, Argentina, and Australia (Queensland) are noteworthy.

The development of new varieties

A study of the history of attempts to improve yields through the development of new varieties reveals four important stages.

STAGE I—SELECTION OF NATURAL (WILD) VARIETIES

Prior to 1887 the varieties planted were basically wild canes which had been selected over many years by planters in sugarcane-producing areas. These wild canes originated in India, New Guinea, and Java, and in most cases, planters relied on a single variety for many years. Occa-

---

[1] The authors are indebted to Mr. John Galstad, Department of Agricultural Economics, University of Minnesota, for assistance in the statistical tabulations and analyses of this section.

Case Studies

TABLE I.1

National Sugarcane Yield and Production Averages for Selected Five-Year Periods

(production in thousands of short tons; yield in short tons per acre)

Area	1910–14 Production	1910–14 Yield	1923–24 Production	1923–24 Yield	1928–32 Production	1928–32 Yield
Brazil	333	–	860	–	956	–
Cuba	2,287	14.5[c]	4,345	19.3	4,389	18.6
India	2,699[a]	11.3	3,563[a]	11.0	3,561[a]	12.4
Mexico	163	–	175	30.2	235	20.5
Australia	216	17.3	409	16.8	450	16.9
Philippine Islands	294	–	502	–	968	20.4
Argentina	194	11.6	260	13.2	410	13.6
Hawaii	567	40.7	614	43.3	951	60.1
United States	311	15.8	229	9.4	149	15.0
Taiwan	192	11.8	450	16.1	869	29.3
South Africa	88	–	181	8.8	312	20.5
Puerto Rico	363	–	414	16.6	795	25.3
Peru	203	22.4	344	24.3	441	40.5
Indonesia	1,513	41.2	1,985	46.5	3,010	56.4
British West Indies[b]	218	–	231	9.6	348	24.0
Dominican Republic	105	–	231	–	419	–
Mauritius	234	15.6	238	14.5	241	15.2
Egypt	67	18.8	93	–	123	35.0

Source: *Yearbook of Agriculture*, USDA, Washington, various issues, 1925-35; *Agricultural Statistics*, USDA, Washington, annual issues, 1936-66; *International Sugar Situation*, USDA, Bureau of Statistics, Bulletin 30, 1904; *Production Yearbook*, FAO, Rome, various issues, 1948-66; *Annual Report*, Bureau of Sugar Experiment Stations, Queensland, annual reports, 1900-64; *South African Sugar Yearbook*, Durban, 1935, 1948-49, 1961-62; *International Yearbook of Agricultural Statistics*, Rome, various issues, 1910-46; *Indian Sugar Manual*, Kalyanur, India, 1962, 1963-64.

[a]Expressed in short tons of low-grade gur.

[b]Countries included are Antigua, Barbados, British Guiana, Trinidad, Tobago, St. Christopher, St. Lucia, St. Vincent.

[c]1913-14 only.

[d]1940-42 only.

[e]1940 only.

[f]1960 only.

[g]1963 only.

| 1938–42 | | 1948–52 | | 1958–62 | | 1963–67 | |
Produc-tion	Yield	Produc-tion	Yield	Produc-tion	Yield	Produc-tion	Yield
1,333	17.1	1,775	17.4	3,726	18.8	5,329	19.8
3,200	17.2	6,378	17.0	6,030	17.0	4,950	16.2
5,508^a	11.5	1,548	13.1	3,364	15.3	4,515	20.8
398	22.4	789	23.1	1,665	26.4	2,319	27.0
746	20.3	865	23.6	1,395	27.5	1,643^g	36.2
1,146	22.6	912	20.3	1,626	26.7	1,584	19.3
509	13.4^d	687	14.9	950	17.0	1,422	23.0
935	65.1	979	76.4	1,048	90.0	1,275	98.7
460	19.3	517	19.5	707	24.5	1,104	25.3
1,357	–	683	27.3	931	33.7	1,100	38.6
534	26.3	612	25.1	1,140	35.3	1,002	35.8
998	32.4	1,264	29.8	1,051	30.4	897	30.6
482	52.6	544	60.0	884	70.4	882	64.2
1,718	61.5	356	40.0	780	49.5	854	39.1
502	17.6	617	38.1	808	39.4$_f$	801	36.4
484	19.0^e	590	–	1,012	19.5^f	800	22.5
337	19.8	490	–	535	24.6	732	24.0
188	–	215	32.8	369	42.6	465	40.0

sionally planters experimented with new varieties but, generally speaking, the only varieties that survived over time were those resistant to the diseases prevailing in the area of production. Techniques of cultivation, irrigation, and processing were well developed in most producing countries by 1887, and sugar was an important world trade commodity by that time.[2]

STAGE II—CROSSING OF VARIETIES

In 1887, in the newly founded experiment station in Barbados, British West Indies and in the experiment station in Java, sugarcane seedlings

[2] The cane sugar industry was a key part of the colonial empires of the nineteenth century. Slavery in the British West Indies was also integrally related to the production of sugarcane. For documentation see [4, 5, 34, 40].

were first produced through a process of sexual reproduction [5, 40, 34]. This was of great importance since it opened the possibility of crossing varieties. The cane plant ordinarily does not flower and produce seedlings readily. Flowering in the cane plant is induced by temperature and light control, and few experiment stations were successful in their attempts to produce seedlings in the early days of cane cross-breeding.[4]

Several experiment stations had notable successes in the development of the first new varieties. The Java station (Proefstatien Oost Java) was the first to develop a new variety (P.O.J. 100) of commercial importance. It later added many more important varieties. Hawaii and Barbados had also developed important commercial cane varieties by 1900. The Coimbatore experiment station in India released the first of its Co. varieties in 1912. This station and the Java station were destined to develop varieties that would be planted commercially in every major cane-producing area of the world by 1930.

STAGE III—BREEDING FOR DISEASE RESISTANCE

Sugarcane disease did not diminish in importance with the introduction of the first new varieties. In many countries, the new varieties which yielded substantially more than the traditional native varieties were invaded by diseases within a few years.[5] The Java station took the lead in developing disease-resistant varieties. In 1921 the variety P.O.J. 2878 was produced. Its grandparent was the first important Java variety, P.O.J. 100. P.O.J. 2878 proved to be resistant to most important cane diseases and to be a high yielding variety as well. More than 50,000 acres were planted to this variety by 1926—a remarkable expansion in

---

[3] Prior to that time cane plants reproduced asexually except for rare instances of sexual reproduction in wild canes. Asexual reproduction is still the means of reproducing all commercially grown cane. Portions of the cane plant (usually the upper portion of the stalk) are planted, and new plants grow from these segments.

[4] The opportunity to reproduce cane both sexually and asexually is important in sugarcane breeding. A successful cross between two cane plants may produce numerous seedlings. A single superior seedling can be reproduced asexually and create a completely new variety. Testing and selection of superior seedlings from thousands of candidates is a major activity in modern cane breeding.

[5] This problem continues to plague cane breeders. Modern varieties tend to undergo a deterioration in yield capability after several years of commercial production. New diseases continually make inroads on the old varieties [5].

plant material from a single seedling in 1921. By 1929 more than 400,000 acres were planted in Java, and it was being planted in many other countries. This "wonder cane" became the most widely planted single variety in the world.

In the period from 1920 to 1940 the Coimbatore station in India also produced a number of important varieties which incorporated disease resistance and high yield. These varieties were planted widely throughout the world. Varieties developed in the British West Indies (Barbados) and Hawaii were also planted extensively outside the regions in which they were developed.

STAGE IV—BREEDING FOR SPECIFIC SOIL AND CLIMATE CONDITIONS
The latest phase in the development of new varietal technology involves the breeding of varieties suited to the specific soil, climate, disease conditions, and cultivating techniques of small regions. For the most part this breeding must be undertaken by the experiment station or stations in a specific region. The scope for international transmission of technical change through varietal transfer is limited. However, information about breeding techniques and the potential of certain varieties as parent stock have been exchanged, as have genetic materials.

More than one hundred sugarcane experiment stations now exist in the world. Almost every important cane-producing country is now using locally developed Stage-IV varieties. This is illustrated by the data in Table I.2. The development of Stage-IV varieties in Queensland, South Africa, Puerto Rico, and Louisiana is reflected in the percentage of acreage planted to locally developed varieties in these areas.

Table I.3 shows the relative importance of the major varieties of sugarcane in the world during the 1940–64 period. The production figures are estimates of the over-all importance of each variety in the major countries of the world during the twenty-five-year period. Argentina and the Philippines are the only major producing countries not included in this calculation.

Almost all the major varieties during this period were bred prior to 1940. Most are examples of the third stage in breeding progress. The widespread planting of the Java (P.O.J.) and Indian (Co.) varieties is

TABLE I.2

Per Cent of Sugarcane Acreage Planted to Varieties Developed by the
Experiment Station of Selected Areas: 1930–65

Area	1930	1940	1945	1950	1955	1960	1965
Hawaii	50	65	82	100	100	100	100
Queensland	20	20	33	54	83	85	85
Taiwan	–	32	46	56	10	4	42
Louisiana	0	23	52	77	65	65	–
Puerto Rico	0	9	12	10	3	35	50
Mauritius	–	8	53	98	93	78	–
South Africa	0	0	0	3	49	78	–

Source: *Annual Report,* Bureau of Sugar Experiment Stations, Queensland, Australia, various issues, 1928-1964; *Proceedings of the Twelfth Congress,* International Society of Sugarcane Technologists, New York, 1967, pp. 867, 1041; *Culture of Sugarcane for Sugar Production in Louisiana,* USDA Agriculture Handbook 262, Washington, D.C., 1964.

evident. Barbados, the British West Indies station, and Hawaii also have produced varieties which have been used extensively in other countries. Only one native variety, Badila of New Guinea, had any commercial importance during this period. The P.O.J. 2364 variety was never a significant commercial variety, but it was important as a parent to P.O.J. 2878 and several other varieties.

Table I.4 indicates the importance of the Coimbatore and Java stations in the generation of new varieties. The Java station has been especially productive of parent and grandparent varieties. Almost all the parent and grandparent varieties were produced in Java, Barbados, India, Hawaii and British Guiana—the successful Stage-II and -III stations. A number of additional stations such as Cuba, Canal Point (Florida), Queensland, South Africa, Taiwan, Mauritius,[6] Brazil, British Honduras, Puerto Rico, and Peru are now important in producing varieties as a result of Stage-IV activity.

[6] Also an important Stage-II station.

International transmission of varietal changes

Reference to Table I.3 indicates that the varieties of the major Stage-II and -III stations were in commercial production in many countries other than their country of origin. What is not obvious, however, is that the experiment station itself was an important factor in the international transmission of the P.O.J., Co., Hawaiian, and British West Indian varieties.

The South African case is instructive in this regard. The sugar industry in South Africa began in 1849. Prior to 1880 several wild varieties imported from Java, Mauritius, and India were cultivated. A wild variety, Uba, was introduced in 1883 and proved to be more disease resistant than the other varieties. For a period of fifty years it was the principal variety grown.

Some experimentation was carried on by planters to find new varieties during this fifty-year period. A number of potentially important Stage-II and -III varieties actually existed. However, it was not until an experiment station was financed by the growers and established at Mt. Edgecumbe that these Stage-II and -III varieties from Java and India were introduced. From 1925 until 1945 the accomplishments of this station were entirely confined to the introduction of new disease-resistant Stage-III varieties, mostly from Java and India.

The percentage of the South African crop consisting of these new varieties rose from 3.3 per cent in 1933–34 to 95.5 per cent in 1942–43, nine years later. An analysis of yield increases indicates that up to 1945 the new varieties introduced outyielded the old Uba variety by about 27 per cent.[7]

By 1947 the experiment station had produced its first South African variety, N:Co. 310 (the first N:Co. varieties were bred in India but the selections for commercial planting were made in South Africa). As

[7] This calculation adjusts for shifts in European and non-European grower percentages and a reduction in the number of ratoon crops (crops grown from the regrowth of the cane plant after cutting—as many as five or six ratoon crops were grown). Since yield declines with the number of ratoon crops harvested, an adjustment was made for the differential age of the Uba cane being phased out and the new varieties being planted. The ratooning, of course, saves the expense of planting cane. It is a factor which slows down the speed of adoption of new varieties.

TABLE I.3

Important Sugarcane Varieties: 1940–64

Variety	Station	Date Bred	No. of Countries where Produced Commercially	As Variety Quantity[a]	As Variety Rank	As Parent Quantity[a]	As Parent Rank	As Grandparent Quantity[a]	As Grandparent Rank
PoJ 2878	Java	1921	12	44.1	1	31.7	1	2.9	13
Co 290	India		7	14.7	2	7.4	7		
Co 213	India	1914	4	10.3	3	11.9	5	13.4	4
ML 318	Cuba	1930	1	10.0	4				
Pepe Cuca	Cuba	1930	1	10.0	5				
Co 331	India		3	8.1	6				
H 371933	Hawaii		3	7.2	7				
PoJ 2883	Java		4	7.1	8				
Co 419	India		3	6.6	9				
N Co 310	S. Africa		5	6.5	10				
Co 312	India		1	6.2	11	3.7	16		
BH 1012	Barbados	1910	4	4.8	12				
Co 313	India		1	4.6	13				
H 328560	Hawaii		3	4.6	14	8.6	6		
B 37161	Barbados		2	3.7	15				
Co 281	India		4	3.5	16	13.1	4		
Badila	(New Guinea) Native variety		1	3.4	17				
H 443098	Hawaii		2	3.1	18				
F 108	Taiwan		1	2.7	19				
PoJ 2364	Java	1911				27.1	2	18.6	2

EK 28	Java	1911		26.0	3	18.6	3
Co 221	India	1918		7.3	8	9.2	6
PoJ 213	Java	1893		6.8	9		
SC 124	Barbados	1912		6.4	10	2.9	14
Co 244	India			5.4	11	3.7	9
Co 291	India			5.1	12		
Co 421	India			4.5	13		
PoJ 2725	Java	1917		4.5	14		
Co 214	India	1914		4.0	15		
Co 270	India			3.0	17		
B 6835	Barbados			2.5	18	3.6	10
B 4578	Barbados			2.4	19	3.6	11
CP 1165	U.S.			2.2	20		
PoJ 100	Java		1			26.5	1
EK 2	Java					11.6	5
Co 206	India					6.6	7
D-74	Demerara					3.7	8
Co 205	India					3.3	12
Co 285	India					2.6	15

Source: *Yearbook of Agriculture*, USDA, Washington, 1936, pp. 561-624; *Proceedings of the Twelfth Congress*, International Society of Sugarcane Technologists, New York, 1967, pp. 844-54; *Agricultural Statistics*, USDA, Washington, various issues; J. T. Rao and Y. Vijayalakshmi, *Improved Canes in Cultivation*, New Delhi, 1967.
[a]Total production in millions of short tons, 1940-64.

TABLE I.4

Varietal Production of Various Sugarcane Experiment Stations: 1940–64
(millions of metric tons)

Experiment Station	Varieties Production[a]	Rank	Variety Parents Production[a]	Rank	Variety Grandparents Production[a]	Rank
Coimbatore, India	64.7	1	75.4	2	53.8	3
Java (P.O.J.)	63.4	2	102.3	1	113.6	1
Hawaii	24.9	3	18.1	4	16.8	4
Cuba	20.4	4	—	—	—	—
Barbados, B.W.I.	10.8	5	18.8	3	59.4	2
Canal Point, Fla.	10.3	6	4.5	6	4.2	7
Queensland	9.1	7	3.3	7	—	—
South Africa	7.3	8	.3	10	.3	9
Taiwan	4.2	9	—	—	—	—
Mauritius	4.2	10	1.7	9	6.0	6
Brazil	3.9	11	1.8	8	1.8	8
British Honduras	3.9	12	—	—	—	—
Puerto Rico	3.8	13	—	—	—	—
Peru	2.2	14	—	—	—	—
British Guiana	.2	15	8.5	5	12.2	5

Source: *Yearbook of Agriculture*, USDA, Washington, 1936, pp. 561-624; *Proceedings of the Twelfth Congress,* International Society of Sugarcane Technologists, New York, 1967, pp. 844-54; *Agricultural Statistics,* USDA, Washington, various issues.

[a]Total production, 1940-64.

shown in Table I.3, this variety came to be commercially produced in four other countries, most notably in Taiwan (a rarity for a Stage-IV cane variety); and from Table I.2 it can be seen that it, along with several additional N:Co. varieties, occupied 78 per cent of the planted acreage in South Africa by 1960. A yield comparison over a five-year period of the N:Co. varieties with the Stage-III varieties from India and Java, which they substantially replaced, showed a 28 per cent advantage for the locally bred canes.[8]

The South African experience with respect to the international transmission of the Stage-II and -III varieties (especially from Java and India) was repeated in most cane-producing countries which had not developed Stage-II and -III varieties. The experiment stations in Queensland, Puerto Rico, Taiwan, Mauritius, and several other countries were instrumental in the testing and introduction of these varieties into their local economies. The exhaustive collection and testing of varieties from other countries also served to provide a basis for the development of breeding programs in these newer stations.

In more recent years the Stage-IV varieties have dominated production in most countries, but only a limited number of these varieties are transferred to other countries. An important element of international transmission of technological change remains, however. Genetic materials such as newly selected seedlings, collections of wild canes, and parent stock varieties of proven merit are freely exchanged between stations. In addition, the technical knowledge regarding improved breeding techniques, superior genetic parent stock, and more efficient selection methods is exchanged.

Intracountry transmission of varietal changes

The South African case again is informative regarding the adoption of new varieties within a given sugar economy. The organization of the industry in South Africa is similar to the organization in a number of countries. Most planters have large acreages (200–1,000 acres) with substantial capital investment. Planters have highly structured relationships with the processing mills and are well organized. As one would

---

[8] The 28 per cent is calculated from actual yield comparisons of old and new varieties under similar production conditions.

expect in South Africa and in most other countries, the organizations of planters which support the experiment stations adopt the new varieties developed by these stations rather quickly. This rapid adoption is heightened by a sense of international competition in achieving comparative advantage in sugarcane production.

In South Africa the variety Co. 331 was introduced in 1946–47 and reached its highest proportion of planted acreage (25 per cent) just eight years later. N:Co. 310 was introduced in 1948–49 and reached its maximum proportion of planted acreage (60 per cent) nine years later. Given that the average age of old cane when ploughed out and replanted in South Africa is now six years, this would seem to be extremely rapid adoption. In fact, planters altered their usual cropping pattern in many cases by ploughing out old cane varieties earlier than usual in order to plant new varieties.

In Australia, each of the varieties, Q50, Pindar, Trojan, and P.O.J. 2878, reached a maximum proportion of planted acreage (25 per cent) approximately ten years after introduction. In Puerto Rico, BH 10-12, introduced in 1920, reached a maximum proportion of approximately 25 per cent fifteen years later. However, PR 980, a locally bred variety introduced in 1955, had reached a proportion of almost 50 per cent by 1965.

This rapid adoption of new varieties does not necessarily hold for all sectors of the sugar-producing economy. The Indian and native planters in South Africa produced yields only two-thirds as high as the European planters' yields in 1959. Planters with small holdings in Java and other countries also have lower yields than the estate or plantation planters. This is not necessarily a consequence of slower adoption of new varieties. India, a country with many small growers, has also experienced relatively rapid adoption of varieties. For example, in 1960 varieties Co. 527 and Co. 449 accounted for 6 per cent and 1 per cent of the acreage of Andra Pradesh. Seven years later the proportions were 14 per cent and 8 per cent, respectively [18].

Changes in sugar trade

Table I.5 presents trade data for sugar. It should be noted that roughly 40 per cent of the world's sugar production is from sugar beets.

TABLE I.5

Net Exports and Imports of Sugar by Countries, Selected Years[a]

Country	Annual Average (thousands of short tons)						
	1909-13	1922-23	1928-31	1937-39	1948-52	1958-62	1963-67
Exporters							
Cuba	2,009	4,725	3,885	2,947	5,790	6,102	5,859
Australia	-76	—	24	477	381	910	1,317
Philippine Islands	175	345	831	960	561	1,106	1,195
Taiwan	5	-20	—	56	413	850	922
Brazil	38	223	40	14	109	766	841
Mauritius	226	285	234	331	465	524	638
Dominican Republic	92	188	388	457	506	878	576
Jamaica	14	42	49	114	220	381	482
Peru	146	306	366	306	317	542	453
South Africa	-29	23	138	240	58	333	330
India	-689	-518[b]	-788	-64	-684	167	281
Indonesia	438	2,066	2,296	1,318	13	43	165
Argentina	-52	-54	9	31	-1,626	59	71
Importers							
U.S.A.	-2,081	-3,787	-2,982	-2,943	-3,521	-4,583	-3,853
U.K.	-821	-1,362	-2,062	-2,151	-1,574	-2,141	-2,036
Japan	-117	-162	-43	94	- 554	-1,429	-1,897
U.S.S.R.						-1,262	-1,723
Canada	-297	-100	-451	-485	-605	-748	-904
Malaysia	—	—	-100	-138	-170	-243	-360
Algeria	-38	-41	-77	-71	-133	-245	-287
New Zealand	-50	-73	-86	-90	-108	-135	-161

Notes to Table 1.5

Source: *Yearbook of Agriculture*, USDA, Washington, 1925-35; *Agricultural Statistics*, USDA, Washington, 1936-66; *International Yearbook of Agricultural Statistics*, Rome, various volumes 1910-46.

[a]Exports are positive numbers; imports are negative.
[b]1924.

With the exception of limited trading of beet sugar between Eastern European countries, world trade figures reflect movements of cane sugar.

The beet sugar production is important in the trade picture because virtually every beet-producing country has instituted a tariff or quota system, or both, to protect the domestic beet industry. The cost of such protection is high and has increased in recent years because of the relatively more rapid technological advances in sugarcane production.

Much sugar is traded under specific agreements between cooperating countries. Prior to 1961 the largest importing country, the United States, imported the bulk of its needs from Cuba, the largest exporting country. Since 1961 this U.S.-Cuban trade has ceased. The United States has allocated Cuba's former quota to other countries. Cuba has shifted her exports to Communist-bloc countries. The United Kingdom, the world's second leading importer, also has agreements with several exporting countries.

From time to time, international sugar agreements have been negotiated among countries in an attempt to control trade and production. They have been only partially effective. The "free" world market for sugar often has been a residual "dumping" market, and price changes have been volatile.

Tables I.1 and I.5 suggest a relationship between changes in sugarcane yields and changes in quantities exported by the major exporting countries. Five exporting countries, South Africa, India, Australia, Argentina, and Taiwan, had yield increases ranging from 32.5 per cent to 41 per cent between the five-year, 1948–52, average and the ten year, 1958–67, average. These five countries increased their average annual exports by 4,069,000 short tons of sugar in this period. This increase in exports was 103 per cent of the 1950 average production in these countries.

A second group of six countries, Philippines, Brazil, Peru, Indonesia, Mauritius, and the Dominican Republic, experienced yield increases ranging from 10 to 20 per cent in this period.[9] Their average annual exports increased by 2,079,000 short tons, 44 per cent of their 1950 average production. Only the Philippines had an export increase (65 per cent) on the order of magnitude of any of the five high-yield-increase countries. Cuba, on the other hand, experienced an actual yield decline for the same period and displayed an almost constant average export volume.[10]

This evidence supports the contention that shifts in comparative advantage have been reflected in the world sugar trade. This relationship is apparent even though world sugar trade has been dominated by (1) intercountry agreements, (2) shifts in the position of competing crops, and (3) changes in the degree of protection offered domestic beet sugar industries.[11]

[9] Indonesia (Java) experienced a yield decline after the 1930–40 period and sharp export reduction beginning in the 1930's and continuing until 1950 when both yields and exports began to increase. Many factors account for this pattern. Prior to the late 1930's Java was second only to Cuba as a sugar exporter and ranked third in production behind Cuba and India. Java and Hawaii had the world's highest sugarcane yields in the 1930's. Today yields in Java are less than half those of Hawaii. Java was acknowledged to have the world's most efficient and modern processing industry in 1930. The depression of the 1930's coincided with relatively high production levels for sugar (to a considerable degree induced by Java-bred canes). Java as the world's major "free" market supplier was forced to cut back exports substantially in 1933. She was not favored in the International Sugar Agreement developed at this time. Aware of the expansion in world supplies as a result of the Java varieties, the government attempted to prevent the release of any new varieties outside of the country. War and Japanese occupation followed the depression. Many of the processing mills were destroyed during this period. From 1945 to 1949 internal revolution took place. This was partially directed against the sugarcane-producing industry which was an integral part of the "dual" structure which existed prior to the war. As a result, by 1950 the processing industry was almost entirely destroyed, cane fields had reverted to jungle and other crops, and what surely was one of the most outstanding agricultural experiment stations in history was closed [5, 9, 34, 40, 45].

[10] Cuba is the only major cane-producing country to have a relatively weak experiment station. Only two commerically produced varieties have originated there. One of these, *pepe cuca,* is of unknown parentage and was produced by an unknown breeder [44].

[11] Factors other than varietal change will affect yields, of course. Yield increases often are due to the interaction of increase in fertilizer use, irrigation, and other inputs with new varieties. It is difficult to measure the extent to which the yield changes were due to new varieties, but it would appear to be the major factor.

Benefits from technological change in the production of sugarcane

The yield increases due to new sugarcane varieties have been substantial and have afforded great benefits to producing and consuming countries. The allocation of these benefits to the economic activity which produced them is difficult for several reasons. As this paper has shown, several different types of activity have been involved. The development of the Stage-II and -III varieties has clearly been important. These benefits must be allocated between the research effort which generated the varieties and the research, testing, and extension effort which speeded up their international transmission to countries other than the originating country.

The early Stage-II varieties were transferred easily, and little formal economic activity was associated with their transfer. New cultural practices were not required. Information regarding the relative profitability of producing the new variety was required, but informal information channels were available through growers' organizations to facilitate this transmission. Producer organizations have been keenly aware of their competitive position in world sugar trade and of their relative comparative advantage. This is one reason that substantial private effort to obtain information about new varieties took place. It also explains why in most countries producers have been willing to finance their own experiment stations privately.[12]

Stage-III varieties were more difficult to transfer because knowledge about specific disease resistance was required. Many new experiment stations (as well as the established stations) contributed to the transfer of these Stage-III varieties. In South Africa, as we have seen, the introduction of Stage-III varieties from other countries increased average yields by 27 per cent. If one wished to attribute this yield increase to the experiment station efforts, a handsome return to such investment could be calculated.[13] But only part of the value of this yield increase

---

[12] Most experiment stations for other agricultural crops have not been privately financed because producer groups have been too difficult to organize and no individual producer is large enough to capture the benefits from research.

[13] All sugarcane research costs in the South African experiment station to 1945 (the ending of the data from the period of introduction of Stage-II and -III varieties from other countries), accumulated at an interest rate of 6 per cent, amounted to 830,782 Rand. After subtracting seed costs associated with the new varieties, a stream of annual benefits can be calculated from the supply function

should be attributed to the experiment station effort since the varieties would eventually have been adopted without it. Also some of the experiment station effort was an investment in a Stage-IV breeding program.

The Stage-IV cane-breeding activity is somewhat more straightforward in terms of the allocation of benefits. Each station typically produces varieties planted only in the region where the station is located, and shifts in the production function and supply curve yield benefits to the producing country which can be attributed to the breeding effort of the local station.[14]

An additional complication is added to the assessment of benefits when one considers the possibility that international transfer of technology means that an experiment station may not only shift the production and supply functions of its own economy, but the production and supply functions of other economies as well. Thus, the exporting country's own demand function for exports will shift, probably to the left.

The Java case is an excellent example of this. The Java station was the leading generator of new varieties from 1900 to 1930. During most of this period, Java was enjoying an increasing relative advantage over other producing countries, including India, which was also a leading generator of new varieties, but whose own varieties were often better suited to other tropical countries than to northern India where much of her production was located. A "technology gap" had been created and reached its widest point around 1930. Yet Java was particularly

shift using a technique developed by Griliches [12]. These measured annual benefits also were accumulated at 6 per cent to 1945. Assuming no further increases in yield, an annual flow of benefits was calculated by assuming the 1945 yields to remain constant and adding to this flow 6 per cent of the accumulated benefits as of 1945. The resultant annual benefit flow was 2.47 times the accumulated research costs of 1945. This could be interpreted as a 247 per cent rate of returns to investment in research. But, for reasons discussed above, such an interpretation may not be correct [1, 8, 7, 11, 39].

[14] If one makes the same calculations and assumptions for the South African case as in footnote 13, except for the 1945–60 period when the station was contributing Stage-IV varieties to the economy, the annual benefit flow is 1.2 times the accumulated costs to 1960. This might more legitimately be interpreted as a 120 per cent rate of return to investment in research. Of course, if one chooses to express this as an "internal" rate of return, it would be much lower. The assumption that yields would remain constant is not fully justified. Yields tend to decline over time with new varieties. Even after making additional adjustments of this sort, we would have to conclude that the South African investment in research has yielded a very high return.

susceptible to the demand effect of this international transmission of her own varieties because of her position as the major free-market supplier. The demand for sugar declined in the early depression years and Java bore the brunt of the reduction in world trade.

II. BANANAS [15]

One of the most dramatic episodes in the long history of banana production and trade in the Central American tropics has been the development and international diffusion of new technologies in response to the devastating inroads of the Panama disease in bananas. In the twenty-year period following World War II, two major technological developments stand out. The first is the selection, diffusion, and adoption of disease-resistant banana varieties. The second is the invention and application of processing and handling techniques specifically designed to accommodate the physical and economic attributes of the new varieties.

The economic impact of this episode on other exporting nations whose banana farms and plantations were not ravaged by Panama disease illustrates side effects that can occur when important techno-logical change directly affects only some producers of an internationally traded commodity.

The postwar setting

During World War II, international trade in bananas shrank drastically because of the extreme shortage of refrigerated, ocean-going ships. But, as Table II.1 indicates when shipping became available after the war, banana production and exports rebounded quickly, attaining prewar levels by the 1948–52 period.

Banana exports from Central America dominated the world trade

[15] Much of the background material for this section is drawn from H. B. Arthur, J. P. Houck and G. L. Beckford, *Tropical Agribusiness: Structures and Adjustments—Bananas*, Harvard Business School, 1968. That study as well as this discussion relies heavily on data kindly provided by private trade sources, especially United Fruit Company and Standard Fruit and Steamship Company. Professor H. B. Arthur of the Harvard Business School offered helpful suggestions on this section of the paper.

TABLE II.1

World Exports of Bananas from South America, Central America,
and the Rest of the World; Five-Year Averages: 1935–39 to 1963–67
(thousands of metric tons)

Region	1935–39	1948–52	1953–57	1958–62	1963–67[a]
Central America[b]	1,130.2	1,157.9	1,120.1	1,227.8	1,401.7
South America[c]	425.4	532.8	974.8	1,424.4	1,739.6
Rest of the World	746.4	640.6	953.5	1,328.0	1,781.9
Total	2,302.0	2,331.3	3,048.4	3,980.2	4,923.2

Source: Food and Agriculture Organization, United Nations (CCP Study Group on Bananas); *Foreign Agriculture Circular,* FDAP-1-67, FAS, USDA, October 1967.

[a]Includes preliminary data for 1967.

[b]Costa Rica, Dominican Republic, Guatemala, Honduras, Mexico, Nicaragua, Panama.

[c]Ecuador, Colombia, Brazil.

picture, accounting for about half the total during the period 1948–52. Most of these Central American shipments went to the United States and Canada. (At this time the United States purchased about two-thirds of all the world's banana exports.) But largely because of rising banana production in Ecuador, South American exports surpassed their prewar levels in the 1948–52 period.

International banana prices were relatively high in this period, and the stage seemed to be set for orderly and profitable growth in the world banana market. United Fruit Company and Standard Fruit and Steamship Company, the two major, fully integrated, banana producing and marketing firms operating in the American tropics, resumed activities on much the same basis as before the war by reactivating and adding to their war-idled resources. These two U.S. firms—United Fruit was by far the larger—had operated plantations, export facilities, and a host of community services (roads, railroads, schools, hospitals, etc.) in Central America since the early 1900's, and their combined banana output accounted for all but a small portion of Central American production.[16] Together, United Fruit and Standard Fruit held 90 per cent to 95 per cent of the U.S. import market during the period 1948–52.

Over the years, these two companies, especially United Fruit, had conducted long-range research programs on banana production and marketing technology. The financing of these continuing programs has varied over time as circumstances in the industry have changed. But the research done by these firms is both basic and applied. In fact, much of the world's scientific and practical knowledge about bananas has been generated by these privately sponsored research programs.

Panama disease

Bananas are subject to a host of deadly plant diseases. Although most now can be controlled, several diseases, at one time or another, have threatened the very existence of large areas of commercial farms and plantations. For example, in the 1930's the rapid spread of sigatoka disease, a wind-borne, leaf-destroying fungus, decimated large banana tracts in Central America. It threatened to wipe out the whole industry. However, frantic research, mainly by United Fruit Company technicians, uncovered an effective treatment based on periodic applications of Bordeaux mixture suspended in water [25, p. 154]. By 1939, most large banana plantations were equipped with elaborate, permanent networks of pipes and spray facilities.[17] In Mexico, where large-scale sigatoka control was not undertaken, partly because of the small size of individual banana farms, this disease virtually killed off the banana industry by 1950.

But no really effective treatment has yet been found for Panama disease. This soil-borne fungus (fusarium wilt) invades the soil, attacks the root system of the susceptible plant, and causes a breakdown in the vascular flow of water and nutrients [37, Chap. 13]. The result is stunting and eventual destruction of the infected plant. Though Panama disease spreads more slowly than sigatoka, the organism remains in-

---

[16] Private producers tied to one or the other of the major companies through production contracts, credit arrangements, and disease control programs are considered as part of company production for this discussion.

[17] Further research and field experience has shown that sigatoka control can be achieved throuᵬh application of either an oil-based or a low-volume organic fungicide spray delivered by aircraft or knapsack sprayer. This development, occurring in the 1950's, has eliminated the need for the cumbersome water-spray installations of the earlier era.

definitely in the soil, rendering infected areas useless for future production of susceptible varieties.

Panama disease does not attack all varieties of bananas; some are highly resistant. However, the Gros Michel variety is quite susceptible. This variety is the traditional commercial banana of Central and South America. Its handling, ripening, and flavor qualities have long been prized by banana men. But it has not been possible to develop a Gros Michel banana with disease resistance. Because, botanically, the banana is a giant herb growing from an underground rhizome, crossbreeding and other known techniques of producing new varieties with selected characteristics of existing varieties are very difficult to apply.

Efforts to "purify" infected acreage by flooding it with water for periods up to a year have proven only temporarily effective. This technique, known as flood fallowing, is very costly and provides immunity from reinfection from only one to five years, depending on soil type and other environmental factors.

Panama disease was identified and widely known in tropical America as early as 1900. Its spread was gradual but inexorable throughout the region's banana lands. By World War II only a few areas, notably Ecuador and Colombia, seemed relatively free of the disease. Since no effective treatment could be found, the spread of the disease was partially offset by abandonment of infected areas. New plantings were then established on previously uncultivated sites. This was a workable practice until the period after World War II when banana production began to exceed prewar levels.

By the 1948–52 period, Panama disease was pervasive, especially in Central America. Relocating and replanting whole farms and plantations had become prohibitively costly. In addition, good disease-free banana land, accessible to existing handling and shipping facilities, was becoming very scarce. United Fruit Company has estimated that since 1900 some 925,000 acres of banana land have been abandoned, mostly because of Panama disease. This averages about 14,000 acres per year. These average annual abandonments amounted to about 10 per cent of United Fruit's owned and controlled banana acreage in the early 1950's. For instance, United Fruit's Quepos Division in Costa Rica had about 25,000 acres in banana production in 1947. By 1956, Panama disease had wiped out all production.

Officials of both United Fruit and Standard Fruit were extremely reluctant to consider abandoning the Gros Michel banana, even though the ravages of Panama disease had reached a critical stage and research on feasible control methods was not especially promising.

The critical stage

The period 1948–52 was the start of the critical stage in the Central American banana industry's confrontation with Panama disease. From this period into the middle and late 1950's the area's banana production and exports dropped. The data in Table II.2 indicate the downward slide in acreage from 1948–52 to 1958–62, and the stagnation in Central American exports in this period is indicated by the data in Table II.1. Abandonments, due principally to Panama disease, exceeded replantings in three of the four major producing countries—Guatemala, Honduras, and Costa Rica. Only Panama showed increased acreage. There, a 12,000-acre flood fallow and replanting program was begun by United Fruit Company in 1950. This experiment was designed to revive one of the company's plantations which had lain idle since Panama disease wiped out production in 1936.

The charts in Figure 1 show banana exports for these four nations annually and as a five-year moving average for about forty years.[18]

TABLE II.2

Areas of Cultivation of Exportable Bananas in Central America:
Five-year Averages 1948–52, 1953–57, and 1958–63

(thousands of acres)

Country	1948–52	1953–57	1958–63
Guatemala	46.7	39.3	31.3
Honduras	55.8	53.5	43.5
Costa Rica	42.8	39.0	30.6
Panama	19.2	26.0	30.8

Note: Major companies and their associated growers only.
Source: Data supplied by major fruit companies.

[18] During this period, Guatemala, Honduras, Costa Rica, and Panama accounted for about 95 per cent of all Central American banana shipments.

FIGURE 1

Volume of Banana Exports from Four Central American Countries, 1925–64
(metric tons)

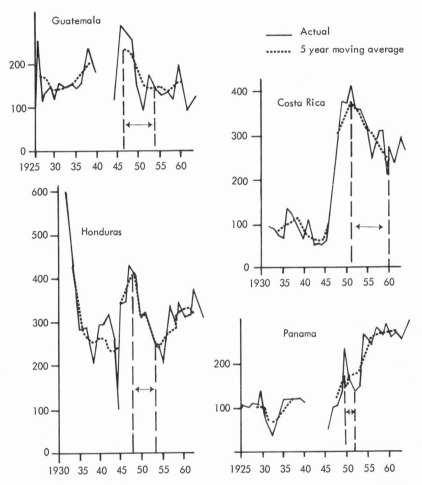

Note: Breaks in Panama and Guatemala indicate that no information is available for the relevant period.

Source: U.N. Food and Agriculture Organization

The drop in exports that can be attributed almost entirely to inroads of Panama disease is shown between the vertical dotted lines. Even in Panama, where the production and export trend generally increased in the 1950's, a major export drop occurred between 1950 and 1952 as the flood fallow and replanting program got underway.

As Central American production faltered in the 1950's, Table II.1 shows that exports from other sources expanded substantially. Banana exports from South America, Ecuador and Colombia, are most relevant in this expansion, because almost all the other major banana exporters operate under the protection of preferential arrangements with major importers (e.g., Jamaica and the Windward Islands with the United Kingdom, Guadeloupe and Martinique with France, the Canary Islands with the Spanish mainland). The dramatic surge of Ecuadorian and Colombian banana shipments to replace lagging Central American exports is shown in Figure 2.

As mentioned previously, both Ecuador and Colombia produced mainly the Gros Michel variety but were relatively free of Panama disease in this period. Colombian bananas were shipped mainly to Western Europe, and up to two-thirds of Ecuador's exports came to the United States where, by 1959, they accounted for over 40 per cent of all U.S. banana imports. Ecuadorian bananas easily filled the gap left by the dwindling supplies and rising costs of Central American bananas. Growing markets, abundant land, and government encouragement fueled this tremendous growth in output. The major banana companies, United Fruit and Standard Fruit, participated in this Ecuadorian expansion mainly as shipping and marketing agents—United Fruit's single, small producing division in that country was expropriated in the early 1960's. Since then, the Government of Ecuador has effectively discouraged the formation of additional foreign-controlled plantations.

A number of smaller exporting and marketing firms, operating with Ecuadorian supplies, flourished during this period. As a result, the combined U.S. market share of the two producing-marketing companies dropped to about 70 per cent in 1959. Ecuadorian banana quality was uneven; seasonal variations in output were sharp. In addition, an export tax was levied, and shipping charges exceeded those for Central American fruit. Yet the demand for Ecuadorian bananas surged ahead as the Central American producers struggled with Panama disease.

During the early portion of this critical stage it seemed likely that, barring a massive Panama disease outbreak, Ecuador soon might corner the relatively open banana markets in North America, Western Europe,

FIGURE 2

Volume of Banana Exports From Ecuador and Colombia, 1925–64
(metric tons)

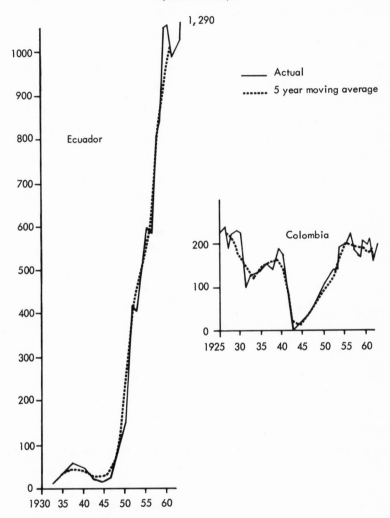

Source: U.N. Food and Agriculture Organization

and elsewhere. Without a major cost-reducing shift in banana production technology, the invested capital, land resources, production knowledge, and skill in quality control of the integrated companies in Central

America might become virtually worthless. Moreover, an important source of vital foreign exchange and tax revenue for the four Central American nations would wither.[19] The companies and their host governments were in trouble with bananas, and they knew it.

Resistant varieties: selection and adoption

Although the Central American trade was built on Gros Michel bananas, a number of Panama-resistant varieties were known to scientists and grown commercially in other areas. The banana industries of Jamaica, French West Indies, Canary Islands, Australia, and others, were based on resistant varieties belonging to the Cavendish group. These varieties had been shunned by the major producing companies because of supposedly lower yields, poorer handling and ripening qualities, and somewhat different management requirements. Another important factor, no doubt, was simply resistance to change within the companies. The firms' producing, shipping, and marketing divisions knew precisely how to grow, transport, and merchandise Gros Michel. Much would have to be relearned if new varieties were adopted.

Resistance to a variety switch gave way faster in the smaller Standard Fruit and Steamship Company, due perhaps to a major management change in 1953 and the existence of smaller disease-free land reserves under company control in producing areas. By 1957, Standard had planted fourteen to fifteen thousand acres in bananas of the Cavendish group. These varieties were selected by researchers from those available in the Caribbean, Africa, and elsewhere. Over time, Standard Fruit researchers focused their attention on one of these varieties, the Giant Cavendish.

In 1960, United Fruit Company botanists began to look seriously at a disease-resistant variety called the Valery, a member of the Cavendish group, which was being grown on the firm's experimental farm in Honduras. This plant had been collected originally in Vietnam by a company expedition several years earlier. In 1962 a major company decision was made to move rapidly into Valery plantings. Even with the problems of multiplying and distributing new seed stock, virtually

[19] In 1955–57, bananas accounted for 13, 34, 54, 72 per cent of export revenues for Guatemala, Costa Rica, Honduras, and Panama, respectively (see Table II.4).

all production by Standard and the majority of United's was in disease-resistant varieties by 1965.

Once begun, the adoption and diffusion of Giant Cavendish and Valery bananas spread quickly. However, this pattern of development and rapid diffusion of disease-resistant varieties should not be interpreted as a clear indication that rapid technical change in tropical agriculture is most likely in sectors or industries dominated by large plantations and vertically integrated firms capable of internal research and development. The diffusion process in the Central American banana case was indeed rapid. But the long delay by the managements of the major companies in selecting, adopting, and marketing resistant strains was nearly disastrous for them. On the other hand, the shift to Cavendish-type bananas already had occurred in the West Indian banana industries of Jamaica, Windward Islands, Guadeloupe and Martinique—areas where small holders and public research facilities predominate.

Diffusion of Giant Cavendish and Valery bananas in Central America was spurred not only by the monolithic decision structures of the two large firms but because of several unexpected advantages with the new fruit which were not apparent at first. As the new varieties were put into commercial production in the Central American lowlands—probably the world's best over-all banana-growing environment—per acre yields were higher than anticipated and even higher than Gros Michel yields.[20]

Heavier bunches and higher planting densities contributed to this yield advantage. Because the new varieties are lower growing, the constant danger of losses due to "blowdowns" is reduced below that for the lankier Gros Michel plants.[21] Though it had always been generally assumed that the Gros Michel was the best-tasting banana in world commerce, some test results in the United States in the early 1960's showed that properly handled and properly ripened Valery bananas were distinctly superior in flavor and aroma to Gros Michel.

However, the skeptics had correctly foreseen a major problem with the new varieties. Bananas of the Cavendish group were not well suited to the commercial methods of handling and shipping then in use. In

[20] The term "new varieties" is not meant to suggest that the adopted varieties were genetically or botanically new. They were simply new to commercial production and export from these areas.

[21] The major companies expected to lose an average of 20 to 25 per cent of their mature Gros Michel banana plants annually due to blowdowns.

the 1950's and early 1960's bananas from Central and South America were still handled as whole stems (bunches) from the moment of harvest until ripening was completed in the importing country. Individual stems, protected by only a thin plastic film bag, were handled up to a dozen separate times en route to the wholesale fruit dealer. The Gros Michel is well suited to this system. However, the individual fingers of fruit on the new varieties are more easily bruised in the green stage than are the Gros Michel. Furthermore, the banana clusters on the new varieties do not lie as close to the stem's center stalk as on the Gros Michel. Hence, they are more easily damaged. With all the handling of exposed stems built into traditional techniques, quality control with the new varieties was very difficult in comparison with the established Gros Michel.

When the first yields of the new varieties were coming onto the North American market, Standard Fruit Company encountered severe quality problems. Outright rejections on arrival were quite high. In addition, prices for the new variety fruit were discounted by wholesale buyers because many banana quality problems do not show up until the fruit is fully ripened and ready for retail merchandising.[22] Standard's response to these quality-control problems probably saved the company and set off a market-induced technological shift that is revolutionizing banana handling in virtually all international markets.

Tropical boxing

During the reign of the Gros Michel in Central and South America, almost all shipments to North American and European markets were cargoes of stem fruit. Bananas remained on the stem until the ripening process was completed in local markets by specialized ripeners, wholesale fruit jobbers, and chain stores. These establishments, of which there were about 1,600 in the United States in 1955, also cut the individual clusters (hands) from the stem, packed them in returnable cartons, and merchandised them to retailers. So, in addition to ripening and retail distribution, these firms performed an important sorting, grading, and packaging function.

---

[22] Legal restrictions prevent the major importing companies from operating their own ripening and distribution facilities. An ownership transfer occurs for virtually all U.S. banana imports at dockside.

In the early 1960's, Standard Fruit began to experiment with the system of cutting, washing, sorting, and packaging individual clusters into 40-pound, labeled, cardboard boxes in the tropics near their production and shipping facilities. The boxed fruit was then shipped to wholesale buyers in the importing country. Under this system, ripeners in the importing country relinquished the cutting and packing functions and part or all of the sorting and grading function, but they retained the ripening and retail distribution functions.

Acceptance of this innovation was unexpectedly rapid in many parts of the U.S. market. Boxed bananas are more easily handled with the typical rail, truck, and warehouse machinery, and the new variety fruit is less likely to be bruised in boxes. Like all other firms in the food-marketing sector, ripeners and jobbers were under severe economic pressure to become larger and more efficient. With boxed bananas, they found that they could reduce per unit costs by eliminating a series of labor-intensive processes and increase the volumes handled. In addition, retailers were pleased with the nonreturnable, one-way cardboard carton. From the producing company's viewpoint, more fruit could be salvaged all along the way than under the old system where whole stems had to be discarded if a single cluster was damaged or had become prematurely yellow. Moreover, the specialized loading and unloading equipment at the seaports was still usable, with some modification, for boxed fruit. Further experience has shown that boxed bananas can be stowed more efficiently in refrigerated cargo ships, and elimination of the center stalk, which is about 15 per cent of the weight of stem bananas, reduces the shipping costs per unit of usable fruit.

The demand by wholesalers for boxed bananas grew so rapidly in the United States that United Fruit Company, which was still shipping Gros Michel in 1962, was forced to develop its own tropical boxing facilities even before its Valery production began. Smaller independent importers, buying on the Ecuadorian market, began to establish boxing facilities in and near the producing regions in order to supply their U.S. customers with boxed fruit, even though their bananas were also Gros Michel variety. Table II.3 shows that in a matter of only four years boxed bananas went from an insignificant portion of the U.S. market to a majority of all imports.

TABLE II.3

Percentage of U.S. Imports of Bananas Arriving as Boxed Fruit: 1960—66

Year	Per Cent in Boxes
1960	2
1961	15
1962	30
1963	50
1964	85
1965	96
1966	99

Source: Estimated from data supplied by major importers.

The trend toward tropical boxing of export fruit is being accelerated in Ecuador. In response to new inroads of Panama disease in Gros Michel plantings, the Ecuadorian government has prohibited new plantings of this susceptible variety [43, p. 21]. Only varieties from the Cavendish group may be used for new farms or for replanting existing farms.

Standard Fruit Company adopted the tropical boxing technology in order to offset quality and handling problems stemming from its earlier decision to adopt the disease-resistant variety, and, as a result, United Fruit and the others adopted the boxing technology much earlier than they would have had to on purely technical grounds. The economic impact of the boxing technology on retail and wholesale channels required Standard Fruit's competitors to begin tropical boxing in order to maintain their previous market position. Several intermediate production processes—cutting, sorting, and boxing—shifted from the developed importing nation to the less developed producing and exporting nations, and new box-making plants came into operation in Central America and Ecuador. Furthermore, the nature of the actual product moving in international commerce was altered from an essentially unprocessed primary product to a commodity substantially closer to the final product sold to consumers.

Economic impacts of innovation

An economist looking at the impact of the disease-resistant varieties in Central America could argue that, as Panama disease spread through the region, the production function for bananas based on traditional inputs shifted slowly but surely downward. Output per unit of the usual inputs eroded at all levels of input application. The main objective of early decisions to adopt new varieties seems to have been to halt this erosion of the function and to stabilize it, even if stabilization was achieved at lower output levels than with Gros Michel. But as the resistant varieties were adopted in the lush Central American banana zone, experience suggested that the production function might be restored to predisease levels and perhaps even beyond them. The extent of this shift is not yet fully known. However, it seems likely that the adoption of new varieties will result in a net increase in the production function for Central American bananas as compared with the disease-free Gros Michel output relationship.

The erosion of banana production relationships in Central America throughout the 1950's no doubt strengthened Ecuador's comparative advantage in banana production and export. This shift in comparative advantage was accelerated by deteriorating production relationships and prices for Ecuadorian cacao and by the slow growth of that nation's coffee-producing industry [46, Chap. 2]. Much of the banana boom in Ecuador during this period can be attributed to this alteration in comparative advantage *vis-a-vis* Central America. Adoption of new varieties has apparently halted this trend and, in fact, may be instrumental in restoring Central America to its preeminent position in the world banana trade.

Tropical boxing of bananas was undertaken initially to facilitate the shift to new varieties. The objective was to maintain quality and reduce waste and transit loss. In effect, the boxing of bananas near the production area was at first a method of sustaining the production function, in terms of output of *marketable* fruit, at levels higher than otherwise would have been the case. The rapid adoption of this new technique in the producing areas where Gros Michel still rules indicates it is a net cost-reducing procedure for bananas moving into the relatively sophisticated marketing channels of North America and Western Europe.

Some calculations for 1963, when stem and boxed bananas shared the U.S. market about equally, indicate that on an equivalent basis and in terms of usable fruit, boxed banana import prices received by major importers were about 13 per cent higher than stem prices. About $1.00 per hundredweight of the approximately $10.00 of value added to boxed bananas from harvest to retail was transferred from establishments in the United States to establishments in producing areas.[23] Though this is only a rough approximation, it does indicate that in terms of foreign exchange earnings and jobs tropical boxing is a significant international shift in handling technology.

The development of box-making and assembly plants in the producing areas, though still in its early stages, can be expected to increase employment and economic growth in those areas. New capital for banana carton factories in Central and South America ran above $50 million in the period 1960–66. This added industrial activity is a direct result of the adoption and diffusion of the banana-boxing technology.

It is clear that the resurgence of the Central American banana industry in response to these two major innovations—the shift in production to new or improved varieties and the tropical boxing technology—has slowed down and altered the growth and development of the Ecuadorian industry. The export data illustrated in Figure 2 indicate this began to occur in the early 1960's. A slowdown of the growth in export volume and continued downward pressure on world prices have resulted in a stagnation in Ecuadorian banana export earnings since about 1963. Banana exports and earnings for Colombia, the other major South American supplier, continue to show only slow growth as Central American boxed bananas become more and more competitive in the European markets which have been Colombia's major outlets.

The data in Table II.4 show the exchange earnings and relative importance of banana exports for Central America and Ecuador in three periods: 1955–57, 1959–61, and 1964–66. The growth in other Ecuadorian export industries reduced that nation's dependence on bananas somewhat since the peak period in 1959–61 and helped to

---

[23] This assumes that the availability of both stem and boxed fruit from the relatively open market in Ecuador kept import prices reasonably close to competitive levels.

TABLE II.4

Value of Banana Exports and Per Cent[a] *of Total Exports Accounted for by Bananas in Four Central American Countries and Ecuador*

Country	Annual average		
	1955−57	1959−61	1964−66
Costa Rica			
Banana exports (mil. dollars)	26.1	20.1	28.6
Per cent of total exports	34	25	24
Guatemala			
Banana exports (mil. dollars)	15.5	15.3	6.5
Per cent of total exports	13	14	3
Honduras			
Banana exports (mil. dollars)	34.0	31.4	53.1
Per cent of total exports	54	46	44
Panama			
Banana exports (mil. dollars)	24.3	20.6	37.8
Per cent of total exports	72	67	48
Ecuador			
Banana exports (mil. dollars)	63.4	86.4	90.1
Per cent of total exports	50	62	52

Source: *International Financial Statistics,* International Monetary Fund, Vols. 15, 17, and 21, and U.S. Department of Agriculture, Foreign Agriculture Service.

[a]Percentages are based on three-year totals.

offset the shift of comparative advantage in bananas back to Central America. Banana earnings in the 1960's generally increased for all the major Central American exporters except Guatemala. However, some new Valery plantings by United Fruit Company in Guatemala are beginning to produce marketable fruit. They will partially offset previous abandonments caused by Panama disease.

Dependence upon bananas for foreign exchange, while still extremely important for several of these nations, especially Ecuador, Panama, and Honduras, declined for all these countries after 1959–61 and for all but Ecuador after 1955–57. In the late 1960's it appeared that much of the future growth in the production and boxing of bananas would be focused in Honduras, Panama, and Costa Rica, because these nations seemed to provide the best over-all environment for the production of disease-resistant varieties and the packing and shipping of boxed bananas to world markets.[24] Both United Fruit and Standard Fruit were engaged in major production-expanding programs with disease-resistant varieties in Honduras. United Fruit, the only major exporter of Panamanian bananas, was expanding Valery output on its fully-owned plantations. In addition, United was being relatively successful with an expanding associate producer program in Central America. (Associate producers grew bananas under contract with United Fruit Company. They received basic services, facilities, and credit from the company, but had to follow specified production practices laid out by the company.) Substantial expansion of production in Costa Rica was being planned, especially by Standard.

Banana prices in several major importing nations drifted downward after the late 1950's. Retail prices in the United States, Canada, and West Germany have dropped about 10 per cent since 1958; "real" prices of course dropped further [42, p. 22], [41, p. 8]. Increased supplies due to the new varieties and the adoption of tropical boxing have intensified the long-run tendency for supplies to increase faster than demand, so that at least part of these price declines can be attributed to technological changes as well as to increased plantings and better management. Measuring the price impact of these changes is difficult, but perhaps the following suggests the magnitudes.

FAO projections of world banana supplies for 1965–70 foresaw an increase of about 40 per cent in the period [26]. Approximately one-third of this increase will come from Central America. If it is assumed that Central American production would remain constant (or possibly decline) in the absence of the technical innovations discussed here, then the effect of these additional supplies on international banana prices is an approximate measure of the price impact of technical change in this area. It is only an approximation, of course, and probably an overestimation since export supplies from other sources, principally

---

[24] There are other economic and political considerations which also favor banana expansion in these countries, but they are beyond the scope of this discussion.

Ecuador, probably would have expanded faster in the absence of Central American competition than they actually will. In any case, the additional supplies from Central America in the last half of the 1960's will exert a downward pressure on retail prices approximately equivalent to 20 per cent of 1965–66 levels. That is, in the absence of any expansion in Central America and assuming all other export availabilities remain as projected, the retail banana prices in world markets would average in 1970 some 10 per cent below 1965–66 levels. When the projected increase in Central American supplies is added, then average retail prices some 30 per cent below 1965–66 levels are required to balance amounts demanded with projected export availabilities [26, Table III.4]. Any supply response to these lower prices naturally would offset at least some of this indicated downward pressure on retail prices. In addition, it is likely that consumers will benefit not only from lower prices but also from the expected rise in average banana quality resulting from the increased use of tropical boxing in most markets.

As in the past, economists and historians will continue to debate the role and contribution of the banana industry to the growth and development of tropical America. Their analyses will have to encompass the long-run impacts of the diffusion and adoption of these two interconnected technological innovations.

III. RICE

In this section [25] an attempt is made to analyze the complex set of technical and economic interactions associated with (1) the diffusion of Japanese rice production technology to Taiwan and Korea, (2) the impact of productivity growth in rice production on rice trade between Japan and Taiwan and Korea, and (3) the impact of rice imports from these two colonial areas on rice prices and production in metropolitan Japan. Specifically, we will test two hypotheses advanced by several Japanese scholars: the transfer of rice production technology from Japan to Taiwan and Korea was responsible for the expansion of exports

[25] The authors are indebted to Yujiro Hayami, Ramon H. Myers, James I. Nakamura, and Henry Rosovsky for review and criticism of an earlier draft of this section of the paper and to Aida Recto and John Sanders for assistance in the statistical tabulation and calculations.

TABLE III.1

*Annual Growth Rates of Output, Inputs, and Productivity in
Japanese Agriculture: 1882–1957*
(per cent per year)

	Phase I (1882-1917)	Phase II (1917-37)	Phase III (1937-47)	Phase IV (1947-57)
Output				
Gross output	1.78	.80	-2.79	4.51
Net output	1.37	.69	-1.78	2.14
Conventional inputs				
Total inputs	.28	.28	-.03	1.41
Labor	.20	.01	1.83	-1.36
Fixed capital				
Including building	.43	.52	-.46	1.70
Excluding building	1.66	1.24	-1.44	3.62
Variable inputs	2.93	1.15	-6.76	12.02
Land acreage total	.60	.15	-.54	.35
Paddy field	.27	.34	-.43	.31
Upland field	1.02	.05	-.67	.39
Productivity per unit of				
Conventional inputs	1.49	.49	-2.77	3.05
Labor	1.86	.81	-4.54	5.84
Fixed capital				
Including building	1.34	.27	-2.35	2.76
Excluding building	.11	-.44	-1.37	.85
Variable inputs	-1.12	-.45	4.25	-6.71
Land	1.17	.64	-2.27	4.14

Source: Saburo Yamada [47], pp. 371-413.

from the colonial areas to metropolitan Japan; these exports in turn
depressed rice prices and dampened the growth of productivity and
farm income in metropolitan Japan.[26]

An alternative hypothesis which might be advanced is that the technical
potential, in the form of biological and chemical innovations, for
continued rapid technical advance in Japanese agriculture was not

[26] "The years after 1920 were difficult years for Japanese agriculture. Cheap
rice began to be imported from Korea and Formosa, where rice cultivation had
been encouraged by the Japanese government following the food shortage of
World War I and the rice riots that resulted in 1918" [36, p. 334].

created during the interwar period. This hypothesis apparently has not been seriously examined in Japan.

Output and productivity growth in Japanese agriculture

The rate of output and productivity growth in Japanese agriculture has varied widely during the one hundred years of "modernization" following the start of the Meiji period in 1868. As outlined in Table III.1, four main periods, sometimes called "technical epochs," are frequently identified. As indicated in Tables III.2 and III.3, the first was

TABLE III.2

Paddy Rice Yields in Japan, 1873–1922; Five-Year Averages of Official and Corrected Figures

	Official Estimates[a]	Yamada – Hayami Estimates[b]	Nakamura Estimates[c]		
			(1)	(2)	(3)
	Koku Per Tan of Brown Rice[d]				
Period					
1873–77	–	–	1.500	1.600	1.700
1878–82	1.166	1.264	1.549	1.636	1.721
1883–87	1.297	1.355	1.599	1.672	1.743
1888–92	1.428	1.425	1.651	1.709	1.764
1893–97	1.371	1.371	1.705	1.747	1.786
1898–1902	1.516	1.516	1.760	1.786	1.808
1903–07	1.626	1.626	1.817	1.826	1.831
1908–12	1.734	1.734	1.876	1.867	1.854
1913–17	1.843	1.843	1.937	1.908	1.877
1918–22	1.927	1.927	2.000	1.950	1.900
Annual average growth rate	1.3	*Per Cent* 1.1	0.6	0.4	0.2

[a]Ministry of Agriculture and Forestry, Agricultural Forestry Economics Bureau, Statistical Section, Reported by Nakamura [27; pp. 66, 228-30].

[b]Kazushi Ohkawa, *et al., Estimates of Long Term Economic Statistics of Japan Since 1868,* Vol. 9, Tokyo, 1963, p. 67.

[c][27; p. 92].

[d]One koku equals 150 kilograms; one tan equals 0.0992 hectares.

TABLE III.3

Production, Area, and Yield of Brown Rice in Japan: 1900–40

Year	Production[a] (thousand metric tons)			Area Planted[b] (thousand hectares)			Yield per Hectare (kilograms)		
	Total	Paddy	Upland	Total	Paddy	Upland	Total	Paddy	Upland
1900–01	6,220	6,122	98	2,805	2,731	74	2,217	2,242	1,325
1901–02	7,037	6,929	108	2,824	2,745	79	2,492	2,525	1,366
1902–03	5,540	5,449	91	2,824	2,740	83	1,962	1,989	1,090
1903–04	6,971	6,872	99	2,840	2,755	85	2,454	2,494	1,162
1904–05	7,713	7,627	86	2,857	2,774	82	2,700	2,749	1,046
1905–06	5,726	5,637	89	2,858	2,783	74	2,004	2,025	1,195
1906–07	6,945	6,842	103	2,875	2,799	77	2,416	2,444	1,363
1907–08	7,358	7,238	120	2,882	2,804	78	2,553	2,581	1,531
1908–09	7,790	7,658	132	2,898	2,815	83	2,688	2,720	1,594
1909–10	7,866	7,732	134	2,914	2,827	86	2,699	2,735	1,545
1910–11	6,996	6,855	140	2,925	2,834	91	2,392	2,419	1,526
1911–12	7,757	7,602	154	2,949	2,852	97	2,630	2,665	1,599
1912–13	7,533	7,389	144	2,978	2,869	109	2,530	2,575	1,322
1913–14	7,539	7,374	165	3,005	2,886	118	2,509	2,555	1,392
1914–15	8,551	8,381	170	3,008	2,886	122	2,842	2,904	1,383
1915–16	8,389	8,189	200	3,031	2,907	124	2,767	2,817	1,607
1916–17	8,768	8,534	234	3,046	2,918	128	2,879	2,924	1,831
1917–18	8,185	8,015	170	3,058	2,928	130	2,677	2,738	1,309
1918–19	8,205	8,022	184	3,067	2,935	132	2,675	2,733	1,392
1919–20	9,123	8,887	236	3,079	2,943	136	2,963	3,019	1,741
1920–21	9,481	9,205	276	3,101	2,960	140	3,058	3,105	1,969
1921–22	8,277	8,055	222	3,109	2,968	141	2,662	2,714	1,572
1922–23	9,104	8,907	203	3,115	2,972	143	2,923	2,995	1,420

Year									
1923–24	8,317	8,120	197	3,121	2,982	139	2,664	2,723	1,411
1924–25	8,576	8,425	150	3,117	2,980	137	2,752	2,827	1,101
1925–26	8,956	8,716	239	3,128	2,993	135	2,863	2,913	1,768
1926–27	8,339	8,150	189	3,132	2,996	136	2,662	2,720	1,385
1927–28	9,315	9,083	232	3,147	3,013	134	2,960	3,014	1,731
1928–29	9,045	8,812	233	3,165	3,030	136	2,858	2,909	1,719
1929–30	8,934	8,802	132	3,184	3,050	134	2,806	2,886	979
1930–31	10,031	9,790	242	3,212	3,079	133	3,123	3,179	1,812
1931–32	8,282	8,098	184	3,222	3,089	133	2,571	2,622	1,383
1932–33	9,058	8,852	206	3,230	3,097	133	2,804	2,858	1,549
1933–34	10,624	10,439	185	3,147	3,022	124	3,376	3,454	1,484
1934–35	7,776	7,634	142	3,147	3,022	124	2,471	2,526	1,138
1935–36	8,618	8,414	205	3,178	3,044	134	2,712	2,764	1,528
1936–37	10,101	9,836	265	3,180	3,042	139	3,176	3,234	1,909
1937–38	9,948	9,766	182	3,190	3,044	146	3,130	3,208	1,246
1938–39	9,880	9,628	252	3,194	3,048	146	3,093	3,159	1,722
1939–40	10,345	10,052	292	3,166	3,016	150	3,267	3,333	1,942
Average									
1900–01 to 1909–10	6,916	6,811	106	2,858	2,777	80	2,419	2,450	1,322
1910–11 to 1919–20	8,104	7,925	180	3,015	2,896	119	2,688	2,686	1,510
1920–21 to 1929–30	8,839	8,627	207	3,132	2,994	138	2,821	2,881	1,505
1930–31 to 1939–40	9,466	9,251	216	3,186	3,187	136	2,972	3,034	1,571

Source: *Japan Statistical Yearbook*, Tokyo, 1949, p. 203; 1961, p. 90; 1964, p. 98.

aConverted from koku to metric tons at 150 kg. per koku.

bConverted from cho to hectares at .991736 ha. per cho.

a period of rapid growth in output and productivity that ended during the 1920's. This was followed by a period of slower growth during the interwar period. The third was a period of decline and recovery associated with World War II. A fourth period of explosive growth in productivity began in the late 1940's or early 1950's [15, 20, 31, 35, 47].

Output and productivity trends both for rice and for the total agricultural sector appear to have followed the same general pattern, reflecting the dominant role of rice in the agricultural economy.[27] The growth in output during the first "technical epoch" was achieved through a combination of increases in land inputs and of growth of land productivity. Yield increases (land productivity) accounted for approximately two-thirds of the growth of output and were achieved primarily through intensification of the "traditional" biological technology; that is, (1) improved crop husbandry, including more intensive use of labor, (2) increases in the application of organic sources of plant nutrients, (3) application of pre-Mendelian methods of crop improvement—primarily through selection rather than breeding, and (4) land improvement projects—principally the replanting of paddy fields and improvement of water delivery and drainage systems [31, pp. 388–409].

Institutions for the rapid diffusion of superior varieties and cultural practices used by the best farmers and in the best regions were developed during the 1880's. This effort was complemented by the development of prefectural (local) experiment stations in the 1890's. By the end of this first period, the research effort was increasingly focused on the development of a "fertilizer-consuming rice culture." This involved the development of rice varieties with shorter stems and more tillers. The application of the more intensive rice production technology was facilitated by small-scale land and water resource development, which contributed to the expansion of the irrigated area and increased the precision of water treatment.

---

[27] The general pattern described above has been challenged by Nakamura [27, 28]. Nakamura argues that agricultural production was underestimated at the beginning of the Meiji period and that the gradual improvement of production estimates between the mid-1870's and the early 1920's has inflated the rate of output and productivity growth during the first "epoch." It appears that Nakamura's criticisms are stimulating review and revision of the "official" estimates. However, these revisions will not destroy the generalizations about the four broad "epochs" described above. For further discussion of this issue see [15, 22, 29].

Technical Change and Agricultural Trade   457

TABLE III.4

Average Price Indexes for Brown Rice and the General Price
Index in Japan: 1878–1912
(1893–97 = 100)

Period	Rice Price Index (R)	General Price Index (G)	R/G
1878–82	92.7	110.9	0.83
1883–87	57.9	81.0	0.71
1888–92	71.8	88.9	0.80
1893–97	100.0	100.0	1.00
1898–1902	129.9	127.3	1.02
1903–07	156.6	152.6	1.03
1908–12	175.1	164.2	1.06

Source: Takekozu Ogura [31], p. 24.

The economic factors for the expansion of the rice area and the adoption of yield-improving technology were favorable throughout the first epoch, so that, as shown in Tables III.4 and III.5, real rice prices rose. By 1900 rice exports, which had risen continuously since the early 1870's, started to decline. Demand was increasing more rapidly than supply. The Japanese government's response was to undertake an intensive program to expand rice production in the northern island of Hokkaido and in the newly acquired colonial areas of Korea and Taiwan.

Output and productivity growth in Korea and Taiwan

Initial efforts to increase rice production in Korea and Taiwan through the transfer of Japanese rice varieties and Japanese cultivation methods were relatively unsuccessful.[28]

In Korea, where the environment for rice cultivation was similar to that in Japan, the transfer of Japanese varieties was rather successful and rapid. Table III.6 shows that by the early 1920's approximately two-thirds of the rice area in Korea was planted to Japanese varieties.

[28] Early efforts to expand rice production on Hokkaido were also relatively unsuccessful. It was not until after World War II that efforts to achieve high and relatively stable average yields were successful in Hokkaido [31, pp. 319, 435–78].

TABLE III. 5

Price Indexes for Rice and Wholesale Price Index in Japan: 1911–40
(1934–36 = 100)

	Wholesale Price Index (G)	Rice Price (1)		Rice Price (2)	
		Index (R_1)	Ratio (R_1/G)	Index (R_2)	Ratio (R_2/G)
Year					
1911	61.0	60.2	.99	60.5	.99
1912	64.6	72.0	1.11	72.2	1.12
1913	64.7	74.9	1.16	74.8	1.16
1914	61.8	56.1	.91	56.4	.91
1915	62.5	45.4	.73	45.6	.73
1916	75.6	47.5	.63	47.7	.63
1917	95.1	68.3	.72	69.1	.73
1918	124.6	113.0	.91	113.4	.91
1919	152.6	159.6	1.05	160.1	1.05
1920	167.8	153.9	.92	154.5	.92
1921	129.6	107.2	.83	107.8	.83
1922	126.7	121.6	.96	122.6	.97
1923	128.9	113.4	.88	113.0	.88
1924	133.6	133.8	1.00	133.7	1.00
1925	130.5	144.5	1.11	145.0	1.11
1926	115.7	130.6	1.13	131.1	1.13
1927	109.9	122.0	1.11	122.9	1.12
1928	110.6	107.2	.97	107.1	.97
1929	107.5	100.7	.94	100.9	.94
1930	88.5	88.0	.99	64.1	.72
1931	74.8	63.8	.85	64.1	.86
1932	83.0	73.3	.88	73.6	.89
1933	95.1	74.5	.78	74.5	.78
1934	97.0	90.5	.93	90.5	.93
1935	99.4	103.1	1.04	103.2	1.04
1936	103.6	106.4	1.03	106.2	1.03
1937	125.8	–	–	112.2	.89
1938	132.7	–	–	119.2	.90
1939	146.6	–	–	129.6	.88
1940	164.1	–	–	150.7	.92
Average					
1911–20	93.0	85.1	.91	85.4	.92
1921–30	118.2	116.9	.99	114.8	.97
1931–40	112.2	–	–	102.4	.91

Source: *Wholesale Price Index: Hundred Year Statistics of the Japanese Economy,* Statistics Department, Bank of Japan, 1966, pp. 76, 77; *Rice Price* (1): *Japan Statistical Yearbook,* 1949, p. 634 – index base has been shifted from 1900 = 100 to 1934-36 = 100; *Rice Price* (2): *Hundred Year Statistics of the Japanese Economy,* Statistics Department, Bank of Japan, 1966, p. 90.

TABLE III.6

*Plantings of Japanese-Type and Ponlai Rice Varieties in
Korea and Taiwan, Selected Years*

Year	Area (thousand hectares)	Per Cent of Total Rice Area	Average Yield of Brown Rice (kg./ha.)
	Plantings of Japanese-Type Varieties		
Korea			
1912	39	3	1,160
1917	590	41	1,354
1922	979	67	1,458
1927	1,163	77	1,633
1932	1,245	80	1,504
	Plantings of Ponlai Varieties		
Taiwan			
1922			
1st crop[a]	.4	.2	1,749
2nd crop	—	—	1,420
1926			
1st crop	111.8	45.2	1,644
2nd crop	11.4	3.9	1,573
1930			
1st crop	80.4	30.6	1,883
2nd crop	54.9	16.6	1,624
1935			
1st crop	186.9	64.8	2,243
2nd crop	118.0	32.0	2,057

Source: Takekazu Ogura[31], p. 190; *Japan Statistical Yearbook,* Tokyo, 1949, pp. 630, 631; *Taiwan Food Statistics,* Taiwan Provincial Food Bureau, 1965 (and earlier issues), Taipei, pp. 18-22.

[a]The first crop in Taiwan is the dry-season crop.

However, as seen in Table III.7, rice yields in Korea did not increase significantly until at least the mid-1920's.

In Taiwan the direct transfer of Japanese varieties was not successful. Japanese rice varieties were not adapted to the Taiwan ecology.

TABLE III.7

Production, Area, and Yield of Brown Rice in Korea: 1912–40

	Production (thous. metric tons)	Area (hectares)	Yield (kg./ha.)
Year			
1912–13	1,630	1,405	1,160
1913–14	1,816	1,445	1,257
1914–15	2,120	1,472	1,440
1915–16	1,927	1,485	1,297
1916–17	2,090	1,506	1,387
1917–18	2,053	1,516	1,354
1918–19	2,294	1,535	1,494
1919–20	1,906	1,525	1,250
1920–21	2,232	1,543	1,447
1921–22	2,149	1,519	1,415
1922–23	2,252	1,545	1,458
1923–24	2,276	1,538	1,480
1924–25	1,983	1,563	1,269
1925–26	2,215	1,572	1,410
1926–27	2,295	1,575	1,457
1927–28	2,595	1,589	1,633
1928–29	2,027	1,505	1,346
1929–30	2,055	1,619	1,270
1930–31	2,877	1,648	1,746
1931–32	2,381	1,661	1,434
1932–33	2,452	1,630	1,504
1933–34	2,729	1,783	1,531
1934–35	2,508	1,698	1,477
1935–36	2,683	1,681	1,596
1936–37	2,912	1,588	1,833
1937–38	4,020	1,626	2,473
1938–39	3,621	1,646	2,200
1939–40	2,153	1,225	1,758
Average			
1912–13 to 1919–20	1,980	1,486	1,330
1920–21 to 1929–30	2,208	1,557	1,418
1930–31 to 1939–40	2,833	1,618	1,755

Source: *Japan Statistical Yearbook,* Tokyo, 1949, pp. 630, 631.

TABLE III.8

Production, Area, and Yield of Brown Rice in Taiwan: 1900–40

	Production (thous. metric tons)	Area (hectares)	Yield (kg./ha.)
Year			
1900–01	307	326	943
1901–02	438	353	1,239
1902–03	403	345	1,168
1903–04	525	395	1,330
1904–05	594	435	1,366
1905–06	622	447	1,390
1906–07	567	459	1,236
1907–08	645	472	1,367
1908–09	665	479	1,389
1909–10	661	479	1,381
1910–11	598	456	1,311
1911–12	642	479	1,340
1912–13	578	481	1,201
1913–14	732	498	1,482
1914–15	658	500	1,317
1915–16	684	491	1,392
1916–17	664	472	1,408
1917–18	691	466	1,481
1918–19	662	483	1,369
1919–20	703	497	1,415
1920–21	692	500	1,383
1921–22	711	495	1,435
1922–23	778	511	1,521
1923–24	695	508	1,369
1924–25	668	531	1,633
1925–26	920	551	1,671
1926–27	888	567	1,565
1927–28	985	585	1,685
1928–29	971	585	1,660
1929–30	926	568	1,630
1930–31	1,053	614	1,714
1931–32	1,069	634	1,686
1932–33	1,278	664	1,924
1933–34	1,195	675	1,768
1934–35	1,298	667	1,947
1935–36	1,303	679	1,920
1936–37	1,366	681	2,004
1937–38	1,319	658	2,006
1938–39	1,402	625	2,242
1939–40	1,307	626	2,088

(continued)

TABLE III.8 (concluded)

	Production (thous. metric tons)	Area (hectares)	Yield (kg./ha.)
Average 1900–10 to 1909–10	543	419	1,281
1910–11 to 1919–20	661	482	1,372
1920–21 to 1929–30	823	540	1,555
1930–31 to 1939–40	1,259	652	1,930

Source: *Taiwan Food Statistics, 1964,* Taiwan Provincial Food Bureau, Taipei, 1964, pp. 2-3.

Furthermore, the official economic policy of the Japanese administration in Taiwan emphasized expansion of sugar production rather than rice production during the first two decades of the colonial period. It was not until the mid-1920's, after thirty years of Japanese rule, that new varieties were developed. These varieties incorporated the high yield potential of the Japanese varieties with the superior adaptation to local conditions of the native *indica* varieties.[29] By the late 1930's half of the

[29] The early Japanese efforts to improve rice yields in Taiwan emphasized selection and diffusion of the highest yielding native *indica* varieties. In spite of a large reduction in the number of inferior varieties grown and substantial diffusion of superior varieties, the average yield showed only modest gains. Early efforts to introduce *japonica* varieties from Japan were not successful. Even after substantial modification in cultural practices, the high yield potentials of the *japonica* varieties were only partially realized under Taiwan conditions. Efforts were then directed to breeding varieties which combined the desirable characteristics of the introduced *japonica* varieties (high fertilizer response, short growing period, nonsensitivity to photo-period, and better quality) with the resistance to disease and the superior adaptation to the local ecology of the native *indica* varieties. The new varieties developed in Taiwan using *japonica* genetic materials are referred to as *ponlai* (or *horai*) varieties.

The first *ponlai* variety was introduced commercially in 1922 when it was planted on 414 hectares in the Hsinchu region. An exceptionally high yield of 2,517 metric tons of brown rice per hectare was achieved. Later the planted areas were increased and extended to the Taipei and Taichung regions. With the diffusion, average yield declined. After 1925 an outbreak of rice blast disease, to which the new varieties were highly susceptible, sharply reduced the *ponlai*

total rice area in Taiwan was planted to the new *ponlai* varieties developed in Taiwan. The average Taiwan rice yield was approaching that in Japan. This rapid diffusion was facilitated by extensive irrigation development.

By the mid-1920's, the increases in rice output in the colonial areas resulted in substantially increased rice exports to Japan (Table III.9). Japanese rice imports rose from an average of 559 metric tons, 6.4 per cent of total Japanese supply, in 1912–20, to 1,754 metric tons, 15.6 per cent of total supply, in 1931–40. During this latter period, imports from Korea accounted for 9.6 per cent and from Taiwan 5.5 per cent of the total Japanese rice supply.

In Taiwan, according to Table III.10, rice exports rose from an average of less than 20 per cent of total production during the 1911–20 period to 31 per cent in 1921–30 and 47 per cent in 1931–40. In Korea, as we see in Table III.11, exports rose from less than 9 per cent in 1912–16 to 30 per cent in 1922–26.

The extent to which the increased rice exports from the two colonial areas were a result of economic incentives generated in the market or administrative pressures has not yet been analyzed. Although data on consumption levels in the two colonial areas are subject to considerable question, it does seem clear that consumption of rice in Korea and Taiwan declined while exports to Japan were rising. As shown in Table III.12, in Taiwan, the per capita supply of rice available for local use declined from 166.5 kilograms per capita in 1920–29 to 133.1 kilograms in 1930–39. In Korea, per capita consumption of rice also appears to have declined sharply while exports to Japan were rising. In contrast, rice consumption in Japan during the 1930's approximated the levels of earlier years.

Impact of rice imports on Japanese prices, production, and productivity

The two decades from 1920 to 1940 have been characterized as a period of relative stagnation in Japanese agriculture. For thirty years prior to World War I, rice prices had risen steadily relative to the gen-

---

yields. Beginning in 1930 other *ponlai* varieties with greater resistance to the rice blast disease were introduced. Over twenty years had elapsed between the introduction of the first *japonica* varieties and the development of the *ponlai* varieties which possessed sufficient advantage over the local varieties to justify rapid diffusion [17, pp. 331–33].

TABLE III.9

Japanese Rice Production and Imports from Korea and Taiwan: 1912–61

Year	Domestic Production		Total Net Imports		Net Imports From Korea		Net Imports From Taiwan		Total Supply[a]
	Thous. metric tons	Per cent of total supply	Thous. metric tons	Per cent of total supply	Thous. metric tons	Per cent of total supply	Thous. metric tons	Per cent of total supply	Thous. metric tons
1912	7,757	95.2	392	4.8	36	.4	91	1.1	8,148
1913	7,533	92.1	642	7.9	44	.5	141	1.7	8,175
1914	7,539	92.8	588	7.2	153	1.9	115	1.4	8,127
1915	8,551	96.1	345	3.9	280	3.2	95	1.1	8,897
1916	8,389	97.3	231	2.7	198	2.3	109	1.3	8,620
1917	8,768	98.6	120	1.4	177	2.0	105	1.2	8,888
1918	8,185	90.0	909	10.0	258	2.8	159	1.7	9,094
1919	8,205	85.6	1,377	14.4	418	4.4	185	1.9	9,582
1920	9,123	95.5	427	4.5	246	2.6	96	1.0	9,550
1921	9,481	93.4	671	6.6	431	4.2	149	1.5	10,152
1922	8,277	89.0	1,024	11.0	447	4.8	72	.8	9,301
1923	9,104	91.7	825	8.3	505	5.1	161	1.6	9,929
1924	8,317	86.4	1,313	13.6	609	6.3	233	2.4	9,640
1925	8,576	84.9	1,525	15.1	552	5.5	281	2.9	10,100
1926	8,956	86.9	1,348	13.1	762	7.4	324	3.1	10,303
1927	8,339	83.0	1,706	17.0	774	7.7	393	3.9	10,045
1928	9,316	85.8	1,537	14.2	1,049	9.7	361	3.3	10,853
1929	9,046	87.8	1,253	12.2	788	7.7	336	3.3	10,298
1930	8,934	88.1	1,207	11.9	763	7.5	327	3.2	10,140

Year									
1931	10,031	87.5	1,429	12.5	1,194	10.4	404	3.5	11,460
1932	8,282	83.5	1,639	16.5	1,073	10.8	516	5.2	9,921
1933	9,059	83.3	1,819	16.7	1,123	10.3	632	5.8	10,877
1934	10,624	84.2	1,997	15.8	1,338	10.6	768	6.1	12,621
1935	7,776	80.9	1,833	19.1	1,249	13.0	676	7.0	9,609
1936	8,618	80.8	2,047	19.2	1,343	12.6	723	6.8	10,666
1937	10,101	85.7	1,685	14.3	1,006	8.5	728	6.2	11,786
1938	9,948	81.9	2,203	18.1	1,519	12.5	744	6.1	12,151
1939	9,880	87.9	1,357	12.1	838	7.5	593	5.3	11,237
1940	10,345	87.1	1,533	12.9	49	.4	417	3.5	11,878
Average									
1912–20	8,228	93.6	559	6.4	201	2.3	122	1.4	8,787
1921–30	8,834	87.7	1,241	12.3	668	6.6	264	2.6	10,075
1931–40	9,467	84.4	1,754	15.6	1,073	9.6	620	5.5	11,221

Source: *Japan Statistical Yearbook*, Bureau of Statistics, 1949, pp. 614, 615. Data converted from koku to metric tons at 150 kg. per koku.

aSupply equals production plus net imports.

TABLE III.10

Rice Supplies, Trade, and Domestic Utilization in Taiwan:
1910–11 to 1939–40

(thousands of metric tons)

Year[a]	Supply			Domestic Utilization	Exports	Exports as Per Cent of Production
	Production	Imports	Total			
1910–11	641	13	654	560	94	15
1911–12	578	18	596	503	93	16
1912–13	732	30	762	601	161	22
1913–14	658	11	669	583	86	13
1914–15	684	9	693	567	126	18
1915–16	664	11	675	564	111	17
1916–17	691	17	708	591	117	17
1917–18	662	48	710	559	156	23
1918–19	703	57	760	591	169	24
1919–20	692	27	719	615	104	15
1920–21	711	21	732	586	146	21
1921–22	778	47	825	718	107	14
1922–23	695	15	710	531	179	26
1923–24	868	18	886	624	262	30
1924–25	920	117	1,037	682	355	39
1925–26	888	67	955	643	312	35
1926–27	985	129	1,115	742	373	38
1927–28	971	46	1,017	678	339	35
1928–29	926	92	1,018	687	331	36
1929–30	1,053	14	1,067	750	317	30
1930–31	1,069	2	1,071	691	380	36
1931–32	1,278	37	1,315	838	477	37
1932–33	1,195	8	1,203	613	590	49
1933–34	1,298	1	1,299	578	721	56
1934–35	1,303	1	1,304	662	642	49
1935–36	1,365	1	1,366	683	683	50
1936–37	1,319	1	1,320	628	692	52
1937–38	1,402	2	1,404	708	696	50
1938–39	1,307	1	1,308	722	586	45
1939–40	1,129	13	1,142	719	423	37
Average 1910–11 to 1919–20	671	24	695	573	122	18
1920–21 to 1929–30	880	57	937	664	273	31
1930–31 to 1939–40	1,267	7	1,274	684	590	47

Notes to Table III.10

Source: Taiwan Provincial Food Bureau, *Taiwan Food Statistics,* Taipei, 1965 (and earlier issues).

[a]The rice year in Taiwan is November 1 to October 31 for years prior to 1945. This was changed to July 1 to June 30 in 1945.

eral price level, and Tables III.4 and Tables III.5 indicate that rice prices rose to their highest relative level in 1913 and their highest absolute level in 1919. The wholesale price of rice in Tokyo more than doubled between 1913 and 1919, and there were consumer riots during the very sharp price rise of 1916–19. As a response to the riots, official policies were designed to encourage rice production in and imports from the colonial areas.

Japanese imports increased sharply in the mid-1920's and remained above 1.2 million metric tons until after 1940 (Table III.12). From 1921 to 1940, the price of rice did not resume its upward drift relative to the general price level but fluctuated below the peak established in 1913. The sharp decline in rice prices in the early 1930's led to protests by farmers against imports. The government limited imports from the two colonial areas in 1933 and again in 1936. Nevertheless, rice imports averaged 1.9 million metric tons in the period 1932–38 and reached their pre-World War II peak of 2.2 million metric tons in 1938.

The impact of rice imports from Taiwan and Korea on rice production, consumption, and prices in Japan during the interwar period depends upon the shape of the rice demand and supply functions in Japan during this period. Estimates of the price elasticity of demand computed by Ohkawa from (1) data on rice consumption by income classes between 1931–32 and 1938–39 and (2) from data on markets between 1920 and 1938 center around −0.20 [32]. Recent income elasticity estimates, summarized by Kaneda, also appear consistent with a price elasticity for rice of −0.20 in the 1920–40 period [22].

Estimates of supply elasticities in rice production are unavailable for Japan. The elasticity of supply depends on both the response of area planted and the response of yield per unit area to changes in the price of rice. Recent reviews of area supply elasticity studies conducted in other Asian countries indicate that the area response to changes in the price of rice typically falls in the +0.20 to +0.30 range [23, 24].

TABLE III.11

*Korean Rice Production and Exports to Japan: Annual
Averages 1912–16, 1917–21, 1922–26*
(thousands of metric tons)

Years	Production	Exports	Exports as of Production
1912–16	1,771	152	8.5
1917–21	2,030	316	15.6
1922–26	2,088	625	29.9

Source: Ki Zum Zo [48], p. 315.

The yield of rice per unit area in Japan was apparently highly responsive to the use of fertilizer, insecticides, and other technical inputs during this period. Estimates of the production function and the demand for fertilizer by Hayami imply an elasticity of yield with respect to price of between $+0.20$ and $+0.25$ [13, 14]. It seems reasonable, therefore, to hypothesize a total supply elasticity for rice of approximately $+0.50$ in Japan between 1920 and 1940.

With these two elasticity estimates it is possible to arrive at an estimate of the impact of rice imports on Japanese rice production, consumption, and price by constructing three simple economic models for the 1921–40 period.

Notes to Table III.12

Source: Japan—*Hundred Year Statistics of the Japanese Economy, Tokyo*, 1966. Taiwan—*Taiwan Food Statistics, 1965* (and earlier issues), Taiwan Provincial Food Bureau, Taipei. The Taiwan data represents per capita supply available for domestic utilization rather than per capita consumption. Korea—*Chosen Beikoku Yoran (Rice Situation in Korea)*, Department of Agriculture and Forestry, Seoul, 1936 and 1940.

[a]1912–19.

[b]1930–36.

[c]1936–38.

TABLE III.12

*Per Capita Annual Consumption of Rice in Japan,
Taiwan and Korea: 1910–40*

(Kilograms)

	Japan	Taiwan	Korea (old series)	(new series)
Year				
1910	162.6	—	—	
1911	147.0	—	—	
1912	160.2	—	115.9	
1913	158.6	—	104.8	
1914	147.2	—		106.8
1915	166.7	—	110.6	
1916	161.6	—	101.0	
1917	168.9	—	108.0	
1918	171.5	—	102.0	
1919	168.6	—		108.7
1920	167.7	192.4	95.1	
1921	173.0	154.2	100.6	
1922	165.0	185.5	95.1	
1923	173.0	134.9	97.1	
1924	168.3	155.6		90.5
1925	169.2	166.7	77.8	
1926	169.5	153.1	79.9	
1927	164.3	173.0	78.7	
1928	169.4	154.5	81.0	
1929	165.0	195.3	66.9	
1930	161.4	162.5	67.6	
1931	167.7	145.7	78.0	
1932	151.8	172.2	61.8	
1933	162.5	122.8	61.5	
1934	170.0	112.7	62.5	
1935	154.1	126.0	58.2	
1936	157.1	126.8	58.2	85.2
1937	166.7	113.6	—	105.5
1938	166.8	124.6	—	116.4
1939	165.5	124.0	—	—
Average				
1910–19	161.3	—	107.2[a]	
1920–29	168.4	166.5	86.3	
1930–39	162.4	133.1	64.0[b]	102.4[c]

TABLE III.13
Actual and Estimated Prices of Rice in Japan: 1921–40
(production, import, and supply figures in thousands of metric tons)

	Actual Data			Partial Isolation		
	Production	Imports	Supply	Price index[a]	Imports	Supply
Year						
1921	9,481	671	10,152	83	559	10,040
1922	8,277	1,024	9,301	97	559	8,835
1923	9,104	825	9,929	88	559	9,663
1924	8,317	1,313	9,630	100	559	8,876
1925	8,575	1,525	10,100	111	559	9,134
1926	8,955	1,348	10,303	113	559	9,515
1927	8,339	1,706	10,045	112	559	8,898
1928	9,316	1,537	10,853	97	559	9,874
1929	9,045	1,253	10,298	94	559	9,604
1930	8,933	1,207	10,140	72	559	9,493
1931	10,031	1,429	11,460	86	559	10,590
1932	8,282	1,639	9,921	89	559	8,841
1933	9,058	1,819	10,877	78	559	9,617
1934	10,625	1,997	12,622	93	559	11,183
1935	7,776	1,833	9,609	104	559	8,335
1936	8,619	2,047	10,666	103	559	9,177
1937	10,101	1,685	11,786	89	559	10,660
1938	9,948	2,203	12,151	90	559	10,507
1939	9,880	1,357	11,237	88	559	10,439
1940	10,345	1,533	11,878	92	559	10,904
Average						
1921–30	8,834	1,241	10,075	92	559	9,393
1931–40	9,467	1,754	11,221	97	559	10,025

Source: See Tables III.5 and III.9 for source of actual data.

[a]1934–36 = 100.

[b]Equals supply.

Model I	Partial Isolation Model II				Isolation Model	
Price index[a]	Production	Imports	Supply	Price index[a]	Production[b]	Price index[a]
88	9,559	559	10,118	84	9,951	91
121	8,598	559	9,157	105	8,983	114
100	9,289	559	9,848	92	9,679	99
139	8,832	559	9,391	112	9,214	122
164	9,250	559	9,809	129	9,612	138
156	9,495	559	10,054	127	9,879	136
176	9,113	559	9,672	133	9,490	143
140	9,983	559	10,542	111	10,364	119
125	9,522	559	10,081	104	9,906	112
95	9,379	559	9,938	79	9,764	85
118	10,628	559	11,187	96	11,012	103
137	9,012	559	9,571	105	9,390	113
123	9,909	559	10,468	93	10,287	99
146	11,600	559	12,159	110	11,978	117
173	8,629	559	9,188	127	9,002	137
175	9,614	559	10,173	127	9,988	136
131	10,869	559	11,428	103	11,250	109
150	11,052	559	11,611	110	11,428	117
119	10,429	559	10,988	98	10,813	105
129	11,013	559	11,572	104	11,395	111
130	9,302	559	9,358	108	9,684	116
140	10,276	559	10,332	107	10,654	115

The first model, identified in Table III.13 as "partial isolation model (I)," illustrates the impact of imports on rice prices when (1) annual domestic production is the same as it actually was in the period 1921 to 1940 (implying a completely inelastic supply function), (2) imports are held at the 1912–20 average level, and (3) the price elasticity of demand is assumed to be −0.20. Under these conditions rice prices would have risen to an average index of 140 for the 1931–40 period, 44 per cent higher than the actual average index of 97 that prevailed during 1931–40.

The second model, identified as "partial isolation model (II)," illustrates the impact on rice prices when (1) the price elasticity of supply is assumed to be +0.50, (2) imports are held at the 1912–20 average level, and (3) the price elasticity of demand is assumed to be −0.20. It differs from model (I) only in the assumption with respect to supply elasticity. Under these conditions, rice prices would have risen to an average index of 107 for the 1931–40 period, 10 per cent higher than the actual average index for the same period.

The third model, called the "isolation model," illustrates the estimated impact of imports on rice prices, production, and consumption when (1) imports are assumed to have been prohibited in the period from 1921 to 1940, (2) the price elasticity of demand is assumed to be −0.20, and (3) the price elasticity of supply is assumed to be +0.50. Under these conditions the average 1931–40 price index would be 115. This is 19 per cent above the actual 1931–40 index of 97.

The prices generated by the "isolation model" are consistent with an estimated rate of growth in rice production in Japan equal to that achieved during the first two decades of this century.[30] The "isolation model" is, therefore, consistent with the hypothesis referred to at the beginning of this section that imports of rice from Taiwan and Korea were responsible for the depressed rice prices and the slow growth of

[30] The actual average rate of rice production growth in the period between 1900–03 and 1919–22 was 1.3 per cent per year. The "isolation model" suggests a similar growth rate of 1.3 per cent for the 1919–22 to 1937–40 period when imports were presumed to be prohibited. The actual production growth rate was 1.1 per cent per year in the presence of imports from other nations. Years before 1900 were omitted from this comparison in order to avoid the data problems raised by Nakamura [27, 28].

rice production in metropolitan Japan during the period 1920–40.[31] However, the data and analysis presented in this paper are inadequate to reject the hypothesis that technical considerations also could have dampened the rate of growth of output even if the calculated equilibrium prices had been obtained.

The impact of the rice imports from Taiwan and Korea on Japanese economic growth is less obvious than their impact on rice production and prices. Clearly one major impact of these rice imports was to reverse the long-run tendency of the terms of trade to favor rice producers by turning it to favor rice consumers. This contributed to higher real incomes for urban consumers, increased the supply of labor in the nonfarm sector, and reduced pressures for wage increases in the industrial sector. One effect was probably to increase the competitive position of Japanese industrial exports in world markets. A second effect was to reduce the growth rate of purchasing power in rural areas. This, in turn, contributed to the slack in domestic private demand for the industrial sector's output [10, pp. 419–42].

The transfer of rice-production technology from Japan to Taiwan and Korea and the Japanese policy on imports from these two countries during the period 1920–40 have important implications for South and Southeast Asian countries for the rest of this century. Approximately two-thirds of the world rice trade today is between Asian countries [2]. Technical change in rice production, similar to the changes that took place in Taiwan and Korea prior to World War II, is underway in several rice-exporting and importing nations of Southeast Asia. Substantial disruptions of trade and price relationships are anticipated in the absence of an effective international stabilization scheme.

IV. SUMMARY

We recognize that it is difficult to draw broad inferences about future patterns of international generation and transmission of technology in

---

[31] The results presented here should be treated more as the statement of a hypothesis than as a final conclusion. Work is currently underway by Yujiro Hayami and V. W. Ruttan to test the colonial trade import hypotheses more vigorously.

agricultural products from the evidence in these three cases. However, we will summarize the common elements that we see in them. We will also draw on this and other related work in making some tentative inferences regarding future patterns of international technical change in agricultural products.

Technical change in all three cases was generated by organized research effort—the more advanced the basic technology, the more highly organized the effort. Early sugarcane breeding, for example, was sometimes accomplished on individual plantations. Virtually all the major canes, however, were the product of experiment station research. The Stage-IV varieties were all produced by scientists using advanced techniques and working in well-organized research establishments. Similarly, advances in rice breeding were and are being produced by experiment stations established for this purpose, and the advances in banana production were generated by researchers working with large private organizations.[32]

Research accomplishments have in many cases followed concentrated effort to solve specific economic problems. The accomplishments in the banana case can be traced to the effort put forth in response to the problems caused by Panama disease. Later, the problems associated with handling and processing the new disease-resistant varieties led to improved methods in that area. The history of sugarcane breeding reveals many instances in which a disease problem was the basis for a sustained effort to find new disease-resistant, higher-yielding varieties.

The international transmission of technical change is a function of both the specific characteristics of the technology and of economic incentives. The technological characteristics that appear to be most important are the sorts of information or knowledge required to insert the technology into the actual production processes. The simplest technology from this point of view might be a new higher-yielding crop variety which is adapted to a wide range of climate and soil conditions and does not require any changes in producing, processing, or marketing techniques. Some of the early transfer of sugarcane varieties was of

[32] In terms of the sugarcane terminology, the banana-breeding effort would be classified as Stage-I research since it involved the selection of natural varieties.

this sort. Only the economic incentive of profitability was needed to encourage rapid international transmission of these varieties.

Information is needed for international transmission even when the technology is embodied simply in the seed of a plant variety. A grower must have some information about the relative yield and quality of a new variety before he can determine whether a change is profitable. This information was relatively easy to obtain for those sugarcane varieties which were adapted to wide climatic and soil conditions, thus Stage-II sugarcane varieties were transferred relatively easily.

But the transmission of technology becomes more difficult as more information is required. For example, the Stage-III sugarcane varieties were not easily transferred because specific information was needed about the diseases to which each of the new varieties was resistant. (A similar amount of information was required on the banana diseases.) Rapid transmission of technology based on this degree of information took place only through the organized testing effort of experiment stations or of large private concerns.

Transmission is further complicated when knowledge is required regarding new production, processing, and marketing techniques. So that, in addition to organized research effort, some form of extension effort often is required to achieve transmission of new technology. In the banana case, the solution to the processing and marketing problems took the form of an important new technical advance. The transmission of rice varieties from Japan to Korea involved knowledge of new cultural practices.

The most complicated and sophisticated forms of technical transfer are those illustrated by the Stage-IV sugarcane breeding effort and the transfer of rice technology from Japan to Taiwan. In these cases, the technology that was transferred was not directly embodied in a tangible input such as a plant seed. It took the form of knowledge or scientific information regarding plant-breeding techniques.

Technology transfer of this kind depends heavily on the existence of effective research organizations and requires a minimum number of competent research scientists committed to the transfer and further development of the technology. In addition, the organization must provide the environment for the communication and complementary interchange of knowledge by scientists within the nation and internationally.

One would expect to find the lag or "technology gap" that exists between the most advanced technology used in the production of a given crop and the least advanced technology to be related to the difficulty of international transmission. Thus, in cases in which the technology is embodied in an input and where little information is needed to determine the profitability of that input, the lag should be relatively short. We would expect the longest lag and the widest technology gap to exist in those agricultural products in which the transfer of information and knowledge is in the "Stage-IV" level. Agricultural development, at the present time, appears to confirm this expectation.

Technology transfer of the easiest sort appears to have been limited to relatively few agricultural commodities. For a few countries, technical change in sugarcane, rice, and a number of the tropical crops has been transferred with limited research activity. In a few additional cases, such as the spread of open-pollinated corn in Thailand, the transfer has involved some extensive activity including added investments in clearing, draining, and irrigating new lands.

However, for most major crops the transfer depends on the existence of research organizations capable of performing Stage-IV-type research. Generally, research organizations with this capability are scarce in the less-developed economies. Exceptions in sugarcane and bananas have been noted. The rice-breeding effort in Taiwan and research efforts in other tropical crops are also exceptions.

The technology gap for many of the major feeds and food grains exists largely because good Stage-IV research organizations do not exist yet in many less-developed countries. This gap has been widened as the research organizations of the developed countries have continuously generated new technology and technical change which have not been transferred to the less-developed countries.

The efforts of the developed countries, particularly the United States, to foster the transmission of agricultural technology to the less-developed nations have not been particularly successful. Where the United States government has failed, however, the Ford and Rockefeller Foundations have partially succeeded.[33] The Rockefeller program in Mexico and the

[33] The economic development efforts associated with the foreign aid and

International Rice Research Institute (IRRI) in the Philippines are examples of the kinds of research organizations which are essential if the technology gap is to be closed.

In addition to the Mexican and IRRI programs, a number of other efforts are underway. It appears that Stage-IV research activity is now being activated on a much broader basis. We would expect this research activity effort to result in a narrowing of the present technology gap and to stimulate a "catching-up" phase by the less-developed economies.[34]

World trade and individual country gains from trade are, or course, both influenced by this catching-up phase. It is difficult to speculate in detail about the specific shifts in trade, but evidence from the three cases in this paper clearly indicates that shifts in technology levels do affect trade patterns. We expect that the less-developed countries, for example, will become more self-sufficient in the production of certain feed and food grains, and that some of the major importers among less-developed nations may shift to an export status in the relatively near future. The food aid and surplus-disposal programs of the United States, Canada, and Western Europe probably will be reexamined as many of the developing countries expand their own food production with newly developed technologies.

This catching-up phase due to the international transmission of technology generally should result in an improvement in the welfare position of the less-developed countries as they become more competitive in world markets. Those developed countries which are presently exporters enjoying a long lead in technology will probably experience a decline in their competitive position. We do not see serious over-all welfare considerations arising from this change since it represents improvement

---

technical assistance programs of the United States have, until recently, given agricultural development low priority. The viewpoint was that the key to economic growth is the development of industrial and urban service sectors, even at the expense of agriculture. This policy of attempting to develop an economy by making it look like a developed economy has not been particularly successful. As interest now turns to searching for "cheap sources of growth" or high-payoff investments, more attention is being paid to the agricultural sector. The establishment of first-rate Stage-IV research stations is likely to be a very high-payoff investment in most of the less-developed countries.

[34] This development of an international technology gap followed by its later reduction is not peculiar to agricultural products [30].

in the welfare of poorer nations relative to rich nations. Nevertheless, the pressure from producers in the developed countries for protectionist trade policies to maintain present trade patterns and price levels will probably be intensified.

REFERENCES

1. Alvord, E. P., and Van de Wall, G., *A Survey of the Land and Feed Resources of the Union of South Africa,* Pretoria, 1954.

2. Arromdee, Virach, *Economics of Rice Trade Among Countries of Southeast Asia,* Ph.D. thesis, University of Minnesota, July 1968.

3. Arthur, H. B., Beckford, G. L., and Houck, Jr., J. P., *Tropical Agribusiness: Structures and Adjustments—Bananas,* Division of Research, Harvard Business School, 1968.

4. Aykroyd, W. R., *The Story of Sugar,* Chicago, 1967.

5. Barnes, A. C., *Agriculture of the Sugar Cane,* London, 1967.

6. Bradfield, Richard, Mandelsdorf, Paul C., and Stakman, E. C., *Campaigns Against Hunger,* Cambridge, 1967.

7. DeKock, M. H., *Economic History of South Africa,* Johannesburg, 1924.

8. Franklin, N. N., *Economics of South Africa,* Capetown, 1948.

9. Geertz, Clifford, *Agricultural Involution,* Berkeley and Los Angeles, 1966.

10. Gleason, Alan H., "Economic Growth and Consumption in Japan," in *The State and Economic Enterprise in Japan,* W. W. Lockwood (ed.), Princeton, 1965, pp. 391–447.

11. Goodfellow, D. M., *A Modern Economic History of South Africa,* London, 1931.

12. Griliches, Zvi, "Research Costs and Social Returns—Hybrid Corn and Related Innovations," *Journal of Political Economy,* October 1958, pp. 419–31.

13. Hayami, Yujiro, "Innovations in the Fertilizer Industry and Agricultural Development: The Japanese Experience," *Journal of Farm Economics,* May 1967, pp. 403–12.

14. ———, "Nogyo Seisanryoku no Hinogyoteki Kiso" (Industrial Basis of Agricultural Productivity), Proceedings of the Fifth Zushi Conference of the Tokyo Center of Economic Research, 1968.

15. Hayami, Yujiro, and Yamada, Saburo, "Agricultural Productivity at the Beginning of Industrialization," *Agricultural Economic Development: A Symposium on Japan's Experience,* Tokyo, 1967.

16. ———, "Technological Progress in Japanese Agriculture." Tokyo Conference on Economic Growth, September 1966.

17. Hsieh, S. C., and Ruttan, V. W., "Environmental, Technological and Institutional Factors in the Growth of Rice Production: Philippines, Thailand and Taiwan," *Food Research Institute Studies,* No. 3, 1967.

18. *Indian Journal of Sugarcane Research and Development,* Vol. VIII, Part 4, July–September 1963.

19. International Society of Sugarcane Technologists. *Proceedings of 9th, 10th, 11th & 12th Congresses* (1956, 1959, 1962, and 1965, respectively).

20. Johnston, Bruce F., "Agricultural Development and Economic Transformation: A Comparative Study of the Japanese Experience," *Food Research Institute Studies,* November 1962.

21. ———, "Agriculture and Economic Development: The Relevance of the Japanese Experience," *Food Research Institute Studies,* Vol. 3, No. 6, 1966.

22. Kaneda, Hiromitsu, "Long-Term Changes in Food Consumption Patterns in Japan," Yale University Economic Growth Center Discussion Paper No. 21, April 15, 1967.

23. Krishna, Raj, "Price Policy for Agricultural Development," in *Agriculture and Economic Development,* B. F. Johnston and Herman Southworth (eds.), Ithaca, 1967.

24. Mangahas, Mahar, Recto, A. E., and Ruttan, V. W., "Market Relationships for Rice and Corn in the Philippines," *The Philippine Economic Journal,* First Semester 1966, pp. 1–27. See also *Journal of Farm Economics,* August 1966.

25. May, Stacy, and Plaza, Galo, *The United Fruit Company in Latin America,* Washington, 1958.

26. "Medium-Term Outlook for World Trade in Bananas," *Monthly Bulletin of Agricultural Economics and Statistics,* February 1967.

27. Nakamura, James I., *Agricultural Production and the Economic Development of Japan,* Princeton, 1966.

28. ———, "Growth of Japanese Agriculture, 1875–1920," *The State and Economic Enterprise in Japan,* W. W. Lockwood (ed.), Princeton, 1965, pp. 249–324.

29. ———, Review of Hayami's and Yamada's Paper on "Agricultural Productivity at the Beginning of Industrialization," *Agriculture and Economic Development: A Symposium on Japan's Experience,* Tokyo, 1967.

30. Nelson, Richard R., "The Technology Gap: Analysis and Appraisal," Rand Corporaton Publication, P-3694-1, December 1967.

31. Ogura, Takekazu (ed.), *Agricultural Development in Modern Japan,* Tokyo, 1963.

32. Ohkawa, Kazushi, *Shokuryo Keizai No Riron to Keisoku* (Theory and Measurement of Food Economy), Tokyo, 1945.

33. Pak, Ki Hyuk, *A Study of Land Tenure System in Korea,* Seoul, 1966.

34. Rosenfeld, Arthur H., *Sugar Cane Around the World,* Chicago, 1955.

35. Sawada, Shujiro, "Effects of Technological Change in Japanese Agriculture, 1885–1960," *Agriculture and Economic Development: A Symposium on Japan's Experience,* Tokyo, 1967.

36. ———, "Innovation in Japanese Agriculture, 1880–1935," *The State and Economic Enterprise in Japan,* W. W. Lockwood (ed.), Princeton, 1965.

37. Simmonds, N. W., *Bananas,* London, 1959.

38. Slichter, Van Bath, B. H., *The Agrarian History of Western Europe,* London, 1963.

39. *South African Sugar Yearbooks.* Published yearly by South African Sugar Association in Durban.

40. Swerling, Boris C., and Timoshenko, Vladimir P., *The World's Sugar,* Stanford, 1957.

41. *Study Group on Bananas: Market Developments in 1967 and Early 1968,* FAO, CCP: BA/ST, 68/2, May 1968.

42. *Trends and Forces in World Banana Consumption,* FAO, CCP/ad-hoc Bananas/CCP/6, 1964.

43. USDA *Agricultural Production and Trade of Ecuador,* ERS-Foreign 218, 1968.

44. USDA *Yearbook of Agriculture,* Washington, 1936.

45. Van Der Kolff, G. H., "An Economic Case Study—Sugar and Welfare in Java," in *Approaches to Community Development,* Phillips Ruopp (ed.), The Hague, 1953.

46. Watkins, R. J., *Expanding Ecuador's Exports,* New York, 1967.

47. Yamada, Saburo, "Changes in Output and in Conventional and Non-Conventional Inputs in Japanese Agriculture Since 1880," *Food Research Institute Studies,* VII, 3, 1967.

48. Zum Zo, Ki, *History of Korean Economy,* Seoul, 1962.

COMMENT

NATHAN ROSENBERG
Harvard University

The paper by Evenson, Houck, and Ruttan is a valuable contribution to our understanding of the forces influencing the success of the generation and international transfer of agricultural techniques. When President Truman announced the Point Four of his 1949 Inaugural Address, the view was widely shared in America that we possessed a cheap "technological fix" for the problems of poverty and backwardness which beset most of the human race. We are, most of us, sadder and wiser today. Of course opportunities exist for raising agricultural productivity by the transfer of existing technology, but most of the very high payoffs may very well have been exhausted. This paper, by focusing on the historical experience of three major crops, provides important insights into the opportunities and the constraints which confront policymakers.

Several factors stand out. First of all, the transfer of agricultural techniques presents certain special difficulties because agricultural activity is always immersed, as manufacturing is not, in a unique ecological environment. The success of an individual crop will often depend on a single quality or a delicate combination of qualities of the natural environment—topography, rainfall, sunlight, chemical composition of soil, temperature variations. Therefore, each region and often each subregion will have to develop, through on-the-spot research, optimal adaptations to local ecological characteristics—as in the breeding of disease-resistant, higher-yielding seed varieties. In most cases the transfer of technology will therefore have to involve not specific tangible inputs, such as a plant seed, but a knowledge of certain scientific principles and techniques, such as genetics, biochemistry, and plant-breeding techniques.

For most of the major crops, large-scale improvements in productivity are going to be dependent on organizations capable of engaging in research of a high scientific quality. In fact, one of the interesting findings of this paper is that, in the case of the three crops, the research efforts had to become more highly organized in an institutional sense as the basic technology became more advanced. The authors conclude that the highest payoff to American technical assistance programs overseas may well be in the establishment of first-rate research organizations.

The discussion of the Japanese effort to raise Taiwan rice yields is very illuminating in this regard. The direct transfer of Japanese techniques failed due to ecological differences between Japan and Taiwan. Success came only after Japanese technical skill was used to breed rice varieties which conformed to the requirement of Taiwanese ecology. It is worth noting that this transfer, which was eventually highly successful, took fully twenty years to accomplish. It is also worth noting, if only in passing, that agriculture's close involvement with nature has another consequence which is significant in inhibiting acceptance of new techniques: because of the importance of even minor variations in rainfall, diurnal rhythms, soil content, etc., there is an unusually high degree of uncertainty concerning the outcome of untried agricultural techniques.

This paper makes it clear that the common practice of treating production functions, involving similar inputs as identical and therefore available to all—much as the information in a cookbook—is not a reasonable characterization of the situation in world agriculture. Abstract bodies of scientific knowledge, such as one finds in biology and genetics, are in some sense available, but these bodies are not capable of direct and easy translations into practical technical applications. One result is that in the case of agriculture what we are calling the *transfer* of technology demands a very high order of talent and scientific training to carry it out successfully—so high, in fact, that one is led to question whether the terminology itself may not be misleading. This paper suggests to me that what we are calling "transfer" (or "diffusion") often involves activities which are very difficult to distinguish, in any meaningful way, from what we ordinarily call "innovation."

A further point which is suggested by a reading of this paper, which the authors do not stress, is the extreme importance of complementarities. First, in order to apply fertilizers successfully to rice crops in southeast

Asia, it has been necessary to breed new rice varieties possessing the appropriate genetic capacities, and, second, the success of the new-varieties-cum-fertilizer approach to higher rice yields has been heavily dependent upon appropriate measures of water control. In addition, the high cost of the required irrigation systems suggests that the gains resulting from new varieties may not come as cheaply as had once been expected. In any case, the whole subject of the exact nature of the complementarities (including regional variations) between (1) new seeds, (2) fertilizer inputs, (3) irrigation systems, and (4) other infrastructure requirements, such as drainage, would seem to be one worthy of a very high research priority. Indeed, it is difficult to see how intelligent allocation decisions can be made in the absence of much more detailed quantitative information than we now have concerning the response of output to the whole range of possible input combinations.

This paper impresses me with the importance of complementarities in a somewhat broader sense. It seems clear that the productivity of a country's agricultural sector will frequently depend not only on resources within that industry, but on the availability and the effectiveness of industries which stand in an important complementary relationship with it. The growing role of a changing technology suggests the increasing importance of the development of new technological inputs (including pure knowledge) by industries outside the agricultural sector. Certainly in the American experience the growth in agricultural productivity was heavily dependent on the machinery sector which developed a whole new mechanical technology appropriate to our special factor endowment, as well as upon the fertilizer industry and upon new educational institutions devoted to the study of such subjects as soil chemistry and genetics. Rapidly changing technology makes it increasingly important that we think in terms of such complementarities instead of in the more static terms of resource endowment and comparative advantage.

Index

INDEX

DATE DUE

4/12/01			

GAYLORD

PRINTED IN U.S.A.